The Business of Winemaking

THE BUSINESS OF WINEMAKING

JEFFREY L. LAMY

Wine Appreciation Guild
an imprint of
Board and Bench Publishing
www.boardandbench.com

Editor: Judith Chien
Book design: TIPS Technical Publishing, Inc.
Cover design: Tressa Pack

Library of Congress Cataloging-in-Publication Data

Lamy, Jeffrey L.
The business of winemaking / Jeffrey L. Lamy.
pages cm
ISBN 978-1-935879-65-7 (hardback)
1. Wine and wine making—Economic aspects. 2. Wineries—
Management. 3. Viticulture. 4. Wine industry. I. Title.
HD9370.5.L36 2015
338.4'76632—dc23
2015019121

Contents

List of Figures

List of Tables

— 1 —

Are you ready for the challenge?

Ownership of a winery continues to be an elite international status symbol. The prestige attached to the production of high-quality wine propels many people to pursue this ultimate challenge.

Many new entrants are driven by a passionate and abiding appreciation for wine. Some are not. Such a love for wine isn't necessarily a prerequisite for assuming the risk of a winery investment. Nor does development of an inspired love for wine always follow as a result of involvement in the industry. That's unfortunate, because a passion for wine can be a very helpful asset in surviving the early years of a winery's establishment.

Among newcomers who don't have a true passion for wine, there are those who feel that winery ownership, in and of itself, or the lifestyle it may enable, is incentive enough to justify accepting the challenge. You might say they have more money than sense, but that wouldn't be entirely fair. Further, and this may be surprising, the pursuit of profit is not always a critical factor in the decision.

Three keys to success

Right at the start of this book, it is essential to state the three elements necessary for success in the winemaking business:

- **Capital**. As with all business enterprises, capital is needed. Without it, the enterprise doesn't get started. Without its timely availability as needed, the enterprise runs the risk of choking on its own burdens, and probably failing.

- **Winemaking skill.** Wine quality is crucial to success. We're talking here about quality as it relates to market segment. Quality is one thing to a $30–60 bottle of wine. It is different and less demanding for standard wines in the $8–12/bottle range. Wherever on the price/quality spectrum you choose to operate your winery business, the winery **has to produce** the appropriate quality of wine. In every case, quality depends on capable grape-growing and winemaking skills.

- **An effective marketing program.** You can make great wine, but if you don't market it properly, you will be stuck with a warehouse full of unsold casegoods. As with any business, you don't make money until the cash register rings.

Winery business is unique

We can marvel at the many ways the wine business is like no other:

- **The production process combines science with art**. Sure, production of consistently high-quality wine requires a fair knowledge of chemistry. But a lot of decisions are based on stylistic preferences, experience and judgment.

- **Winemakers, who are the key people in determining the competitiveness of the winery's products, meet routinely with their peers** (competitors?) to critique each other's wines and swap processing secrets . . . er, effective winemaking techniques.

- **Technical knowledge about winemaking at the highest management level**, not just administrative skills and access to money, is important to delivering consistently high product quality, and to achieving marketing success.

- **The pursuit of short-term profits often denies the achievement of impressive long-term profits**, or the accomplishment of any profit at all.

- **Effective marketing tactics differ greatly between the high and low ends of the price/quality spectrum**. High-quality wine is best hand sold, with lots of personal selling and very little media advertising. Lower-priced wines are sold like beer and soda pop: lots of advertising and expensive in-store displays.

- **The ways in which the winery and its key people conduct themselves in full view of the industry and its marketplace exert a strong influence on the winery's marketing success**. In other words, this is a business where style points count . . . heavily.

- **Patience is supremely important to success**. Those who wish easy or immediate gratification in the wine business had better look somewhere other than a winery or vineyard. Perhaps a retail wine shop or restaurant would be better suited for near-term results.

The following insights, offered for those hardy souls who wish to venture forth in the winery acquisition and/or development game, are particularly applicable to wineries in the 3,000 to 30,000 case range. As we travel through this journey together, the author begs your understanding. Efforts have been made to balance the serious with a few of the humorous aspects of the wine business, some factual and some based on myth with regard to the humorous.

Please take these asides in the spirit in which they are offered; harm is meant for no one nor any group.

Respect for the challenge

First, the winery buyer or developer needs to comprehend the complexities of quality wine production and marketing. Success is not easy nor simple. Outstanding wines seldom happen by accident, and rarely does a great wine result from good intentions in the absence of technical capability. If the buyer/investor doesn't possess strong technical knowledge, then he or she would be well-advised to employ a skilled and experienced winemaker, to seek the services of a capable consultant, or to "partner up" with such knowledge.

Then, there's the "ritual" side of the wine business: the glamour, the romance, the hero worship, the fol-de-rol, the wine geeks, the winemaker dinners, the symposia, the charity events, the wine competitions, the wine writers. In America, wine represents a new arena for pontification, and where there's opportunity, there will be opportunists. But, if you're cynical about these trappings of the business it'll show, and your cynicism will work against your success. That's why you must have "respect for the challenge." You have to play the game on its terms, not yours.

There's a reason why the wine business has such attributes. It's because wine has earned a ceremonial place in most cultures and religions of the world that is unmatched, going back more than twenty centuries.

When is the last time you saw a bunch of lumber judges, gathered around a table, licking two-by-fours and making comments like: "Hmmm . . . sturdy and smooth, yet angular, with a clean finish and aroma redolent of retsina (Greek wine that is made with pine pitch)?"

America is a latecomer to the world of pervasive wine appreciation. Wine represents a wonderful world of cultural enrichment, of endless opportunities for cross-cultural enjoyment of foods and people. Wine is magic. If you had an opportunity to hear Robert Mondavi's sermon on the wonders of wine, consider yourself among the fortunate. His passion for wine was truly inspiring.

Essentials for success

All of the following factors must come together to consistently produce top quality wine:

- **High-quality grapes** produced at a good site by advanced (sometimes "ancient") vineyard techniques, and picked at the right moment.
- **Skilled and dedicated winemaking** at the center of the process.
- **Record keeping** to compile a reference database of experience and to assuage the bureaucratic concerns of the regulators.
- **The curse of the accountant**, to assure that the financial underpinnings will be there to enable doing what needs to be done.
- **Marketing savvy** to move the wine through distribution channels to the consumer.

- **Staff able to perform well in technical and management functions** so the operation meets its objectives, and they need good facilities to enable their work.

- **A vineyard and/or winery, acquired or developed at a cost that is suitable for production of an acceptable return to investment.**

- **Effective management**, including expertise and skills of the owner or managing partner, to guide and balance productive efforts.

The production of wine can be a tremendously fascinating and rewarding endeavor. In the following chapters, we will explore each of these factors.

ᘓᘗ

A supportive marketplace

Bullish consumer demand

Opportunities for the creation of new wineries depend on two main factors: growth of wine consumption by Americans and the rate at which Americans upgrade their wine preferences from *jug* and *standard* wines to *premium* and *better* wines.

America's consumer wine market is growing at a rapid and steady rate. During the period from 2000–2014, annual consumption of *all* wines increased by 335 million gallons, an average annual gain of 22.3 million gallons, or 3.9 percent. Annual per capita consumption increased from 2.03 to an estimated 2.85 gallons in the same period.

In large part, our attention is directed at the category "table wines", because it is there that most opportunities for new smaller and medium-size wineries are to be found. The same can be said for acquisitions and expansions of existing wineries.

As Figure 1 shows, more moderate annual growth occurred in 2008, following the aggressive increases between 2001 and 2007. In 2001, the nation reacted to the terrorist attacks on New York's Twin Towers. How could an event that occurred in September affect the year's consumption so strongly, you may ask? For most wineries, the holiday season accounts for 50–65 percent of annual sales.

A Tribute

Robert Mondavi
1913–2008

Robert Mondavi was one of the world's greatest men of wine. His unrelenting efforts to improve his own brand led a revolution in California winemaking. His untiring efforts to promote his and other California wines grew the American market for quality wines.

On the several occasions when I had the honor of visiting with him, his demeanor was always the same. He extended friendship, encouragement and a respect I had done nothing to earn. Eventually, he would get around to the same question: "What are you doing with pinot noir in Oregon?"

If you were one of the many people to hear him talk about wine and its importance to food and society, you are very fortunate.

In a way, it is partly because of Robert Mondavi that we are experiencing such an explosion of American wineries, and I am writing this book.

—Jeffrey L. Lamy

The slower growth year of 2008, was caused by the financial market collapse and recession. A resurgence resumed in 2009, with an aggressive uptick in 2011. a long-term market reality still exists: the demand for wines in the U.S. does not experience an absolute decrease during recessions. The growth rate may slow, but does not turn negative, and this characteristic has been true for at least the past sixty years.

All Wines includes several sectors. *Table Wine* is the largest, at about 70 percent of the market. *Sparkling Wines* and *Dessert Wines* make up most of the difference between *All Wines* and *Table Wines*.

Table Wines are defined as dry and sweet still wines that are not more than 14 percent alcohol. *Dessert Wines* have more than 14 percent alcohol. *Sparkling Wines* have retained carbon dioxide greater than 0.5 pounds pressure in the bottle.

There are some additional sub-categories of wines, including *Other Special Naturally-Flavored Wines* and *Vermouth*. They are ignored because they are extremely small and unlikely to represent significant opportunities in the American market.

The movie *Sideways*, released in 2004, appears to have had only a minor impact on total U.S. table wine consumption, but it created a boomlet of interest in Pinot Noir. For Oregon wineries, who arguably make the best Pinot Noir in the world outside of Burgundy, the movie stimulated a demand for Pinot Noir that quickly cleaned out winery inventories and resulted in substantial price increases. It also significantly boosted the sales of the other varietals made in the state.

Explosive winery growth

The number of wineries in America has literally exploded in the past twenty years, before trailing off in 2009, then resuming high growth during 2010-2014. A glance at Figure 2 shows that the number of wineries has grown steadily

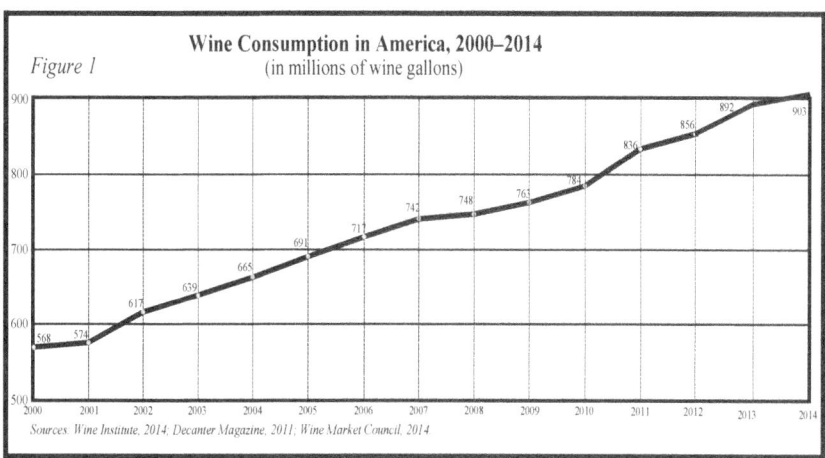

Figure 1

Wine Consumption in America, 2000–2014
(in millions of wine gallons)

Sources: Wine Institute, 2014; Decanter Magazine, 2011; Wine Market Council, 2014

Figure 2

**Explosive Growth of Winery Licensees
National Total, 1995–2014**

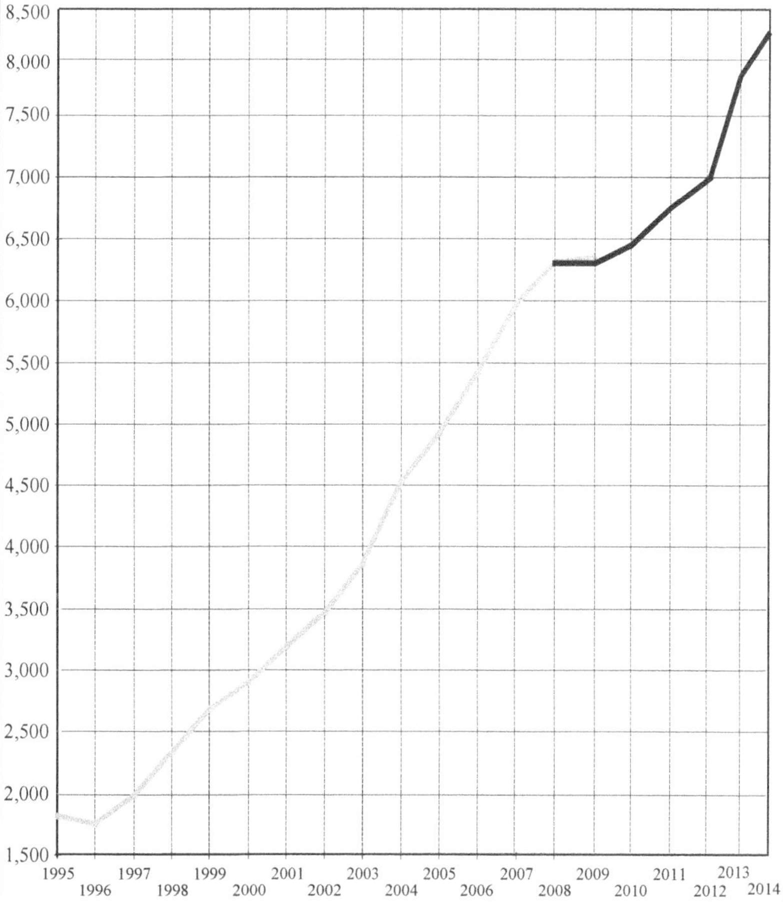

Sources: Wine Institute, 1995–2009; Wines & Vines, 2008–2015.

between slight decreases in 1996 and 2009. The average increase over the period was about 11.0 percent per year. It is equally impressive that the number of new winery licenses issued during the 2000–2001 recession did not decrease from the annual trend. Many winery developers took their money out of underperforming areas, like the stock market, and invested in winery facilities and equipment during those periods. In contrast, the 2009 decrease reflects the recession, an abrupt shift in wine consumer buying habits, some consolidation of ownerships and failures of marginal performers. The situation is discussed in more detail in Chapter 10.

These statistics include another class of licensees called "virtual wineries," which perform like wineries in several respects. One example is Oregon's Growers Sales Privilege Permit, by which a grower can contract with a winery to make the wine from the grower's grapes and bottle it with the grower's label. Then, the grower takes possession and markets the wine. Similar versions operate in some other states under custom crush regulations.

In 2012, there were 1,059 of these operations in America, amounting to 16.5 percent of total wineries.

Small wineries outnumber large ones

Wineries making less than 150,000 gallons annually in 2004 turned out only 8.8 percent of U.S. wine production in aggregate, but the 2,322 of them (in 2004) represented 93.6 percent of the number of all America wineries.

The distribution by winery size in 2015 is shown in Table 1. In that year, 96.2 percent of the wineries made less than 50,000 cases (118,924 gallons), and 77.8 percent made less than 5,000 cases (11,892 gallons). The distribution suggests one can start small and stay small, and still achieve success.

California still leads number of new licensees, but other states in chase

Since 1975, states other than California have experienced impressive growth in the number of bonded wineries. California's share of licensees has dropped from 57.0 percent in 1975 to 43.0 percent in 2010. (Figure 3).

From 1995–2012, the total number of bonded wineries in America grew by 412.7 percent from 1,817 to 7,498. During that seventeen-year period, the

TABLE 1   **Wineries by Production Size, January 2015**

		Wineries		
Cases Produced	**Gallons**	**Number**	**Percent of Total**	**Cumulative Percent**
<1,000	<2,378	3,030	36.6	36.6
1,000–4,999	2,379–11,892	3,465	41.7	78.3
5,000–49,999	11,893–118,924	1,480	17.9	96.2
50,000–499,000	118,925–1,189,249	254	3.0	99.2
>500,000	>1,189,250	58	0.7	100.0
Totals		8,287	100	100

Source: Wines & Vines

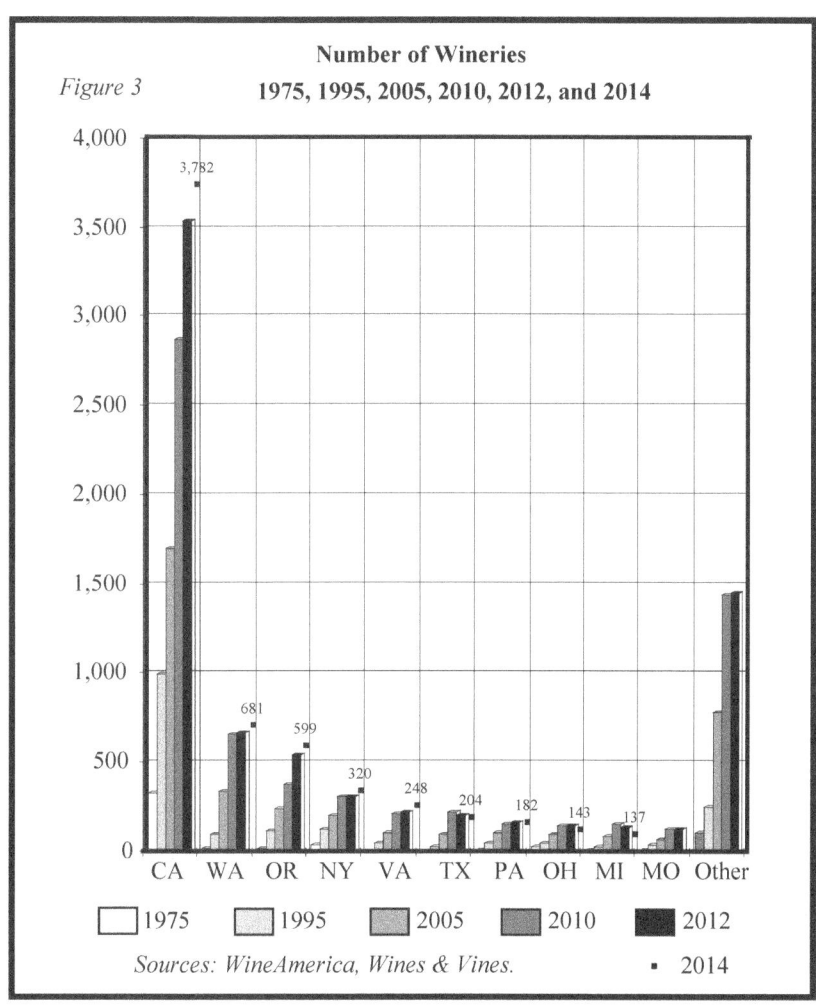

Figure 3

Number of Wineries
1975, 1995, 2005, 2010, 2012, and 2014

Sources: WineAmerica, Wines & Vines.

annual average increase was 334 new wineries. Washington and Oregon led the non-California states, averaging 33.8 and 25.4 new wineries formed annually, respectively.

It is equally impressive that the number of states containing bonded wineries increased from thirty-four in 1975 to all fifty by 2005.

Establishment of new wineries is not the only measure of rapid growth. Wine production is increasing rapidly, too.

The development of new wineries has a stimulating effect on wine consumption. The novelty of visiting local wineries to taste locally-made products introduces new consumers to the pleasures and health benefits of wine.

There's no question; much of the new winery cachet is the novelty of locally-grown wine. That acknowledged, operation of a winery does not depend entirely on locally-grown fruit. Crushed and uncrushed fruit, as well as pressed juice (sometimes frozen), are frequently shipped from grower sites to wineries in other states. The ability to utilize fruit from "ideal" climates to make wines closer to retail markets is a significant factor contributing to winery growth in states that are too hot, or too cold, to grow the best grape varieties.

Refrigerated semi-trailer trucks are used for uncrushed fruit, even over relatively short distances. It is widely agreed that shipping grapes further than 10–15 miles can be damaging to wine quality. Refrigerated tanker trucks are used for juice and destemmed crushed fruit.

Vitis vinifera grapes dominate the industry and marketplace

America is two wine regions. In general, wineries to the west of the Rockies make wine almost entirely from European grape varieties. In states to the east of the Rockies, wineries rely on native American varieties and French hybrids, as well as tree fruits and berries, with only a relatively small part of wine production based on *Vitis vinifera* grape varieties.

Table 2 presents production and growth data for the three Pacific States: California, Oregon and Washington. A focus on these three states is warranted because, taken together, they accounted for almost 90 percent of America's 2012 winegrape crush.

The list of grape varieties presented in Table 2 is noteworthy for its near absence of non-vinifera grape varieties. French Colombard, Rubired and Ruby Cabernet are hybrids developed from vinifera crosses by UC-Davis. The absence of Thompson Seedless grapes from the list is a mystery, inasmuch as the triple-use cultivar finds its way into many California jug wines.

The pattern of winery production that has occurred in California (typically 84–85 percent of U.S. production) since 2000 illustrates the agricultural nature of the industry. Figure 4 tracks the California winegrape crush over the past fifteen years. After a huge crush in 2005 and again in 2009 and 2012, 2013 outdid them all. The longer-term trend is obvious. Although many wineries try to scale vineyard production according to their marketing goals it is apparent that overall, at least in California's large wineries, volumes tend to be production driven by the harvest. In large part, that is due to the practice of allowing the vines for jug wine use to overproduce in good years. The vine responds by setting a smaller crop in the following year.

Rapid increases in wine production do not appear to have been damaging to wine prices, as was the experience of Australian wineries in 2006–2008. There, the problem was gross over-planting of new vineyards. In contrast, American wineries seem capable of absorbing harvests such as in 2005, and adjusting their market production schedules as needed for the short turn-around jug wines, with minimal downward pressure on wine prices.

Increases worth noting in Table 2 for Washington and Oregon include, Pinot Gris, Viognier and White Riesling among the whites; and Cabernet Sauvignon, Merlot, Pinot Noir and Syrah among the reds.

In the other states west of the Continental Divide—Idaho, Utah, Colorado, Arizona, New Mexico and Texas—the list of grape varieties is similarly populated with *Vitis vinifera* grapes.

To the east of the Rockies a different wine industry emerges. With the exception of New York State, the winery scene is characterized by small family-run

TABLE 2   Winegrapes Crushed by Wineries in Pacific Coast States

	2012 California Winegrape Crush				2012 Washington Winegrape Crush			2012 Oregon Winegrape Crush		
	Tons Crushed	% Share of Total Crush	% Increase 2011–2012	% Increase 2007–2012	Tons Crushed	% Share of Total Crush	% Increase 2007–2012	Tons Crushed	% Share of Total Crush	% Increase 2007–2012
Chardonnay	735,778	18.3	31.7	24.8	36,900	19.6	38.2	2,998	6.2	44.1
Chenin Blanc	58,080	1.4	6.6	–31.0	900	0.5	–18.2			
Gewürztraminer	16,839	0.4	50.7	73.6	3,500	1.9	–14.6	501	1.0	–16.8
French Colombard	311,612	7.8	–0.7	–2.4						
Sauvignon Blanc	113,269	2.8	–43.2	6.7	5,300	2.8	26.2	665	1.4	552.0
Muscat of Alexandria	78,418	2.0	19.5	42.7						
Pinot Gris	195,453	4.9	12.6	146.3	6,400	3.4	146.2	8,351	17.4	33.7
Viognier	24,157	0.6	34.2	53.3	1,900	1.0	58.3	336	0.7	–13.0
White Riesling	36,926	0.9	33.0	166.0	36,700	19.5	41.2	1,994	4.2	28.6
Barbera	56,272	1.4	24.1	–25.5						
Cabernet Franc	13,959	0.3	28.5	–8.8	3,400	1.8	25.9	325	0.7	26.5
Cabernet Sauvignon	496,774	12.4	29.3	16.8	35,900	19.1	64.7	959	2.0	13.8
Carignane	14,043	0.3	7.7	–36.6						
Grenache	65,519	1.6	–6.5	9.8	1,100	0.6	na			
Merlot	334,917	8.3	17.0	10.1	34,000	18.1	59.6	780	1.6	–21.2
Petite Syrah	66,065	1.6	12.8	40.0						
Petit Verdot	18,007	0.4	27.2	91.3	1,000	0.5	na			
Pinot Noir	248,469	6.2	45.8	177.6	800	0.4	0.0	29,953	62.3	–29.3
Rubired	226,504	5.6	–11.6	53.4						
Ruby Cabernet	71,257	1.8	–4.4	–2.0	800	0.4	0.0			
Sangiovese	9,419	0.2	30.2	20.3	1,200	0.6	71.4			
Syrah	132,486	3.3	21.1	4.4	11,800	6.3	26.9	1,035	2.2	22.9
Zinfandel	448,039	11.2	–29.8	9.9	na	na	na	119	0.3	–25.2
Total Crushed	4,017,800	100.0%	20.0%	23.7%	188,000	100.0%	48.0%	48,016	100.0%	616.1%

Notes: na = not available because of disclosure of source.

Source: National Agricultural Statistics Service; USDA. Oregon survey discontinued after 2010.

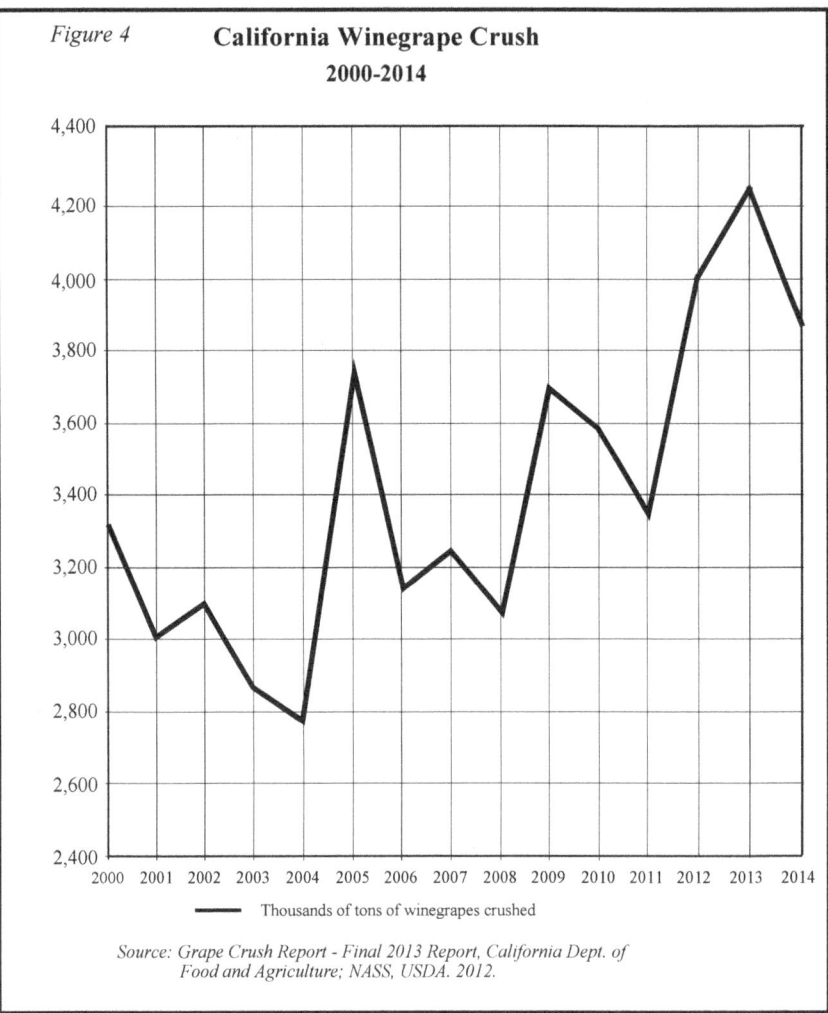

Figure 4 **California Winegrape Crush**
2000-2014

— Thousands of tons of winegrapes crushed

*Source: Grape Crush Report - Final 2013 Report, California Dept. of
Food and Agriculture; NASS, USDA. 2012.*

operations succeeding by making wines from Native American varieties,
French hybrids, a smattering of *Vitis vinifera* vines, and a wide selection of
tree and berry fruits. Table 3 lists winegrape varieties, along with indicators of
their importance, utilized in three states considered typical of the Midwest and
Eastern states. These figures are the most recent available; Midwestern and
Eastern states do not survey their vineyards as frequently as those on the West
coast.

The figures are distorted for Concord and Niagara in New York and Michigan.
Most of the tonnage is utilized for juice and table grapes, the rest for wine.

Sparkling/champagne wines

Beginning in the mid-1970s, European sparkling wine producers began building
American operations. It is not clear whether the movement was undertaken to
establish corporate images here or to pursue expansion in what they considered to be an emerging American market for sparkling wines. Whatever it was,
they built exotic wineries, most of them in prestigious Napa Valley. Moët &
Chandon began with Domaine Chandon in 1975. That was followed by Sonoma

TABLE 3   Leading Grape Varieties Three Midwest and Eastern States

Variety	Class	2011 New York Prod. Tons	2011 New York % of Crush	2008 Virginia Util. Tons	2008 Virginia % of Crush	2011 Michigan Acres	2011 Michigan % of Acres
Aurora	Fr.hybrid	4,225	2.2			3	0.0
Baco Noir	Fr.hybrid	1,069	0.6			12	0.1
Cabernet Franc	Vinifera	1,779	0.9	885	13.0	155	1.0
Cabernet Sauvignon	Vinifera	742	0.4	518	7.6	36	0.2
Chambourcin	Fr.hybrid	182	0.1	218	3.2	49	0.3
Chancellor	Fr.hybrid	234	0.1			46	0.3
Chardonel	Fr.hybrid					28	0.2
Catawba	Amer.hybrid	5,674	3.0			15	0.1
Cayuga	Hybrid	2,068	1.1			21	0.1
Chardonnay	Vinifera	2,889	1.5	1,264	18.6	215	1.4
Concord	Nat.American	120,382	64.0			9,030	57.5
DeChaunac	Fr.hybrid	490	0.3			30	0.2
Delaware	Nat.American	662	0.4				
Elvira	Amer.hybrid	5,528	2.9				
Fredonia	Amer.hybrid	281	0.1			6	0.0
Frontenac	Fr.hybrid					20	0.1
Gamay Noir	Vinifera					12	0.1
Himrod	Table grape					6	0.0
Lemberger	Vinifera					18	0.1
Gewürztraminer	Vinifera	491	0.3			60	0.4
Marechal Foch	Fr.hybrid	483	0.3			62	0.4
Marquis	Table grape						
Merlot	Vinifera	2,357	1.3	807	11.9	105	0.7
Moore's Diamond	Nat.American	426	0.2				
Muscat	Vinifera					9	0.1
Niagara	Nat.American	19,558	10.4			3,480	22.2
Norton	Amer.hybrid			170	2.5		
Petite Verdot	Vinifera			225	3.3		
Pinot Blanc	Vinifera					25	0.2
Pinot Gris	Vinifera	278	0.1			210	1.3
Pinot Meunier	Vinifera					4	0.0
Pinot Noir	Vinifera	952	0.5			235	1.5
Regent	Fr-Amer.hybrid					8	0.1
Sauvignon Blanc	Vinifera	297	0.2			22	0.1
Syrah	Vinifera					17	0.1
Seyval Blanc	Fr.hybrid	1,473	0.8			65	0.4
Traminette	Fr.hybrid	361	0.2	214	3.1	49	0.3
Ventura	Hybrid	575	0.4				
Vidal Blanc	Fr.hybrid	1,223	0.7	480	7.1	130	0.8
Vignoles	Fr.hybrid	508	0.3			80	0.5
Viognier	Vinifera			464	6.8	4	0.0
White Riesling	Vinifera	4,052	2.2			595	3.8
State Totals		188,000	100.0%	6,800	100.0%	15,700	100.0%

Note: "Prod. Tons" is "Production Tons"; "Util. Tons" is "Tons Utilized by Wineries."
Source: NASS, USDA; most recent reports for respective states.

Piper (Piper-Heidsieck), Domaine Carneros (Taittinger), Mumm Napa (G.H. Mumm), Roederer Estate (Louis Roederer) and Gloria Ferrer (Spain, now part of Freixenet). Then there are several premium quality California companies: Schramsberg, Hanns Kornell, Iron Horse, Jordan and Korbel. Add in three long-time New York producers, all owned by Seagrams: Taylor, Great Western and Gold Seal, and Washington State's Chateau Ste. Michelle, and you have a severe case of overcrowding. In the last twenty years, as America's wine consumers did not get excited about sparkling wines, most of those producers turned to making still wines in order to survive financially. Table 4 shows a steady decline of U.S. sparkling wine production's market share to 53.6 percent of total U.S. sparkling wine sales in 2014.

Fruits other than Vinifera wine grapes

It should be obvious by now that the primary focus of this book is on wines made from the European *Vitis vinifera* grape varieties. The reason for this bias is that *vinifera* is "where the action is" in America's metropolitan wine markets. National status for the winery, success in securing good distributors, access to the shelves of retailers and restaurant wine lists, ability to survive the clear preferences of the upcoming generations of wine consumers and sustainable profits are characteristics that argue in favor of *vinifera* wines.

The foregoing is not to say that wines made from non-vinifera fruits are without merit. To the contrary, many small wineries in newly emerging wine-producing states are doing quite well in quality and price by producing fruit and berry wines (see Chapter 7) and wines from locally-grown non-vinifera grapes (see Table 3).

TABLE 4   Sparkling Wines Share of Total U.S. Wine Shipments

	Millions of Gallons			Sparkling Wines as Percent of All Wines	
			Sparkling Wines		
	All Wines	Table Wines	All	U.S. Produced	All	U.S. Produced
2000	568.2	507.1	28.1	17.8	4.9	63.3
2005	692.4	609.4	30.9	19.5	4.5	62.9
2006	717.4	627.9	32.3	19.5	4.5	60.4
2007	746.4	650.5	32.8	19.4	4.4	59.1
2008	751.1	653.4	32.1	19.6	4.3	61.0
2009	767.8	669.5	33.1	20.7	4.3	62.6
2010	784.2	681.2	36.6	21.6	4.7	59.0
2011	836.0	749.0	41.4	22.7	5.0	54.8
2012	856.5	724.0	42.1	23.2	4.9	55.1
2013	886.4	769.1	43.7	23.6	4.9	54.0
2014	892.5	768.9	46.8	25.1	5.2	53.6

Sources: Wine Institute; U.S. Department of Commerce; Gomberg, Fredrikson & Associates.

U.S.-produced sparkling wines from TTB Production Reports' "Taxable Withdrawals." 2012.

A lesson in market demand

The West Coast offers an important lesson, however. Fruit and berry wines are almost nonexistent in California, Oregon and Washington. Some prominent Oregon wineries made fruit and berry wines during the early years of the state's wine industry in the 1960s and 1970s. Almost all of those wines have since disappeared, as well as some of the wineries that made them, owing to declining market demand. Marketing is discussed further in Chapter 10.

Current market conditions

As this book is written, there is some turmoil in the wine market. The recession of 2008–2013 is having an impact on wine demand and prices that can be expected to continue through 2014—and perhaps 2015—if the bunch in the nation's capitol don't change their policies.

Generally, consumers have cut back on dining out and travel, while increasing dining and entertaining at home. Those who do dine out have been paring back their wine buys from higher-priced wines to medium-priced premium wines and, even carafe wines. The impacts are fairly simple. Wineries who base their marketing programs heavily on the hotel and restaurant trade are experiencing cutbacks in demand, some severe. Restaurant chains are demanding lower wholesale wine prices and, in some cases, are even dropping from their lists prominent wineries that don't go along with their wishes.

On the other hand, some supermarkets are selling so many lower- and medium-priced wines that they are allocating more shelf space to wines. Some Costco stores, the nation's largest wine retailer, recently have doubled the floor space devoted to wines.

As we saw in Figure 2, the issuance of new winery licenses continues. Further, history has demonstrated that U.S. wine consumption of premium and super-premium wines does not decline in recessions, although the growth rate and prices may decrease. There are reasons for this.

During a recession, investors don't have many really good investment opportunities, except maybe gold. And, by mid-2011, gold appeared to have stalled its significant growth in value. A recession seems like a very good time to get those winery establishment years out of the way, and to be ready to ride the upswing when the wines come to market. Further, a recession offers advantageous development costs, particularly in construction of facilities and some types of equipment, perhaps even payroll.

In regard to wine consumption, some people will retrench to cheaper wines, and some of them will return to beer and mixed drinks for their alcoholic beverages. Historically, the wine segment experiencing the biggest, and only negative impact is jug wines, the low end of the price/quality spectrum.

The price and cost trends shown in Figure 5 offer a telling portrayal of wine price inflation since 1999. To assist in this analysis, each of the indices has been recalculated to a base value of 100.0 in 1999. These are the significant observations:

- The *Producer Price Index—Wineries* (PPI-W) indicates that wineries have been very conservative in raising their prices in response to inflation of food prices in general.

- We use the *Consumer Price Index—All Items, All Urban Consumers* (CPI-AI) as the overall measure of food price inflation. In almost every year, winery prices have been a better buy than other food purchases.

- The *Consumer Price Index—Wine Consumed at Home* (CPI-WCH) illustrates that wine prices in supermarkets and wine shops followed the trend of winery prices (*Producer Price Index—Wineries*, or PPI-W) closely between 1999 and 2005. Thereafter, wine prices through these outlets did not reflect the slowing of winery price increases in 2007, nor the winery price **reductions** in response to the national recession in 2010 and 2011.

Prevailing wine-pricing behavior at the retail level favors pricing through these outlets that is much more reflective of winery pricing than the pricing methods of establishments where the wine is consumed on the premises. That is because distributors and retail stores tend to stay with the same markup percentages year after year.

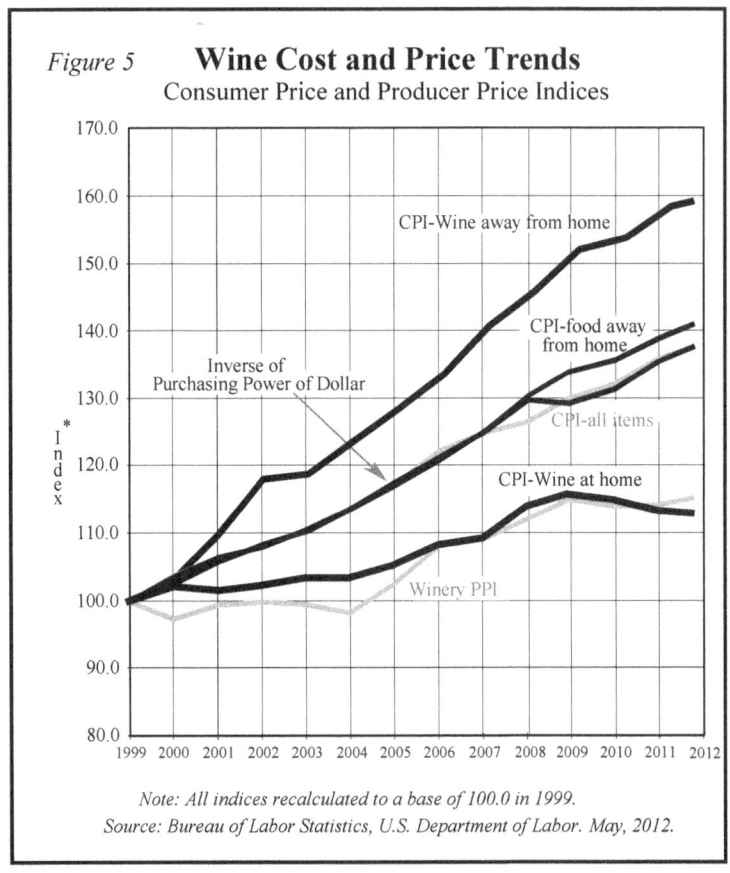

Figure 5 **Wine Cost and Price Trends**
Consumer Price and Producer Price Indices

Note: All indices recalculated to a base of 100.0 in 1999.
Source: Bureau of Labor Statistics, U.S. Department of Labor. May, 2012.

- Comparison of the *CPI—Food away from Home* (CPI-FAFH) with CPI-AI shows an amazingly close correlation during 1999–2008 between the pricing of non-alcoholic food items on restaurant menus and retail prices charged by food stores.

- Comparison of *CPI—Wine away from Home* (CPI-WAFH) with CPI-FAWH illustrates how wine prices charged by full service restaurants have been growing much more rapidly than food price inflation in general (CPI-AI), non-alcoholic foods consumed in restaurants (CPI-FAFH), and wines consumed at home (CPI-WAFH).

- Evaluation of CPI-WAFH reveals a slowing of wine price inflation in 2003 (9/11 recession) and 2010 (2007–2009 recession). Then, there has been a **decrease** in wine prices by restaurants since 2011.

Some clarification is needed for the trend during the period from 2009–2012. It is now well known that a strong consumer response to the 2009–2012 recession was a movement of wine consumers away from dining out in favor of dining and entertaining at home. Accordingly, there was a large shift in wine-buying away from restaurants and toward retail stores, particularly Costco, the nation's largest wine retailer. So, the hesitation of wine price inflation in restaurants, at least partially, is due to a shift in the mix of wine values purchased at each type of outlet: fewer but higher-priced wine in restaurants, and more lower-priced wines at Costco, supermarkets and wine shops.

The 1999–2012 trends are summarized thus:

Price trend of	Inflation 1999–2012
Wines consumed at home	+12.4%
Winery prices	17.7%
Inverse purchasing power of dollar	**37.0**%
CPI-All Food Items	**39.7**%
Food in restaurants	41.8%
Food at home	41.9%
Wines in restaurants	+59.4%

Has the restaurant trade been contributing to its own sales problems?

Conclusions about market conditions

Various industry reports indicate that, while wine sales measured in dollars decreased from 2009 to 2010 by as much as 6–8 percentage points, the volume sold, in gallons, increased by as much as 2 percent. A recent survey of CEOs of twenty-one leading wineries[1] confirmed the consumer shift to lower-priced wines, dropping sales revenues and profits and distributor consolidations. However, most of them felt a turnaround is at hand and advised for sharper management in terms of forward planning, pricing strategies and cost controls.

All things considered, and taking into consideration the long-term situation, the wine market outlook is relatively strong and positive with respect to the

---

1. "Responding to Trends in a Difficult Market: 2010 Wine Industry CEO Survey"; Wine Industry Financial Symposium Group and UC-Davis Graduate School of Management. Published in *Practical Winery & Vineyard* magazine; November-December 2010 issue. Page 27.

establishment and/or expansion of small wineries. **The most fertile market segment to pursue is better-than-standard quality wines from noble *Vitis vinifera* grape varieties.** To a large extent, the feasibility of starting/acquiring small wineries will depend on availability of suitable climates and sites for vineyards within reasonable distances from the winery. Those wineries planning on importing grapes from vineyards that have the right climates, topographies and soils need to seriously evaluate refrigerated transportation costs as a significant component of raw materials costs.

Further reading

Stevenson, Tom. *Champagne*. The Wine Appreciation Guild; Sotheby's Publications; Harper and Row, Publishers, 1986.

TTB, Alcohol and Tobacco Tax and Trade Bureau, U.S. Department of the Treasury, Washington, DC. Website: http://www.ttb.gov/wine/

Wasserman, Sheldon, and Pauline Wasserman. *Sparkling Wine*. New Century Publishers, 1984.

The Wine Institute, The Advocacy Group for California Wineries. Website: http://www.wineinstitute.org

WineAmerica, The National Association of American Wineries, Washington, DC. Website: http://www.wineamerica.org

80 03

–3–

Importance of the grape

The production of high-quality wine begins in the vineyard, where desirable characteristics of the finished wine must be "grown" into the fruit before it is harvested and brought to the winery.

At the beginning, we identified eight major factors that must come together to make a winery venture a success. This chapter will focus on the raw material: the grapes and other fruits used to make wine.

High-quality grapes

Site topography and soils, climate, many aspects of vineyard management and design, and timing of harvest all contribute to success in the vineyard. Failure in any of these elements will weaken prospects for a great wine. Certainly, ideal weather can reduce the task of mold control, but it won't eliminate the need for all of the other tactics of vineyard management. Further, skilled hedging and leaf-pulling may or may not be required to reach a perfect balance among the many aromatic and flavor components in every year. But, even in that occasional "ideal" year, the winemaker still has to get the grapes picked at the right time or the balance provided by Mother Nature will go unrealized.

The importance of grape quality is well expressed in this statement by one accomplished winemaker: "If it isn't in the grape when it hits the crush pad, it'll never be in the wine." How true this simple statement is. Some winemakers have tried to reduce the perfect moment of harvest to numbers. They are fond of reciting: "I like to consider sugar, total acidity and pH"; or "the ratio between acidity and pH is particularly important."

The problem with the "numbers approach" is that the vine adjusts to changes in the growing season's heat. Grapes will achieve biological ripeness at lower sugar and higher acid levels in a cool season, and vice versa in an abnormally warm season. *Biological ripeness* is the stage where aromas and flavors typical for the variety have developed in the fruit.

Ask the world's greatest winemakers and they'll tell you that the aroma and taste of the grapes are the most important determinants of harvest timing. When you come right down to it, the subjective sensory abilities of the wine-maker are more important than laboratory tests in determining the readiness of the fruit to make the transition into high-quality wine.

Sugar and acid levels can be adjusted in the winery.

It starts with vineyard siting

Let's back up to the vineyard's origin. Many characteristics of the fruit are established in the very first stage of the vineyard's development: selection of the microclimate. Location with respect to latitude, elevation, slope direction and severity, and macroclimate (area temperature patterns, amount of precipitation and its timing, cloud cover and seasonal prevailing wind direction) all contribute. So do soil characteristics, such as pH (throughout the rooting depth, not just the 8–15 inches of topsoil), water holding capacity, drainage, texture, rooting depth, color, fertility (cation exchange capacity coupled with pH) and essential nutrients.

Three very important factors must be considered right up front:

1. A large number of aspiring grape growers take the real estate agent's word for the property's grape-growing suitability. Or, they listen to a new grower just down the road, who recently stuffed his first vines into the ground and still has a lot to learn. A handful of real estate agents are outstanding grape growers and know what they are talking about. The same can be said for growers "just down the road." But, the knowledge-able ones are few and far between. The author wouldn't take a realty salesman's or newbie grower's word for the property's potential, nor should you.

   In your best interest, and that of the large investment of money, time and labor you are about to make, **get the opinion of someone who has the grape knowledge and does not have a financial stake in your land trans-action**. Such expertise may, or may not, reside with an extension agent, depending on how much experience that agent has with quality grape growing.

2. Almost every person starting a new vineyard wants to produce some-thing special. Many farmers think growing grapes is as simple as growing berries or vegetables and feel they can excel with grapes. Not all of them say it right out, but they say it indirectly. You can hear it. Especially, the ones who aspire to starting a winery wish to achieve great things.

   Therefore, this chapter on establishing the vineyard is extremely important. That's why it is accorded so many pages, so many observations and words of advice. It must be said: **What you do in the vineyard is the most crucial part of all that you will do to make outstanding wine.**

3. There are still some unknown factors relating to wine excellence in the vineyard. You can take advantage of all the knowledge available about vineyard siting and its effects on wine quality, either gained through your own experience in grape growing **and** winemaking, or the employment of a knowledgeable consultant, but you are still only about 80 percent of the way home, in this writer's opinion, to growing outstanding wine. Otherwise, every vineyard on a given hillside, sharing the same soils, topography, microclimate, design and cultural practices would be of equal quality. Why do all of the vineyards above Vôsne-Romanée in Burgundy's Côte d'Or, for example, not have *Grand Cru* status like those owned by Domaine de la Romanée-Conti?

   There is still an empirical element, one of trial and error and mystery, involved in achieving wine greatness.

Heat and light

Temperature is not the only energy source to be considered. Two forces drive photosynthesis in the vine's leaves: ambient temperature and solar radiation, or light. To some extent, one may substitute for the other. But, it is the combination of the two that determines the photosynthetic rate. And, the latter factor, solar radiation, offers opportunities for modifying the energy captured by the vine canopy. Further, the author's extensive research over almost forty years indicates that the shape of the energy input curve over the course of daylight hours has a lot of influence on taste and aroma characteristics in the resulting wine, depending on the grape variety. More of this subject will be pursued later.

The microclimate on a hillside can be modified by changing row direction and trellis design, and by planting windbreaks. Adjustment of soil acidity and addition of essential minerals and nutrients are additional controllable elements. Foliar spray applications enable precision timing of nutrient availability.

Determinants of wine quality

In America, heat summation (degree-days) and soil characteristics generally serve to describe good growing areas for winegrapes. The French revere the term *climat* to describe the best growing areas. *Climat* includes the total microclimate environment in which the grapes are grown: heat, sunshine, precipitation, soil and slope, but also everything the grower does in the vineyard. Germans take yet a different approach. Soil characteristics are important, but "hours of sunshine" reign supreme.

Climate indicators

The "heat summation" method is usually used in America to classify areas as to their suitability for growing winegrapes. The method was devised by professors at the University of California at Davis (UC-Davis).

Heat Summation totals the degree-days over 50°F during the growing season of April 1 through October 31. The calculation for one day's contribution is:

$$\text{Degree-days} = \frac{(\text{daily high temperature} + \text{daily low temperature})}{2} - 50°\text{F}$$

In Table 5, heat summations are shown for well-known viticulture areas worldwide, as well as for established locations in America. The rank-ordered listing of 178 sites may be used as a rough guide for selecting grape varieties to be grown. Just look to nearby famous growing areas in the listing. Heat summation does have its shortcomings for this task. It is true that budbreak usually occurs at the time the average temperature exceeds 50°F. Once the leaf is unfurled, though, photosynthetic activity occurs all the way down to 41°F, if sunlight is present.

Evaluation of growing sites according to total available energy would provide a better comparison than that provided by air temperature alone. Remember, the photosynthetic rate is determined by both ambient temperature and solar irradiance.

German viticultural sites are evaluated according to the total hours of sunshine during the growing season. That appears to be an argument in support of considering the solar energy input to the site, as well as temperature. Hours of sunshine are in different units than photons (light) or watts/sq. meter (solar radiation), but both can be used as rough scalars for light energy.

Solar radiation data can be found for some areas. The recording of such data is coordinated by the U.S. Bureau of Reclamation. This topic will be discussed more under "Topography."

A more widely available measure is the **potential evapotranspiration index,** or PET, which is commonly used in farm areas to estimate daily irrigation needs. PET represents the total water transpired from all plant surfaces, as well as evaporation from the land and bodies of water. Many mathematical equations have been developed. Some work better than others in specific applications, such as crop irrigation versus watershed water management. However, all are attempts to integrate the many forces in the climate, including temperature, humidity, barometric pressure, wind speed, etc., in relating them to plant activity.

Thornthwaite's Index was the first PET formula, developed by C.W. Thornthwaite and published while he was Chief of Climactic and Physiographic Research of the USDA Soil Conservation Service. The innovation inspired dozens of refinements, the most popular of which seems to be the Penman equation.

There are difficulties in obtaining comparable PET values from state to state, however. Not all states use the same evapotranspiration models. Some states, particularly California, have developed multipliers for use on specific crops. Other states have chosen grass to be representative of all plants. Therefore, unless you are a mathematics wonk, PET will have limited use, except in comparing sites within the same state.

Matching varieties and climates

Each grape variety has its own heat and light energy requirements to achieve ripeness, or biological maturity. Analysis of the world's greatest vineyards reveals a consistent characteristic: the grape varieties that are grown there just reach full maturity in most years, but not in every year. The climate is marginal,

TABLE 5 **Heat Summation—Degree-Days, Selected Sites Worldwide**

Location	Degree-Days	Location	Degree-Days	Location	Degree-Days
Nanaimo, BC, CAN	1,598	Whenuapai, Aukland, NZ	2,509	Bloomington, IN	3,343
Flathead Lake, MT	1,701	Middletown, RI	2,510	Livermore, CA	3,348
Christchurch, NZ	1,716	Parma Exp. Sta., ID	2,533	Nebraska City, NE	3,368
Sturgeon Bay, WI	1,732	New Philadelphia, OH	2,545	Cape May, NJ	3,371
Reims, Champagne, FR	1,744	San Luis Obispo, CA	2,548	Warrenton, VA	3,382
Wurzburg, Germany	1,802	Danbury, CT	2,574	Dahlonega, GA	3,389
Aigle, Switzerland	1,816	Elgin, IL	2,586	Los Lunas, NM	3,404
Trier, Mosel, Germany	1,825	Odessa, Ukraine	2,620	Capetown, South Africa	3,435
Geisenheim, Reingau, DEU	1,839	Bordeaux, FR	2,622	Festus, MO	3,454
Cottage Grove, OR	1,849	Lebanon, PA	2,631	Orange, Rhone, FR	3,545
Puyallup, WA	1,872	Canberra-Hunter Valley, AUS	2,638	Yadkin Valley, NC	3,552
Chandler. Apt., MN	1,884	Milan-Malapensa Airport, IT	2,639	Healdsburg, CA	3,578
Taos, NM	1,902	Hollister, CA	2,648	Lexington, KY	3,588
Geneva, SUI	1,944	Maquoketa, IA	2,649	Palisade, Grand Valley, CO	3,593
Nelson, NZ	1,947	Glenns Ferry, ID	2,662	Carbondale, IL	3,605
Orleans, Loire, FR	1,998	Cave Junction, OR	2,671	Livingston, TN	3,654
Penticton, BC, Canada	2,020	Paonia, CO	2,691	Jefferson City, MO	3,679
Colmar, Alsace, FR	2,045	Loudoun-Mt.Weather, VA	2,730	Tblisi, Georgia (Russia)	3,688
Hood River, OR	2,066	Prosser, WA	2,826	Florence, IT	3,699
Dijon-Longvic, Burgundy, FR	2,068	Budapest, Hungary	2,845	Lodi, CA	3,716
Geneva, NY	2,091	Kalamazoo, MI	2,848	St. Charles, MO	3,728
Mulhouse, Alsace, FR	2,125	Porto, Portugal	2,867	Sao Paolo, Brazil	3,729
Dundee, OR	2,141	Riverhead , LI, NY	2,876	Faywood, NM	3,736
Tours, Loire, FR	2,156	Sunnyside, WA	2,882	Split, Croatia	3,742
Auxerre, FR	2,158	Norfolk, Airport, NE	2,913	Warrenton, MO	3,802
Pomfret, CT	2,162	Adelaide Hills, AUS	2,923	Lewes, DE	3,803
Chalk Hill, PA	2,163	Keyser Exp. Station, WV	2,924	Mendoza, Argentina	3,822
South Hero, VT	2,167	Parkton, MD	2,929	Charlottsville, VA	3,829
Vienna, Austria	2,185	Villa Real, Portugal	2,945	Frederick, MD	3,856
Carlton, OR	2,217	Morgantown-Hart Airport, WV	2,948	Algiers, Algeria	3,885
Oliver, BC, Canada	2,247	Spencer, WV	2,976	Placerville, Amador. Co., CA	3,926
Penn Yan, NY	2,255	Santiago, Chile	2,987	San Fernando, Jerez, Spain	4,009
Yakima, WA	2,255	Ephrata, WA	2,994	Las Cruces, NM	4,018
Huntley, WY	2,255	Bucharest, Romania	3,006	Kofu, Japan	4,086
Ashland, OR	2,267	Ankara, Turkey	3,015	Modesto, CA	4,160
Leelanau Peninsula, MI	2,269	Santa Barbara, CA	3,019	Lawrence, KA	4,178
Niagara, ONT, Canada	2,273	Caldwell, ID	3,020	Tularosa, NM	4,281
Forest Grove, OR	2,273	Udine, Friuli, IT	3,023	Kansas Settlement, AZ	4,285
Beaune, Burgundy, FR	2,311	Santa Rosa, CA	3,034	Wellington, South Africa	4,333
Roseburg, OR	2,331	Weston, WV	3,113	Sedona, AZ	4,369
Santa Maria, CA	2,336	Westchester, PA	3,119	Moab, UT	4,376
Bridgehampton, LI, NY	2,351	Napa State Hosp., CA	3,131	Vinita, OK	4,394
Macon, Burgundy, FR	2,359	Ashville Regional Airport, NC	3,137	Catania, Sicily, IT	4,410
Medford, OR	2,369	Logrono, Rioja, Spain	3,156	Lubbock Regional Airport, TX	4,426
Kingston, RI	2,369	Walla Walla, WA	3,157	Ozark, AR	4,471
McMinnville, OR	2,370	Atlantic City Airport, NJ	3,166	Clanton, AL	4,508
Napa, CA	2,380	Siena, Tuscany, IT	3,169	Lordsburg, NM	4,508
Lincoln, MA	2,387	Clearlake, CA	3,177	Palermo, Sicily, IT	4,540
Grants Pass, OR	2,391	Montelimar, Rhone, FR	3,185	Aiken, SC	4,625
Martha's Vineyard, MA	2,393	Vermillion, SD	3,203	Pahrump, NV	4,779
Prairie de Sac, WI	2,404	Cincinnati-Ripley Ex.Farm, OH	3,212	Post, TX	4,815
South Hampton, NH	2,416	Lambertville, NJ	3,219	Lawton, OK	5,042
Fredonia, NY	2,422	Dallesport, WA	3,222	Natchez, MS	5,186
Freiburg, Germany	2,437	Pisa, Tuscany, IT	3,234	Fredericksburg, TX	5,248
Santa Maria, CA	2,438	Hanover, PA	3,234	Fort Stockton, TX	5,293
Salinas, CA	2,443	Sonoma, CA	3,241	Covington, LA	5,314
Kutztown, PA	2,465	King City, CA	3,245	St. Augustine, FL	5,385
Lyon-Satolis, FR	2,481	Middleburg, VA	3,258	Clermont, FL	5,654
Eltopia, WA	2,485	Paso Robles, CA	3,301	College Station, TX	5,788
Santa Cruz, CA	2,498	Soledad-Pinnacles, CA	3,307		

Notes: (1) Heat Summation Degree-Days are base 50°F for April-October. Daily average temperature minus 50 degrees = Degree-Days for that day. (2) Annual Degree-Days are calculated by the author from monthly average temperatures using the double triangle method. In most cases, the average temperatures used are 30-year averages.

Sources: Climatography of the United States No. 81; National Climatic Data Center, *NESDIS, National Oceanic and Atmospheric Administration*, 2002; *WorldClimate.com*, 2006; *The Weather Channel; The Weather Underground*, 2008; *Burgundy*, by Anthony Hanson; *Canadian Climate Normals and Averages, National Climate Data and Information Archive*, Revised 2006. Some estimates by the author based on several nearby weather stations.

i.e., ripening occurs when the ambient temperature and solar input are both declining in magnitude, approaching the level at which photosynthesis no longer occurs. Therefore, final ripening of the grapes progresses slowly. Final ripening is the period when the fruit esters and other flavor and aroma components of the grape are elaborated or created. A prolonged time period enables the development of concentration and complexity.

A clue as to which varieties are best for a given site is provided by the heat summation in degree-days. Certain growing areas are generally considered to represent an ideal for specific grape varieties. Table 6 presents a summary of many of those areas. While it is advisable to consider also the typical solar radiation received by the site, heat summation is a rough shortcut to the best matches. Also, one has to consider the wine style produced, as well as the grape variety.

The principle is fairly simple: Grow the grapes in a climate that is too cold, and the flavors don't have a chance to develop completely. The resulting wine is acidic and thin, lacking in full varietal character. If you grow them in a climate that is too warm, the final ripening period is too short, flavors don't develop complexity, but advance to overripe and acidity plummets. The resulting wine is flat, insipid, flabby, "out of balance."

Grow grapes in a climate that has a very small difference between daytime and nighttime temperatures, and you will get colorless, flavorless grapes.

The trick, then, is to select grape varieties that achieve full ripeness in most years within the vineyard's microclimate. Or, because most new viticulturists wish to produce certain types of wines, start with the grape varieties and then choose an appropriate vineyard location. Does that sound too complicated? Nobody said this was going to be easy.

Soils
The suitability of soils for growing grapes can be analyzed using information available from the U.S. Department of Agriculture's Soil Conservation Service, and published in *Soil Survey* books for each agricultural county. Grapevines are adaptable to many soils. The most important soil characteristics are discussed in Table 7.

Topography
Topography can have a profound effect on the quality of grapes. It is well-known that a slope can overcome the effects of frost. On a sloped hillside, cold air flows down, preventing the settling that is necessary for frost to accumulate. Flat sites will probably need a mist system, wind machines, or to be planted with a variety that recovers extremely well from frost damage.

There are some differences of opinion about vine suitability based on which direction the slope faces. In the 1960s, Oregon's vineyard pioneers thought a south-facing slope was the only one on which one could grow grapes. Justifiably, they reasoned that, because the climate was cooler than in Burgundy's Côte d'Or, they had to take maximum advantage of available sunlight. So, almost everyone planted north-south rows on south-facing slopes, a practice that still

TABLE 6   **Wine Growing Areas Considered Best Leading Varieties and Heat Summation**

Region	Leading Varieties	Other Varieties	Degree-Days	Nearest Weather Station
Champagne	Pinot Noir, Chardonnay	Pinot Meunier	1,744	Rheims
Alsace	White Riesling, Pinot Gris	Pinot Blanc	2,045	Colmar
	Gewürztraminer	Müller-Thurgau		
Burgundy				
Vôsne Romanée	Pinot Noir		2,126	Nuits-St.-George
Montrachet	Chardonnay		2,250	Beaune
Loire Valley				
Atlantique	Muscadet (aka Melon de Bourgogne)		2,001	Nantes
Chinon-Bourgueil	Cabernet Franc		2,018	Bourgueil
Vouvray	Chenin Blanc		2,156	Tours
Sancerre	Sauvignon Blanc		1,992	Sancerre
Beaujolais	Gamay Noir au Jus Blanc		2,359	Macon
Bordeaux	Cabernet Sauvignon, Merlot,	Cabernet Franc,	2,622	Bordeaux
	Sauvignon Blanc, Semillon	Malbec, Petite Verdot		
Cognac	St. Emillion (aka Trebbiano, Ugni Blanc)		2,587	Cognac
Rhone Valley				
Côte Rôtie	Syrah	Grenache, Viognier	2,681	Vienne
Italy				
Piedmont	Nebbiolo, Barbera	Arneis	2,994	Torino
		Muscat Blanc a Petits Grains		
Tuscany	Nebbiolo, Sangiovese		3,169	Sienna
Friuli	Pinot Griggio (aka Pinot Gris)		3,023	Udine
Germany				
Rheingau	White Riesling		1,839	Geisenheim
Franconia	Sylvaner		1,802	Wurzburg
Rheinhessen	Müller-Thurgau		1,849	Nierstein-Oppenheim
Portugal	Touriga Nacional	Bastardo	2,945	VillaReal
Spain				
Jerez	Palatino		4,009	San Fernando
Rioja	Tempranillo		3,156	Logroño
California				
Napa Valley	Cabernet Sauvignon, Merlot		3,364	St. Helena
Amador County	Zinfandel		3,831	Placerville

TABLE 7   **Soil Guidelines for Winegrapes**

Soil Property	Guidelines for Suitability
Rooting depth to bedrock	Soil structure that permits rooting to 5 feet preferably, or 3 feet minimum. If rooting depth is less than 3 feet, irrigation will be needed. Check high water table or perched water table conditions that can kill roots. Deep subsoiling, or riping, may be necessary to break up plow pans or mineral pans that would limit rooting. Grapevine roots can penetrate to 40+ feet if allowed, and if needed to seek water.
Available water capacity	The soil should be able to hold 10–12 inches of water (0.2 in/in over 5 feet) through its rooting depth. If less than 10 inches, irrigation will be needed. Most grape varieties need about 16–18 total inches of water to get through the growing season. The vine's water supply comes from precipitation plus water stored in the soil (plus irrigation).
Clay content (particles less than 0.002 mm)	Clay above 20 percent is desirable for good vine nutrition, but clay exceeding 50 percent is questionable because of hindered root penetration.
Drainage	Another name is "permeability." Measured in in/hr of water movement through saturated soil. 0.6–2.0 in/hr is good. Slower, and roots can become waterlogged. Faster, and the soil dries out too quickly.
Acidity	Measured as pH, which is the negative logarithm for the hydrogen ion count. pH < 5.5 is too acidic; liming may be needed. pH > 8.4 is too calcareous; downward adjustment may be needed. In either case, special attention must be paid to rootstock selection.
Nutrient capacity or soil fertility	Called "cation exchange capacity," it is soil's capacity to exchange ion with the plant's roots. 20–25 Meq (millequivalents) per 100 grams.

prevails in Oregon today. After all, why argue with success? As growers gained experience, though, they demonstrated that other slopes do well with certain varieties, even Pinot Noir. Further, slight north slopes can be used to grow Pinot Noir and Chardonnay for sparkling wine.

Strong empirical messages about slope direction are provided by the world's most famous vineyards. Perhaps the strongest messages come from Burgundy and Champagne. Almost all of the Côte d'Or's Grand Cru and Premier Cru Pinot Noir vineyards are on east and southeast slopes. Over some 15 centuries, trial and error have demonstrated that Pinot Noir grows its best wines on these slopes in Burgundy. Who would want to argue with the monks?

Chardonnay does not seem to be so emphatically affected by slope direction. All but one of Burgundy's Chardonnay *Grand Cru*, however, are on east-southeast slopes: Les Montrachet, Chevallier-Montrachet and Bâtard-Montrachet. Further north, on Corton hill above Aloxe-Corton, is the other *grand cru* Chardonnay vineyard. It is on a south and southwest slope: Corton-Charlemagne.

One look at a contour map of the area from Aloxe-Corton to Santenay reveals plenty of east-facing slopes producing *Premier Cru* Chardonnay. However, many flat or slightly hilly vineyards in every direction produce excellent Pinot Noir and Chardonnay. But, they are not necessarily the best.

In Champagne, the same patterns do not prevail. The Montagne de Reims is an expansive south-facing ramp above the Marne River to the north of Épernay. It is all planted with Pinot Noir and Pinot Meunier, both black grapes. To the east of Épernay is the Côte des Blancs, in a side valley off the Marne River, all east-facing, all white grapes: Chardonnay and Pinot Blanc.

To fully comprehend the importance of topography, one needs to understand photosynthesis and solar radiation. Photosynthesis is the process that occurs in the leaves of plants in which carbon dioxide is absorbed from the air through the stoma on the leaf bottoms and, powered by solar radiation (photons of light), it is converted within the leaf into carbohydrates and oxygen by a two-stage process. The oxygen is released to the atmosphere. The most important carbohydrate at this stage is sugar, which is transformed in the leaves and elsewhere in the vine, in what are called *dark reactions* (also known as light independent reactions or Calvin-Benson Cycle), into all of the building blocks of the vine and its fruit.

No photosynthesis can occur in the absence of light. It can be said that solar radiation is the creator of the basic food of all plant life, and of all heat energy realized on earth. Solar radiation, or irradiance, or insolation, or light, is mass-free energy transmitted in electromagnetic waves. It travels to the leaf surface by several paths: direct, reflected and diffuse.

Figure 6 illustrates several ways in which solar radiation can be analyzed, depending on the task at hand. **Radiation available to the site** is the solar radiation that has made it through the atmosphere and is available for providing light energy to the site and vine. **Radiation impacting the site** is the amount of radiation making contact with the bare soil surface, and its magnitude is affected by the site's slope angle. **Radiation impacting the vine canopy** is the amount of light energy that contacts the surface area of the vine canopy, and its magnitude is affected by the angle at which the direct, reflected and diffuse radiation components strike the canopy's surface. **Radiation absorbed by the vine canopy** is the amount of light energy that the leaf cells put to use. Its magnitude is affected by the distribution of light wavelengths within its spectrum and how they are utilized by the two types of chlorophyll.[1]

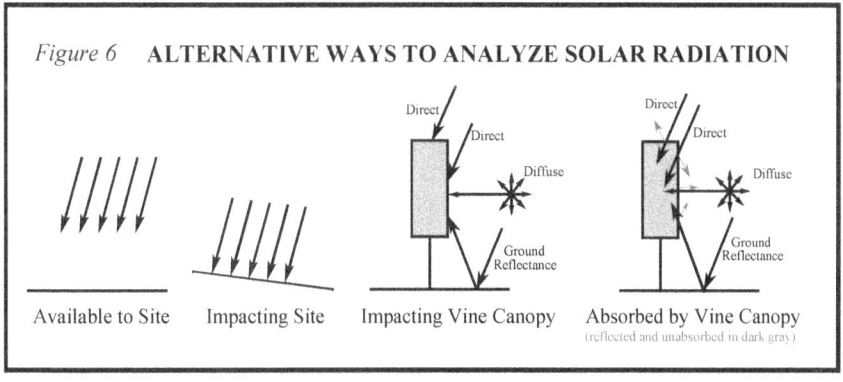

Figure 6   **ALTERNATIVE WAYS TO ANALYZE SOLAR RADIATION**

Available to Site   Impacting Site   Impacting Vine Canopy   Absorbed by Vine Canopy
(reflected and unabsorbed in dark gray)

---

1. A more detailed presentation of photosynthesis is made in Chapter 4.

Some definitions are in order:

Solar radiation	Energy that is emitted by the sun in electro-magnetic waveform. It exists in a wide array of visible and invisible wavelengths. As it passes through earth's atmosphere, some is reflected back into space (albedo), some is absorbed by the atmosphere and the rest gets through. It is worth noting that, on a typical cloudy day, as much as 30–35 percent of the solar radiation still gets through. Also called solar irradiance, solar insolation and light.
Photons	Frequently, light is measured in photons. The amount of energy in a photon varies with the wavelength. As used in horticulture, light typically is measured in photons or foot-candles.
Vectors	Because the relative positions of the sun and a vineyard site are changing all day and throughout the growing season, it is necessary to break the radiation down into vectors. Then, available radiation can be applied to topographic conditions of the site, and vineyard design parameters like row direction and trellis configuration. The vectors that best simplify this analytical process are: vertical, north-south, and east-west.
Direct solar radiation	Direct solar energy reaching the land or leaf surface. Also called "beam radiation," it is measured at the bottom of a black tube to eliminate diffuse and reflected radiation from other sources.
Diffuse radiation	Solar radiation that is deflected by the atmosphere, mostly reflected by, and refracted within, water droplets. It reaches the vine from all directions.
Global solar radiation	The total from all solar radiation sources. Total direct solar radiation plus diffuse radiation.
Total solar radiation	Global solar radiation plus ground reflectance.
Ground reflectance	Solar radiation reflected off the ground surface onto the vine canopy.

Figure 7 illustrates how solar radiation can be broken down into three vectors for analysis of the ways in which radiation impacts a vineyard site: vertical, east-west and north-south. Also shown, to the right, is conversion to the vectors that relate to the specific site. In this latter form, the vertical vector is perpendicular to the soil surface at the site and the north-south component is parallel to the soil surface. The east-west component is zero because the slope faces due south.

In Figure 8, available solar radiation is analyzed over the course of 16 hours of sunlight on a mid-July day. Latitude is 45.6° North. Direct solar radiation is assumed at 650 watt-hours/square meter/hour. Cloud cover is six percent. Diffuse light is 30 percent. Soil reflectivity is 0.70.

In the graph, data is presented with morning on the right, afternoon on the left, as a concession to our habit of orienting maps with north at the top. It is as if we are viewing the site from the south, watching the day progress from sunrise on the right to sunset on the left.

In Oregon's Willamette Valley, the peak of diffuse radiation lags about 30 minutes behind the direct radiation vectors.

If we add the heat energy owing to ambient temperature to the energy presented by solar radiation, we have the **total energy driving photosynthesis** in the grapevine. Figure 9 does just that.

The total energy curve is shifted slightly to the left because of the heat component curve.

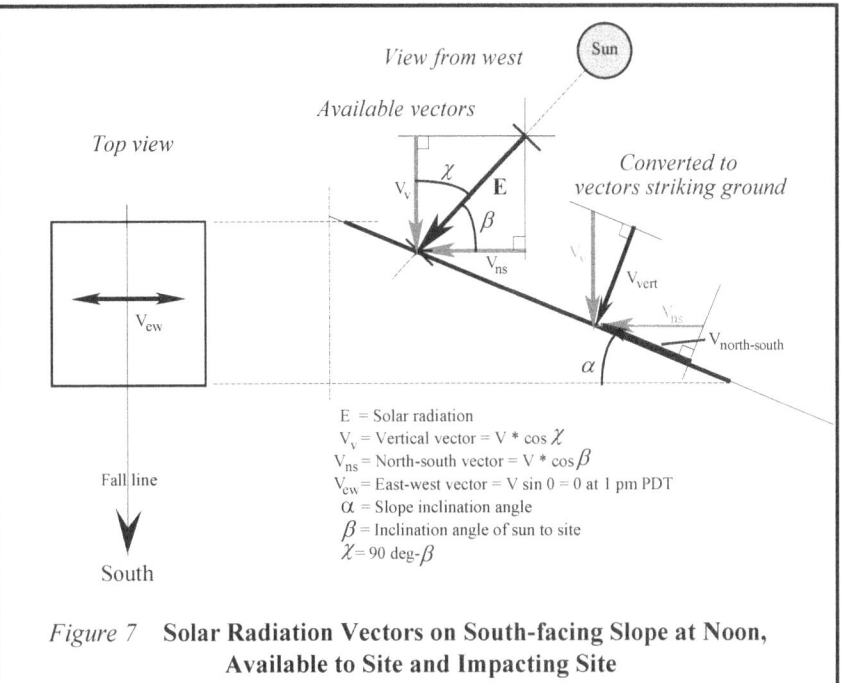

E = Solar radiation
V_v = Vertical vector = $V * \cos \chi$
V_{ns} = North-south vector = $V * \cos \beta$
V_{ew} = East-west vector = $V \sin 0 = 0$ at 1 pm PDT
α = Slope inclination angle
β = Inclination angle of sun to site
$\chi = 90 \deg - \beta$

Figure 7   **Solar Radiation Vectors on South-facing Slope at Noon, Available to Site and Impacting Site**

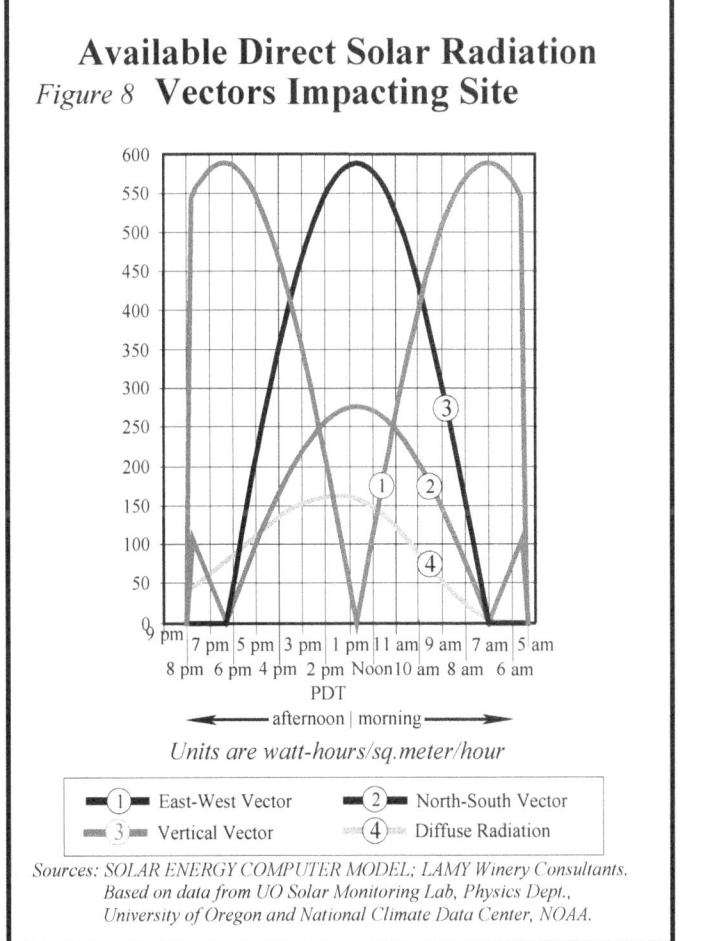

Available Direct Solar Radiation
Figure 8 **Vectors Impacting Site**

Units are watt-hours/sq.meter/hour

1 East-West Vector   2 North-South Vector
3 Vertical Vector   4 Diffuse Radiation

*Sources: SOLAR ENERGY COMPUTER MODEL; LAMY Winery Consultants.
Based on data from UO Solar Monitoring Lab, Physics Dept.,
University of Oregon and National Climate Data Center, NOAA.*

Figure 9 depicts all of the solar radiation components striking bare ground on a 15 degree south slope, as well as the energy equivalent contributed by temperature.

Figure 10 compares total energy curves for east-, south-, and west-facing slopes. The shift in the pattern of total radiation energy from the symmetry of the direct solar vectors available to the south slope is obvious in the total energy curve. The reason is that the east-west direct radiation vector applies over more hours, east slope in the morning, west slope in the afternoon. On a south slope, the east-west vector is zero.

The east-facing and west-facing slopes receive a more moderate pattern of total energy than the south slope. That is, the maximum energy peak on them is less than it is on the south-facing slope.

It is the author's belief that the blue curve (east slope) reveals one of the significant factors behind the greatness of Côte d'Or Pinot Noir. This contention is analyzed further in Chapter 4.

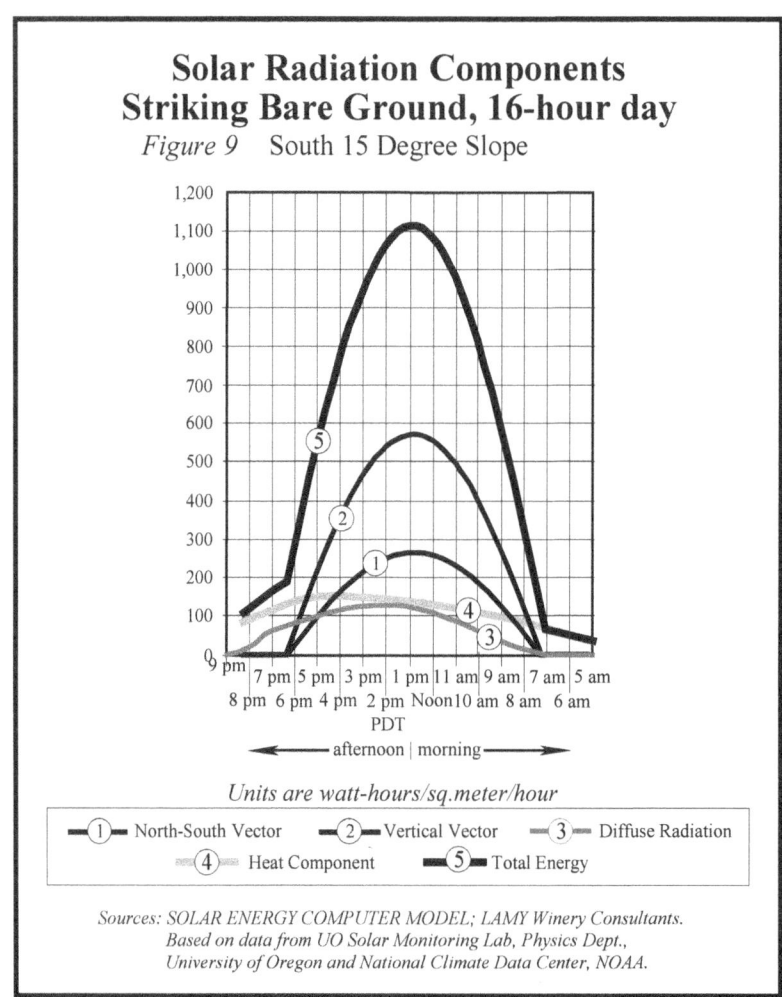

Solar Radiation Components Striking Bare Ground, 16-hour day

Figure 9   South 15 Degree Slope

Units are watt-hours/sq.meter/hour

1 — North-South Vector   2 — Vertical Vector   3 — Diffuse Radiation
4 — Heat Component   5 — Total Energy

Sources: SOLAR ENERGY COMPUTER MODEL; LAMY Winery Consultants.
Based on data from UO Solar Monitoring Lab, Physics Dept.,
University of Oregon and National Climate Data Center, NOAA.

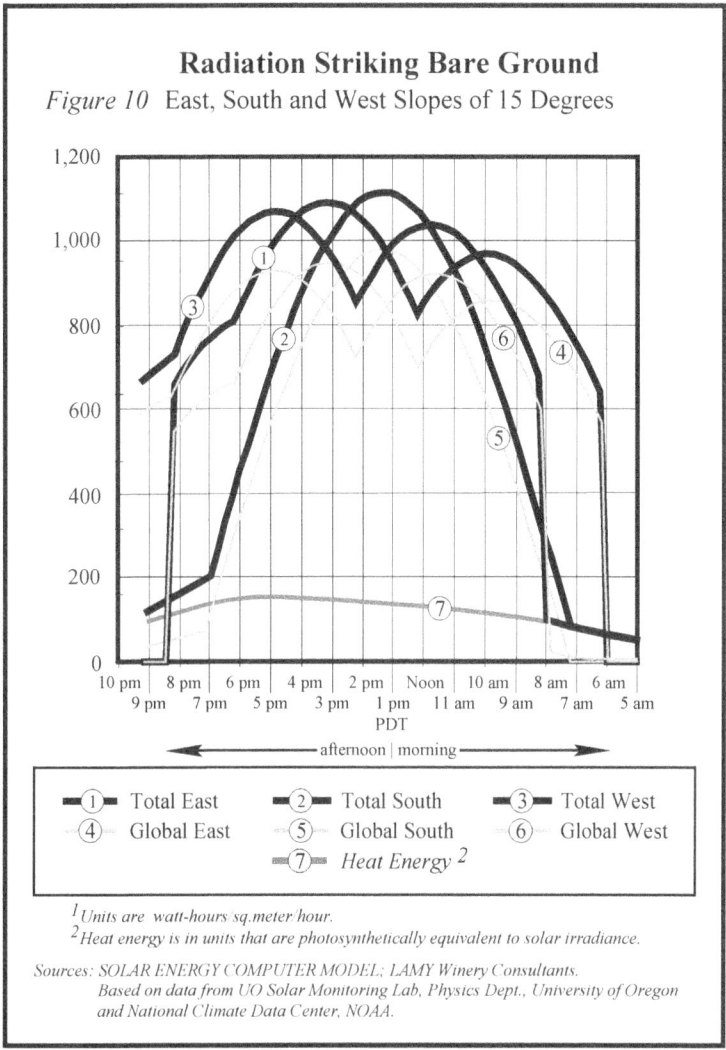

Radiation Striking Bare Ground

Figure 10   East, South and West Slopes of 15 Degrees

For all of the hype about the south slope being superior, the total solar radiation received per day (encompassing 64 readings over 16 hours) is one-third greater for both east- and west-facing slopes than for the south slope on this mid-July day:

Slope Direction	Maximum (watts/sq.m/hour)	Percent of South	Cumulative over 16 hrs (watts/sq.m/(hour)	Percent of South
East	1,090.0	97.9	13,122.2	136.8
South	1,113.8	100.0	9,395.8	100.0
West	1,071.5	96.2	12,605.6	131.4

Completing this brief initial study of solar radiation's effects relative to topography is Figure 11. It depicts how total direct solar radiation varies by the severity of the slope. The amount of radiation received by the plot, at this latitude, increases between flat and a 22.2° incline, then decreases after 22.2°.[2]

Slope Severith	Maximum (watts/sq.m/hr)	Percent Increase	Full day over 16 hrs (watts/ sq.m/hr)	Percent Increase
0 degrees	602.2		4,599.2	
5 degrees	621.3	3.2	4,744.4	3.2
10 degrees	635.6	2.3	4,853.6	2.3
15 degrees	645.0	1.5	4,925.8	1.5
20 degrees	649.6	0.7	4,960.5	0.7
25 degrees	649.2	−0.1	4,957.5	−0.1

Similar evaluations can be done on other world-famous wine areas of France, Germany, Italy and California.

The manipulation of a vine canopy's receipt of solar radiation is very likely to be the next important frontier of viticultural and winemaking research. For this reason, solar radiation input will be discussed further in Chapter 4, where the analysis will focus on the amount of energy captured by the vine canopy.

Selection of grape varieties

Then come varietal and rootstock selection, vine spacing, trellis configuration, and cover crop decisions. Or, ideally, you start with the determination of the varieties to be grown, then proceed to looking for the best site to grow your selections.

As we have already said, the ideal microclimate for each grape variety is one where the grapes just attain maturity in most years.

What about climate change?

Concern about an ongoing increase in global temperatures has prompted a call to convert vineyards to warmer climate varietals. One possible scenario being voiced is that over the span of 100 years the perfect climate for Cabernet Sauvignon will migrate northward by several hundred miles.

For winegrape growers, the debate over replanting requires some perspective. First, each degree Fahrenheit of temperature increase (both high and low) would elevate heat summation for the growing season by 214 degree-days annually. It is currently believed by the United Nation's International Panel on Climate Change (IPCC) that an increase in global temperature could run about

---

2. Solar radiation energy captured by the site increases up to a slope angle of 22.2° at this vineyard site. Then, it decreases. This example is drawn on June 21, the summer solstice, when the sun is at its northernmost position relative to earth (23.5°). On this day, the angle between the solar plane (plane described by the earth's orbit relative to the sun) and the site's latitude is 22.2°. The overall effect may be described as follows: increasing the slope's southern inclination increases the solar radiation capture up to a slope equal to the site's latitude (45.7°) minus the tilt of earth's axis relative to the solar plane (23.5°); thereafter, the radiation capture decreases with increasing slope inclination. It may also be said that southern slope increases result in greater radiation capture the further north the site is situated (at least in the northern hemisphere). The progression of increases in solar capture follows a sine wave. These comments apply only to south-facing slopes.

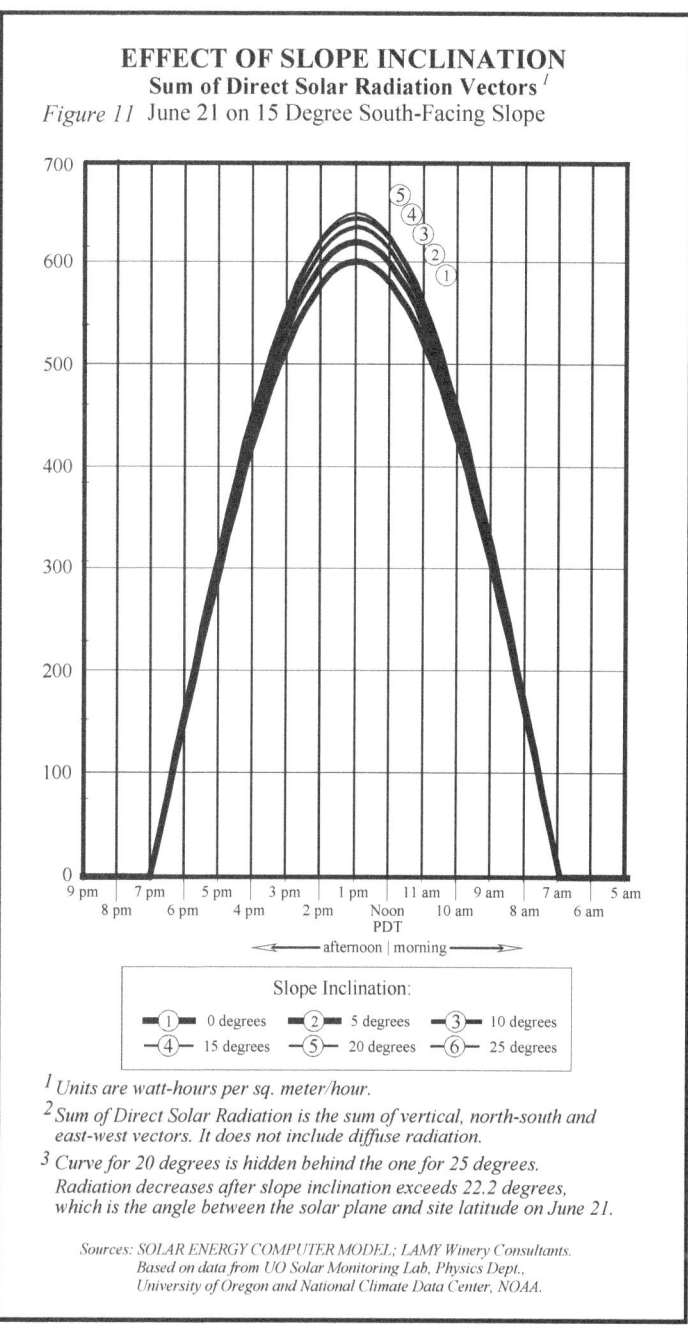

EFFECT OF SLOPE INCLINATION
Sum of Direct Solar Radiation Vectors [1]
Figure 11 June 21 on 15 Degree South-Facing Slope

Slope Inclination:
① 0 degrees   ② 5 degrees   ③ 10 degrees
④ 15 degrees   ⑤ 20 degrees   ⑥ 25 degrees

[1] *Units are watt-hours per sq. meter/hour.*

[2] *Sum of Direct Solar Radiation is the sum of vertical, north-south and east-west vectors. It does not include diffuse radiation.*

[3] *Curve for 20 degrees is hidden behind the one for 25 degrees. Radiation decreases after slope inclination exceeds 22.2 degrees, which is the angle between the solar plane and site latitude on June 21.*

Sources: SOLAR ENERGY COMPUTER MODEL.; LAMY Winery Consultants. Based on data from UO Solar Monitoring Lab, Physics Dept., University of Oregon and National Climate Data Center, NOAA.

two degrees Fahrenheit between 1990 and 2025.[3] That is a rise of 12.2 degree-days annually.

---

3. Climate Change—The IPCC Scientific Assessment, 1990.

Another forecast projects an increase of 5.4 degrees Fahrenheit in large cities between 2025 and 2050.[4] This last forecast reflects the uniqueness of large cities as urban heat islands.[5] It does not apply to most vineyard locations.

Varietal conversion is an action not to be taken lightly. It is expensive. The cost of plant material and labor needed to replant has to be considered, as does the loss of income during the multi-year period during which the vines do not produce at full yield.

Several factors should frame the debate:

- **Changes in the average global temperature will not occur equally in all locations.** Wind and oceanic currents move too much heat energy around the globe for that. Attention should focus on empirical changes being experienced by discrete winegrape-producing regions.

- **Solar radiation captured by each vineyard microclimate should also be considered.** The vine's metabolic rate, i.e., photosynthetic rate, is driven by both heat and light (see Chapter 7 discussion on solar radiation). Existing research information suggests that light energy may have four to five times as much impact on photosynthesis as does ambient temperature, as asserted in the rate of carbon dioxide assimilation (see discussion on photosynthesis).

- Movement to higher elevations should be considered, as well as horizontal relocations. As a general rule, each 100 feet of elevation reduces the temperature by 0.378 degrees Fahrenheit, or ~90 degree-days from April 1 through October 31.

Vineyardists can take some very important actions for the immediate future:

1. **Install recording high-low thermometers** in the vineyard and begin tracking actual microclimate changes as they occur. Vineyards that are situated on complex topography will require more than one monitoring station. Such microclimate tracking would have provided valuable information even before the vineyard was first planted. It's not too late to start.

   Figure 12 illustrates the recording of degree-days at three *Agrimet* sites in Oregon. FOGO and ARAO bracket the famous Dundee Hills and are on the valley floor, much lower than most hillside vineyard sites. MDFO is in southern Oregon's Rogue Valley. Note the pronounced year-to-year fluctuations.

2. **Review the appropriateness of the current planting scheme** to determine whether the existing varietals are planted in the best on-site microclimates. It is possible that better varietal-microclimate matches already exist, and they may be implemented in the near term by top-grafting.

3. **Avoid a stampede to follow "forward-thinking" vineyard operators in switching to different locations.** There will be some growers who are willing to gamble on making changes, feeling it represents a competitive advantage or investment hedge. Others may be motivated by

---

4. McCarthy, M.P., M.J. Best, and R.A. Betts. "Climate Change in Cities Due to Global Warming and Urban Effects," *Geophysical Research Letters* 37/9 (2010). http://onlinelibrary.wiley.com/doi/10.1029/2010GL042845/full.

5. Temperatures in large cities are significantly warmer than in the surrounding countryside. The reasons include paved areas, buildings, heating and air conditioning, vehicular emissions and reduced vegetation, all of which result in greater heat generation/absorbtion during the day and radiation back into the atmosphere during the night.

panic, swept long by the actions of others. Always bear in mind: these phenomena take place over relatively long periods of time.

4. Great winemakers are not part of the herd.

Burgundy and Rhone varieties lead in California and Oregon

In the selection of varieties, one needs also to consider where the market is going and the profit-making opportunities offered by each variety. The financial aspects of an array of varieties grown in various climates will be addressed in a later chapter. We'll deal here with winery demand for grapes.

The demand for new vines experienced by nurseries provides an indication of where the industry is headed. Table 8 shows the number of new vineyard acres planted in 2008 through 2014. It reflects the collective wisdom of new and expanding winegrowers regarding future demand for wine.

The Burgundy varieties, Pinot Noir and Chardonnay, are the most popular for new plantings in California. It is interesting to note that nurseries report considerable interest in the "Rhône" varieties: Syrah, Viognier, Mourvedre, Cinsault and Grenache. Although the orders at these three nurseries aren't reflecting it, sharply increasing sales volumes indicate that California vineyards

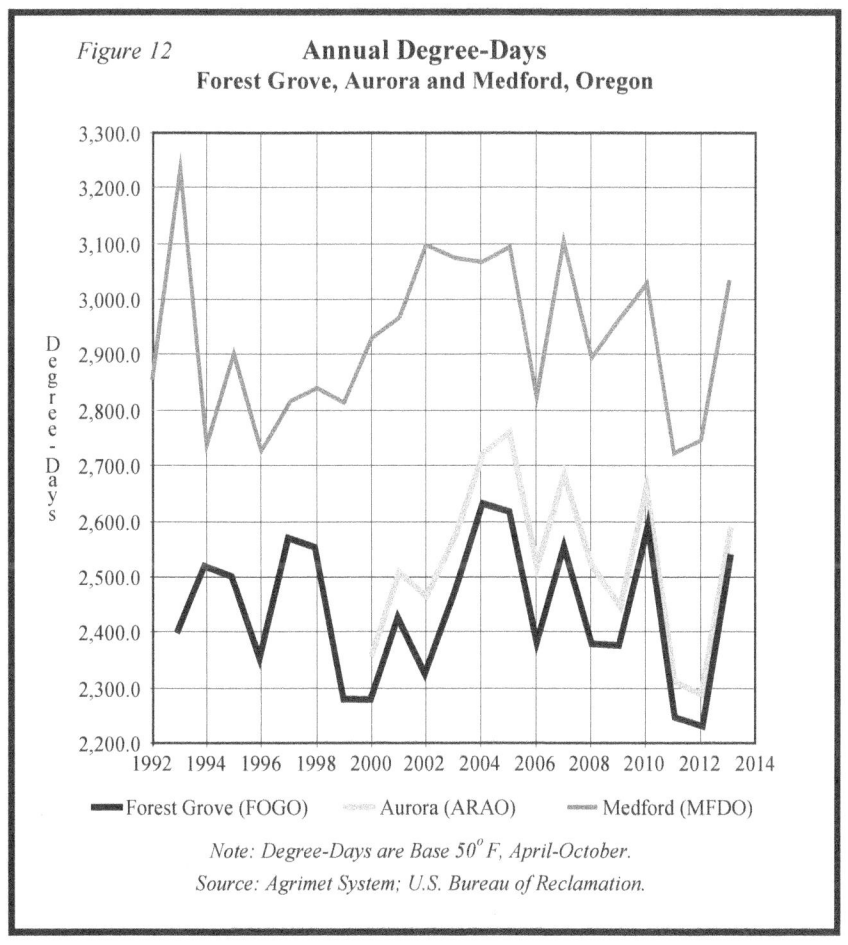

Figure 12　　**Annual Degree-Days**
Forest Grove, Aurora and Medford, Oregon

Note: Degree-Days are Base 50° F, April-October.
Source: Agrimet System; U.S. Bureau of Reclamation.

TABLE 8   New Vineyard Plantings in California, 2008–2014

Variety	2008	2009	2010	2011	2012	2013	2014
Chardonnay	2,230	1,145	272	315	292	1,779	846
Chenin Blanc	0	10	0	81	48	21	43
French Colombard	46	12	148	270	759	409	243
Gewürztraminer	5	62	0	65	0	23	3
Muscat of Alexandria	0	103	115	313	200	210	9
Pinot Gris	1,725	524	189	121	107	526	1,216
Sauvignon Blanc	202	97	100	90	70	127	59
Viognier	113	22	23	28	12	7	44
White Riesling	155	94	45	0	143	158	17
Barbera	94	14	17	7	15	17	73
Cabernet Franc	63	26	17	3	8	45	58
Cabernet Sauvignon	686	984	1,033	634	1,693	3,147	1,723
Carignane	50	0	1	5	7	7	1
Grenache	76	49	34	52	578	56	22
Merlot	48	358	52	246	83	345	335
Petit Syrah	136	179	140	177	176	388	346
Petit Verdot	83	11	44	2	16	96	50
Pinot Noir	2,616	841	490	493	390	1,200	1,555
Rubired	76	453	265	237	155	32	263
Ruby Cabernet	7	0	34	80	9	0	70
Sangiovese	17	46	17	29	6	5	9
Syrah	120	46	33	27	91	51	224
Zinfandel	304	226	171	39	365	773	187
Total Acres Planted	**9,634**	**5,639**	**4,189**	**4,434**	**5,474**	**9,422**	**7,396**

Source: Tables 4 & 5, *2012–2014 California Grape Acreage Report*; California Department of Food and Agriculture. April, 2013.

are investing heavily in Pinot Grigio, known in other states by its French name, Pinot Gris.

Oregon varieties

In the 1960s and 1970s, Oregon wineries made approximately equal volumes of Pinot Noir, Chardonnay and White Riesling (Figure 16). Small amounts of Gewürztraminer, Cabernet Sauvignon, Pinot Gris, Müller-Thurgau and several others also were made. During the 1980s, Pinot Gris was established as a popular contender for the future, increasingly an alternative to Chardonnay. In the 1990s, the availability of top clonal material from Burgundy for Pinot Noir and Chardonnay pushed Pinot Noir to greater heights, and perhaps saved Chardonnay from an uncertain future in Oregon. At the same time, White Riesling's continuing price dilemma (mired at low supermarket prices by the flood of White Zinfandel) has driven many vineyards to top-graft their Riesling vines to other varieties, even though vineyards in Oregon's Willamette Valley have proven they can produce outstanding White Rieslings, comparable to those of Germany's Rheingau.

Figure 13 illustrates the dominance of Pinot Noir and Pinot Gris in Oregon's expansion plans. Together, the two varieties accounted for 2,746 acres, or 78.3 percent of the total 3,505 acres of new plantings in the three-year period of 2005-2007. According to the *2013 Oregon Vineyard and Winery Census Report*, the dominance continues through 2013 where these varietals accounted for 78.7 percent of the new acres planted.

Oregon has three distinct producing climates. We have reviewed the Willamette Valley above. In the state's southwest corner, the Rogue and Umpqua Valleys have a warmer climate nearer to California conditions. In the state's north central region, along the south bank of the Columbia River, several counties share the same desert climate profile as Washington's Columbia Valley: a hot, dry and short growing season.

Washington State varieties

In Washington State, the experience differs from Oregon's. White Riesling and Syrah led the 2,999 acres of new plantings in 2003-2005 with 1,588 acres, 53.0 percent of the total (Figure 14, most recent survey available).

Interestingly, Washington's confidence in the market for White Riesling is reflected in the addition of 1,144 acres of it during 2003-2005. At the same time, Oregon growers have been tearing out White Riesling, generally in favor of Pinot Noir and Pinot Gris.

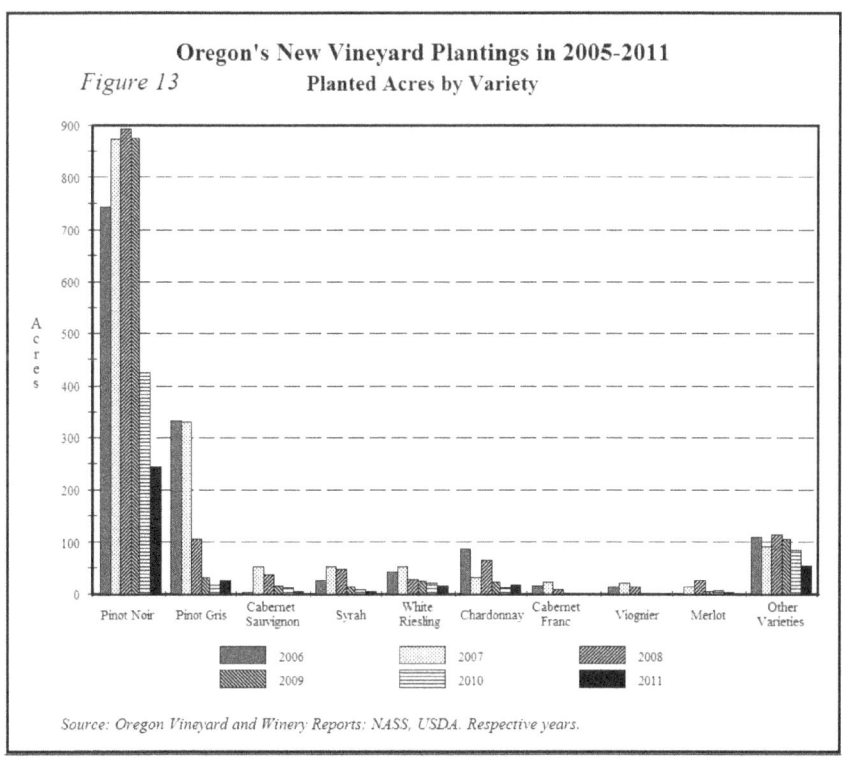

Oregon's New Vineyard Plantings in 2005-2011
Figure 13 — **Planted Acres by Variety**

Source: Oregon Vineyard and Winery Reports: NASS, USDA. Respective years.

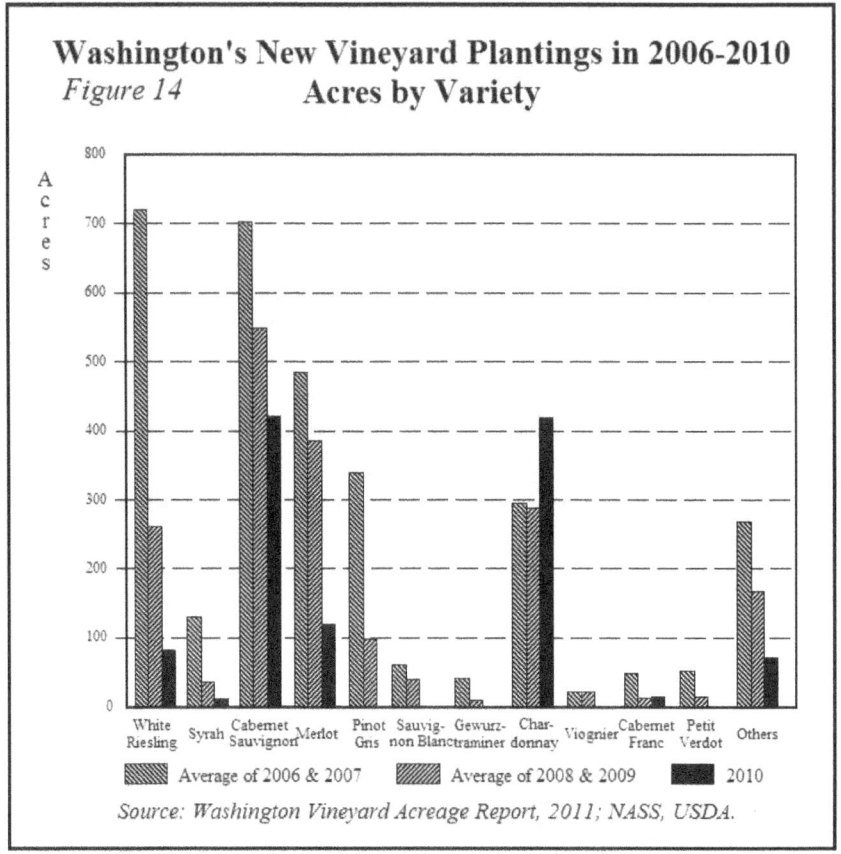

Washington's New Vineyard Plantings in 2006-2010
Figure 14   Acres by Variety

Source: Washington Vineyard Acreage Report, 2011; NASS, USDA.

Midwestern and eastern states

The three West Coast states, California, Washington and Oregon, will dominate the pattern of varietal production in the future, although winemakers from the Midwest and East may disagree. But, as the dynamics of national wine marketing and trend-setting now exist, that claim must stand.

The following observation is going to provoke some dissension. The wine media and wine writers play to the nation's major metropolitan markets, in particular New York, San Francisco, Miami, Washington, DC and Las Vegas. That's where most fervent wine consumers live (or consume, as is the case of DC and Las Vegas), wine writers write, and top restaurants draw attention. Boston, Atlanta, Philadelphia, Detroit, Chicago, Denver, Dallas, Houston and Los Angeles tend to follow. If you can get distribution in the top markets, access to lesser markets will be much easier, if you work it right.

Midwestern and Eastern states do not conduct vineyard surveys as Western states do. Some who do, notably Michigan and Pennsylvania, only gather data every five years. Information is available for 2011 and 2014 in New York and Virginia, to provide a glimpse into new planting trends. The top ten new varietal plantings in each of those states are shown in Table 9. Cabernet Franc, Chardonnay, and Merlot are the only similarities.

TABLE 9   New Plantings in Eastern States, Acres

Rank	New York intentions to plant, 2011	Rank	Virginia bearing acres, 2014
1	Concord	1	Chardonnay
2	Niaga	2	Cabernet Franc
3	Catawba	3	Merlot
4	White Riesling	4	Cabernet Sauvignon
5	Chardonnay	5	Viognier
6	Merlot	6	Petit Verdot
7	Aurora	7	Vidal Blanc
8	Elvira	8	Chambourcin
9	Cabernet Franc	9	Norton
10	Cayuga White	10	Traminette

Source: Grape Report, respective states; NASS, USDA. New York 2011 Vineyard Survey; NASS, USDA. Virginia 2014 Commercial Grape Report; Virginia Wine.

Rootstock selection

It no longer makes economic sense to plant winegrapes on their own roots, unless your vineyard site has soil with extremely high sand content. The root louse, phylloxera, has spread too widely to take the chance on having to replant after an infestation.

Phylloxera resistance is not the only property of rootstocks that is of interest. Compatibility with soil pH and rooting depth, diameter, compatibility with scion variety, and effect on vine growth and production are all worthy of consideration. A detailed presentation of rootstock varieties and application in specific plantings will not be made here. The reader is referred to state extension services and vineyard consultants for recommendations. West Coast consultants have the most experience in matching rootstocks with *vinifera* grape varieties.

No one achieves 100 percent vine survival with new plantings. It is common practice to purchase 5–10 percent more vines than the design calls for. They should be heeled into nursery rows (about one foot apart) in a convenient location where they are easy to irrigate.

Beware of recommendations by nurseries who may be trying to unload unsold inventory; the pairings of rootstock and scion may not be the best for your vineyard site or quality goals.

The normal timetable for obtaining grafted rootstock in the Northern states of America is:

Timing	Task
December–January, Year 1	Order grafted rooted vines
January–February, Year 1	Nursery makes grafts, plants grafted cuttings
December–March, Year 2	Nursery digs and prunes plants, delivers
January–April, Year 2	Grower plants rooted grated vines in vineyard

Note: Applies to cool climates. Timing varies in warmer regions.

Vineyard design

Row direction, vine spacing, trellis design, and hedging all influence wine quality. A detailed evaluation of microclimate at the site is very helpful to productive vineyard design. If you are interested in quality, the task is not as simple as installing north-south rows and standard VSP trellising. Ambient temperature, solar radiation, slope direction and severity, elevation, prevailing wind direction, and the grape varieties to be planted all come into play.

Row direction

If you were to go to Burgundy, Champagne, Alsace or Germany, you would see that the vine rows follow the hill's *fall line*. It means the rows go straight downhill, whichever way the slope faces, even north. To some extent, rows are aligned that way because it enables safer tractor work. Driving crosshill on a steep slope with a high center-of-gravity tractor can be a deadly experience.

Growers in Burgundy use over-the-row tractors that put the center of gravity for the tractor and its driver very high off the ground. Growers have been killed by tractor rollovers while turning around at the end of a row.

German engineers have devised ingenious devices to transport workers and the harvest up and down the hillside. They also bulldoze level crosshill roadways at intervals up and down the slope, and pave them with asphalt. Between those roadways, the rows are still straight up and down the slope.

In mountainside locations, California growers terrace their steep hillsides in efforts to control runoff (prevent erosion), make tractor work safer, and simplify the mechanics of irrigation. The rows run with the contour lines. Rows on the terraced hillsides of France's Rhône Valley, Portugal's Duoro Valley and the island of Madeira, for example, follow whatever directions permit survival.

Rows that are aligned north-south "maximize the solar intercept," as the college professors like to say. To you and me, that means getting the most out of available sunlight. North-south rows allow the vine canopy to intercept the same amount of solar energy in the morning as in the afternoon. In some growing areas, it is not necessary to "maximize the intercept," because there is enough heat energy to offset a reduction in interception of light energy. Previously in this book, we considered the bare hillside as the area under analysis. That approach enables calculation of all, or "global," energy received by the site. That analysis suggests that orchards whose canopies present a virtually flat, horizontal surface to the sun, do not "maximize the solar intercept." In the next chapter, the amount of radiation received, or captured, or intercepted by the vine canopy will be analyzed. The results are surprisingly different from the radiation profile of the flat, horizontal plane.

Now, a new concept is introduced. Dr. Richard Smart, a well-known vineyard authority, has raised the subject of orienting rows so as to avoid sunburn of the fruit in warm climate areas. High berry temperatures are detrimental to wine quality. He recommends lining up the rows so the sun strikes only the tops of the canopy when the air temperature is at a maximum.[6] Thus, the vine

---

6. "Row Orientation and Sunburn," *Practical Winery & Vineyard* (November–December 2010): 42.

canopy shades the fruit so maximum solar radiation does not hit the grapes directly in the warmest hours. There's a simple test to determine what that orientation is, unless of course, you have a computer model that tells you the sun's position at the temperature peak. Insert a stake in the ground. When the temperature hits its daily peak, somewhere around 3–5 pm, the stake's shadow will define the proper row alignment.

All the rest of you, who are in climates that seldom experience temperatures over 100°F, can look to other reasons for row orientation.

Vine density

Among winemakers, there is a generally understood relationship between vine spacing (i.e., density) and wine quality: **the tighter the spacing, the more concentrated the wine**. The vines must compete for available nutrients and water, and the resulting stress makes the wine more intense. The concept goes hand in hand with the principle that wine quality is inversely related to the crop level: **the lighter the crop load, the more concentrated the wine**.

The author's experience with growing Pinot Noir at various spacings has led to a slightly different understanding of those relationships. High vine density requires frequent hedging of the canopy to minimize shading. Hedging removes the apical bud tissue at the ends of the shoots, thus denying the shoots' ability to elongate until the vine can establish new apical tissue, which it does at the leaf axils. During that period, about 7–10 days, the vine redirects its nutrients and growth to the remaining parts of the vine, rather than devoting its energies to growing longer shoots and more leaves. With frequent hedging, the vine's trunk and canes increase substantially in diameter, and the retained leaves grow much larger. Clusters are larger and have more berries, but the berries remain small, i.e., the skin:juice ratio remains the same, which is desired by winemakers.

In effect, hedging keeps the vine from wasting its energies on growing new leaves, and the carbohydrates manufactured by the older leaves are directed to the grapes and the "permanent" parts of the vine. In the grapes, the increased activity produces greater concentrations of the fruit esters and anthocyanins that give the wine its characteristic aromas and flavors.

Greater vine density causes another beneficial effect. Competition among the root systems reduces the vine's green growth, minimizing the required amount of hedging.

Row spacing in America has been dictated by available farm equipment. Therefore, it is common to find rows spaced nine, ten, or even twelve feet apart. In recent years, availability of narrower tractors and awareness of European practices has inspired some smaller American vineyards to install narrow row spacings. But, the limited observations of some wine writers notwithstanding, it is still rare to find rows spaced closer than seven feet.

American vineyards use wide in-row spacings. In general, in-row spacings are chosen to suit the growth and fruiting habits of the variety. The objective is to fill the trellis, but avoid overlapping canopies. Accordingly, in-row spacings of six to eight feet are common for most noble grape varieties, and as wide as ten feet for very vigorous vine types.

For the popular vinifera varieties, current viticultural thinking favors densities of 60–70 square feet per vine, or 622–726 vines per acre for premium table wines.

An international vineyard consultant roams the globe advising clients with high-vigor sites to **increase** vine spacing yields as a means of achieving high yields, large pretty fruit and acceptable phenological numbers: i.e., sugar, acid and pH.

There is a big difference between the fruit quality concepts held by agriculturists and those of winemakers.

In some states that are new to the winegrape business, agricultural college crop specialists and extension agents tend to be biased toward table grapes and fresh fruit, where large, attractive fruit is the objective . . . it is not so with winemakers. For them, the phenological numbers are still important (sugar, acid and pH), but winemakers are focused more intently on intensiveness of flavors and aromas, and true-to-type varietal characteristics. Those results are more likely to be produced by higher density plantings, restricted yields and frequent hedging to "force" the vines into balance with the reduced fruit load.

So, if you wish to produce grapes for "jug" and "standard" wines, you can probably benefit in profits by following the globe-trotting vineyard consultant. On the other hand, if you have higher ambitions to grow "premium" and "super-premium" wines, and most new wineries do, then you would be better advised to look to Burgundy, Bordeaux, Alsace, Rheingau and Tuscany for guidance.

In France, vine rows are typically 1.0–1.2 meters apart in the best quality areas. And vines are one meter apart in the rows. Converted to American measures, those spacings of 3.3–3.9 feet by 3.3 feet define vine densities of 10.7–12.9 square feet per vine, or 3,378–4,053 vines per acre.

Ground preparation

The timing of ground preparation depends on where you are, and what organisms inhabit the soil. Soil infested with phylloxera by a previous vineyard planting will have to be fumigated, and the process may require two years before replanting.

Most new vineyard sites can be prepared in one season before planting. The site should be plowed, then disked and harrowed in both directions. Weeds that germinate after the soil is leveled can be eliminated with glyphosate (Roundup™).

If the site has been farmed before, and the soil contains some clay, there will be a plow pan at 14 inches deep that needs to be broken up. Dense clay content builds up in a film where the plow sole slides, and it makes a plow pan that is impenetrable by the vine's roots.

Good preparation includes deep subsoiling. If it is done right, it will break through the plow or mineral pan (if there is one) and mix some topsoil down into the lower soil horizons to the depth of the shank. Timing is important.

The soil should be dry so the topsoil can mix freely into the V-shaped area of soil disturbance. That occurs in late July and all of August in most temperate growing areas in the northern hemisphere. Depth depends on soil properties. Note, winegrapes will root to 30–50 feet if allowed to, and if forced to reach for water in late summer.

Most soils can be adequately prepared by subsoiling to 30–32 inches deep. If you are working more than 10 acres, it will save time and work to use two adjustable shanks on a toolbar, and rig a foam marker to locate the center of the next track.

If the soil has a solid rock or basalt ledge at 20–30 inches, obviously you will not be able to subsoil very deeply. But, do something to stir up the soil past 14 inches.

In the alluvial soils of Napa Valley, mineral pans have forced subsoiling to depths of 6–8 feet.

If subsoiling is run across the hillside, it will eliminate most erosion problems, unless the soil has a perched water table or other erosion-inducing properties. That means subsoil east-west on a south slope and space the cuts on the vine spacing. North-south subsoiling on a south slope is guaranteed to cause future erosion problems. The soil-loosening effect of the subsoiling, coupled with the love gophers have for burrowing in the soft soil can result, literally, in vines being blown out of the ground in a good rainstorm.

Vineyard layout

Many owners of smaller vineyards like to plant grapes as one would plant roses. Drive wooden pegs at each vine location, then come along with an auger. Throw some fertilizer in the bottom of the hole, mound up some topsoil, then one person holds the vine with the roots spread out on the mound as another person shovels in the dirt.

That method, though romantically appealing, will cost more than $400/acre, if you value your time.

The author favors using a rope system and dividing the vineyard into manageable sub-blocks. The sub-blocks might measure five rows by five plants, or as large as twenty rows by 20–25 vines . . . it depends on your vine densities and your ability to handle long planting ropes.

In planning the vineyard, it pays dividends to anticipate operating needs. Of course, the vine density is important, but so are the setbacks around the vineyard margins (Figure 15).

Along the edge at the row ends, a tractor driver will need about 30 feet of clear space to turn the tractor around. Most tractor activities are spraying, which require towing an airblast sprayer through the turns. The usual practice for turning is to come out of a row and turn left, then skip six aisles and turn left for the return. At the other end of the row, skip five aisles and turn left. Repeat the procedure, skipping six rows at one end and five at the other. You will be doing sets of fourteen rows (seven loops), which works out nicely because you will have to cover seventy rows, a multiple of fourteen, in the example vineyard

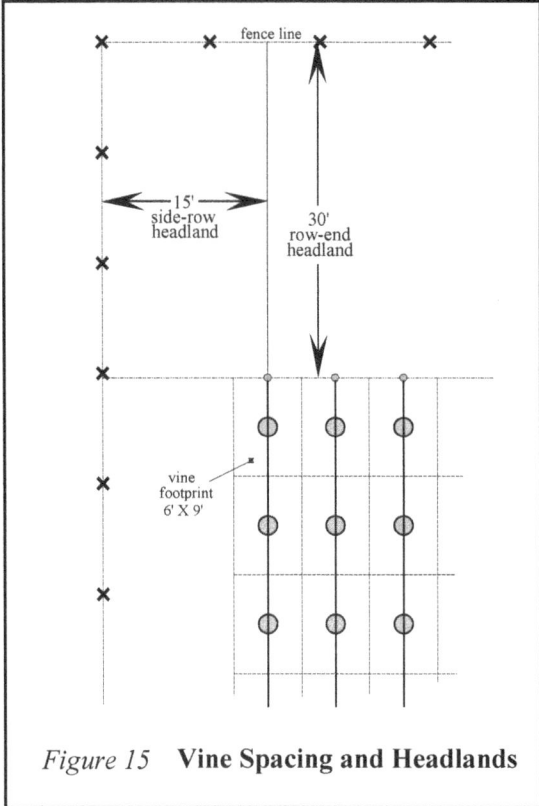

Figure 15 **Vine Spacing and Headlands**

block. If you prefer to turn right all of the time, do it that way . . . it makes no difference.

Any number of rows may be chosen for the sets, depending on the headland setback and aisle width. This method requires that the tractor make a half-circle turn at the row-end, rather than backing up at each turn. This radius is 5 feet less than the head-land width (the tractor centerline is tracking the arc). So, the diameter defined by the diameter of the half-circle turn, divided by aisle width, gives you the minimum number of aisles that can be traversed without backing up. It's all a matter of economics and efficiency. The calculation is shown in Figure 16.

If your vineyard has a number of aisles that isn't a multiple of fourteen, you can enlarge the last set to adjust.

The minimum number of aisles per set can be reduced if your tractor-sprayer assembly has a shorter turn radius, or if your sprayer is 3-point hitch-mounted (25–50 gallon tank). You can even traverse every row, one by one, with a 3-point sprayer, by standing on one of the brakes to turn around, but then those turns will tear up the soil and cover crop in the headlands.

Along the sides parallel to the rows, fifteen feet is a good minimum clear-ance. Some vineyards get away with ten feet, but you'll need more during harvest for tractors, trucks and picker vehicles.

Let's use a square ten-acre parcel as an example. This is a fairly common starter vineyard size, and even more common partitioning of a larger parcel. Property dimensions are 660 ft. by 660 ft. Figure 17 illustrates the simplicity.

Row direction is up and down in Figure 19. Deducting the headlands (660–30–30) leaves 600 feet for vines. At 6 feet between vines, that's 100 vines per row.

Spacing between rows will be 9 feet. There's 630 feet available for vines (660–15–15). The number of aisles is 70; number of rows is 71 (630/9 + 1).

The calculations are different for rows than for vines. The distance used for vines is endpost to endpost. For rows, it is row center-to-row center. You're actually counting aisles rather than rows.

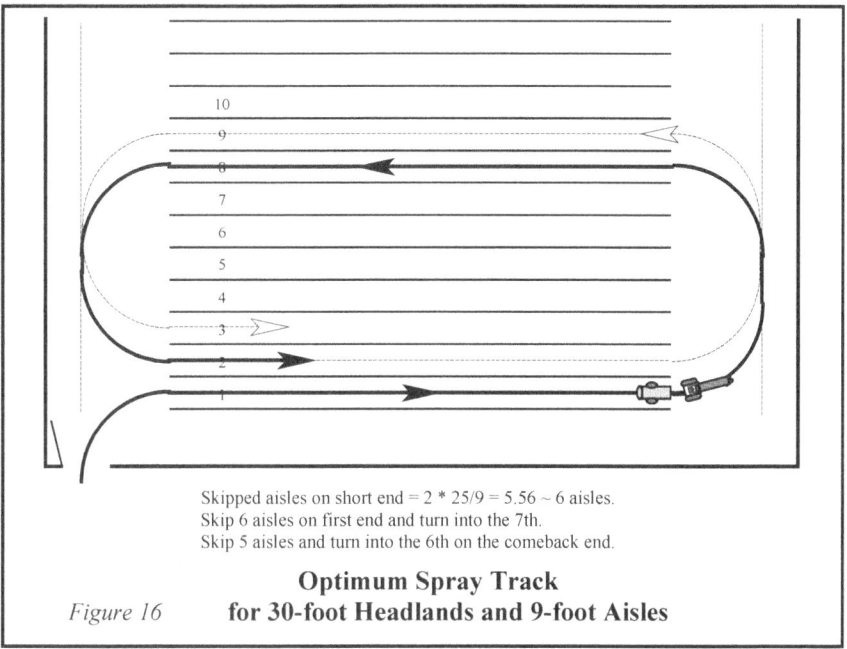

Skipped aisles on short end = 2 * 25/9 = 5.56 ~ 6 aisles.
Skip 6 aisles on first end and turn into the 7th.
Skip 5 aisles and turn into the 6th on the comeback end.

Optimum Spray Track

Figure 16   **for 30-foot Headlands and 9-foot Aisles**

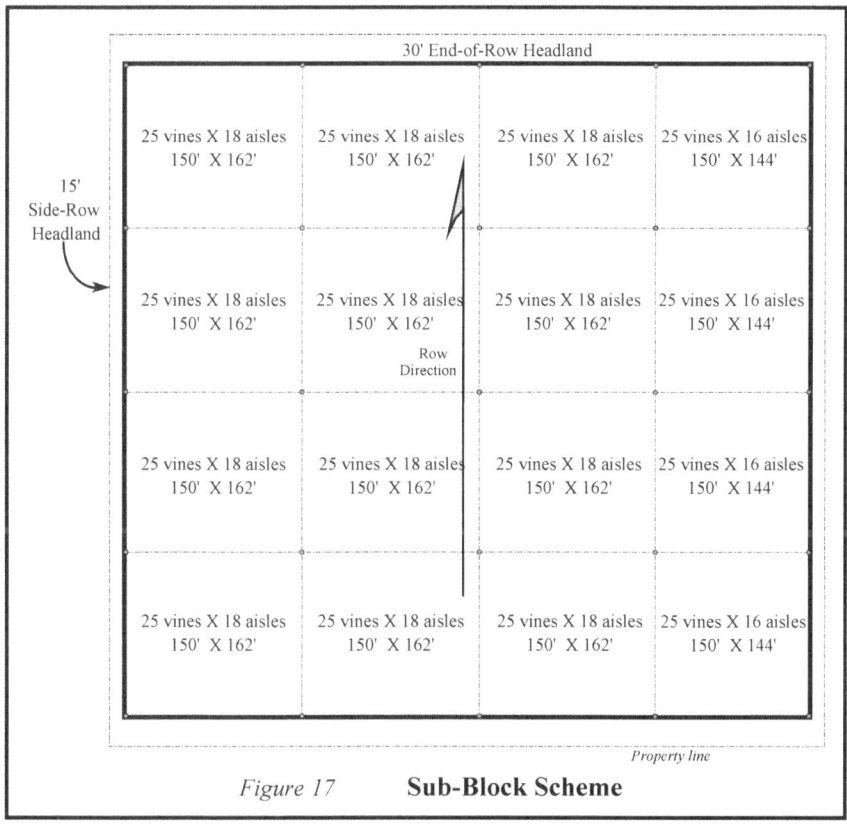

Figure 17   **Sub-Block Scheme**

Now, we can calculate some important numbers:

Gross Vineyard Acres = 660 ft. × 660 ft./43,560 =10.0 acres

Headlands: End-of-Row = 30 ft.; Side-Row = 15 ft.

Net Planted Acres = 71 rows × 9 ft. × 100 vines/row × 6 ft. = 8.80 acres

Land Use Efficiency = 8.80 acres/10.0 acres = 88.0%

Vine footprint = 9 ft. between rows × 6 ft. between vines = 54 sq. ft.

Number of vines = 71 rows × 100 vines/row = 7,100 vines

Vine Density = 7,100 vines/8.80 acres = 806.8 vines per acre

Note that the net planted acres are less than the gross acres. One has to be careful when counting acres for statistical purposes. If someone says they have 20 acres of vineyard, they're probably including a homesite, farm buildings and access roads, maybe even a winery. Their net planted vineyard acres are likely closer to 15–18 acres.

Marking and the rope system

To mark the ground for planting, the rope system has proven to be efficient. No doubt there are many variations that have been used for many years, but this one was devised for the daunting task of planting ~400 gross acres at Montinore Vineyards (Forest Grove, OR) by hand in 1983–84. It was later used for planting many smaller vineyards, too. It is based on the concept of breaking up the job into manageable sub-blocks. If the corners of the sub-blocks are lined up with each other, then everything else will line up. The method works equally well for smaller projects.

Historically, the planting of many small vineyards begins with pounding posts and stringing wire. The author doesn't support that method because of economics. Why install the posts and wire two years before they are needed to support the vines? You're going to invest about $2,800 an acre in materials and labor for part of the trellis just to use it for alignment purposes. Interest alone on that expenditure for two years at a reasonable cost-of-capital interest rate of 12 percent is almost $4,900 for the nominal 10-acre vineyard used as the example above. Why spend that kind of money at the start when you don't have to? You can buy a lot of 4-foot bamboo stakes for much less.

First, mark the corners for the sub-blocks. If you do this right, the same marks can be used for subsoiling. Use 12-inch long pointed 1" × 1½" wood stakes and a really bright-colored surveyor's flagging tape.

You will need a flexible, non-stretchy cable for measuring the distances between sub-block corners. Aluminum airplane cable works well. Inexpensive key tags with the plastic tags and steel rings can be used for the markers. To splice the end loops of the wire, and to attach the key rings to it, use Nicopress sleeves.

Find a common size for most of the sub-blocks. For this vineyard, 18 rows by 25 vines is the best compromise between the ability to manage the ropes and cost efficiency.

The sub-block cross-row dimension is 18 aisles for the first three sub-blocks, left-to-right, then one sub-block of 16 aisles. That makes 70 aisles, or 71 rows.

All four sub-blocks in the row direction are 25 vines apiece, for a total of 100 vines per row (Figure 17).

If the entire site is a ramp with no undulations, it doesn't matter if you lay the cable flat on the ground while marking the sub-block corners. However, if there are any undulations, the corners have to be measured on a flat plane that is at constant elevation, so all of the vines line up in both directions. Figure 18 shows why this is so.

The example uses a 15-degree slope. The horizontal distance is 150 feet, but the ground surface measures 155.3 feet; or 155 feet, 3.5 inches. That's a difference of 5.3 feet! The vertical drop is 40.2 feet.

To set the marker for 150 feet on a 15 degree slope, use the cable to find 150 feet on the ground, then use a steel tape measure to add another 5 feet, 3.5 inches. That's where to drive the stake.

Prepare, and carry in your pocket, a laminated index card with a table referencing the length to be added to the on-ground dimension versus slope angle (see Table 10).

A pocket-size carpenter's protractor can be used to visually estimate the slope degrees.[7]

After the corner markers are set, go back and visually sight along each line, and adjust the markers into line based on the two corners in which you have the most confidence. Do it in both cross-row and with-row directions. 10-power binoculars work well for this task.

If you can borrow or rent a surveyor's transit to set the sub-block corners, do it. A GPS device can also be used.

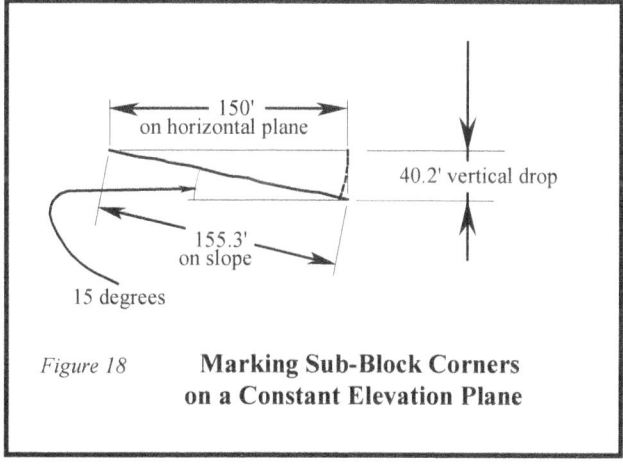

150'
on horizontal plane

40.2' vertical drop

155.3'
on slope

15 degrees

Figure 18   **Marking Sub-Block Corners
on a Constant Elevation Plane**

---

7. Craftsman Magnetic Universal Protractor, plastic, Model No. 39840, Sears Item No. 119398–40000; or equivalent.

TABLE 10   Sub-Block Adjustment Card, Adjustments for 150-foot Horizontal Distance

Slope Angle in Degrees	Distance on Ground	Add to Cable Length		Vertical Drop (ft)
		Feet	Inches	
0	150.0	0	0.0	0.0
2	150.1	0	1.1	5.2
4	150.4	0	4.4	10.5
6	150.8	0	9.9	15.7
8	151.5	1	5.7	20.9
10	152.3	2	3.8	26.0
12	153.4	3	4.2	31.2
14	154.6	4	7.1	36.3
16	156.0	6	0.5	41.3
18	157.7	7	8.6	46.4
20	159.6	9	7.5	51.3
22	161.8	11	9.4	56.2
24	164.2	14	2.3	61.0
26	166.9	16	10.7	65.8

Preparing the ropes

For the ropes, use a stretchy polyethylene type of braided rope. The elasticity is needed to adjust to changing dimensions on the ground. You will need three baseline ropes and one planting rope (more, if you re going to plant blocks on different in-row spacings).

The baseline ropes have marks at the row spacing intervals. Steel lock washers can be crimped onto the rope as markers. You can paint these marks, but mud has a way of obliterating everything in the field. Crimp the lock washers tightly so they won't slide, but not so tight as to cut into the rope. Splice loops into both ends so they can be held by stakes.

Nail down baseline ropes at each end of the sub-block. (See Figure 19 for the overall planting scheme.) The third baseline rope will enable you to set up the adjacent sub-block while you're planting this one.

The planting rope has marks set for the in-row vine spacing.

Vines are planted using D-handle drain spades with 5½ × 16-inch blades (Figure 20). For the example vineyard there are twenty-five vines per row in the sub-block. You can use five laborers (each plants five vines) or twenty-five on shovels. If you have a different size sub-block at the end of the field, you can have the planters rotate positions and let one or more sit out on each set.

Set the planting rope. Place the shovel over the top of the rope and drive it into the soil on a 45-degree angle, starting immediately on the other side of the rope. If you did the subsoiling properly the preceding fall, the shovel will penetrate easily. Lift the shovel handle enough to pry open a wedge-shaped hole and shove the vine in. Don't worry about getting the roots fanned out perfectly, or avoid bent roots. The new roots will grow every which way anyway. Pull the shovel out and step on the loose soil. You're planted! The bud that will produce the vine's trunk should be facing up, right over the mark on the planting rope.

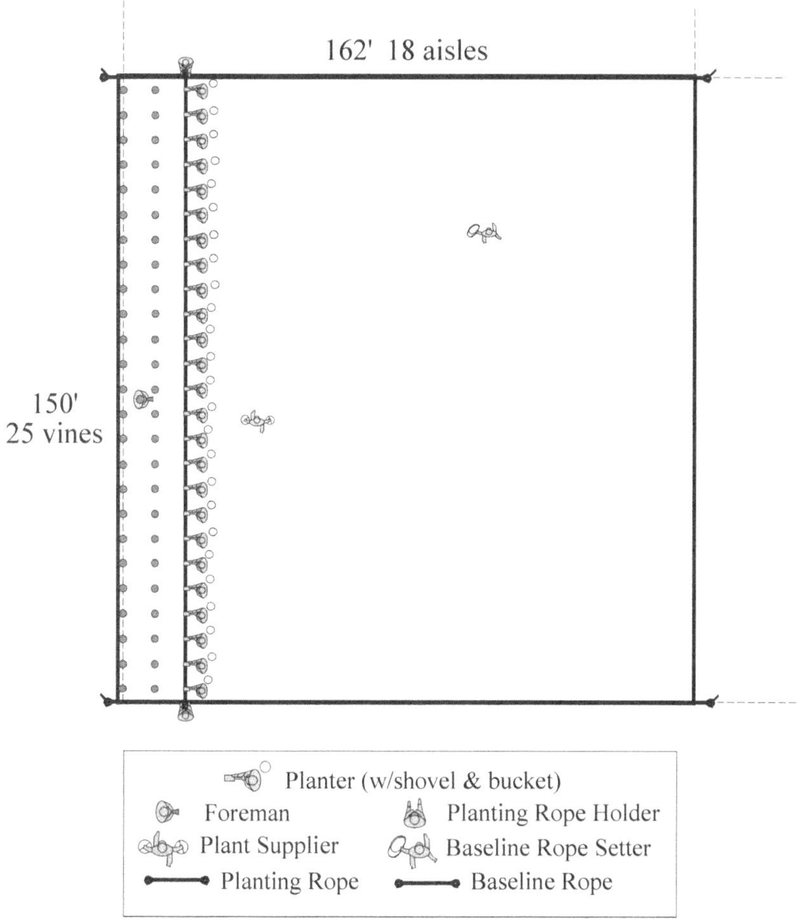

162' 18 aisles

150'
25 vines

Planter (w/shovel & bucket)
Foreman   Planting Rope Holder
Plant Supplier   Baseline Rope Setter
Planting Rope   Baseline Rope

Figure 19 **Planting**

Planting rope

Figure 20 **Planting by Shovel**

With twenty-five shovels, twenty-five vines are planted every forty seconds

Come back after planting and place a 3/8" @ 4' bamboo stake at each vine, then install a ½-gallon milk carton around it.[8]

Whew! Finally, we have the vineyard planted!

Using this method, Montinore Vineyards was planted at a direct labor cost of $75 per acre, at a time when most new vineyards in Oregon were incurring close to $300 per acre. Some mechanized planting methods can come close, but then their vine placement is nowhere near as precise. Precision is important to achieving uniform fruit production and quality.

Based on experience and ease of handling, the practical limitations for rope lengths are: baseline ropes, 200 feet; planting ropes, 160 feet. On sites with extreme undulations, shorter lengths would apply.

Annual tasks come next

Each year thereafter, variables such as the type of training system, number and location of buds left at pruning, tying, hedging, cluster thinning, mowing the cover crop, application of nutrients, herbicides, fungicides (and sometimes insecticides) have to be dealt with. All of them affect characteristics of the wine.

Then comes the harvest. Do you prefer propane cannons, electronic bird call emitters, bird net, shotgun shells, balloons, reflecting metallic ribbons, or whacking on pie pans for bird control? Next, sample clusters must be gathered to determine progress toward perfect ripeness. Initially, juice is analyzed in the laboratory for total acidity, sugar and pH. Plot the values on a graph to project the likely harvest date. When the phenological data are nearing ideal targets, it is time to switch over to tasting samples in the vineyard to pinpoint the perfect moment of harvest. How fast is the weather deteriorating to winter patterns? Did it rain last night? Will there be a few dry days to let the leaves pull some of that water out of the grapes? Where can we find pickers? Are molds starting to develop in the clusters? Have the grapes reached the point where they're losing more each day by dilution and molds than they're gaining in flavor by more "hang time?" For independent growers, what are the grape purchase contract incentives for targeted ripeness measures, such as sugar in degrees Brix?

After a year of dedicated care, it all comes down to this game of brinkmanship, this annual "winemaker's dance with Mother Nature."

---

8. A handy tool can be made of a 40" length of ¾" PVC pipe, with a cap glued on one end. It'll keep the bamboo stick straight, and provide a measuring device so every stick is exactly eight inches into the ground. Another tool can be made to help in setting the milk cartons. Make it out of steel, same footprint as the end of the carton. Attach a convenient handle and a foot rest if you like, and make it so the groove it cuts will enable the carton to lean about 10–15 degrees to the south.

Further reading

Aney, Warren W. "Oregon Climates Exhibiting Adaptation Potential for Vinifera," *American Journal of Viticulture and Enology* 25/4 (1974). Mr. Aney was a research biologist with Oregon Department of Fish and Wildlife, and a grape grower.

Division of Agricultural Sciences, University of California. *Grape Pest Management*. Rev. ed. Publication No. 4105. Berkeley, 1982.

Donahue, R.L., R.W. Miller, and J.C. Shickluna. *Soils: An Introduction to Soils and Plant Growth*. Prentice-Hall, 1983.

Galet, Pierre. *A Practical Ampelography; Grapevine Identification*. Translated by Lucie T. Morton. Cornell University Press, 1979.

Hanson, Anthony. *Burgundy*. Rev. 2nd ed. Faber and Faber, 1995.

Oregon LIVE Program (Low Input Viticulture and Enology, Inc.). Website: http://liveinc.org

Oregon Winegrowers Association. *Oregon Winegrape Growers Guide*. 4th ed. Portland, OR, 1992.

Pesticide Action Network. *PAN Pesticide Database—Chemicals*. Website: http://www.pesticideinfo.org

Reisch, Bruce I., and Steve Luce. *The Less Risky Varieties, Old and New*. NYS Agricultural Experiment Station, Cornell University, 2005. Website: http://www.hort.cornell.edu/reisch/grapegenetics/winehandout.html

Robinson, Jancis. *Vines, Grapes and Wines*. Alfred A. Knopf, 1986.

Shaffer, R., T.O. Sampaio, J. Pinkerton, and M.C. Vasconcelos. *Grapevine Rootstocks for Oregon Vineyards*. Oregon State University Extension Service, 2004. Website: http://ir.library.oregonstate.edu/xmlui/bitstream/handle/1957/20368/em8882.pdf

Skuratowicz, Eva. *2013 Oregon Vineyard and Winery Census Report, October 2014*. Southern Oregon State University Research Center. Website: http://www.sou.edu/assets/research/2013_Oregon_Vineyard_and_Winery_Report.pdf

Wilson, James E. *Terroir: The role of Geology, Climate, and Culture in the Making of French Wines*. Octopus Publishing Group Ltd; University of California Press; The Wine Appreciate Guild, 1988/1999.

Winkler, A.J., J.A. Cook, W.M. Kliewer, and L.A. Lider. *General Viticulture*. Rev. and enlarged ed. University of California Press, 1974.

The solar factor

In the preceding chapter, we were introduced to solar radiation to the extent that it impacts bare ground on a vineyard site. Now, we move on to the way in which the grapevine puts radiation to work in growing the vine and producing fruit.

Solar radiation, or irradiance, is the energy, in electromagnetic waveform, emitted by the sun. Its magnitude anywhere in the solar system is related to distance from the sun and several other factors. As measured at the outer limits of earth's atmosphere (top of atmosphere, or TOA) by NASA satellites, the magnitude varies with earth's distance from the sun (earth's orbit is not perfectly round) and sunspot activity. Sunspots are visual evidence of eruptions from the sun's surface that eject massive amounts of radiation energy (coronal mass ejections, or CME) into the universe.[1]

Top of atmosphere radiation

Total solar energy arriving at TOA is known as the "solar constant," although in Figure 21 it appears to be anything but constant. According to NASA, the intensity varies in an 11-year cycle over the range 1,364.7–1,367.2,[2] depending on the

---

1. A technical paper is posted on NASA's website, suggesting that an intense CME may be responsible for triggering the March 11, 2011 9.0 Richter earthquake and its tsunami off the Japanese coast near Sendai.

2. The composite is assembled from readings by several satellites: Nimbus/ERB and ACRIM 1, 2 & 3 by NASA.

sun-earth distance. There is some difference of opinion regarding the annual average of solar radiation reaching earth. Even NASA appears to have a mixed position on the issue. Various analyses, all based on NASA's satellite measurements, result in amounts varying from 1,362 to 1,370 watts/square meter. Based on readings of long standing, we shall take the TOP irradiance to be 1,366.92, rounded to 1,367 watts/square meter. This is the standard adopted by the World Meteorological Organization.

Light is also expressed as Langleys, a unit of measurement that varies with wavelength. While Langleys may be useful in working with optics and the visible part of solar radiation, the unit of measurement is not practical for dealing with measurements of the entire spectrum of solar radiation.

All of the foregoing discussion does not affect the analyses conducted herein. All figures are based on actual readings of "direct" (or beam) radiation and "diffuse" radiation made on the ground by the most accurate instruments available.

Technically, solar radiation at TOA is called *irradiance* and the radiation that penetrates to earth's surface is called *insolation*. More simply, all references in our analyses are called "solar radiation." Figure 21 illustrates how solar radiation is reflected and diffused as it passes through the atmosphere. About 54 percent of TOA radiation makes it to earth's surface as direct or "beam" radiation, and some of that is reflected back into the atmosphere.

The average 1,367 watts per square meter of radiation that reach the outer limits of earth's atmosphere (TOA) are comprised of a spectrum of wavelengths that varies from 100 nm (nanometers, or 10^{-10} meter), at the shortwave end (gamma rays) to about one nm (10^{-12} meter) at the longwave infrared end.

The light gray-shaded area in Figure 22 shows TOA radiation.

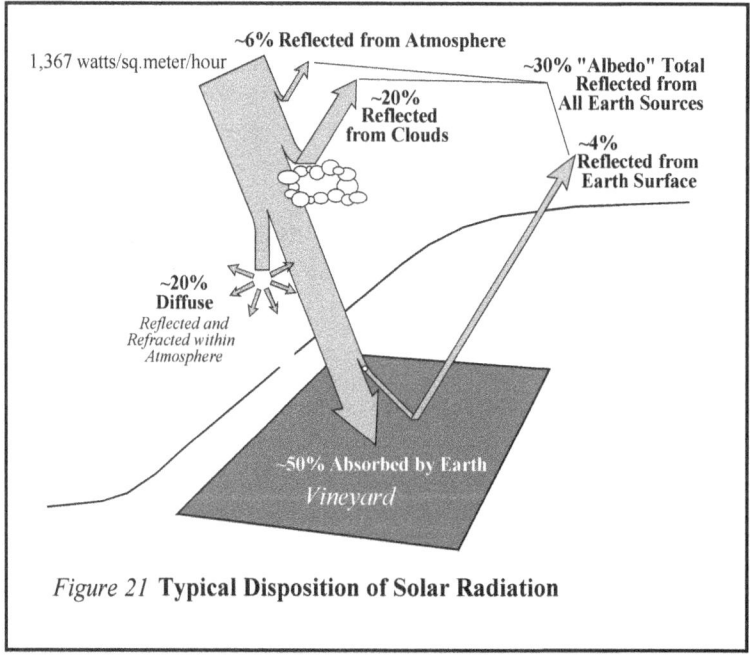

Figure 21 **Typical Disposition of Solar Radiation**

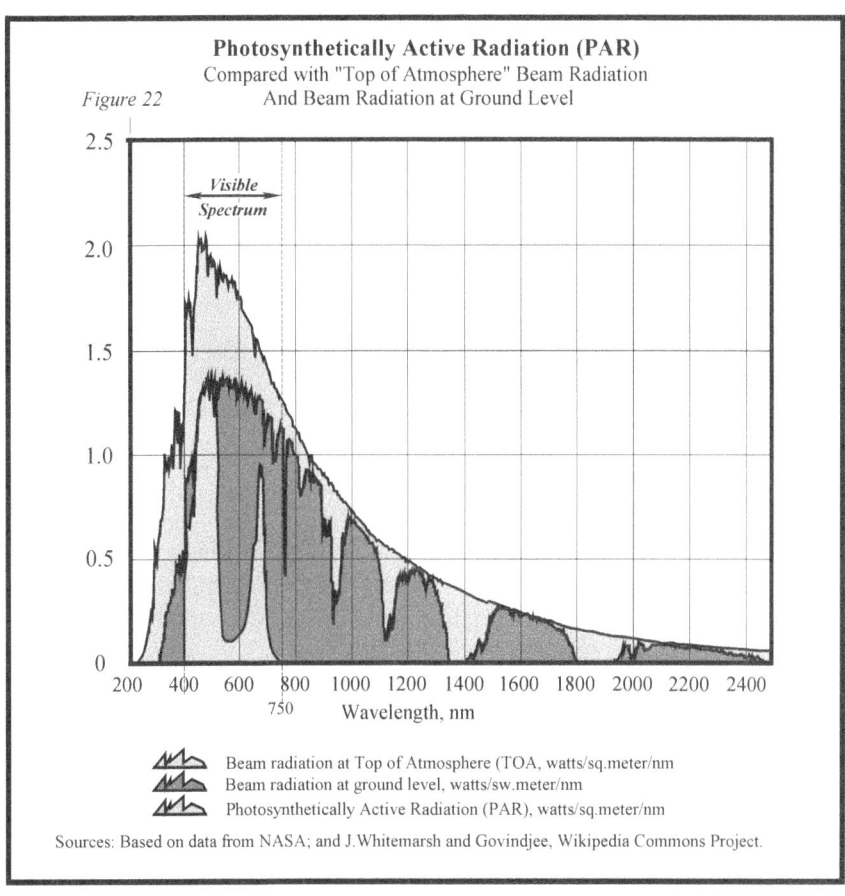

Photosynthetically Active Radiation (PAR)
Compared with "Top of Atmosphere" Beam Radiation
Figure 22   And Beam Radiation at Ground Level

Beam radiation at Top of Atmosphere (TOA, watts/sq.meter/nm)
Beam radiation at ground level, watts/sw.meter/nm
Photosynthetically Active Radiation (PAR), watts/sq.meter/nm

Sources: Based on data from NASA; and J.Whitemarsh and Govindjee, Wikipedia Commons Project.

Radiation reaching earth's surface

The amount of solar radiation that penetrates earth's atmosphere depends on latitude, sun angle, elevation, humidity, and quantity of particulates and gases in the air. The influence of these factors can be appreciated by comparing several solar monitoring sites in Oregon (Table 11).

TABLE 11   Comparison of Solar Radiation Received at Oregon Monitoring Stations

	Portland Airport	Hermiston	Eugene	Burns	Whitehorse Ranch
Altitude, meters MSL	45	180	150	1,265	1,325
Latitude	45.45	45.82	44.05	43.52	42.33
Longitude	122.64	119.28	123.07	119.02	118.23
Monthly average in July:					
Direct Normal*	577	752	644	769	773
Peak hour, PST	3 pm	noon	3 pm	11 am	11 am
Diffuse*	220	181	215	165	162
Peak hour, PST	noon	noon	noon	1 pm	3–4 pm

Note: *units are watt-hours/square meter/hour.

Source: Pacific Northwest Solar Radiation Data, UO Solar Monitoring Lab, Physics Dept., University of Oregon. April, 1998.

Portland and Eugene are large metropolitan areas with all of the air particulates and gases associated with dense population. Additionally, their maritime climates have relatively high humidity. Hermiston and Burns are at higher elevations in arid and sparsely-populated eastern Oregon. Whitehorse Ranch is the epitome of pristine conditions, 1,325 meters elevation and 11 inches of precipitation annually. It has the highest direct radiation and lowest diffuse radiation. The same conditions that permit a high rate of penetration by direct radiation also cause a lower diffuse radiation rate.

In Figure 22, the dark gray-shaded area depicts solar radiation reaching ground level. The four major valleys in the curve are caused by absorption of certain gases and water vapor in the atmosphere. From left to right they are centered at: O_3 (below 300 nm); O_2 (760 nm); H_2O (925, 1,125, 1,350, 1,875 and over 2,500 nm). CO_2 causes minor dips at 2,000 and 2,650 nm).

Photosynthetically active radiation

Of the light spectrum reaching ground level, only light waves in the range of 400–700 nm are visible to the human eye. This is also the range within which solar radiation causes photosynthetic activity. All wavelengths do not have

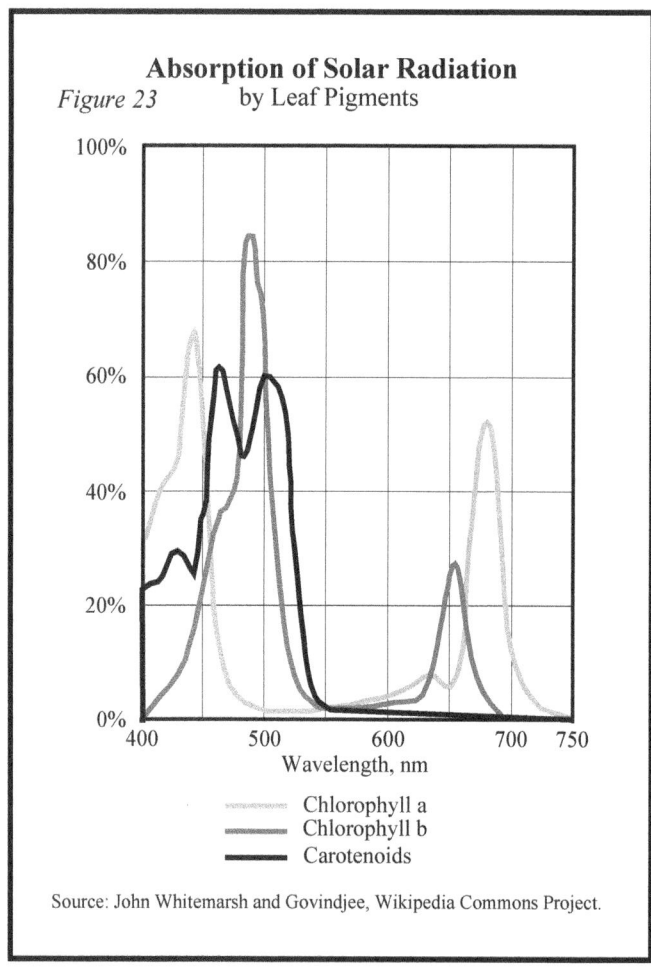

Absorption of Solar Radiation by Leaf Pigments

Figure 23

Source: John Whitemarsh and Govindjee, Wikipedia Commons Project.

the same effects, however. The absorption rates by wavelength for the most important pigments are plotted in Figure 23. Most of the photons that participate in photosynthesis are in the blue part of the spectrum. The chlorophylls also utilize some energy in the red part for photosynthesis.

Most of the green wavelengths are reflected away by plant tissue, which is what makes plants appear green.

The solar radiation utilized for photosynthesis is indicated by the light gray color with cross-hatch in Figure 22. More specifically, the wavelengths utilized for photosynthesis are those shown on Figure 23, which are absorbed by leaf pigments: Chlorophyll a, Chlorophyll b, and the Carotenoids.

Even though the infrared part of the light spectrum does not participate directly in photosynthesis, it does have some effect. Infrared wavelengths transmit heat energy to the atmosphere and all of the surfaces on earth. Because the photosynthetic rate, i.e., carbon assimilation, is increased by an ambient temperature increase, the effect is on the speed of the reaction and not in the supply of additional electrons to the process.

A simplified primer on photosynthesis

The process by which carbohydrates are generated in the vine leaf is not a simple one. We usually think of the overall photosynthesis equation as:

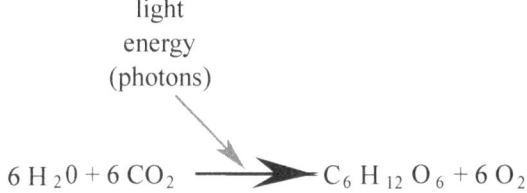

$$6\,H_2O + 6\,CO_2 \longrightarrow C_6\,H_{12}\,O_6 + 6\,O_2$$

This is a pared-down discussion of photosynthesis. For a complete detailed discussion, see the suggested references at the end of the chapter.

The process has three main reactions, depicted in Figure 24:

1. **First light-dependent reaction—Photosystem II.** The first step begins when *chlorophyll a* (P680) absorbs light energy and converts ADP into ATP. An electron is recruited for this task from the splitting of a water molecule, which releases oxygen and hydrogen. Photosystem II was discovered later than Photosystem I, hence the reverse numbering.

2. **Second light-dependent reaction—Photosystem I.** The second step receives its energy in a photon (another electron) from P700, another form of *chlorophyll a*. Here, the ADP is converted to NAPD and NAPDH.

3. **Light-independent reaction.** Also known as the dark reactions, the light-independent processes nonetheless are stimulated by light energy. This phase is also called the *Calvin-Benson Reaction*.

Solar radiation intercepted by vine canopies

Now, let's carry the analysis of solar radiation to the next logical step.

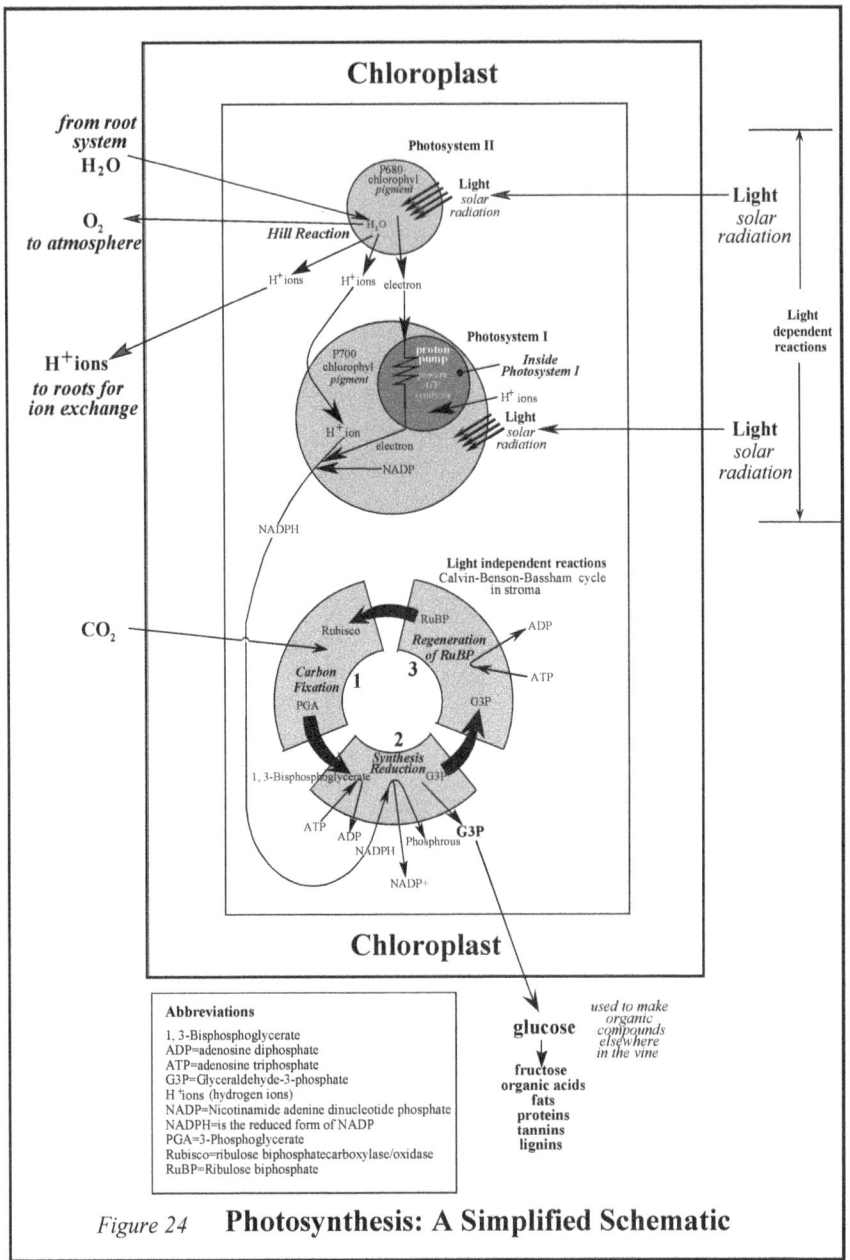

Figure 24   **Photosynthesis: A Simplified Schematic**

Think of the individual vine canopy as a solar energy panel. The same principles of absorption apply. Dust off the trigonometry you learned in high school, that subject you thought you'd never use again.

In the preceding chapter, Figure 10 showed that solar radiation can be broken down into vertical, north-south and east-west vectors to analyze a bare site.

Now, we will apply those vectors to the trellis canopy in order to determine the amount of solar radiation absorbed by the vines. A south-facing slope at noon is used because it simplifies the depiction.

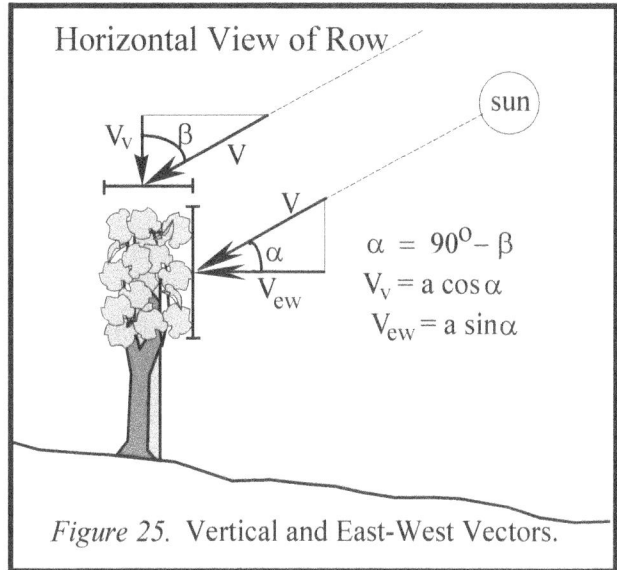

Figure 25. Vertical and East-West Vectors.

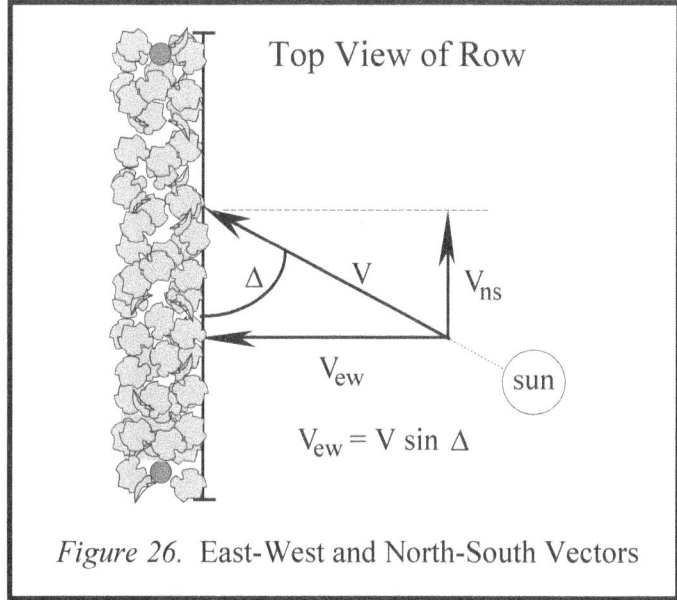

Figure 26. East-West and North-South Vectors

The main objective of vineyard design is to provide the vine canopy with sunlight in the way that is best suited to the grape variety. The following example shows how this can be done.

Figures 25 and 26 assist by illustrating trigonometric relationships among the solar vectors and vine canopy.

The best relationships between grape varieties and the hillside direction on which they grow can be deduced by the settings of the world's best vineyards for each variety. Sometimes it is possible to select the best slope direction for the grapes you want to grow, and sometimes it is not, depending on whether you acquire the site before or after you select the grape varieties. Don't lose hope, however, because you can change the row direction and/or trellis config-uration to bring a desired energy profile to vine canopies.

Growers in Burgundy attribute the greatness of their wines to the *terroir*. That term includes everything in the vine's environment: temperature, solar radiation, precipitation, soils, topography, vine density, canopy configuration, and what the *vigneron* does to care for the vines. The emphasis is on climate and soils.

You are about to learn about a factor that heretofore has not been addressed.

To illustrate how valuable a tool the analysis of solar interception by the vines is, let's compare two leading Pinot Noir producing locations. Almost everyone who knows about Pinot Noir knows about Domaine de la Romanée Conti at Vosne-Romanée in Burgundy. Their wines command the highest prices year-in and year-out. Retail prices run $100–400 per bottle upon release. DRC's vineyard holdings include: La Tâche, La Romanée, La Romanée-Conti, Le Richebourg, Romanée-St.Vivant, Les Échézeaux and Les Grands Échézeaux. We'll analyze one of their vineyards without identifying which one.

Since Oregon is compared with Burgundy these days, let's look also at the Dundee Hills AVA, currently considered Oregon's best. Comparing them side by side should be interesting. Although we will be viewing two different training

Table 12	**Vineyard Parameters**	
	Oregon Dundee Hills AVA	*Côte d'Or Vosne-Romanée*
Latitude	45.6° N	47.17° N
Longitude	123.1°	4.75°
Elevation	600 ft.	285 meters (934.3 ft.)
Spacing:		
Between Rows	9 ft. (2.75 meters)	1.0 meter (39.37 in.)
Between Vines	7 ft. (2.14 meters)	1.0 meter (39.37 in.)
Land area/vine	63.0 sq.ft.	1 sq.meter (10.7 sq.ft.)
Vines/acre	691.4	4,053.0
Canopy:		
Topped at	6 ft. 2 in. (1.88 meters)	1.0 meter (39.37 in.)
Thickness	15 in.	15.0 in.
Vertical length	44 in. (1.12 meters)	0.76 meters (30.0 in.)
Slope direction	South	East
Slope inclination	15°	15°
Solar radiation:		
Direct, at solar noon	650 watt-hrs/sq.m./hr	700 watt-hrs/sq.m./hr
Diffuse radiation	32.6%	28.6%
Ground reflectance	0.20	0.15
Cloud cover	6.0%	6.0%

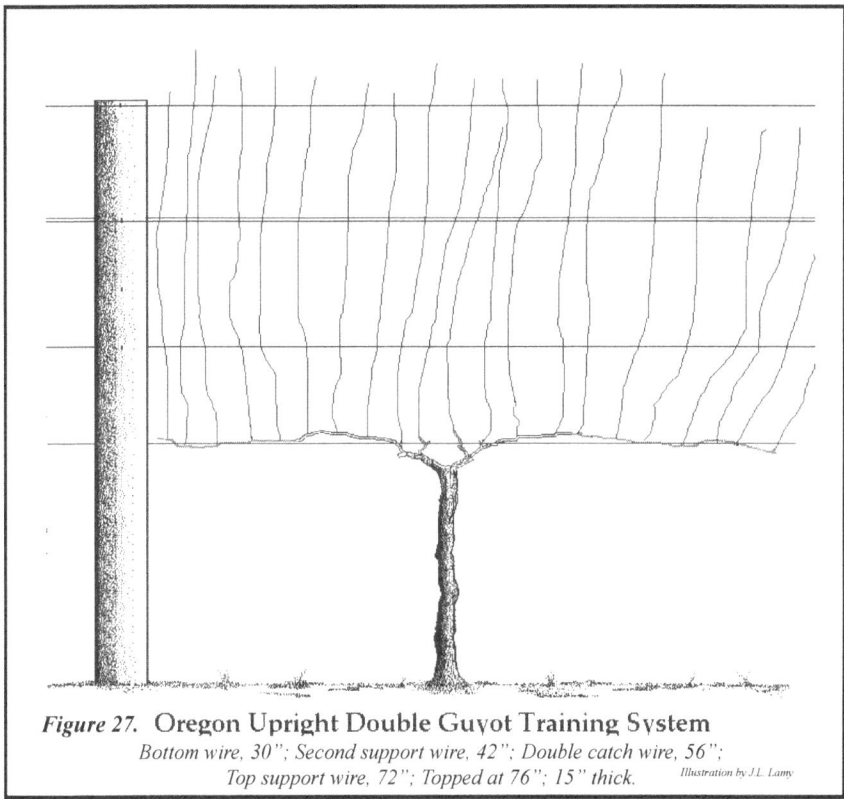

Figure 27. Oregon Upright Double Guyot Training System
Bottom wire, 30"; Second support wire, 42"; Double catch wire, 56";
Top support wire, 72"; Topped at 76"; 15" thick.   *Illustration by J.L. Lamy*

systems and slopes facing in different directions, the exercise is, nonetheless, illuminating.

Table 12 presents the pertinent parameters for the comparison.

Figure 27 depicts the traditional Oregon Upright Single Curtain trellis.[3] There are variations, especially in regard to one or more fixed wires in place of the double catch wires. The canopy configuration is consistent. Older vineyards placed a grape stake at each vine. Since the early 1980s, the New Zealand Hi-Tensile System is a more common practice. Line posts are placed approximately every 30 feet, depending in intra-vine spacing. Support of the vine's weight depends on the tension placed on the wires by strainers.

Generally, no adjustment is made to row height in order to match a ratio with the intra-row spacing, as is done in Europe. Top and side hedging at about two-week intervals is done by the best producers between bloom and *veraison,*[4] the frequency depending on how fast the vines are growing.

The best growers also practice shoot positioning, and removal of leaves on the east side of the fruit zone after *veraison.* The floor management programs of most growers include maintaining a bare soil zone under the vines, and cultivating a grass crop on the rest of the vineyard floor. Much research has been

---

3. In France, the training system would be referred to as "double Guyot."

4. Veraison is the stage of berry development when the color changes.

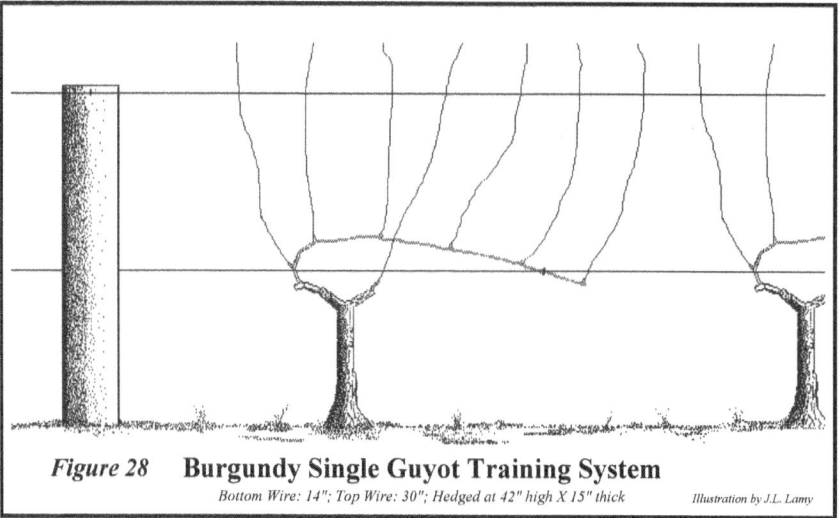

Figure 28   **Burgundy Single Guyot Training System**
Bottom Wire: 14"; Top Wire: 30"; Hedged at 42" high X 15" thick   *Illustration by J.L. Lamy*

devoted to using a cover crop to wick water out of the soil after *veraison* in order to stress the vines and hasten ripening.

Figure 28 illustrates the traditional Burgundy trellis system. In the best vineyards, the intra-row spacing is maintained at one meter, matching the row height. Only six-seven buds are left on each vine at pruning. Frequent hedging is standard practice.

Most Côte d'Or vineyards maintain bare soils under their vines. Some grow a cover crop every third or fourth row, leaving the soil bare between. At pruning, the lone fruiting cane is twisted to split its brown bark, and bent over to the opposite side of the trunk. The tactic balances the early growth rate of vines by slowing the naturally more rapid elongation of new vines out toward the end of the cane, thus allowing shoots closer to the trunk to catch up.

Equivalent units for ambient heat

Photosynthesis is driven by both light and heat. In order to estimate the total photosynthetic energy capture by the leaf canopy, a conversion factor for heat has to be developed. Data from light box studies at UC-Davis were used to calculate a conversion factor based on the amount of carbon respiration (mg CO_2/square meter/hour) produced by temperature and light differences.[5]

In one experiment, light was held constant at 4,000 foot-candles while temperature varied. In another, temperature was constant at 77°F while light intensity was varied.

There are some shortcomings to using this data for the task. First, the testing was done on Sultana (Thompson Seedless) and Shiraz grapes, both suited to the hot climate of California's Central Valley. The selection shows how UC-Davis at that time (1968–1971) focused its research efforts on large-production crops rather than the high quality wine grape varieties later grown in Napa Valley and the coastal counties. Second, the CO_2 assimilation rate varies from one grape

5. *General Viticulture*; Winkler et al.; University of California Press; Berkeley, CA. Revised and enlarged edition. 1974, 97–98.

variety to another. This is, however, the only data available, so we'll have to go with it.

There is a redeeming factor. We're interested in the rate of gain in assimilation produced by a gain of light or heat. The curves are approximately parallel in the operating range that is of interest to us. In the operating range for vineyards in moderate climates (58.9–76.7°F and 2,000–4,000 foot-candles) where vineyards spend most of their growing season time, assuming linearity in the relationships is reasonably valid.

The result is a simple formula:

Solar radiation equivalent of ambient temperature = 3.27165 • (T_L − 41°F)

Where:

$T_L = T_A + 6°F$

T_L is the average leaf temperature for the day.

T_A is the average ambient (air) temperature for the day.

Solar radiation equivalent is in watt-hours/square meter/day

Leaf temperature is assumed at six degrees above ambient (air) temperature. This value will vary among wine grape varieties.

The base of 41°F is used because, although an average temperature above 50°F is required for budbreak to occur, after some leaves have unfurled, carbon assimilation occurs as low as 41°F.

Oregon—Dundee Hills AVA solar profile

Solar radiation vectors for the vine canopy in Oregon's Dundee Hills AVA are shown in Figure 29. All of them, except the heat equivalent, show the morning-afternoon symmetry produced by north-south row alignment. The north-south vector is for the projected area of the top of the row on this south-facing slope. The diffuse radiation peak is shifted about thirty minutes into the afternoon, a recorded phenomenon.

Notice the radiation reflected off the ground between rows and up onto the sides of the canopy (curve 5).

The radiation (per meter of row length), *including the equivalent units for ambient heat*, intercepted by the Oregon canopy peaks twice a day: 1,050.8 watt-hours/sq meter/hr at 9:42 AM and 1,205.8 watt-hours/sq meter/hr at 3:12 PM sun time.

Total energy captured, per meter of row, over the course of all daylight hours on this mid-July day (total area under curve 6) is 11,772.5 watt-hours/sq meter.

Burgundy—Vosne-Romanée solar profile

Solar radiation vectors for the vineyard in Vôsne-Romanée, Burgundy are shown in Figure 30. The curves for the solar vectors are symmetrical and centered on solar noon, except the curve for diffuse radiation. It is shifted to the left because diffuse radiation is multidirectional and largely independent of slope direction.

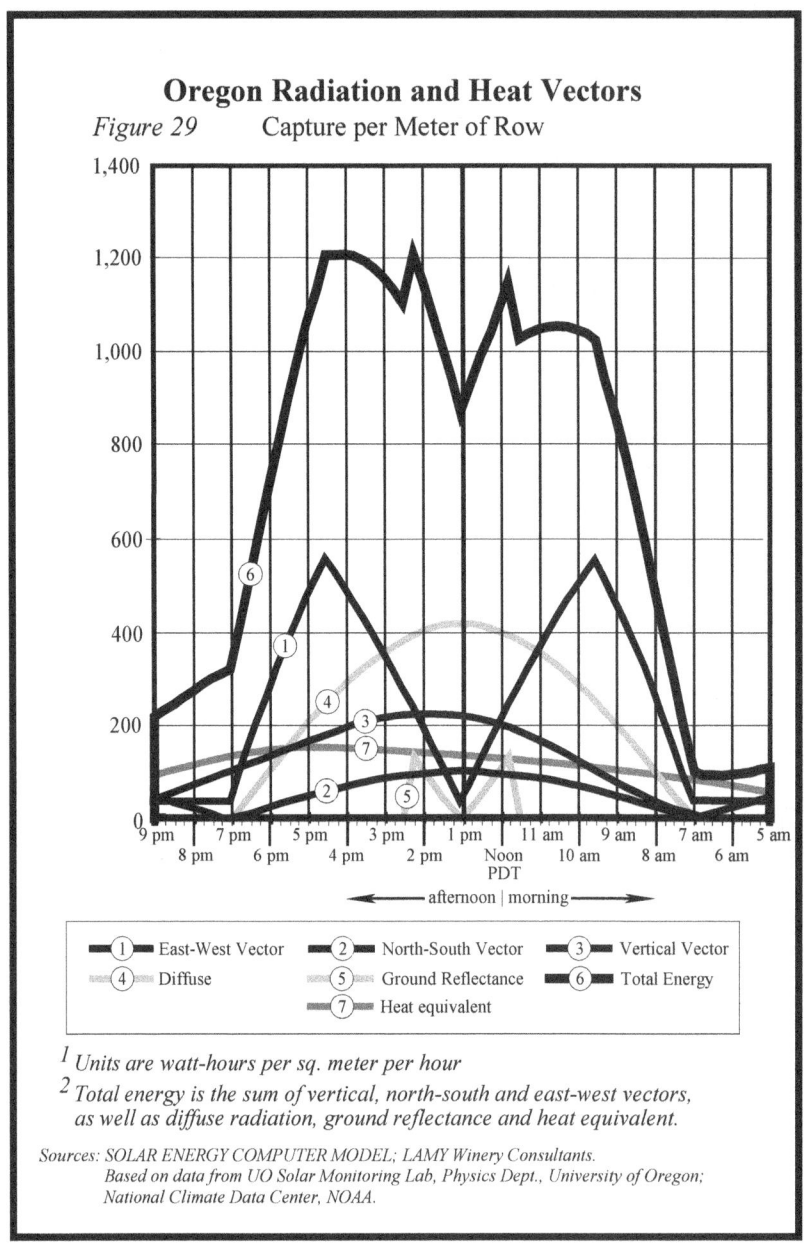

Oregon Radiation and Heat Vectors

Figure 29   Capture per Meter of Row

The east-west vector is absorbed by the top of the canopy on this east-facing, 15° hillside.

Total energy captured by the canopy peaks (per meter of row length) at 1:12 PM in sun time is 967.5 watt-hours/sq meter/hour.

Total energy captured over the full sunlit day is 10,889.1 watt-hours/sq meter.

Total daily energy comparison

When viewed in terms of radiation per meter of row length (see Figure 31), vine canopies on the Oregon site captured more radiation energy, 8.1% greater than did the Côte d'Or canopies.

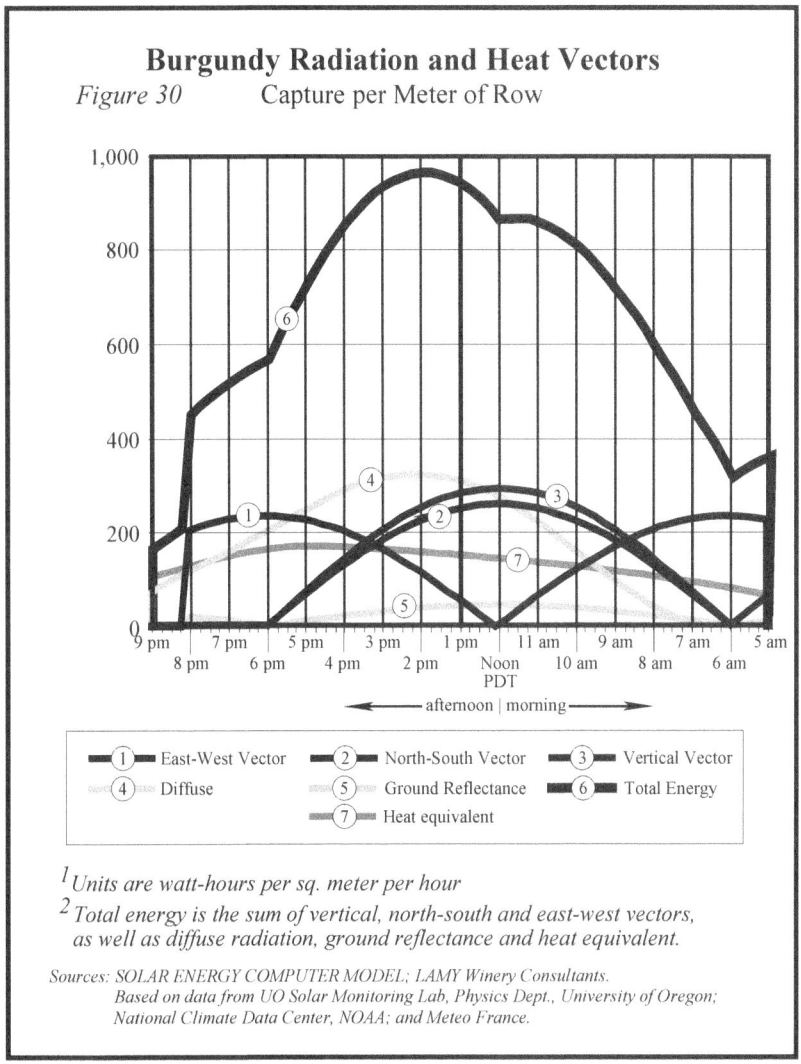

Burgundy Radiation and Heat Vectors

Figure 30   Capture per Meter of Row

[1] Units are watt-hours per sq. meter per hour

[2] Total energy is the sum of vertical, north-south and east-west vectors,
as well as diffuse radiation, ground reflectance and heat equivalent.

Sources: *SOLAR ENERGY COMPUTER MODEL; LAMY Winery Consultants.*
Based on data from UO Solar Monitoring Lab, Physics Dept., University of Oregon;
National Climate Data Center, NOAA; and Meteo France.

*But, is this, watt-hours per meter of row length, the most meaningful measure
for comparing the two?*

To answer this question, we will explore capture rates using other denominators: (1) per square meter of vineyard; (2) per vine; and (3) per pound of fruit produced.

Alternative rates

Figure 32 compares total energy capture in terms of watt-hours/sq meter/hour per square meter of vineyard land.

Total energy for the Oregon example peaks at 415.9 watt-hours/sq meter/hour at 10:57 AM and 439.6 watt-hours/sq meter/hour at 3:12 PM. Burgundy peaks at 1:12 PM solar time at 967.5 watt-hours/sq meter/hour.

Total energy captured per day in mid-July in the Burgundy example is 10,889.1, 153% greater than 4,291.5 in the Oregon vineyard. The reason: the Burgundy layout has more canopy surface area than the Oregon VSP.

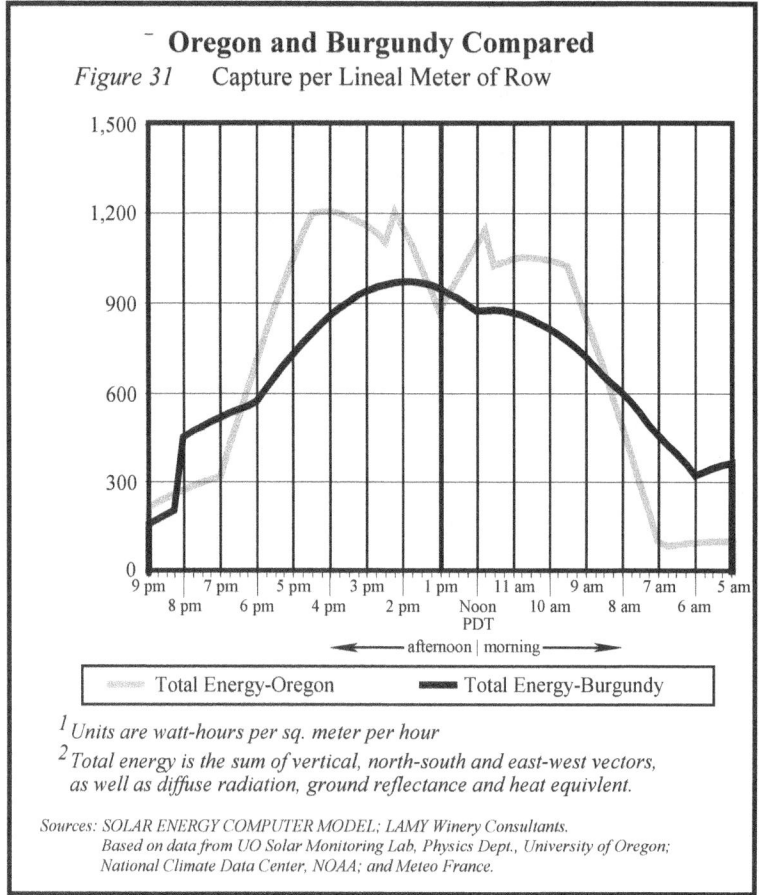

Oregon and Burgundy Compared

Figure 31   Capture per Lineal Meter of Row

Total Energy-Oregon   Total Energy-Burgundy

[1] *Units are watt-hours per sq. meter per hour*

[2] *Total energy is the sum of vertical, north-south and east-west vectors, as well as diffuse radiation, ground reflectance and heat equivlent.*

Sources: SOLAR ENERGY COMPUTER MODEL; LAMY Winery Consultants. Based on data from UO Solar Monitoring Lab, Physics Dept., University of Oregon; National Climate Data Center, NOAA; and Meteo France.

TABLE 13   Effect of Yield in Dundee Hills AVA

		Watt-hours/square meter/day		
		wh/sm/day	Maximum ¼ hr.	Time
Dundee Hills AVA				
	2.0 tpa	**4,341.8**	**444.7**	**3:12 pm**
	3.5 tpa	2,481.0	254.1	3:12 pm
	4.0 tpa	2,170.9	222.4	1:27 pm
Vôsne-Romanée				
	2.0 tpa	**11,016.7**	**978.8**	**1:12 pm**

In Figure 33, the radiation capture per vine is greater in the Oregon vineyard. Its 25,117.7 watt-hours/sq meter for the day are 130.7% larger than Burgundy's 10,889.1. Why? There are far fewer vines per unit area in the Oregon example.

Figure 34 depicts the radiation capture per pound of fruit produced. We have used a yield of 2 tons/acre for the Burgundy vineyard, although records indicate that 2.1–2.2 might be more appropriate. The Dundee Hills vineyard is assumed to yield 3.5 tons/acre, although some newer clones, rootstocks and ambition have pushed some plantings to 4 tons/acre in good weather years.

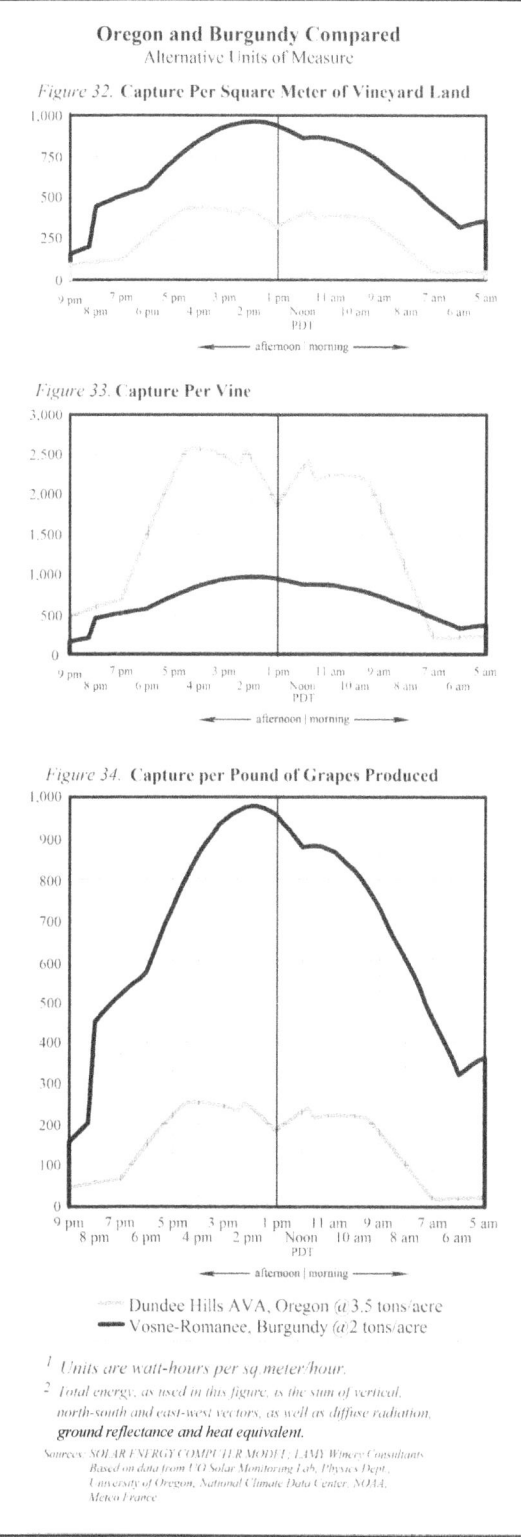

Oregon and Burgundy Compared
Alternative Units of Measure

Figure 32. **Capture Per Square Meter of Vineyard Land**

Figure 33. **Capture Per Vine**

Figure 34. **Capture per Pound of Grapes Produced**

Dundee Hills AVA, Oregon @ 3.5 tons/acre
Vosne-Romanee, Burgundy @ 2 tons/acre

[1] *Units are watt-hours per sq.meter/hour.*

[2] *Total energy, as used in this figure, is the sum of vertical, north-south and east-west vectors, as well as diffuse radiation,* **ground reflectance and heat equivalent.**

Sources: SOLAR ENERGY COMPUTER MODEL; LAMY Winery Consultants
Based on data from UO Solar Monitoring Lab, Physics Dept.,
University of Oregon; National Climate Data Center, NOAA;
Meteo France

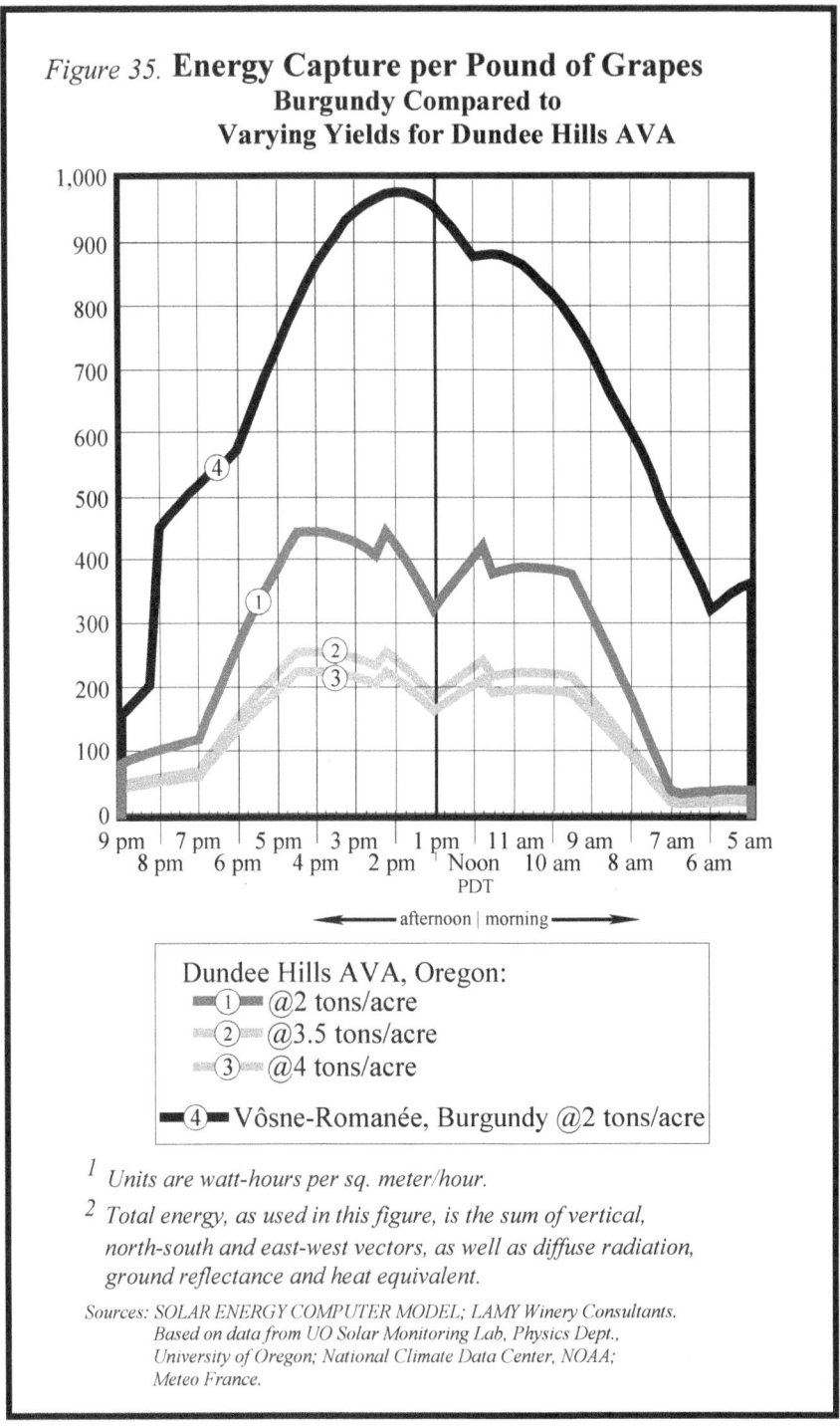

Figure 35. **Energy Capture per Pound of Grapes**
Burgundy Compared to
Varying Yields for Dundee Hills AVA

Dundee Hills AVA, Oregon:
1 @2 tons/acre
2 @3.5 tons/acre
3 @4 tons/acre
4 Vôsne-Romanée, Burgundy @2 tons/acre

1 Units are watt-hours per sq. meter/hour.
2 Total energy, as used in this figure, is the sum of vertical, north-south and east-west vectors, as well as diffuse radiation, ground reflectance and heat equivalent.

Sources: SOLAR ENERGY COMPUTER MODEL; LAMY Winery Consultants. Based on data from UO Solar Monitoring Lab, Physics Dept., University of Oregon; National Climate Data Center, NOAA; Meteo France.

The Burgundy vineyard has the greater amount of radiation captured, at a stunning 11,016.7 watt-hours/sq meter/hour, 4.44 times as much as the 2,481.0 watt-hours per sq meter/hour captured by the Oregon VSP. There are four reasons: greater vine density, trellis configuration, row alignment, and very low fruit load per vine.

This discovery may alter the way winegrowers think about high density plantings.

Varying yields in the Dundee Hills AVA

Can the total energy capture per pound of grapes in the Dundee Hills vineyard be increased to parity with that of the Vôsne-Romanée vineyard by reducing its yield? To place the effect of reducing yields in the Oregon vineyard in perspective, Figure 35 compares the total energy capture for 2.0, 3.5 and 4.0 tons/acre to the constant Burgundy yield of 2 tons/acre.

Reducing the Dundee Hills AVA's yield to 2.0 tons/acre increases the 24-hour energy capture to 4,341.8 watt-hours/sq meter/day. Even at yield parity, the total energy capture for Vôsne-Romanée is 153.7 percent greater than for Dundee Hills.

Further reading

Bledsoe, Karen. *Photosynthesis*. Biology 102, Chapter 7.

Calvin Cycle. Website: http://en.wikipedia.org/wiki/Calvin_cycle

Hanson, Anthony. *Burgundy*. Rev. 2nd ed. London: Faber and Faber, 1995.

Casteel, Ted. *Oregon Winegrape Growers Guide*. 4th ed. Portland, OR: Oregon Winegrowers Association, 1992.

Donahue, R.L., R.W. Miller, and J.C. Shickluna. *Soils: An Introduction to Soils and Plant Growth*. Englewood Cliffs, NJ: Prentice-Hall, Inc., 1983.

Grape Pest Management. Publication No. 4105. Rev. ed. Berkeley: Division of Agricultural Sciences, 1982.

The Light Independent Reactions.
Website: http://kentsimmons.uwinnipeg.ca/cm1504/calvincycle.html

Photosystem II. Website: http://en.wikipedia.org/wiki/Photosystem_II

Photosynthesis. Website: http://www.emc.maricopa.edu/faculty/farabee/biobk/biobookps.html

Robinson, Jancis. *Vines, Grapes and Wines*. New York: Alfred A. Knopf, 1986.

Winkler, A.J., J.A. Cook, W.M. Kliewer, and L.A. Lider. *General Viticulture*. Rev. and enlarged ed. Berkeley: University of California Press, 1974.

— 5 —

Managing the vineyard

There are so many publications available on how to manage the vineyard that the rudiments need not be covered here. Instead, let's look at issues that are rarely covered in print or are the subject of frequent misunderstanding. The *Further Reading* list at chapter's end provides many publications for the reader's perusal.

Trellis installation

Trellis design is part of vineyard design. However, because installation of the trellis after planting is favored for economic reasons, the operation is integrated with other vineyard management tasks. The facets of vineyard design are considered in the order in which they are encountered.

The choice of trellis configuration is one issue, selection of materials is another. Design alternatives illustrated in Figure 36 are **high tensile** (hi-ten), or **conventional** (grapestake at every vine). There are many other trellising systems in use, some going back many years, others relatively new. Research efforts continue around the globe to discover the perfect trellis system in each setting. However, the majority of the industry has virtually settled on the vertical-shoot-positioned profile (VSP) on hi-ten and long line post spacing.

You will also decide whether to use hi-ten or the old cheap, softer stuff. The case can be made that hi-ten will cost less, because it requires far fewer line posts, generally every 25–30 feet depending on in-the-row spacing. End-post

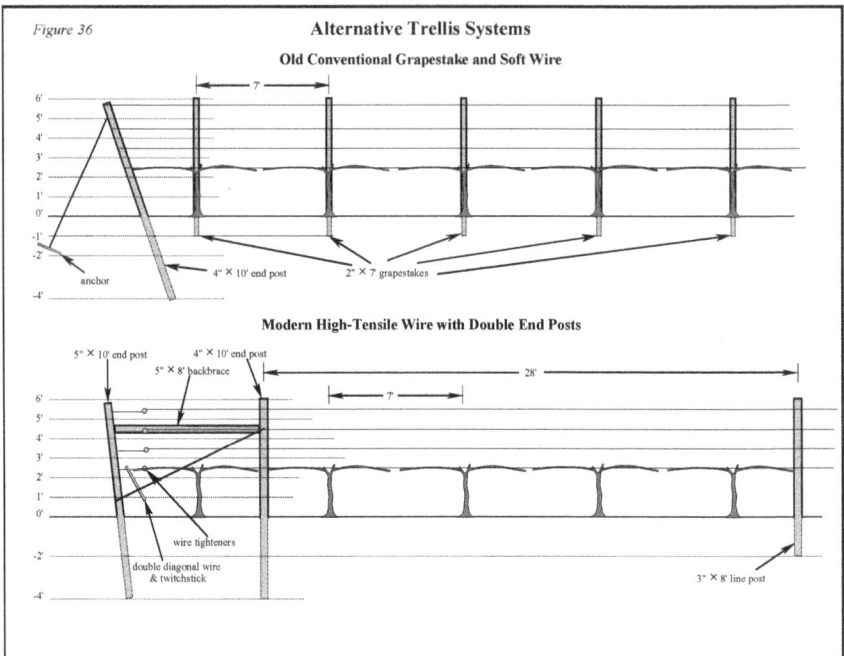

Figure 36

Alternative Trellis Systems

Old Conventional Grapestake and Soft Wire

Modern High-Tensile Wire with Double End Posts

assemblies have to be stronger to hold the tension. That means double end-post assemblies with a horizontal brace post. Both of the end posts are longer (4' in the ground). These embellishments add to the cost, but not enough to cancel out the materials, labor and hardware savings afforded by fewer grapestakes or line posts.

You can use treated wood posts, steel fence posts, recycled plastic, or concrete like the Italians. Many vineyards have gone to steel posts because of the poor preservative treatment of wood posts, or because they fear environmental effects of the wood preservatives.

Most wood posts are treated with a process called CCA, chromated copper arsenate. The wood moisture has to be reduced to 21–22 percent prior to treating for the preservative salts to stay in the wood after the pressure is removed. Otherwise, the water compressed inside the post will shove the salts back out again as soon as the retort pressure is reduced.[1] Most growers install "catch wires" with the vertical-shoot-positioned (VSP) trellis system. Installed in pairs, one on each side of the line posts, catch wires allow the canopy to sprawl through bloom. Shortly after bloom, the wires are moved up in several steps to gather the canopy into its eventual vertical profile.

Why is this done? Immediately after the bloom period, the fruiting canes develop their *bud primordia* for next year's crop. Bud primordia contain miniature versions of the clusters and shoots that will emerge next year.[2] German researchers discovered that the fruiting canes for this year's crop, if positioned

---

1. According to Timber Products Inspection, Inc., a compliance inspection and consulting firm that audits pressure treater compliance with specifications.

2. To see this phenomenon, use a razor blade to slit a bud protrusion down the middle and look at it through a strong magnifying glass or microscope. Some vineyardists excise dormant buds during the winter to forecast the coming season's yields.

for full sun exposure during this bud-setting phase, will set clusters for next year's crop that are significantly more fruitful than normal. So, leaving the vines in a sprawl through this period will accomplish good sunlight exposure.

Annual purchase contracts

A purchase agreement, or contract (APC), is a purchasing method that is useful for acquiring materials and supplies in large quantities over all or part of the year. It is a significant tool of "just in time" inventory management. Annual contracts are used extensively in manufacturing industries. In general, suppliers are willing to grant price discounts based on the commitment of large quantity.

Here is how annual contracts work. The buyer issues a *Request for Quotation* (RFQ) to prospective suppliers. The RFQ stipulates that the buyer will buy a certain amount during the year, but the RFQ provides that the product be shipped in installments, called *releases*, at regular intervals. Releases can be any number of shipments, spaced to accommodate the buyer's production schedule. When the successful bidder (there may be one or several competitively) is selected, the buyer draws up the APC, which becomes the contract upon signing by the supplier.[3]

For example, let's say a vineyard wishes to use an APC to buy treated posts for trellises. Let's say we have a 20-acre parcel (660 ft E-W by 1,320 ft N-S) and wish to divide it into two vineyard blocks. Deducting for 30-ft headlands at row end and 15-ft avenues on the sides, each block measures 615 ft N-S by 630 ft E-W.

We're going to install the hi-ten trellis system with double end-post assemblies and VSP vine training. Vine spacing is 9 ft. between rows and 7 ft. between vines in the row. Those numbers convert to 71 rows of 89 vines (Figure 37). Line posts are spaced at 28-foot intervals.

By our calculations, and adding a 10 percent allowance for breakage and early replacements, the need for posts is:

8' × 3" tops, line posts	4,530
10' × 5" tops, end posts	312
10' × 4" tops, end posts	312
5' × 4" tops, brace posts	312

An example purchase order is illustrated in Figure 38. The method can be used to advantage for trellis wire, wine bottles, corks, capsules and, perhaps, labels. In all of these supplies, quantities are large, and the vineyard or winery does not normally need full quantities all at once. Further, the prices for those items are relatively stable through a year's time. On the other hand, the dealer cost of vineyard spray chemicals can be volatile. For that reason, a wholesaler may not be willing to enter into an agreement that commits to a long-term price schedule.

---

3. The author is not an attorney. Readers are cautioned to consult an attorney for legal nuances that might apply in each state.

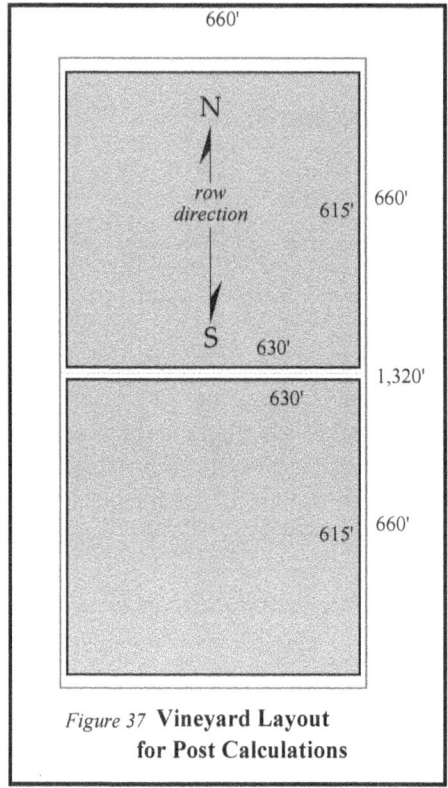

Figure 37 **Vineyard Layout
for Post Calculations**

The vendor may want to specify a price penalty, such as a 5 percent upcharge, if the purchaser fails to meet or exceed the quantities specified in the APC.

Annual cultural activities

Vineyard management activities are many over the course of the year. The major groups include winter pruning and tying, herbicide sprays in the strip beneath the canopy, fungicide sprays, insect sprays, nutrient sprays or applications, shoot positioning, hedging, leaf pulling, harvest, and post-harvest applications of boron. These activities are depicted in Figure 39.

Winter pruning

Most of the pruning is done during the winter months when the vines are dormant. Pruning should not start too soon after harvest. It is best to wait for cold weather to harden off the vines for winter. Further, as long as the leaves are green, they are still contributing something to the vine's winter storage of nutrients and carbohydrates in the permanent parts of the plant.

Winter pruning should be accomplished before the buds begin to push in the spring, about April 1 in moderate growing areas, March 1 in California and other warmer areas. The only exception to this rule is *double pruning*, a tactic to delay budbreak. In areas where late frost is an issue, all of the pruning cuts except the ends of the surviving canes are executed during dormancy, but the tips are left untrimmed. Pruning the tips of the canes shortly before budbreak

Example Purchase Order
Figure 38   **Using Annual Purchase Contracting**

PURCHASE ORDER

Date: 9/16/2010   P.O. No. 2011-23

Purchaser: Grand Eagle Estate Winery, Inc.
                   27600 West Avenue of the Vineyards
                   West Paradise, OR 97116
                   (503)357-XXXX

Vendor: Durable Treated Post Company
                  Harvard, ID 83834

	Release Date**	Quantity	Price***
All are CCA-treated wood posts of lodgepole pine*:			
Item #1: 8' length X 3" tops	12/1/2010	2,400	$4.00/ea
	2/1/2011	1,200	$4.00/ea
	4/1/2011	930	$4.00/ea
Item #2: 10' length X 5" tops	4/1/2011	312	$12.60/ea
Item #3: 10' length X 4" tops	4/1/2011	312	$10.00/ea
Item #4: 5' length X 4" tops	4/1/2011	312	$5.15/ea

*All posts to be pressure-treated with chromated copper arsenate
  (CCA) in accordance with AWPA specification C-16.
  All posts subject to incoming inspection for conformance.

**Delivery will be made within ten days
  of specified release dates.

***Failure to meet or exceed full contract quantities of each
    release will be charged a 5% price penalty on that release.

Grand Eagle Estate Winery | 27600 Avenue of the Vineyards | West Paradise, OR 97116
Phone: (503)357-XXXX | FAX: (503)357-XXXX | pa@grandeagle.com

will delay budbreak for two weeks from the time the pruning cuts are made. This tactic will not help after the buds have produced green tissue.

Fungicides, insecticides and nutrients

Warning! *The pest control programs presented herein are based upon personal experience with site-specific vineyards, coupled with recommendations presented by the respective states' extension services. Growers should be aware that departures from these schedules may be appropriate, particularly in regard to timing and materials utilized, as dictated by their own site-specific conditions.*

Plant disease, insect pests and nutrient deficiencies vary widely across America. It is impossible to lay out a single program covering all sites in the country or even within a region. There are too many variables among sites that change the challenge. The same array of disease pathogens does not exist in all growing areas. Likewise, damaging insect populations vary from place to place. Finally, nutrient deficiencies depend on the soil pH and structure, and soil evolution is affected by climate conditions. Therefore, we will consider a "best case"–"worst case" pair of scenarios to illustrate the range.

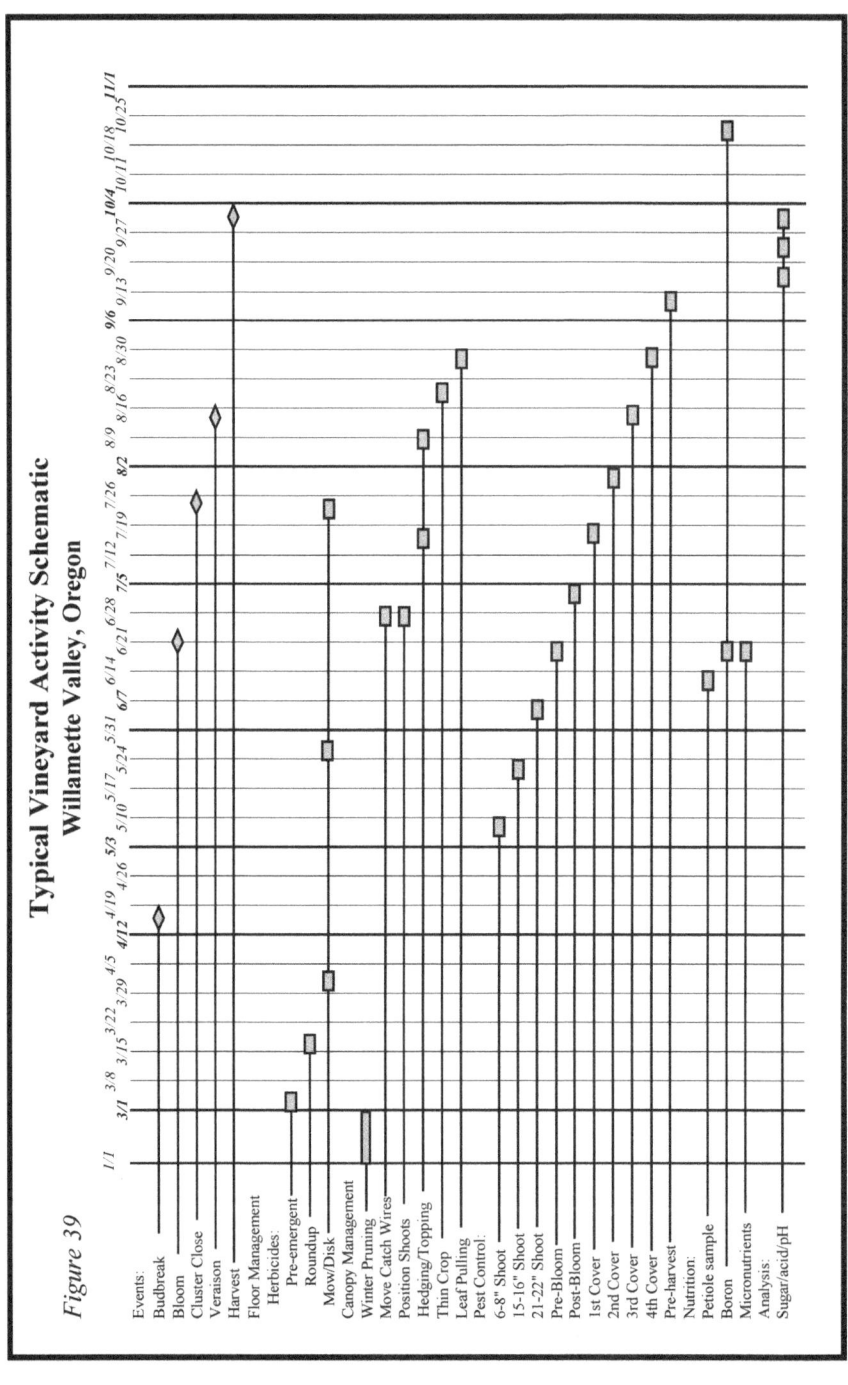

Figure 39

Oregon's northwest Willamette Valley is chosen as the "best case" scenario. For the time being, it presents the fewest pathogen and insect challenges of any American grape growing area. Part of the reason is that the humidity is moderate-to-low when the temperature is high, thus reducing powdery mildew pressure and extending the effectiveness of some systemic fungicides to as long as 21 days.

Figure 40 is a graphical portrait of the disease and insect problems faced by growers in Oregon's Willamette Valley.

Most vineyards utilize a combination of systemic and contact fungicides. The advantage of systemics is that they last longer between applications, are generally more effective, cost less in the long run, and are not externally obnoxious. If the waiting period before harvest is observed, there will be no harmful residue in the grapes or wine.

For some applications, contact materials have been discovered that can be effective on powdery mildew. JMS Stylet oil, detergent and baking soda are among them.

Organic growers favor using a lot of sulfur dust for powdery mildew control. This approach has its disadvantages. Excessive buildup of sulfur in the soil is one of them. Another is the irritation it causes to eye and nasal linings and lungs. Then, a little wind and/or rain, and you'll be making another application, adding to your costs. If you have a small vineyard, you may not mind spraying every week at times, but it's economic suicide for a larger vineyard. Of course, protective clothing and masks are vitally important, as is the case with all spray materials. But, this stuff hangs on the skin and must wear off despite your best efforts to wash it off.

There is another side effect of sulfur that demands attention in these environmentally-conscious times. Repeated sulfur applications will kill many of the beneficial insects.

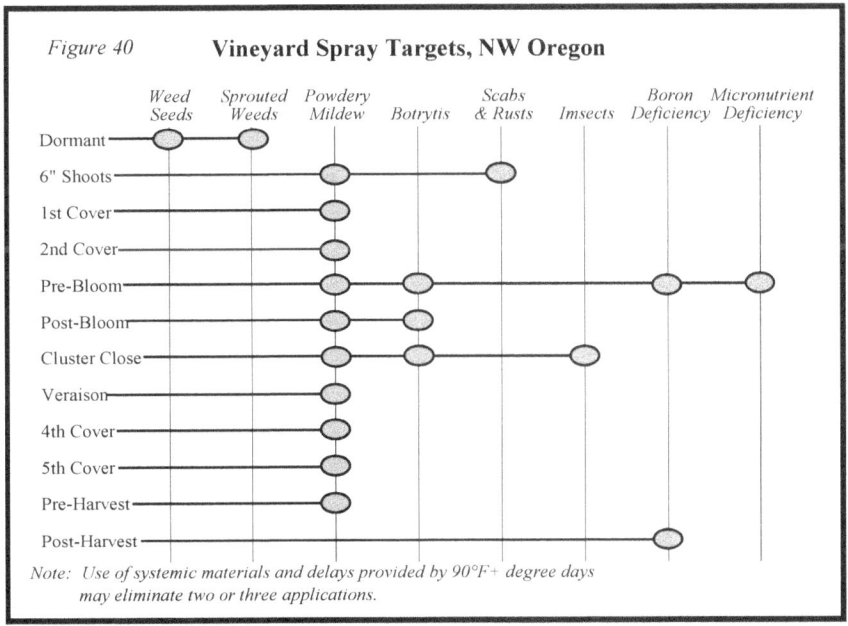

Figure 40   **Vineyard Spray Targets, NW Oregon**

Note: *Use of systemic materials and delays provided by 90°F+ degree days may eliminate two or three applications.*

Some grape varieties are sensitive to sulfur, and it should not be used on them. The sensitive varieties are all American cultivars and French-American hybrids, commonly grown in vineyards east of the Rocky Mountains:

Definitely sensitive (do not use sulfur)—Chambourcin, Chancellor, Concord, De Chaunac, Marechal Foch and Rougeon.

May be sensitive to sulfur (use with extreme care, if at all)—Canadice, Couderc Noir, Esprit, Glendora, LaCrosse, Leon Millot, Rayon d'Or, Reliance, Saint Croix, Saint Pepin, Traminette, Venus, Villard Blanc, Villard Noir, Vincent, Vinered and Vivant.

In Table 14, a spray program typical for Oregon's Northwest Willamette Valley is detailed. This full program would apply to varieties like Chardonnay and White Riesling, which ripen later than Pinot Noir and Pinot Gris. The pre-harvest application would likely not be needed for Pinot Noir or Pinot Gris, as they ripen around October 1 in most of this region's vineyards.

The hypothetical spray schedule of Table 14 includes four systemic fungicide applications, but no delays of sprays for powdery mildew because of 90°F+ days. Temperatures over 90°F interrupt the propagation of fruiting spores by the mildew for 7 to 10 days, so powdery mildew sprays can be delayed for the same period.

That brings us to the "worst case" scenario. Growing areas in the Midwest, South and East have fungi and vine diseases that are not prevalent in states west of the Rocky Mountains. Historically, those problems have limited the planting of European *Vitis vinifera* grape varieties. Instead, growers have tended to rely on Native American and French hybrid varieties, and on aggressive experimentation with new hybrid varieties. Trials and production of some *Vitis vinifera* varieties have been pursued for almost fifty years. However, growers in those regions need to do more experimentation with *vinifera* grapes to determine effective control materials. In most areas with climates suitable for growing grapes, those problems should be manageable.

Let's look at one of these viticultural areas for the "worst case" comparison: the Ohio River Valley of Indiana, Ohio, Kentucky and West Virginia. A thriving wine industry existed there as long ago as the 1820s. By 1860, Cincinnati was the center of American wine production, then based on the Catawba grape. Eventually, disease and insect damage combined with labor shortages during World War I and Prohibition to destroy the industry. Today, the region is experiencing a rebirth of winemaking.

The Ohio River Valley's climate may be described as *humid subtropical*. Conditions favor heavy disease pressure and burgeoning insect populations. Over the past fifty years, however, many new fungicides and insecticides have been developed to cope with those problems.

Figure 41 lays out the challenges facing a typical vineyard in the Ohio River Valley in the vicinity of Cincinnati. Compare the greater number of targets shown in Figure 42 with those in Figure 41 for the Willamette Valley.

The *Midwest Commercial Small Fruit and Grape Spray Guide: 2015* was produced cooperatively by the agricultural universities in eleven states. The

TABLE 14   Typical Spray Program, Oregon's Willamette Valley

Chardonnay or White Riesling on 9' Row Spacing; 2014 Dollars

Stage/Material	Approximate Date	Application Rate	Units	Material Cost	Labor Cost	Equipment Cost	Total Cost	Target
Dormant*					$6.34	$18.36	$24.70	banded
Princep 4L	3/6	2.39	lbs/acre	$3.10			$3.10	weeds
Roundup 41	3/20	1	lb/acre	$3.67			$3.67	weeds
6–8" Shoot**	5/6				$3.11	$13.48	$16.59	alt.rows**
Dithane M-45		4	lbs/acre	$5.19			$5.19	broad
Sulfur, Wettable		5	lbs/acre	$4.62			$4.62	PM
Nu-Film 17PS		0.5	pints/acre	$1.62			$1.62	
15" Shoot	5/20				$6.22	$26.96	$33.17	
Sulfur, Wettable		5	lbs/acre	$10.39			$10.39	PM
Nu-Film 17PS		0.5	pints/acre	$3.23			$3.23	
23" Shoot	6/3				$6.34	$29.35	$35.69	
Rally 40WP		4	oz/acre	$20.01			$20.01	PM
Pre-bloom	6/19				$6.22	$26.96	$33.17	
Pristine 38WG		10.5	oz/acre	$36.88			$36.88	PM + BC
Solubor		1	lbs/acre	$2.02			$2.02	nutrient
Bonide Liquid Iron Plus		0.5	pints/acre	$1.95			$1.95	nutrient
Post-bloom	7/7				$6.34	$29.35	$36.89	
Flint		12.4	oz/acre	$55.73			$55.73	PM + BC
1st Cover	7/25				$6.34	$29.35	$35.69	
Sulfur		5	lbs/acre	$10.39			$10.39	PM
R-11 Spreader		6	oz/acre	$1.50			$1.50	
Sevin 80WP		2	lbs/acre	$11.89			$11.89	insects***
2nd Cover	8/8				$6.34	$29.35	$35.69	
Endura		8	oz/acre	$57.41			$57.41	PM + BC
3rd Cover	8/22				$6.34	$29.35	$35.69	
Rally 40WP		4	gal/acre	$20.01			$20.01	PM
4th Cover	9/5				$6.34	$29.35	$35.69	
JMS Stylet Oil		2	gal/acre	$33.72			$33.72	PM
Pre-harvest	9/19				$6.34	$29.35	$35.69	
Sulfur, Wettable		5	lbs/acre	$10.39			$10.39	PM
Nu-Film 17PS		0.5	pints/acre	$3.23			$3.23	
Post-harvest	10/20				$3.17	$14.68	$17.85	alt.rows**
Solubor		2	lbs/acre	$2.02			$2.02	nutrient
Totals per acre				$299.17	$69.74	$311.87	$680.78	

* Banded on 3' width.
** Alternate rows.
*** Yellow jackets and spiders.
Abbreviations: broad = broad spectrum; PM = powdery mildew; BC = botrytis cinerea.

Guide presents all of the alternative treatments possible for areas from Nebraska to Ohio across the north, down through Oklahoma to West Virginia across its southern extreme. It is a daunting task to cover all of the varying conditions of macroclimate, soils and topography that pertain to the growing areas of such a vast region. The eleven universities are to be commended for working cooperatively to get ahead of the needs of the new wine industry emerging in these states.

Further complicating the situation is the abundance of sulfur-intolerant American and French Hybrid grape varieties grown by so many vineyards in this region

In all honesty, the *Guide* must be seriously intimidating to novice grape growers. It is literally a smörgåsbord of treatments, an "equal opportunity program" for farm chemical dealers. All materials are not equal in their control of diseases, though. Growers in each of the widely-varying areas will discover through experience which materials work best in each situation, and they will differ, as established producing areas including California, Oregon, Washington, Texas and New York have learned.

Here is a challenge for the eleven universities to address: comparison research of the efficacies of the alternative treatments and methods, area-by-area within each state. If the establishment of AVAs (American Viticultural Areas) has any validity, the uniqueness of each area in optimum pest and disease control will be discovered.

A typical annual pest control program for the Ohio River Valley is given in Table 15.

In some states, viticulture guidelines published by state extension services recommend applying almost everything every two weeks, regardless of disease pressure or material effectiveness. In some growing areas, that practice is excessive in environmental impact and overly expensive. For some treatments, it is necessary to "read" the vines and make applications only as called for. Almost all systemics are effective in most areas with low-to-moderate disease pressure

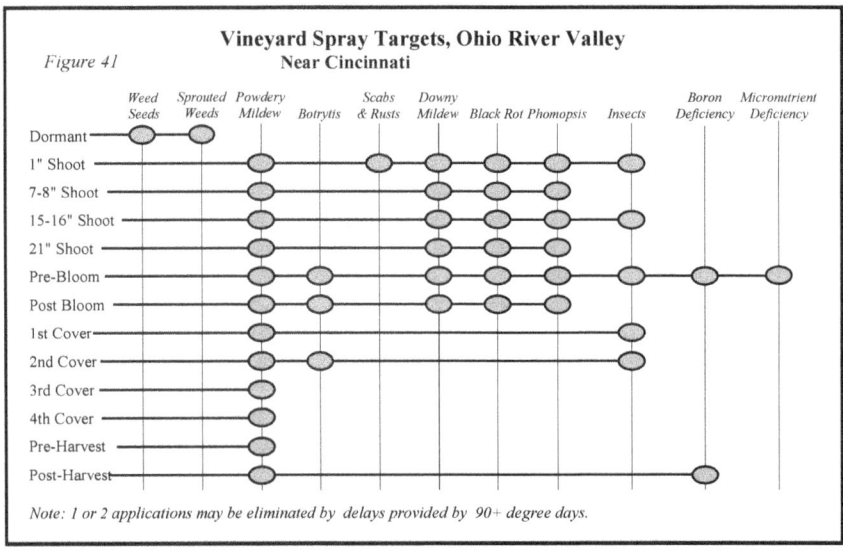

Vineyard Spray Targets, Ohio River Valley
Near Cincinnati

Figure 41

Note: 1 or 2 applications may be eliminated by delays provided by 90+ degree days.

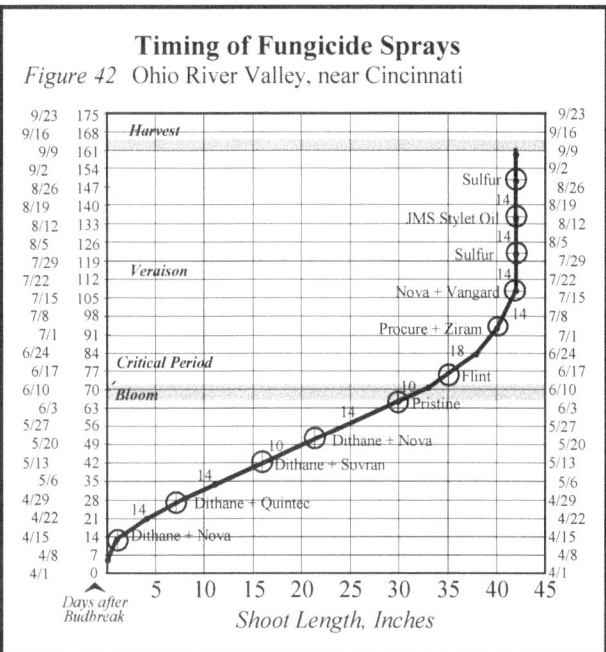

Timing of Fungicide Sprays

Figure 42 Ohio River Valley, near Cincinnati

for up to three weeks, regardless of the weather. Most protect new growth, as well as what was showing at the time of application.

When sulfur dust is applied, its effectiveness can be increased by addition of a sticker-spreader. But, use only one-third to one-half of the recommended sticker-spreader rate, or the sticker will encapsulate the sulfur particles and render them ineffective. Sulfur works through the gas it gives off, and the gas is what prevents powdery mildew from sporulating.

Because the spray program for the Ohio River Valley site is so complex, it may help to envision it graphically, as is done in Figure 42. The graph plots vine shoot length against days after budbreak. Key target-related events shown are budbreak, bloom, veraison and harvest. The "critical period" for the vine's susceptibility to disease is also highlighted. Each of the eleven fungicide/pesticide applications is plotted along the vine growth curve.

Parameters observed in the design of the Ohio River Valley spray program are:

- No systemic fungicide is repeated consecutively, and *strobilurins* are alternated with *sterol inhibitors*, both measures executed to avoid development of resistant fungus strains;

- Dithane is used repeatedly in the early vine development to prevent black rot, downy mildew and phomopsis cane and leaf spot. *Dithane* and the other *mancozeb*-based products utilize copper for disease control;

- No *mancozeb*-based products are applied within sixty-six days of harvest, which is the required pre-harvest interval;

- *Pristine* and *Vangard* are applied pre-bloom and before veraison, respectively, both to prevent botrytis infection and broad coverage at these critical times;

TABLE 15   **Typical Spray Program, Ohio River Valley**

Varieties Not Sensitive to Sulfur on 9' Row Spacing; 2014 Dollars

Stage/Material	Approximate Date	Application Rate	Units	Material Cost	Labor Cost	Equipment Cost	Total Cost	Target
Dormant*					$7.04	$18.6	$25.40	banded
Princep 4L	3/1	2.39	lbs/acre	$2.76			2.76	weeds
Roundup 41%	3/15	1	lb/acre	2.78			2.78	weeds
1" Shoot	4/15				3.52	14.68	18.19	alt.rows
Dithane M-45		4	lbs/acre	4.29			4.29	BR,DM,Ph
Nova 40WSP		4	oz/acre	6.90			6.90	PM,BR
Sevin 80WSP		2	lbs/acre	5.29			5.29	FB,CW
7–8" Shoot	4/29				3.52	14.68	18.19	
Dithane M-45		4	lbs/acre	4.29			4.29	BR,DM,Ph
Quintec 2.08F		4	oz/acre	6.00			6.00	BC
Nu-Film 17PS		0.5	pints/acre	1.44			1.44	
15–16" Shoot	5/13				7.04	29.5	3.6.39	
Dithane M-45		4	lbs/acre	8.58			8.58	BR,DM,Ph
Sovran 50WG		5	oz/acre	25.50			25.50	broad
Sevin 80WSP		2	lbs/acre	10.58			10.58	FB,RLR,RC
Nu-Film 17PS		0.5	pints/acre	2.87			2.87	
21" Shoot	5/23				7.104	29.35	36.39	
Dithane M-45		4	lbs/acre	8.57			8.58	BR,DM,Ph
Nova 40WSP		4	oz/acre	13.79			13.79	PM,BR
Pre-Bloom	6/6				7.04	29.35	36.39	
Pristine 38WG		10.5	oz/acre	32.81			32.81	broad
Sevin 80WSP		2	lbs/acre	10.58			10.58	GBM
Solubor		1	lb/acre	1.80			1.80	nutrient
Bonide Liquid Iron Plus		0.5	pints/acre	1.74			1.74	nutrient
Post-Bloom	6/16				7.04	29.35	6.39	
Flint		4	oz/acre	49.58			49.58	broad
1st Cover	7/4				7.04	29.35	36.39	
Procure 50WS		8	oz/acre	26.00			26.00	PM,BR
Ziram 76DF		4	lbs/acre	16.80			16.80	BR,Ph,DM
Acramite 50WS		1	lb/acre	10.50			10.50	Mites
2nd Cover	7/18				7.04	29.35	36.39	
Vangard		10	oz/acre	38.00			38.00	BC
Losban 4E		4.5	pints/acre	25.43			25.43	GRB
3rd Cover	8/1				7.04	29.35	36.39	
Sulfur, Wettable		5	lbs/acre	9.24			9.24	PM
R-11 Spreader		16	oz/acre	3.56			3.56	
4th Cover	8/15				7.04	29.35	36.39	
JMS Stylet Oil		2	gal/acre	30.0			30.00	PM
Pre-Harvest	8/29				7.04	29.35	36.39	
Sulfur, Wettable		5	lbs/acre	9.24			9.24	PM
Nu-Film 17PS		0.5	pints/acre	2.87			2.87	
Post-Harvest	10/1				3.52	14.68	18.19	
Solubor		2	lbs/acre	3.60			3.60	nutrient
Totals per acre				**$375.38**	**$80.92**	**$326.57**	**$779.27**	

* Banded on 3' width.

** Alternate rows.

Abbreviations: broad = broad spectrum; PM = powdery mildew; BC = botrytis cinerea; BR = black rot; DM = downy mildew; Ph = phomopsis cane & leaf spot; FB = flea beetle; CW = cutworm; RLR = rebounded leaf roller; RC = rose chafer; GBM = grape berry moth; GRB = grape root borer.

- Sulfur and *JMS Stylet Oil* are alternated after veraison to get away from systemics, and when endangerments by diseases are past their acute periods, except for powdery mildew and botrytis cinerea. The minimum separation time before and after the JMS Stylet Oil is fourteen days. Only sulfur represents a cost-saving material;

- Although nutrients are not shown in Figure 43, they are included in both Tables 13 and 14. Boron is applied as Solubor before bloom and after harvest. The former is to enhance development of pollination tubes in the inflorescences. The latter is done (at twice the previous rate) at the optimum time to be stored in the vine's permanent parts for the next growing season;

- *Bonide Liquid Iron Plus* is also applied in the pre-bloom spray, to provide a wide range of micronutrients necessary for healthy vine and grape development. Petiole sampling a week before the pre-bloom application may indicate a more specific micronutrient supplementation for individual materials;

- Insecticides are also included. In Oregon, the insect threat is usually limited to the nuisances of yellow jacket hornets and spiders. On rare occasions, tomato hornworms and mites present a threat. In the Ohio River Valley, there are many insect predations, as indicated in the footnotes of Table 15.

It is advisable to avoid sulfur applications during the pre-bloom and bloom periods. Sulfur hardens the *calyptra* (crown) that covers the inflorescences. The points of the calyptra stiffen and don't roll up as easily. So, the calyptra doesn't eject normally, interfering with a successful pollination.

Micronutrients are applied by foliar spray rather than by incorporation into the soil. Foliar application permits greater control over when the vine takes in the nutrient, and avoids the detrimental effects that soil pH may have in binding some nutrients.

For the first two spray applications of the season, consider aerial application for any vineyard larger than twenty acres. The objective is to kill any overwintering organisms on the ground as well as on the vines, and there is not yet a significant vine canopy to penetrate. If you need more acres to make it work economically, buddy up with some neighbors. You're all in the same boat, so to speak.

Spray program cost comparison—Willamette Valley versus Ohio River Valley

Now, it's time to compare costs for the spray programs, the "best case" versus the "worst case." Summed by cost category, the comparison is shown in Table 16. The "Difference/acre" is how much more it costs in Ohio River Valley than Willamette Valley.

Hedging

When grape leaves grow in the shade, they produce green vegetative flavors in the wine. Sauvignon Blanc is one of the worst varieties in this regard. Hedging is done to prevent this effect. Dr. Nelson Shaulis, of New York's Geneva Experiment Station, demonstrated how sunlight penetrates the vine canopy. Each leaf absorbs 91 percent of the direct sunlight presented to it, passing 9

TABLE 16   Comparison of Spray Program Costs Willamette Valley versus Ohio River Valley, 2014 Dollars

	Materials	Labor	Equipment	Total
Willamette Valley	$299.17	$69.79	$311.89	$680.86
Ohio River Valley	$375.38	$80.92	$326.57	$782.87
Difference/acre	$76.21	$11.12	$14.68	$102.01

percent through to the next leaf. The third leaf in line gets almost nothing, theoretically 0.073 percent. Of course, additional diffuse and reflected light is received, but they are minor amounts. It is true that leaves don't stand still in the breeze and they don't overlap exactly. But, the point is made: don't let the canopy keep more than 5–7 leaves from one side to the other. Poke a stick through the canopy and count how many leaves it touches. The appropriate thickness for the canopy varies depending on the vine's ability to grow a dense canopy, and your trellis configuration. A relatively open canopy may not need any hedging.

Fifteen inches is a good thickness for the canopies of most popular grape varieties trained to a single upright curtain system. The optimum thickness will be different for divided canopies, and for ballerina-style canopies. Hedge-trimmers that mount on the front of the tractor, adjustable as to width and powered hydraulically by a PTO pump, are available for this task.

When you top the vines, which is common practice, it will force new lateral shoots to grow from the leaf axils up and down the cane. The same result occurs when the canopy is hedged on its sides. The laterals will grow more leaves, contributing to canopy density and setting of a second crop of small clusters on the laterals. Usually, these second-set clusters are removed at veraison, because they rarely get ripe and just provide a drag on available nutrients and growth energy.

Leaf pulling

The practice of removing leaves from the east side of the fruit zone during final ripening is done to permit increased air flow (thus reducing fungus pressure) and better light exposure for the fruit. Leaves on the west side are not removed to avoid sunburning fruit in hot afternoons.

Grape contracts

The standard way of documenting the sale of grapes is the grape contract. Grower and winemaker should both have a voice in negotiations. Price is not the only issue to be decided. Properties of the grapes at picking, and the methods and materials used during the growing season are all of interest. Growers who value a long-term working relationship with a winery are well-advised to review these issues before the growing season.

The simplest stipulation regarding ripeness at picking is the sugar level, expressed in degrees Brix. The winemaker should be the one controlling this condition, because the sugar level affects the style and quality of wine to be produced, and the right figure will differ among grape varieties. There needs to be an escape provision, however, because not all seasons are capable of achieving a desired sugar content. Historically, this has been accomplished by giving bonus or penalty points to the price depending on whether it is over or under the targeted sugar level. Beware, however it may be advantageous to the grower to delay picking so more revenue can be gained at the expense of a decline in wine quality. More sugar means more tonnage. The winery has to understand, too, that the grower can't just turn on and off the availability of a picking crew, and some growers have to juggle picking with another job.

Wineries have also attempted to establish ideal pH and acid levels for the timing of harvest. All of these efforts notwithstanding, however, the most important qualities are taste and smell, if the winemaker is interested in high wine quality. Adjustments to sugar and acid can be made in the winery. So, the ideal winery/grower relationship is one of mutual understanding and cooperation.

A trend that is gaining popularity in high-quality wine production is purchase of grapes by row or acre. Under this system, the winemaker designates the vines from which he/she wants to purchase the fruit. Then, vine cultivation and fruit loads are managed according to the winemaker's specifications. It is not unusual for the winery to supply some labor and management for extra shoot positioning, cluster thinning and leaf pulling tasks. The fruit is priced per ton as if the yield were a normal quantity.

For example, assume the normal yield for a block of Merlot is four tons per acre, the fruit is usually priced at $1,800/ ton, and the winemaker wants to cut the fruit load to 3 TPA. Normally, the grapes would produce revenue to the grower of $4 \times $1,800 = $7,200 per acre. So, if the harvest is reduced to 3 TPA, the price per ton would be $1,800 \times 4/3 = $2,400 per ton.

The grape contract should also state the terms of payment. Payment in three installments is common, with the first one-third paid on delivery, one-third thirty days later, and the final one-third by December 31. This scheme allows the winery to get through the high revenue holidays before completing payment. Yes, the winery is requiring the grower to finance winery operations.

Another method of payment is called the bottle price contract. Under this method, the grower helps finance the winery, but shares in the added value if the wine brings an unexpected higher price in the marketplace. Typically, the first two payments are made as above, but the last payment is made when the wine is released for sale. The final price per ton is a multiple of the shelf price of the wine, say 100 times the price per bottle. The escalation in value is all reflected in the final payment.

For example, say the winery expects to price a Cabernet Franc at $18/bottle retail and negotiates a price of $1,800/ton for the grapes based on a bottle price multiplier of 100. The first two payments are made on schedule at $600/ton each. But, the wine turns out to be much better than expected and *Wine Spectator* gives it a 91 score. The winery decides to price the wine at $24/bottle retail. According to the contract, the grape price jumps to $2,400/ton, and the final grape payment is $1,200/ton (100 × $24 – $1,200 already paid).

Yields

Yields vary from variety to variety. Further, yields will vary from one season to another, will depend on buds left at pruning and will be reduced by any cluster thinning done prior to harvest.

Figure 43 plots the typical yield progression for several varieties. They are not all on the same vine spacing and trellis system. VSP trained vines are cane-pruned. See the footnote in Figure 43.

Figure 44 illustrates how yield progressions can be affected by the spacing, training system and cluster thinning on Pinot Noir. The Burgundy training system enables more rapid yield buildup than VSP because of greater vine density per acre. Cluster thinning is necessary to achieve good quality. With either system, VSP or Burgundy, leaf hedging is needed to avoid vegetative flavors and otherwise enhance wine quality.

Harvest

Then comes the harvest. Do you prefer propane cannons, electronic bird call emitters, bird net, shotgun shells, balloons, reflecting metallic ribbons, or

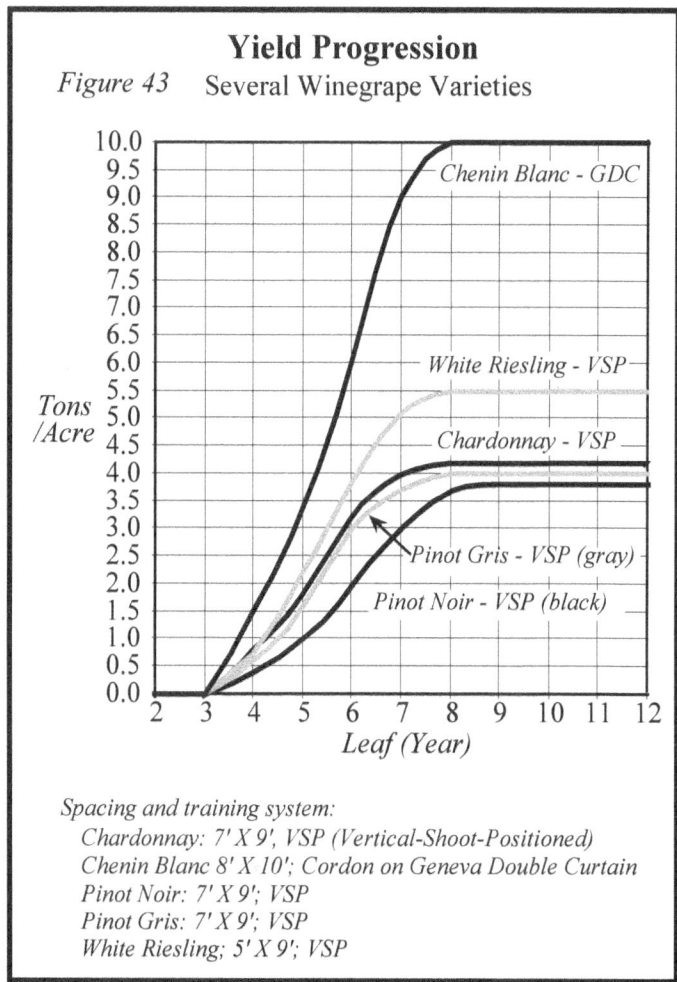

Yield Progression

Figure 43 Several Winegrape Varieties

Tons /Acre — *Leaf (Year)*

Chenin Blanc - GDC
White Riesling - VSP
Chardonnay - VSP
Pinot Gris - VSP (gray)
Pinot Noir - VSP (black)

Spacing and training system:
  Chardonnay: 7' X 9', VSP (Vertical-Shoot-Positioned)
  Chenin Blanc 8' X 10'; Cordon on Geneva Double Curtain
  Pinot Noir: 7' X 9'; VSP
  Pinot Gris: 7' X 9'; VSP
  White Riesling; 5' X 9'; VSP

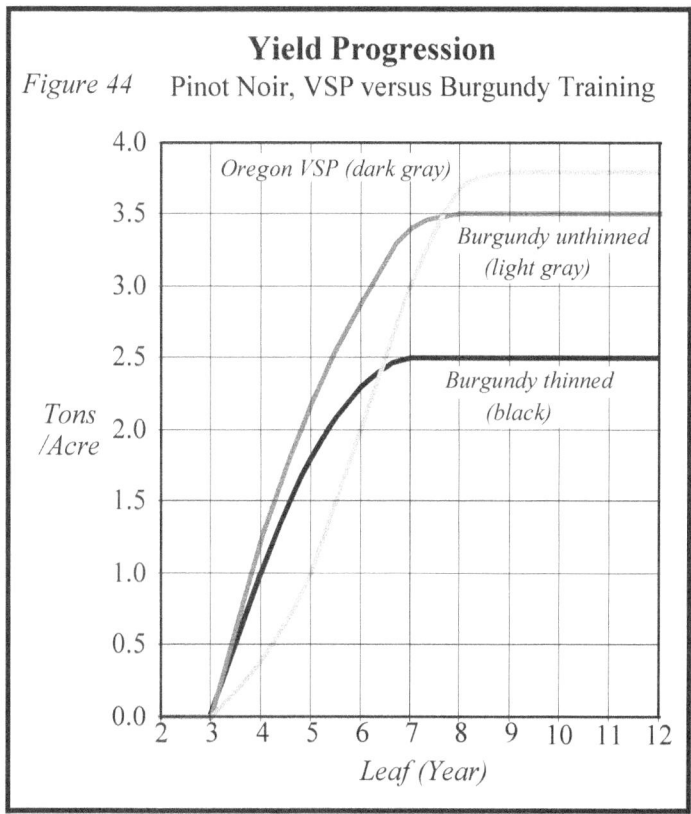

Yield Progression

Figure 44   Pinot Noir, VSP versus Burgundy Training

Oregon VSP (dark gray)

Burgundy unthinned (light gray)

Burgundy thinned (black)

Tons /Acre

Leaf (Year)

whacking on pie pans for bird control? Next, sample clusters must be gathered to determine progress toward perfect ripeness. Grapes are tasted in the vineyard to pinpoint the perfect moment of harvest. How fast is the weather deteriorating to winter patterns? Did it rain last night? Will there be a few dry days to let the leaves pull some of that water out of the grapes? Where can we find pickers? Are molds starting to develop in the clusters? Have the grapes reached the point where they're losing more each day by dilution and molds than they're gaining in flavor by more "hang time"? For independent growers, what are the grape purchase contract incentives for targeted ripeness measures?

After a year of dedicated care, it all comes down to this game of brinkmanship, this annual "winemaker's dance with mother nature."

Wineries and independent growers are divided in opinion regarding the type of container to be used for harvest. Five-gallon plastic buckets that hold about 25 lbs of grapes are the most common. Two may be carried easily to collection points at row's end.

The traditional container for transporting grapes to the winery is a wood or plastic bin, 4' × 4' × 4'. Some vineyards have gone to 4' × 4' × 2' in order to minimize crushing of grapes by weight in the bin.

The next advancement has been to pick directly into plastic lug boxes that hold about 20 lbs each. The grapes are kept in the lugs all the way to the crush pad. This last practice is common to producers of sparkling wines, and has also been adopted by some producers of high-quality red and white wines. Each winery has to make the choice for themselves in terms of wine quality. Lugs are more expensive to handle in the field and on the crush pad and may require specialized equipment to handle at the winery.

Picking machines are gaining in popularity as other wine costs escalate. They offer the lowest harvest costs and simplification of labor relationships, but they must also be evaluated for their impact on wine quality. For lower-priced wines in almost every variety, the effect on wine quality is likely to be negligible. For high-quality wines, however, the use of picking machines is probably detrimental.

Disposal of grape pomace

After the grape skins, stems and seeds have been pressed, particularly the red varieties, the best place for them is back in the vineyard they came from. A refurbished old manure spreader works marvelously for the job (without the manure). It doesn't matter if some of the pomace hangs up on the canes and leaves. There's a whole winter coming to wash it to the ground. What does the pomace add to the vineyard?

- About 25 percent of the nutrients required for next year's crop;

- The viable yeast cells are those that survived fermentation. That makes them well-qualified to work future fermentations. They may be "wild" or natural in origin, or they may be selected and cultured; it doesn't matter. Just think. Europe's old producing areas have topsoil that is made up mostly of decayed grape debris and yeast cells. No wonder they do so well with wild yeast fermentations!

Migrant labor

It is fair to say that the vineyard business depends on the availability of migrant labor. Find a supply of U.S. resident labor that is willing to work a full day in the vineyards in wet and cold February-March, and a very hot July-August, for $8–10/hour, and you will have freedom from migrant labor. The same can be said for orchards, nurseries, row crops and meat packers.

It should not surprise anyone that every migrant worker who comes looking for work bears what looks like the required legal documentation. There is a thriving industry in providing such documentation, stolen identity or just fabricated. At this writing, all that is legally required of an employer is the same as for any new hire: an I-9 form with photocopies of the documentation attached, and then validation from the Department of Homeland Security's E-Verify system.

The required documents are described in detail on the form *I-9, Employment Eligibility Verification*. Basically, a qualified passport is enough. If a passport is not available, one document from List B (establishing identity) and one from List C (establishing employment authorization) are needed. The most common are: driver's license or state ID card for List B, plus a Social Security card or valid U.S. birth certificate for List C.

The U.S., Congress created the *E-Verify* Internet system in 1997. It is administered by Department of Homeland Security. Employers enter identifying documents and other information from the I-9 form, and the program compares the data with several computerized registries. DHS claims that most inquiries are answered within seconds, but verification problems may extend that time to three days. DHS has an audit that indicates an error rate of 8 percent. But, an independent survey by research firm Westec finds the system failed to identify illegal workers half of the time.

So, it is totally disingenuous of politicians to flog businesses for hiring illegal aliens, when there is no foolproof method available for verifying the validity of I.D. papers. The following is excerpted from a May 30, 2010 editorial by the *Yakima* (WA) *Herald-Republic*:

> *What was missing during the discussion was an honest appraisal of E-Verify's track record. It's abysmal. A recent study of the free online service by the research firm Westec showed that E-Verify failed to flag illegal workers more than half the time. That's hardly what you would call a fool-proof process. The reason for this is simple: The U.S. does not have a coun-terfeit-proof identification system. A Social Security card doesn't guarantee a person's legal status due to its corruptibility. Fake Social Security cards abound. So it really doesn't matter what system the City of Yakima uses for its employees or requires of its contractors, because determining who's here legally is, at best, a roll of the dice.*

The following conclusion is unavoidable. Unless and until the federal government comes up with the following reforms, there is no justification for bashing employers:

1. A foolproof identification card that cannot be falsified
2. An accessible and reliable database so employers can readily check validity
3. A workable guest worker program
4. Crack down on producers of falsified documents.

Sustainability and organic farming

Sustainability has become the buzzword of the day in the wine business, all the way from the vineyard to the retail shelf and wine publications. *Sustainability* has an official definition, provided by that great authority on the environment and agriculture, the *U.S. Congress:*

Sustainable Agriculture as defined by the U.S. Congress

Sustainable Agriculture is an integrated system of plant and animal production practices having site-specific applications that will, over the long term:

- Satisfy human food and fiber needs
- Enhance environmental quality and the natural resource base upon which the agricultural economy depends

- Make the most efficient use of non-renewable resources and on-farm resources

- Integrate, where appropriate, natural biological cycles and controls

- Sustain the economic viability of farm operations

- Enhance the quality of life for farmers and society as a whole.

To put it simply, Sustainable Agriculture is economically viable, socially supportive and ecologically sound.

That list of objectives looks like good, sound management, doesn't it? It is.

But, like any government-promoted program, we have to add bureaucracy—registration, application for approval, paperwork, fees, etc.

As with any movement, there are extremists. In the case of vineyards, the practices identified as *organic* and *biodynamic* are the extreme.

Biodynamic is the name for the most extreme, a system derived from beliefs held by a 1920s philosopher, Rudolf Steiner, of Austria. In the 1980s, a Burgundian soil scientist promoted Steiner's system to rejuvenate the region's soils, which had been mostly sterilized of soil organisms by centuries of severe chemical abuse.

In Oregon, generally considered to be in the forefront of matters environmental, there is a measure of the extent to which growers are buying into the sustainable/organic growing regimen. The annual vineyard/winery survey in 2006 (Table 17) asked the question about programs in use and produced these results:

The 2006 survey returns on this question represented 14,263 (91.4 percent) of the 15,600 acres estimated for the state in that year. The 15,600 acres Figure includes estimates for nonrespondents; the 14,263 Figure does not include estimates for nonrespondents to that specific question. The question has not been asked in subsequent surveys.

The data shows that owners of 5.8 percent of the state's acreage bought into "biodynamic" farming by 2007. That's the form that includes doing certain things according to the phase of the moon and burying manure-filled cow horns in the vineyard, which are later dug up and the rotted manure incorporated into

TABLE 17   Certified Vineyard Acres in 2006

Vineyard Management Practice	Number of Acres	Percent of Total
Conventional	7,415	52.0
Sustainably Certified	3,631	25.5
Organic Certified	656	4.6
Biodynamic Certified & Non-certified	832	5.8
Organic Non-certified and Sustainable Non-certified	1,729	12.1
Total Oregon Respondents	**14,263**	**100.0**

Note: Sustainable Certified includes LIVE (Low Input Viticulture & Enology, Inc., and VINEA, The Winegrowers' Sustainable Trust.

Source: 2006 Oregon Vineyard and Winery Report; National Agricultural Statistics Service and Oregon Wine Board. February, 2007.

a compost tea and sprayed on the vines. Is it a good idea to spray cow poop on the vines?

The same question was not pursued in subsequent surveys. However, the 2010 survey solicited the number of cases of 2009 wines that were labeled with environmental certifications (see Table 18). The classifications deny any meaningful detailed analysis, because of multiple certifications. If these numbers are correct, then only 2.5–4.2 percent of the wine produced in 2009 was labeled with organic or biodynamic certifications. Further, only 167,148 cases out of the estimated total of 2,331,900 cases produced, or 2.5–8.3 percent, bore *any* certification logo. One may be able to argue the accuracy of the figures shown, but their *approximate* magnitude is enough to gain a rough picture of the extent of the industry's participation with 2009 wines. The practice is not pervasive, as some wineries and wine writers would have us believe.

There is another problem with the organic/biodynamic approach. One of the objectives of both belief systems calls for encouraging maintenance of a natural population of insects. Specifically, that population in many growing areas includes yellow jacket hornets and spiders containing toxic venoms. Some diligent wineries have installed vacuum cleaners on their sorting belts to suck the critters off the grapes. But, have you noticed how tenaciously both kinds of insects cling to things? Surely, you wouldn't want those insects to get into the fermentation. It's a strong argument in favor of at least one insecticide application, probably *Sevin,* just before cluster close to get rid of the offenders.

Those growers who are dedicated to the insect population may find solace in the fact that the insects will move back into the vineyard from neighboring properties, just as soon as harvest is over.

Numerous well-respected winemakers observe that there is no proof that environmentally-attuned vineyard practices produce better tasting wine. Many of them, however, have joined the sustainability ranks as a marketing and public relations necessity.

TABLE 18   Certified Wine Labels in 2009

Certifications on Label	Number of Cases	Percent of Certified	Percent of Total Produced
Oregon Certified Sustainable	100,897	60.4	4.3
Limited Input Viticulture & Enology	131,835	78.9	5.7
Certified Organic	11,300	6.8	0.5
Made with Organic Grapes	57,808	34.6	2.5
Demeter-Certified Organic	4,289	2.6	0.2
Made with Biodynamic Grapes	39,650	23.7	1.7
USDA Food Alliance	2,290	1.4	0.1
Other	21,096	12.6	0.9
Total Cases Certified	**167,148**	**100.0**	7.2
Total Cases Produced	**2,331,900**		100.0

Source: 2009 Oregon Vineyard and Winery Report; National Agricultural Statistics Service and Oregon Wine Board. Revised March, 2010.

It is of interest to observe that Lalou Bize-Leroy was one of the first to embrace biodynamic practices. Madame Bize-Leroy formerly was managing director of Domaine de la Romanée-Conti, commonly recognized as the pinnacle of Burgundy's wine estates. After leaving DRC in a management dispute (although her family still owns half), she acquired the vineyard holdings that are now Domaine Leroy. Although she fervently advocates for biodynamic methods, all of these vineyards were at the top of Burgundy's wine estates before biodynamic farming was implemented. Further, the question must be asked: how effective are biodynamic methods when applied only to part of a vineyard, when other ownerships continue to use conventional management methods on the rest of the contiguous vineyard block?

Oregon Winegrowers Association has adopted a certification program that incorporates LIVE (Limited Input Viticulture and Enology) along with "Salmon Safe." The former includes guidelines that make sense, and surveillance by competitors. Salmon Safe addresses prevention of toxic runoff.

Further reading

2005 Southeast Regional Bunch Grape Integrated Management Guide. Cooperative publication of the University Extension Services of Georgia, North Carolina, Tennessee, and Clemson University.

University of Tennessee website:
http:// www.smallfruits.org/SmallFruitsRegGuide/Guides/2006/

2008 Berry & Grape Information Network. Oregon State University, University of Idaho, Washington State University and USDA-ARS. Website: http://berrygrape.oregonstate.edu/

Ball, Trent, and Raymond J. Folwell. *Wine Grape Establishment and Production Costs in Washington, 2003*. Cooperative Extension, Washington State University.
Website: http://www.agribusiness-mgmt.wsu.edu/AgbusResearch/winegrape.htm

Crop Profile for Wine Grapes in Washington—2003; WSU Cooperative Extension, College of Agriculture, Human & Natural Resource Sciences, Washington State University.
Website: http://www.ipmcenters.org/cropprofiles/docs/WAgrapes-wine.pdf

DeMarsay, Anne. *Guidelines for Developing an Effective Fungicide Spray Program for Wine Grapes in Maryland—2007*. University of Maryland Cooperative Extension.
Website: http://www.grapesandfruit.umd.edu/Grapes/Pages/MDWineGrapeSprayGuidelines2007.pdf

Diseases of Grapes in Michigan. Michigan State University website:
http://www.grapes.msu.edu

Ellis, Michael A. *Developing an Effective Fungicide Spray Program for Wine Grapes in Ohio—2005*. OARDC, The Ohio State University.
Website: http://www.oardc.ohio-state.edu/grapeweb/OGEN/20070511/2007fungspray.pdf

Enterprise Budget, Wine Grapes, Willamette Valley Region, EM 8537, April 1993. Oregon State University Extension Service.
Website: http://arec.oregonstate.edu/oaeb/files/pdf/EM8537.pdf

Growing Grapes in Missouri, MS-29, June 2003. State Fruit Experiment Station, Missouri State University, Mountain Grove.
Website: http://mtngrv.missouristate.edu/Publications/GGIMpub.htm

Hamman, Richard A., Steven D. Savage, and Harold J. Larsen. *Colorado Grape Growers Guide, Bulletin 550A, 1998 Edition*. Colorado State University Extension.
Website: http://www.ext.colostate.edu/PUBS/Garden/550a.pdf

Hellman, Edward. *The Texas Winegrape Network*. Texas A & M University; Texas AgriLife Extension Service, Texas Tech University.
Website: http://winegrapes.tamu.edu/

Kamas, Jim. *Growing Grapes in Texas Hill Country*. Texas Agricultural Extension Service, Fredericksburg, Texas.
Website: http://aggie-horticulture.tamu.edu/hillcountry/grapes/GrowingGrapes.htm

Larsen, H.J. *Grape Pest Management Options for Colorado—2006*. Colorado Research Center, Grand Junction; Colorado State University Cooperative Extension.
Website: http://www.colostate.edu/programs/wcrc/pubs/viticulture/grapepestmgmtguide06.pdf

Midwest Commercial Small Fruit and Grape Spray Guide—2015. Cooperative publication of the University Extension Services of Arkansas, Illinois, Indiana, Iowa, Kansas, Kentucky, Minnesota, Missouri, Nebraska, Ohio, Oklahoma, West Virginia and Wisconsin.
Website: https://ag.purdue.edu/hla/Hort/Documents/ID-169.pdf

New York and Pennsylvania Pest Management Guidelines for Grapes—2008. Cornell University Cooperative Extension. Website: http://ipmguidelines.org/grapes/

The North Carolina Winegrape Grower's Guide. North Carolina Department of Commerce.

Pest Management Strategic Plan for the North Central Region Grape Industry. (Midwest States). Website: http://www.ipmcenters.org/pmsp/pdf/NorthCentralGrapePMSP.pdf

A Pocket Guide for Grape IPM Scouting in the North Central and Eastern US; Michigan State University website: http://www.grapes.msu.edu

Roper, Teryl R., Daniel L. Mahr, Patricia S. McManus, and Brian R. Smith. *Growing Grapes in Wisconsin, A1656—2006*. University of Wisconsin Cooperative Extension.
Website: http://learningstore.uwex.edu/pdf/A1656.pdf

Seavert, Clark F., Jenny Freeborn, and Steve Castagnoli. *Vineyard Economics: Establishing and Producing Wine Grapes in Hood River County (Oregon)—October, 2007*. Oregon State University Extension Service.
Website: http://extension.oregonstate.edu/catalog/pdf/em/em8878-e.pdf

Sharp, Rod, Horst Caspari, and Dana Hoag. *The Cost of Growing Wine Grapes in Western Colorado—July, 2002*. Western Colorado Research Center, Colorado State University;
Website: http://www.colostate.edu/programs/wcrc/pubs/viticulture/resource.htm

Skinkis, Patty. *A Quick Start Guide Establishing a Vineyard in Oregon*. Oregon State University Extension Service.
Website: http://berrygrape.oregonstate.edu/wp-content/uploads/2008/08/osu-vineyard-establishment-resources.pdf

Smith, Rhonda J., Karen M. Klonsky, Pete Livingston, and Richard L. De Moura. *Sample Costs to Establish a Vineyard and Produce Wine Grapes, Chardonnay, North Coast Region, Sonoma County, 2004, GR-NC-04*. University of California Extension.
Website: http://coststudies.ucdavis.edu/current.php

Statewide Integrated Pest Management Program. Agriculture and Natural Resources, University of California. UC IPM Online.
Website: http://www.ipm.ucdavis.edu/PMG/selectnewpest.grapes.html

U.S. Citizenship and Immigration Services Website: http://www.uscis.gov/i-9

Vinewise, the Washington Guide to Sustainable Viticulture—2006. Washington Association of Wine Grape Growers, Cashmere, WA. Available on WAWGG's website:
http://www.vinewise.org/ Also see: http://www.liveinc.org

Vineyard and Winery Report. National Agricultural Statistics Service; February, 2007 and March, 2010. Website: http://www.nass.usda.gov/Statistics_by_State/Oregon/Publications/Vineyard_and_Winery/index.asp

Vineyard Management. New England Grape Growers' Resource Center; University of Massachusetts Extension Service, Amherst. NEGGRC website:
http://www.newenglandwinegrapes.org/

Weber, Edward A., Karen M. Klonsky, and Richard L. De Moura. *Sample Costs to Establish a Vineyard and Produce Wine Grapes, Cabernet Sauvignon, North Coast Region, Napa County, 2003, GR-NC-03*. University of California Extension.
Website: http://coststudies.ucdavis.edu/current.php

White, Gerald B. *Cost of Establishment and Production of Vinifera Grapes in the Finger Lakes Region of New York—2007, E.B. 2008-5, May, 2008.* College of Agriculture and Life Sciences, Cornell University; Website: http://aem.cornell.edu/outreach/extension/eb0506.pdf

Wine-Grower News #36. Midwest Grape & Wine Industry Institute, Iowa State University. Website: http://www.extension.iastate.edu/ag/newsletters/winegrowers/winegrowers08_36.pdf

৪০৫৪

—6—

Vineyard financial analysis

Vineyard development costs

The cost of developing a vineyard varies with the vineyard location, vineyard design, trellis configuration, and grape varieties planted. In some cases, the differences between locations can be quite dramatic. Land use restrictions, labor rates, material costs, transportation costs, climate conditions and topography are among the main factors that change from area to area.

Effect of trellis system and vine density

One of the great debates in recent years relates to the way trellises are designed and how close together the vines are spaced. The costs of different trellis configurations need to be compared but, for the most part, we will leave that to the various states' agricultural economists.

No one seems to want to place analyses of the costs relating to vine density side by side for comparison, either. But, the issue of European superiority in wine quality compels attention to the subject, so we will do it here.

Let's analyze the same training alternatives used in Chapter 3 for the solar radiation analysis. Further, since there is still some reluctance to go to the New Zealand High-Tensile System, we'll also compare to the old upright canopy system with a grapestake at every vine.

Parameters for the comparison are given in Table 19. All three are vertical shoot-positioned curtains (VSP).

TABLE 19   Trellis Comparison Design Details

	Original Grapestake VSP	Hi-Tensile VSP	Burgundy Single Guyot
Vine spacing	6' × 9'	6' × 9'	1 meter × 1 meter
Vines per acre	806.7	806.7	4,040.7
Max. canopy height	78"	78"	42"
Fixed wires	3@11 ga. soft	3@12.5 ga. hi-ten	3@12.5 ga. hi-ten
Catch wires	2@14 ga. soft	2@14 ga. soft	none
End posts	1@4" × 10'	2 @4" × 10'	1 @4" × 7'
Backbrace	none	4" × 6'	none
Anchor	yes	no	yes
Line posts	grapestakes	3" × 8' every 24'	3" × 5' every 9 vines

Notes: The vineyard is 10 gross acres, or 8.8 net planted acres. All posts are lodgepole pine, CCA-treated to AWPA Standard P23-08 (0.4" penetration). Vines are nursery-produced #1 plants grafted onto phylloxera-resistant rootstock. They are root-pruned, fungicide-dipped and ready to plant. Vine material costs include 3/8" × 4' green bamboo stakes and 24" vine tubes.

The vertical shoot-positioned 6' × 9' trellis is a versatile system. It is commonly used for red and white varieties that are cane-pruned and yielding 3.5–4.5 tons per acre. Different trellis configurations are usually needed for high vigor sites and varieties that are very vigorous, high-yielding, and that respond well to long-cane or cordon-spur pruning.

The Burgundy Single Guyot System is used with excellent results on Pinot Noir, Chardonnay and Pinot Gris (Pinot Beurot) in Burgundy. A similar system is used for the Carmenet family of varieties in Bordeaux (Cabernet Sauvignon, Cabernet Franc, Merlot, Malbec and Petite Verdot).

Trellis and planting costs for the three situations are given in Table 20. There are additional direct costs incurred in establishment. Weed control is the largest of these. Also, some fungicides and nutrition supplements are needed to enable vigorous new vine growth. The comparison of the three trellis systems in Oregon's Willamette Valley is summarized here.

	Original Grapestake VSP	Hi-Tensile VSP	Burgundy Single Guyot
Vine spacing	6' × 9'	6' × 9'	1 m × 1 m
Trellis & planting costs—8.8 acre planting	$64,302	$56,857	$185,320
Per acre	$6,987	$6,141	$20,474
Weed & pest control	2,016	2,016	3,686
Total direct cost of Establishment	$64,302	$56,857	$185,320
Per acre	$7,307	$6,461	$21,059

In order to derive the amount that will have to be capitalized and amortized over time, we have to add the indirect costs of vineyard establishment. Those costs are management, insurance, property taxes and other charges incurred during the first three years, prior to the first year of fruit production.

TABLE 20   Comparison of Trellis Systems

Original Grapestake Vertical System compared with New Zealand Hi-Tensile System and Burgundy Single Guyot System. Location: Willamette Valley, Oregon. Dollars per Acre, 2014

	Original Grapestake Vertical Curtain				Vertical Single Curtain High-Tensile System				Burgundy Single Guyot System			
	Unit Cost	Year 2	Year 3	Total	Unit Cost	Year 2	Year 3	Total	Unit Cost	Year 2	Year 3	Total
Materials												
End Post Assy	$10.40	$168	$0	$168	$35.56	$574	$0	$574	$6.81	$301	$0	$301
Anchors	6.06	98	0	98	0.00	0	0	0	6.06	268	0	268
Line Post/Stake	2.08	1,661	0	1,661	4.78	955	0	955	3.73	1,867	0	1,867
Wire, 12.5 ga. Hi-Ten	0.03	378	0	378	0.02	314	0	314	0.03	1,380	0	1,380
Wire, 14 ga. soft galv.	0.018	261	177	438	0.018	0	177	177	0.000	0	0	0
J Nails	0.103	20	91	111	0.103	14	24	38	0.103	383	0	383
Strainers	2.77	67	0	67	8.31	134	0	134	2.77	45	0	45
Nicopress Sleeves	0.15	8	3	11	0.15	16	11	27	0.15	28	0	28
Total Materials		**2,661**	**271**	**2,932**		**2,007**	**212**	**2,219**		**4,272**	**0**	**4,272**
Labor												
End Posts		30	0	30		30	0	30		83	0	83
Line Posts		451	0	451		364	0	364		524	0	524
Anchors		30	0	30		30	0	30		83	0	83
Wire		46	46	92		23	23	46		62	62	124
Strainers		0	15	15		0	15	15		0	0	0
Total Labor		**557**	**61**	**618**		**447**	**38**	**485**		**752**	**62**	**814**
Total Trellis		**3,218**	**332**	**3,550**		**2,454**	**250**	**2,704**		**5,024**	**62**	**5,086**
Vines												
Material		3,227	0	3,227		3,227	0	3,227		14,547	0	14,547
Labor		210	0	210		210	0	210		842	0	842
Total Vines		**3,437**	**0**	**3,437**		**3,437**	**0**	**3,437**		**15,388**	**0**	**15,388**
Total Trellis + Vines	**per acre**	**$6,655**	**$332**	**6,987**		**$5,8911**	**$250**	**6,141**		**$20,412**	**$62**	**20,474**
Pest Control 1st 2 yrs				320				320				585
Total Direct Cost				**7,307**				**6,461**				**21,059**
Vineyard Total		8.8	acres:	$64,302		8.8	acres:	$56,857		8.8	acres:	$185,320

Source: LAMY Winery Consultants, 2013

By comparison, vineyard establishment costs for the Burgundy Single Guyot System are impressively high. No doubt, that is what explains the general reluctance of American growers to embrace the system. But, that system and its high costs are the norm in Burgundy's Côte d'Or for Grand Cru and Premier Cru appellations for Pinot Noir and Chardonnay. Perhaps we should not begrudge the high prices their wines bring in the marketplace.

While we're on the subject of high-density plantings, it would be well to address the reasons for Oregon's recent success with Pinot Noir. Why, it is reasonable to ask, can Oregon produce such great Pinot Noirs, when a mere handful of winemakers/growers have installed Burgundy-type spacings?[1]

Based on the author's observations, the significant reasons why Pinot Noirs in Oregon's northwest Willamette Valley have improved so dramatically include:

- Restriction of yields in the neighborhood of 2–3 tons per acre, achieved by winter pruning and fruit thinning at veraison, sometimes forced by cool growing conditions;

- Availability of the Dijon clones because of a close working relationship between Oregon and Burgundy producers;

- Tighter vine spacings (5' × 7' for 1,245.0 vpa and 6' × 8' for 907.5 vpa, for example) than the previous norm of 8' × 8' for 680.6 vpa and 8' × 9' for 605.0 vpa, but still not as dense as in Burgundy's 4,040.7 vpa;

- Aggressive hedging of the vine canopy;

- Employment of more Burgundy winemaking tactics;

- The helping hand offered by Robert Drouhin and Domaine Drouhin Oregon.

Vineyard areas used in comparisons

In order to apply the perspective of vineyard costs to the regional areas across America, twenty growing areas have been selected in eighteen states. Most of them are defined differently than official American Viticultural Area (AVA)[2] designations that may have similar names. The reason is that many approved AVAs are so large that they include localities that do not share characteristics relating to selection of grape varieties and viticulture methods. There is no intent to denigrate any growing area, nor express favoritism or endorsement for one locality over another. Wine people are sensitive about these things.

Many other areas were considered for financial analysis, but brevity argued for twenty. Indeed, it was thought initially that only ten sites were needed to represent price and cost regions. But, early in the analysis it became apparent

---

1. There are two notable exceptions. Montinore Vineyards (now Montinore Estate) established a 5.2-acre block of Pinot Noir on 3.5' × 5' spacing (2,489.1 vpa) in 1986. Domaine Drouhin Oregon planted on standard Burgundy spacing three years later in 1989. Several more truly high-density plantings have been added since then.

2. American Viticultural Areas are designated by the federal Alcohol and Tobacco Tax and Trade Bureau (ATTTB) in response to applications received from local areas that share climate, geographical and other characteristics.

that more were necessary to represent significant cost differences between states, particularly in wage levels.

The twenty selected areas are listed in Table 21 and depicted on a map of the United States in Figure 45. For those readers who are interested in delving further into the subject of AVAs all over the U.S., see the "Further Reading" references at the end of this chapter.

There may be localities within a Vineyard Area where irrigation is not required. Also, there is no cost included for deer fencing. Again, that is a local situation.

Vineyard sites are assumed to have been plowed, disked, harrowed and subsoiled, perhaps even limed, prior to planting, and those costs are not included. Using the same methodology as was used in the comparison of three trellis systems, vineyard establishment costs for the twenty sites across America are calculated in Table 22. All of them feature high-tensile VSP trellis systems and 6' × 9' vine spacing.

It is worth noting that pest control programs, particularly fungicide sprays, account for approximately 25 percent of any vineyard's total direct costs. In Table 22, drip irrigation systems are included for locations where irrigation is common. All irrigation installations include sand filtration, although individual situations may not require it. Because the twenty selected Vineyard Areas differ significantly in regard to climate, prevalent diseases and grape varieties grown, a separate spray program was designed for each of the twenty sites.

TABLE 21   **Selected Vineyard Areas, 20 Areas in 18 States**

Columbia Valley, WA	Columbia River drainage from Yakima through Walla Walla
Willamette Valley, OR	Western half of valley, from Forest Grove to Eugene
Southern Oregon	SW Oregon, Rogue Valley and Umpqua Valley AVAs
Snake River Valley, ID	Snake River drainage, Twin Falls to Payette
Sonoma Valley, CA	Inland southern part of Sonoma County
Central Coast, CA	Coastal valleys between Santa Cruz and Santa Barbara
Sonoita, AZ	Basin southeast of Tucson
Grand Valley, CO	Colorado River Valley around Grand Junction
Texas Hill Country	Area around Fredericksburg
Central Missouri	Central Missouri
Shawnee Hills, IL	Southern tip of Illinois
Leelanau Peninsula, MI	Near Traverse City, on east side of Lake Michigan
Ohio River Valley, OH-IN-KY-WV	West Virginia through Indiana
Lake Erie, NY-OH-PA	South shore of Lake Erie
Finger Lakes, NY	North Central area around Finger Lakes in Upper NY State
Lancaster Valley, PA	Lancaster and Chester Counties
SE New England, CT-MA-RI	Along Long Island Sound from New Haven, CT through Cape Cod, MA
Piedmont Plateau, MD	North Central Maryland, around Fredericksburg
Central Blue Ridge Mtns., VA	Blue Ridge Mountain foothills around Charlottesville
Yadkin Valley, NC	NW North Carolina, Surrey, Wilkes and Yadkin Counties

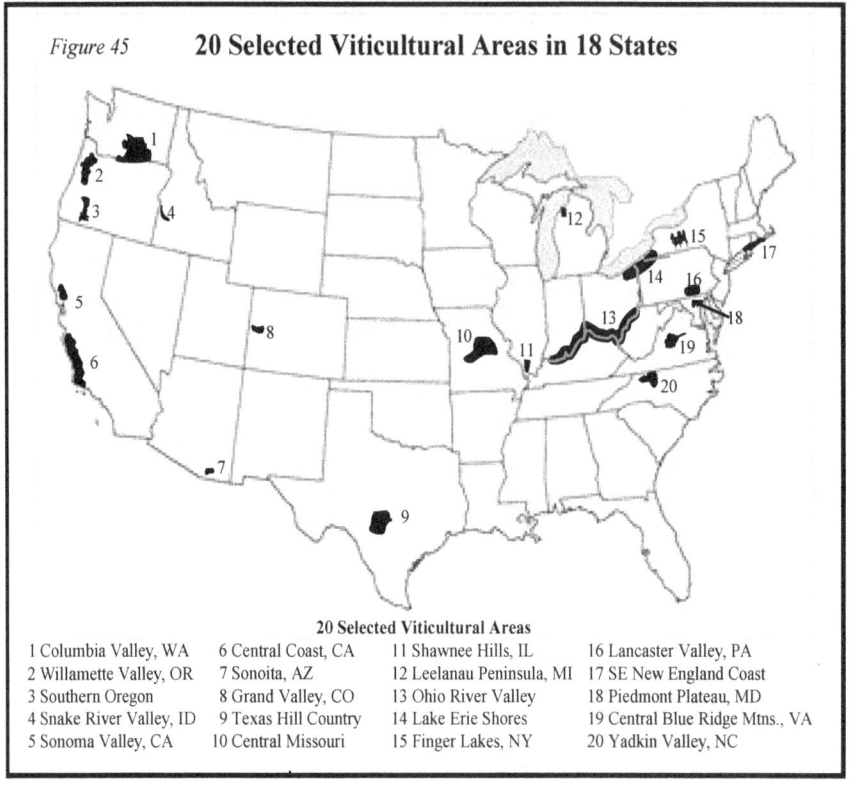

Figure 45   **20 Selected Viticultural Areas in 18 States**

20 Selected Viticultural Areas

1 Columbia Valley, WA	6 Central Coast, CA	11 Shawnee Hills, IL	16 Lancaster Valley, PA
2 Willamette Valley, OR	7 Sonoita, AZ	12 Leelanau Peninsula, MI	17 SE New England Coast
3 Southern Oregon	8 Grand Valley, CO	13 Ohio River Valley	18 Piedmont Plateau, MD
4 Snake River Valley, ID	9 Texas Hill Country	14 Lake Erie Shores	19 Central Blue Ridge Mtns., VA
5 Sonoma Valley, CA	10 Central Missouri	15 Finger Lakes, NY	20 Yadkin Valley, NC

TABLE 22   **Comparison of Vineyard Development Costs, Twenty Sites across America**

8.8 Net Acres of VSP Trellis on 6' × 9' Spacing, 2014 Dollars

	Trellis Materials	Trellis Labor	Trellis Total	Drip Irrigation	Vines	Total per Acre	Vineyard Total
Columbia Valley, WA	2,263	539	2,802	3,382	3,460	9,644	84,869
Willamette Valley, OR	2,218	486	2,704	---	3,437	6,141	54,042
Southern Oregon	2,241	476	2,716	3,322	3,433	9,471	83,347
Snake River Valley, ID	2,285	493	2,778	3,322	3,440	9,541	83,957
Sonoma Valley, CA	2,218	490	2,708	3,191	3,439	9,338	82,177
Central Coast, CA	2,218	426	2,644	3,107	3,411	9,162	80,629
Sonoita , AZ	2,330	424	2,754	3,231	3,410	9,395	82,675
Grand Valley, CO	2,442	488	2,930	3,443	3,438	9,811	86,332
Texas Hill Country, TX	2,442	447	2,889	3,262	3,420	9,571	84,224
Central Missouri	2,442	550	2,992	---	3,465	6,457	56,821
Shawnee Hills, IL	2,442	406	2,848	---	3,403	6,250	55,003
Leelanau Peninsula, MI	2,442	436	2,878	---	3,416	6,294	55,383
Ohio Valley, OH-IN-KY-WV	2,442	543	2,985	---	3,462	6,446	56,729
Lake Erie, NY-OH-PA	2,397	434	2,831	---	3,415	6,246	54,963
Finger Lakes, NY	2,352	484	2,836	---	3,436	6,273	55,199
Lancaster Valley, PA	2,330	558	2,888	---	3,468	6,356	55,935
SE New England, CT-MA-RI	2,442	410	2,852	---	3,404	6,256	55,052
Piedmont Plateau, MD	2,218	532	2,751	---	3,457	6,208	54,627
Central Blue Ridge Mtns.,VA	2,263	601	2,864	---	3,487	6,350	55,883
Yadkin Valley, NC	2,442	493	2,935	3,195	3,440	9,570	84,215

Source: LAMY Winery Consultants; 2013

Napa Valley is not included in the list. Because of its fantastic success, almost nonexistent opportunity for new operations, and extremely high land prices, Napa Valley does not represent any kind of opportunity for most aspiring vineyard and winery developers. The same may be said of New York's Long Island. The objective of this book is to provide information that is helpful to most prospective developers and investors in new vineyards and wineries. Hence, Napa Valley and Long Island are not included.

Vineyard operating costs

A pro forma analysis of revenues and costs when the Oregon example vineyard reaches full production are detailed in Table 23. Full maturity is expected by the seventh leaf in this climate and at this spacing. The variety is Pinot Noir, grown in Oregon's northwest Willamette Valley. The grape price is $2,500 per ton. Because establishment costs are capitalized, then amortized over twenty years, the financial pro forma indicates a net profit of $25,196.23:

Gross revenue	$66,000.00
Total costs	40,803.77
Net profit	**$25,196.23**
Add back depreciation	1,010.08
Add back interest	10,63.45
Add back amortization	2,702.04
Deduct owner management	2,420.00
Cash flow	**$37,122.80**
Capitalization rate	13.0%
Capitalized value	**$285,500**
per acre	32,443
Land residual value per acre	**$26,302**
Return non investment	31.8%
Average annual profit	34.5%

The cash flow of $37,122.80 supports a capitalized value of $285,500 at a capitalization rate of 13.0 percent. The cap rate reflects the high risk of an agricultural investment, where harvest quality and quantity can vary beyond the grower's control. After deducting establishment costs, the residual value imputed to the land is $26,302 per acre. (See Table 27 for present worth values.)

The Return on Investment (ROI) is 31.8 percent. Average Annual Profit, if this performance is repeated year after year, is 34.5 percent. These are handsome financial returns, indeed.

Now, we progress to analytical comparisons of vineyard operating costs at the twenty selected Vineyard Areas. Tables 24 and 25 present operating statements for red grapes. Tables 26 and 27 are for white varieties. Grape varieties were chosen on the basis of two factors: what varieties have proven to be good performers in the vineyard and marketplace; and what cultivars have demonstrated that they have good potential to be outstanding after some initial success.

TABLE 23 Detailed Vineyard Operating Statement, North Willamette Valley, Oregon

8.8 Net Planted Acres of Pinot Noir at Full Production,, 2014 Dollars (per acre)

	Labor			Equipment		Total Vineyard			Line Totals
	Hours	Cost	Materials	Hours	Cost	Labor	Materials	Equipment	
Production:									
Nutrients				627.90				5,525.52	5,525.52
Pruning & Tying	43.1	486.30	6.40			4,279.46	56.29	0.00	4,335.75
Herbicides	0.5	7.22	72.81	0.5	8.30	63.52	640.70	73.04	777.26
Fungicides	3.7	50.52	256.58	3.7	136.55	444.62	2,257.95	1,201.66	3,904.22
Move Catch Wires	5.0	56.45				496.76	0.00	0.00	496.76
Shoot Positioning	8.0	90.32				794.82	0.00	0.00	794.82
Disbudding	16.0	180.64				1,589.63	0.00	0.00	1,589.63
Hedging	1.8	24.84		1.8	28.57	218.64	0.00	251.43	470.07
Leaf Removal	3.3	37.63				331.17	0.00	0.00	331.17
Floor Management	2.0	27.63		1.0	15.89	243.15	0.00	139.81	382.96
Bird Control	1.0	13.70	22.00	0.5	4.95	120.57	193.60	43.56	357.73
Frost Control						0.00	0.00	0.00	0.00
Irrigation						0.00	0.00	0.00	0.00
Supervision	10	206				1,809	0	0	1,809
Subtotals	**94.5**	**1,180.78**	**985.69**	**7.5**	**194.26**	**10,390.90**	**8,674.05**	**1,709.50**	**20,774.45**
Harvest:									
Pick		423.38	9.01			3,725.70	79.28	0.00	3,804.98
Load/Haul	2.9	39.19	3.39	1.0	35.30	344.83	29.83	310.66	685.32
Supervision	3.0	49.32				434.06	0.00	0.00	434.06
Grape Tax			37.50				330.00	0.00	330.00
Subtotals	**6**	**512**	**50**	**1.0**	**35**	**4,505**	**439**	**311**	**5,254**
Total Variable Costs	**100.3**	**1,692.67**	**1,035.59**	**8.5**	**229.56**	**14,895.49**	**9,113.16**	**2,020.16**	**26,028.81**
Misc. Overhead			172.50				1,518.00		1,518.00
Insurance & Real Estate Taxes			88.06				774.91		774.91
Interest on Borrowed Funds			1,111.36				9,780.01		9,780.01
Amortization of Establishment Costs			307				2,702		2,702
Total – All Costs					229.56	14,895.49	23,888.12	2,020.16	40,803.77
NET PROFIT									$25,196.23

The results show a couple of noteworthy things. First, red wine varieties, in general, outperform white varieties. Contributing factors include:

- The demonstrated trend in preference from whites to reds as wine consumers become more sophisticated at including wine in their cuisine;

- Influence of the movie *Sideways*;

- Generally very good economic conditions, with increased wine consumer disposable incomes, during the 1990s and from 2002 through 2008.

Another result stands out: the poor financial performance of White Riesling grown in Washington, and to a lesser extent in Upper New York State. The example is made not to pick on Washington, but to illustrate a market condition relating to White Riesling. Wines of the variety are generally viewed as "picnic wines" by the wine-consuming public. That is, they are wines for informal, casual dining occasions and not regarded for serious consumption by the wine trade and the consumers they influence. White Zinfandel is the dominant wine of this genre, and the flood of White Zin that hit the market in the 1980s set the low price standard.

It is indeed a shame that the noble White Riesling has been relegated to such a common existence. The variety has produced wines of great character, comparable with those of Germany's best growing areas, in places like Central Washington, Oregon's Willamette Valley and Upper New York State. And these accomplishments have been made in the absence of any financial incentive for winemakers to strive for excellence in the styles of the Rheingau and Alsace.

The problem is one of price. The costs in the example in Tables 26 and 27 apply to a relatively small-sized vineyard operation of ten total acres (8.8 net acres) because that is the focus of this book. In Washington, White Riesling production is dominated by very large operations like Columbia Crest, where vineyard acres number in the thousands. There, sizable economies of scale are realized by mechanization, such as spray equipment that covers four rows on a pass and machine harvesting. Those measures improve financial returns considerably.

Columbia Crest and its sister brand, Chateau Ste. Michelle, have made heroic efforts for more than twenty years to stimulate the American market for White Riesling wines, but with limited success. So, while we knock ourselves out pursuing alternatives to Chardonnay, like Pinot Gris/Grigio and Viognier, the noble and versatile White Riesling languishes among the also-rans.

In the opinion of this writer, there is no better match for the varied seafood cuisine of America than White Riesling.

Present worth of land residual value[3]

Because the calculated land residual value doesn't occur until the vineyard reaches full yield, the amount that was derived applies to that year in the

3. The concept of present worth enables us to relate an amount received in the future to what it is worth today. For example, if we expect to receive $100.00 ten years from now, that's the same as investing $55.84 today at a compound interest rate of 6 percent for ten years To compute the present worth of an amount at a discount rate of 6 percent per annum, divide the amount by 1 + 0.06 once for each of the ten years. The formula is $100.00/(1 + .06)^{10} = 55.84.

TABLE 24 **Vineyard Operating Statements, Red Varieties**

8.8 Net Planted Acres. High-Tensile VSP Trellis on 6' × 9' Spacing, 2014 Dollars

Vineyard Area / Variety	Columbia Valley, WA Cabernet Sauvignon	Willamette Valley, OR Pinot Noir	Southern Oregon Syrah	Snake River Valley, ID Syrah	Sonoma Valley, CA Cabernet Sauvignon	Central Coast, CA Syrah	Sonoita Arizona Syrah	Grand Valley, CO Cabernet Sauvignon	Texas Hill Country Cabernet Sauvignon	Central Missouri Norton
Tons/Acre	4.0	3.0	4.0	4.0	4.0	4.0	4.0	4.0	4.0	5.0
$/Ton	$1,550	$2,500	$2,000	$1,900	$2,500	$2,000	$1,425	$1,750	$1,600	$1,300
Total Revenues	**$54,560**	**$66,000**	**$70,400**	**$66,880**	**$88,000**	**$70,400**	**$50,160**	**$61,600**	**$56,320**	**$57,200**
Production Costs:										
Nutrients	894	634	890	889	894	887	886	891	891	896
Pruning & Tying	552	498	488	503	502	440	439	500	458	417
Herbicides	91	90	89	90	90	88	88	90	88	87
Fungicides	458	452	451	453	453	447	447	453	448	444
Move Catch Wires	63	57	56	58	58	50	50	57	52	48
Shoot Positioning	101	91	89	92	92	80	80	92	84	76
Disbudding	202	182	179	184	184	161	161	183	168	153
Hedging	59	54	53	55	54	48	48	54	50	46
Leaf Removal	42	38	37	38	38	34	33	38	35	32
Floor Management	48	44	43	44	44	39	39	44	41	37
Bird Control	43	41	41	42	41	40	40	44	43	42
Frost Control	0	0	0	0	0	0	0	0	0	0
Irrigation	0	0	0	0	0	0	0	0	0	0
Supervision	229	208	204	210	209	185	185	208	192	176
Total Production Costs	**2,783**	**2,389**	**2,620**	**2,658**	**2,660**	**2,499**	**2,497**	**2,654**	**2,551**	**2,453**

Harvest Costs:

Pick	645	437	571	589	587	515	515	585	537	611
Load/Haul	89	79	84	85	85	80	80	85	82	85
Supervision	55	50	49	50	50	44	44	50	46	42
Grape Tax	51	38	51	51	51	51	51	51	51	63
Total Harvest Costs	**840**	**603**	**754**	**775**	**773**	**690**	**690**	**771**	**715**	**801**
Total Variable Costs	**3,623**	**2,992**	**3,374**	**3,433**	**3,433**	**3,189**	**3,187**	**3,424**	**3,267**	**3,254**
Misc. Overhead	174	174	174	174	174	174	174	174	174	174
Insurance & Real Estate Taxes	115	89	114	115	113	112	114	117	115	90
Interest on Borrowed Funds	1,218	1,123	1,100	843	1,853	1,230	990	1,119	1,001	631
Amortization of Establish. Costs	487	310	478	482	472	463	474	495	483	316
Total-All Costs	**5,618**	**4,688**	**5,241**	**5,047**	**6,045**	**5,169**	**4,939**	**5,330**	**5,040**	**4,465**
NET PROFIT	**582**	**2,812**	**2,759**	**2,553**	**3,955**	**2,831**	**761**	**1,670**	**1,360**	**1,035**
Add back Depreciation	122	118	118	119	119	116	116	119	117	116
Add back Interest	1,312	1,221	1,180	869	2,081	1,343	1,054	1,201	1,065	621
Add back Amortization	487	310	478	482	472	463	474	495	483	316
Less Owner Management	278	278	278	278	278	278	278	278	278	278
Cash Flow	**2,225**	**4,182**	**4,258**	**3,746**	**6,348**	**4,475**	**2,128**	**3,208**	**2,747**	**1,811**
Capitalization Rate	13.0%	13.0%	13.0%	13.0%	13.0%	13.0%	13.0%	13.0%	13.0%	13.0%
Capitalized Value	17,100	32,100	32,700	28,800	48,800	34,400	16,300	24,600	21,100	13,900
per Acre	17,100	32,100	32,700	28,800	48,800	34,400	16,300	24,600	21,100	13,900
Land Residual/Acre	**7,456**	**25,959**	**23,229**	**19,259**	**39,462**	**25,238**	**6,905**	**14,789**	**11,529**	**7,650**
Return on Investment	*14.0%*	*31.2%*	*28.9%*	*30.8%*	*28.6%*	*28.1%*	*15.6%*	*21.3%*	*19.9%*	*21.4%*
Average Annual Profit	*4.9%*	*33.8%*	*31.0%*	*29.9%*	*36.8%*	*31.9%*	*8.5%*	*19.9%*	*16.9%*	*13.8%*

TABLE 25 Vineyard Operating Statements, Red Varieties

8.8 Net Planted Acres. High-Tensile VSP Trellis on 6' × 9' Spacing, 2014 Dollars

Vineyard Area	Shawnee Hills, IL	Leelanau Peninsula, MI	Ohio River Valley	Lake Erie Shores	Finger Lakes, NY	Lancaster Valley, PA	SE New Engl. Coast	Piedmont Plateau, MD	Cen. Blue Ridge Mountains, VA	Yadkin Valley, NC
Variety	Chambourcin	Cabernet Franc	Cabernet Sauvignon	Cabernet Franc	Cabernet Franc	Cabernet Franc	Cabernet Franc	Cabernet Franc	Cabernet Franc	Cabernet Sauvignon
Tons/Acre	5.0	4.0	4.0	4.0	4.0	4.0	4.0	4.0	4.0	4.0
$/Ton	$1,100	$1,600	$1,300	$1,600	$1,600	$1,675	$1,615	$1,700	$1,600	$1,520
Total Revenues	**$48,400**	**$56,320**	**$45,760**	**$56,320**	**$56,320**	**$58,960**	**$56,848**	**$59,840**	**$56,320**	**$53,504**
Production Costs:										
Nutrients	896	892	896	893	893	896	896	892	890	887
Pruning & Tying	417	448	551	445	496	571	421	545	614	505
Herbicides	87	88	91	88	90	92	87	91	93	90
Fungicides	444	447	458	447	452	459	445	457	464	453
Move Catch Wires	48	51	63	51	57	65	48	62	70	58
Shoot Positioning	76	82	101	82	91	105	77	100	113	93
Disbudding	153	164	202	163	182	210	154	200	226	185
Hedging	46	49	59	49	54	61	46	59	66	55
Leaf Removal	32	34	42	34	38	44	32	42	47	39
Floor Management	37	40	48	40	44	50	38	48	54	45
Bird Control	42	42	45	42	43	44	42	45	45	44
Frost Control	0	0	0	0	0	0	0	0	0	0
Irrigation	0	0	0	0	0	0	0	0	0	0
Supervision	176	188	229	187	207	236	178	226	253	210
Total Production Costs	**2,453**	**2,525**	**2,786**	**2,521**	**2,645**	**2,833**	**2,463**	**2,766**	**2,933**	**2,663**

Harvest Costs:

Pick	611	524	644	522	580	667	493	637	717	591
Load/Haul	85	81	89	81	85	91	79	89	94	86
Supervision	42	45	55	45	50	57	43	54	61	51
Grape Tax	63	51	51	51	51	51	51	51	51	51
Total Harvest Costs	**801**	**701**	**839**	**698**	**765**	**865**	**665**	**830**	**923**	**778**
Total Variable Costs	**3,254**	**3,226**	**3,625**	**3,219**	**3,411**	**3,698**	**3,128**	**3,596**	**3,856**	**3,441**
Misc. Overhead	174	174	174	174	174	174	174	174	174	174
Insurance & Real Estate Taxes	90	90	91	90	91	90	90	89	91	115
Interest on Borrowed Funds	631	809	804	731	688	802	829	816	806	931
Amortization of Establ. Costs	316	318	326	315	317	321	316	314	321	483
Total-All Costs	**4,465**	**4,617**	**5,020**	**4,529**	**4,679**	**5,086**	**4,538**	**4,990**	**5,248**	**5,144**
NET PROFIT	**1,035**	**1,783**	**180**	**1,871**	**1,721**	**1,614**	**1,922**	**1,810**	**1,152**	**936**
Add back Depreciation	116	117	122	116	119	123	115	121	125	119
Add back Interest	621	836	815	742	683	809	864	831	809	974
Add back Amortization	316	318	326	315	317	321	316	314	321	483
Less Owner Management	278	278	278	278	278	278	278	278	278	278
Cash Flow	**1,811**	**2,775**	**1,165**	**2,767**	**2,562**	**2,590**	**2,940**	**2,798**	**2,129**	**2,235**
Capitalization Rate	13.0%	13.0%	13.0%	13.0%	13.0%	13.0%	13.0%	13.0%	13.0%	13.0%
Capitalized Value	13,900	21,300	8,900	21,200	19,700	19,900	22,600	21,500	16,300	17,100
per Acre	13,900	21,300	8,900	21,200	19,700	19,900	22,600	21,500	16,300	17,100
Land Residual/Acre	**7,650**	**15,006**	**2,454**	**14,954**	**13,427**	**13,544**	**16,344**	**15,292**	**9,950**	**7,530**
Return on Investment	21.4%	27.0%	11.5%	29.3%	28.5%	25.7%	28.1%	27.5%	21.1%	17.1%
Average Annual Profit	13.8%	23.5%	−1.9%	24.9%	22.6%	19.9%	25.5%	22.5%	13.7%	10.8%

TABLE 26 **Vineyard Operating Statements, White Varieties**

8.8 Net Planted Acres. High-Tensile VSP Trellis on 6' × 9' Spacing, 2009 Dollars

Vineyard Area	Columbia Valley, WA	Willamette Valley, OR	Southern Oregon	Snake River Valley, ID	Sonoma Valley, CA	Central Coast, CA	Sonoita Arizona	Grand Valley, CO	Texas Hill Country	Central Missouri
Variety	White Riesling	Pinot Gris	Viognier	Chardonnay	Chardonnay	Chardonnay	Sauvignon Blanc	Chardonnay	Chardonnay	Vidal Blanc
Tons/Acre	5.0	4.0	4.0	4.5	4.5	4.5	5.0	4.5	4.5	6.0
$/Ton	$1,100	$1,500	$1,750	$1,300	$1,950	$1,450	$1,378	$1,550	$1,500	$1,000
Total Revenues	**$5,500**	**$6,000**	**$7,000**	**$5,850**	**$8,775**	**$6,525**	**$6,890**	**$6,975**	**$6,750**	**$6,000**
Production Costs:										
Nutrients	965	770.50	881	919	926	918	956	921	914	927
Pruning & Tying	573	492.70	483	500	497	433	478	495	454	454
Herbicides	90	88.67	88	89	89	87	86	89	87	86
Fungicides	453	447.81	447	449	448	442	428	448	444	426
Move Catch Wires	63	56.45	55	57	57	50	50	57	52	47
Shoot Positioning	70	90.32	88	92	91	79	88	91	83	83
Disbudding	200	180.64	177	166	165	143	159	164	150	151
Hedging	31	53.42	52	54	54	47	70	54	49	66
Leaf Removal	0	37.63	37	255	253	220	33	252	231	31
Floor Management	48	43.52	43	44	44	39	39	44	40	37
Bird Control	43	40.65	41	42	41	40	40	43	42	41
Frost Control	0	0.00	0	0	0	0	0	0	0	0
Irrigation	0	0.00	0	0	0	0	0	0	0	0
Supervision	159	206	202	188	186	164	110	186	171	105
Total Production Costs	**2,694**	**2,507.83**	**2,594**	**2,853**	**2,850**	**2,660**	**2,536**	**2,842**	**2,719**	**2,455**

Harvest Costs:										
Pick	736	576.51	565	624	621	541	634	618	567	753
Load/Haul	93	84.22	83	86	86	81	101	86	82	117
Supervision	54	49.32	48	50	50	44	44	50	46	42
Grape Tax	63	50	50	56	56	56	63	56	56	75
Total Harvest Costs	**946**	**760.05**	**747**	**817**	**813**	**722**	**841**	**810**	**752**	**986**
Total Variable Costs	**3,640**	**3,267.88**	**3,341**	**3,670**	**3,663**	**3,382**	**3,377**	**3,652**	**3,471**	**3,441**
Misc. Overhead	173	172.50	173	173	173	173	173	173	173	173
Insurance & Real Estate Taxes	91	88.06	113	114	112	111	85	116	114	85
Interest on Borrowed Funds	1,052	1,120.91	1,089	843	1,842	1,225	802	1,116	998	605
Amortization of Establ. Costs	328	307	474	477	467	458	286	491	479	286
Total-All Costs	**5,283**	**4,956**	**5,189**	**5,276**	**6,257**	**5,348**	**4,722**	**5,546**	**5,234**	**4,588**
NET PROFIT	**217**	**1,044**	**1,811**	**574**	**2,518**	**1,177**	**2,168**	**1,429**	**1,516**	**1,412**
Add back Depreciation	112	117.62	117	118	118	115	113	118	116	119
Add back Interest	1,113	1,208.46	1,168	860	2,060	1,330	823	1,189	1,054	583
Add back Amortization	328	307.05	474	477	467	458	286	491	479	286
Less Owner Management	250	250	250	250	250	250	250	250	250	250
Cash Flow	**1,520**	**2,426.73**	**3,320**	**1,780**	**4,913**	**2,829**	**3,140**	**2,976**	**2,915**	**2,149**
Capitalization Rate	13.0%	13.0%	13.0%	13.0%	13.0%	13.0%	13.0%	13.0%	13.0%	13.0%
Capitalized Value	11,600	18,600	25,500	13,600	37,700	21,700	24,100	22,800	22,400	16,500
per Acre	11,600	18,600	25,500	13,600	37,700	21,700	24,100	22,800	22,400	16,500
Land Residual/Acre	**5,047**	**12,459**	**16,029**	**4,059**	**28,362**	**12,538**	**18,389**	**12,989**	**12,829**	**10,789**
Return on Investment	*12.0%*	*18.3%*	*22.8%*	*14.8%*	*22.4%*	*17.9%*	*32.0%*	*19.9%*	*21.3%*	*27.4%*
Average Annual Profit	*-0.6%*	*13.2%*	*22.3%*	*5.5%*	*25.8%*	*14.2%*	*27.8%*	*16.9%*	*18.8%*	*19.4%*

TABLE 27   Vineyard Operating Statements, White Varieties

8.8 Net Planted Acres. High-Tensile VSP Trellis on 6' × 9' Spacing, 2009 Dollars

Vineyard Areas	Shawnee Hills, IL	Leelanau Peninsula, MI	Ohio River Valley	Lake Erie Shores	Finger Lakes, NY	Lancaster Valley, PA	SE New Engl. Coast	Piedmont Plateau, MD	C. Blue Ridge Mnts., VA	Yadkin Valley, NC
Variety	Chardonnel	Pinot Gris	Chardonnay	Chardonnay	White Riesling	Vidal Blanc	Vidal Blanc	Chardonnay	Chardonnay	Viognier
Tons/Acre	4.0	4.0	4.0	4.0	5.0	6.0	6.0	4.0	4.0	4.0
$/Ton	$1,500	$1,350	$1,500	$1,500	$1,215	$1,200	$1,200	$1,600	$1,600	$1,330
Total Revenues	**$6,000**	**$5,400**	**$6,000**	**$6,000**	**$6,075**	**$7,200**	**$7,200**	**$6,400**	**$6,400**	**$5,320**
Production Costs:										
Nutrients	927	984	988	986	964	988	988	982	883	879
Pruning & Tying	413	443	546	441	515	622	459	608	608	500
Herbicides	86	87	90	87	89	90	86	92	92	89
Fungicides	440	443	453	443	448	441	426	459	459	449
Move Catch Wires	47	51	63	50	56	65	48	70	70	57
Shoot Positioning	76	81	100	81	63	114	84	112	112	92
Disbudding	136	162	181	146	180	208	152	202	202	183
Hedging	45	48	59	48	28	89	67	65	65	54
Leaf Removal	210	34	278	224	0	43	32	310	310	38
Floor Management	37	39	48	39	43	50	37	53	53	44
Bird Control	41	42	45	42	42	44	41	44	44	44
Frost Control	0	0	0	0	0	0	0	0	0	0
Irrigation	0	0	0	0	0	0	0	0	0	0
Supervision	157	186	204	167	143	140	105	226	226	208
Total Production Costs	**2,615**	**2,601**	**3,054**	**2,754**	**2,571**	**2,893**	**2,525**	**3,222**	**3,123**	**2,637**

Harvest Costs:

Pick	463	519	607	491	663	823	911	681	675	585
Load/Haul	81	80	88	80	88	124	125	101	93	85
Supervision	42	45	54	44	49	56	42	60	60	50
Grape Tax	50	50	50	50	63	75	75	50	50	50
Total Harvest Costs	**637**	**694**	**799**	**666**	**863**	**1,078**	**1,154**	**892**	**879**	**770**
Total Variable Costs	**3,252**	**3,295**	**3,853**	**3,419**	**3,434**	**3,970**	**3,679**	**4,114**	**4,002**	**3,407**
Misc. Overhead	173	173	173	173	173	173	173	173	173	173
Insurance & Real Estate Taxes	89	89	90	89	91	85	85	90	90	114
Interest on Borrowed Funds	626	804	804	730	695	771	812	808	804	922
Amortization of Establ. Costs	313	315	322	312	328	286	286	318	318	479
Total-All Costs	**4,451**	**4,676**	**5,242**	**4,723**	**4,720**	**5,284**	**5,034**	**5,501**	**5,386**	**5,093**
NET PROFIT	**1,549**	**724**	**758**	**1,277**	**1,355**	**1,916**	**2,166**	**899**	**1,014**	**187**
Add back Depreciation	115	115	121	115	111	125	122	126	123	118
Add back Interest	615	828	807	735	693	763	823	801	801	964
Add back Amortization	313	315	322	312	328	286	286	318	318	479
Less Owner Management	250	250	250	250	250	250	250	250	250	250
Cash Flow	**2,341**	**1,732**	**1,757**	**2,189**	**2,236**	**2,839**	**3,146**	**1,893**	**2,006**	**1,498**
Capitalization Rate	13.0%	13.0%	13.0%	13.0%	13.0%	13.0%	13.0%	13.0%	13.0%	13.0%
Capitalized Value	18,000	13,300	13,500	16,800	17,200	21,800	24,100	14,500	15,400	11,500
per Acre	18,000	13,300	13,500	16,800	17,200	21,800	24,100	14,500	15,400	11,500
Land Residual/Acre	**11,750**	**7,006**	**7,054**	**10,554**	**10,647**	**16,089**	**18,389**	**8,150**	**9,050**	**1,930**
Return on Investment	*28.0%*	*17.0%*	*17.5%*	*23.4%*	*24.4%*	*30.4%*	*32.0%*	*19.0%*	*20.1%*	*11.6%*
Average Annual Profit	*21.6%*	*8.8%*	*8.5%*	*17.1%*	*18.2%*	*23.1%*	*26.6%*	*10.1%*	*11.9%*	*-1.2%*

future. To estimate what the land residual value is, in terms of 2014 dollars, future values at full yield have to be discounted to the year 2014. That is done in Table 28.

Land Residual Value is computed by subtracting the cost of improvements from the capitalized value of the operating vineyard. The discount rate chosen is 6.0 percent, which is more likely to apply to the future time period than the approximately 3.25 percent that would be warranted based on recent three-month Treasury Bill rates. No reduction for inflation is needed because all of the operating revenues and costs are already expressed in constant 2014 dollars.

Cumulative cash flow

Frequently, we hear that vineyards take a long time to pay out. Yes, unequivocally, they do.

TABLE 28   **Present Worth of Land Residual Value**
20 Selected Sites Across America. Per Acre of Planted Area, 2014 Dollars

Vineyard Area	Red Variety	Year	Present worth	White Variety	Year	Present worth
Columbia Valley, WA	Cabernet Sauvignon	6	$5,256	White Riesling	5	$3,771
Willamette Valley, OR	Pinot Noir	7	17,264	Pinot Gris	7	8,286
Southern Oregon	Syrah	7	15,449	Viognier	7	10,660
Snake River Valley, ID	Syrah	6	13,577	Chardonnay	6	2,861
Sonoma Valley, CA	Cabernet Sauvignon	5	29,488	Chardonnay	5	21,194
Central Coast, CA	Syrah	5	18,859	Chardonnay	5	9,369
Sonoita, AZ	Syrah	5	5,160	Sauvignon Blanc	5	13,741
Grand Valley, CO	Cabernet Sauvignon	6	10,426	Chardonnay	6	9,157
Texas Hill Country	Cabernet Sauvignon	6	8,127	Chardonnay	5	9,586
Central Missouri	Norton/ Cynthiana	6	5,393	Vidal Blanc	5	8,062
Shawnee Hills, IL	Chambourcin	5	5,717	Chardonnel	5	8,780
Leelanau Peninsula, MI	Cabernet Franc	7	9,980	Pinot Gris	7	4,659
Ohio River Valley	Cabernet Sauvignon	6	1,730	Chardonnay	6	4,973
Lake Erie, NY-OH-PA	Cabernet Franc	6	10,542	Chardonnay	6	7,440
Finger Lakes, NY	Cabernet Franc	7	8,930	White Riesling	6	7,506
Lancaster Valley, PA	Cabernet Franc	7	9,008	Vidal Blanc	5	12,023
SE New England	Cabernet Franc	7	10,870	Chardonnay	6	12,964
Piedmont Plateau, MD	Cabernet Franc	6	10,780	Chardonnay	5	6,090
Central Blue Ridge Mtns., VA	Cabernet Franc	6	7,014	Chardonnay	5	6,763
Yadkin Valley, NC	Cabernet Sauvignon	6	5,308	Viognier	6	1,361

The number of years required to break even varies depending on climate, vine spacing, grape variety, water supply, vine cultural practices and several other factors. For example, Pinot Noir may require eight years to reach yield maturity in 7 ft. × 10 ft. spacing in Oregon's Willamette Valley, but as rapidly as five years in 1 meter × 1 meter layout and the same location. The reason: many more vines contribute to the runup before serious root competition begins.

In another example, Chardonnay may need seven-eight years to achieve full yield in Oregon's Willamette Valley, but five years in California's Sonoma Valley. Why? Sonoma's growing season is about one month longer on both ends of the season and the temperatures are higher.

Just to show this is an equal opportunity book, some French-American hybrids can develop to full yields in four years in warmer eastern and Midwest state settings, such as Arkansas, Iowa, Kentucky and Upstate New York, where most *Vitis vinifera* varieties require seven or eight. Among those hybrids are: Aurore, Cayuga White, Chelois, De Chaunac, La Crosse, Seyval Blanc and Vidal Blanc. There are more, and some of them may perform differently in some climates. Some are so vigorous that they have to be restrained by pruning and cluster-thinning in order to maintain desirable, or "targeted," crop levels. The term "desirable crop levels" is used because, if allowed to grow unchecked, some varieties will run up yield to seven-nine tons/acre, resulting in serious diminishment of wine quality and then severe unwanted crop reduction in the following year.

Forecasting crop levels for each variety can be a complex challenge. Let's use Oregon-grown Pinot Noir to analyze the break-even point for a vineyard, since that variety is so tempting to many growers these days. The series of pro forma operating cost statements for the first ten years is detailed in Table 29. The "first leaf" is the year the vines are in nursery. They are outplanted in "leaf 2." Other assumptions are shown in the table. The break-even point occurs with the harvest in leaf year 6. The payback period, when cumulative cash flow turns positive, ends with year 7. The Internal Rate of Return for the first ten years is 29.8 percent.

Further reading

American Viticultural Area; *Wikipedia* website: http://en.wikipedia.org/wiki/American_Viticultural_Areas

Appellation America website: http://wine.appellationamerica.com/

The Economics of Wine Production in Virginia; Capps, Smith, Wolf and Walker; Virginia Cooperative Extension, Virginia Tech University.

ஐᏮ

TABLE 29   **Vineyard Operating Statements, First Ten Years**

8.8 Acres of Pinot Noir in Oregon, 2014 Dollars

	Pre-production Years	4	5	6	Leaf Year* 7	8	9	10
Tons Harvested		5.3	12.3	22.9	26.4	26.4	26.4	26.4
Price/Ton	---	$1,800	$1,900	$2,000	$2,500	$2,500	$2,500	$2,500
Total Revenues		**$9,504**	**$23,408**	**$45,760**	**$66,000**	**$66,000**	**$66,000**	**$66,000**
Production Costs:								
Nutrients		1,105	2,763	4,144	5,526	5,526	5,526	5,526
Pruning & Tying		867	3,035	3,902	4,336	4,336	4,336	4,336
Herbicides		777	777	777	777	777	777	777
Fungicides		3,123	3,904	3,904	3,904	3,904	3,904	3,904
Move Catch Wires		248	497	497	497	497	497	497
Shoot Positioning		397	596	795	795	795	795	795
Disbudding		1,590	1,590	1,590	1,590	1,590	1,590	1,590
Hedging		235	353	470	470	470	470	470
Leaf Removal		0	0	199	331	331	331	331
Floor Management		383	383	383	383	383	383	383
Bird Control		179	358	358	358	358	358	358
Frost Control		0	0	0	0	0	0	0
Irrigation		0	0	0	0	0	0	0
Supervision		1,447	1,628	1,809	1,809	1,809	1,809	1,809
Subtotals		**10,352**	**15,883**	**18,827**	**20,774**	**20,774**	**20,774**	**20,774**

Harvest Costs:								
Pick		571	1,332	2,473	3,805	3,805	3,805	3,805
Load/Haul		103	240	445	685	685	685	685
Supervision		65	152	282	434	434	434	434
Grape Tax		50	116	215	330	330	330	330
Subtotals		788	1,839	3,415	5,254	5,254	5,254	5,254
Total Variable Costs		**11,140**	**17,722**	**22,242**	**26,029**	**26,029**	**26,029**	**26,029**
Misc. Overhead		759	1,139	1,366	1,518	1,518	1,518	1,518
Insurance & RE Taxes		620	697	775	775	775	775	775
Interest on Borrow. Funds		6,357	7,824	9,291	9,780	9,780	9,780	9,780
Amort. of Establ. Costs		3,314	3,314	3,314	2,702	2,702	2,702	2,702
TOTAL-ALL COSTS	54,041	22,190	30,695	36,988	40,804	40,804	40,804	40,804
NET PROFIT (LOSS)		**($12,686)**	**($7,287)**	**$8,772**	**$25,196**	**$25,196**	**$25,196**	**$25,196**
Add Depreciation		859	960	1,010	1,010	1,010	1,010	1,010
Interest		9,571	10,103	10,634	10,634	10,634	10,634	10,634
Amortization		2,702	2,702	2,702	2,702	2,702	2,702	2,702
Net Cash Flow	$54,041	$446	$6,477	$23,118	$39,543	$39,543	$39,543	$39,543
Cum. Cash Flow	**(54,041)**	**(53,595)**	**(47,118)**	**(24,000)**	**15,543**	**55,086**	**94,629**	**134,171**

*Includes one year in nursery before outplanting.

Source: LAMY Winery Consultants. 2014.

—7—

Alternative fruits and products

Some other fruits

The foregoing is not to say that wines made from non-vinifera fruits are without merit. To the contrary, many small wineries in newly emerging wine-producing states are doing quite well in quality and price by producing fruit and berry wines, and wines from locally-grown non-vinifera grapes. Most of their patronage comes from locals and tourists visiting tasting rooms. An Oregon Marionberry wine is presented as an example. The fermentation analysis is in Chapter 8, the financial analysis in Chapter 14.

A winery in Maui (Tedeschi Vineyards) makes an outstanding white wine from pineapple juice; it tastes remarkably like an off-dry white grape wine. A winery in Key West, Florida (Key West Winery) makes a French roasted coffee bean-infused orange wine. The concept works well with some other white wines, such as Chenin Blanc and Chardonnay.

Hey! Anytime you can get $15–$18 a bottle for a non-grape wine, you have a money-making deal!

The array of berries and tree fruits used for wine is extensive. Here are the most common used by commercial wineries:

> **Tree fruits:** apple, apricot, banana, cherry, cranberry, elderberry, guava, key lime, mango, passion fruit, orange, peach, pear, pineapple, plum, tangerine.

Berries: blackberry, blueberry, currant, elderberry, gooseberry, huckleberry, marionberry, raspberry, strawberry.

Non-fruit: rhubarb, classified as a vegetable, and mead, made from honey.

Fruit and berry wines are almost always diluted before fermentation. The reason is simply that nature does not produce non-grape fruits with sugar-to-acid balances that are acceptable for winemaking. Federal regulations in America limit the amount of dilution, called *amelioration*, to 35 percent of the finished wine's volume. This is usually a good level of dilution, and is more concentrated than most home winemakers use to make acceptable wines.

Calculations for fruit and berry wines are discussed in detail in the next chapter.

Liqueurs

Liqueurs are distilled alcohol products. Ethanol is combined with sugar and concentrates or extracts. They are not wines.

Distilled products

We won't get into grain-based distilled products here. Nor will we discuss potato vodka or cactus-based tequila. The focus is on fruit-based brandies, or eaux-de-vie, because they are a logical extension of winemaking activities.

Brandies are distilled from wine. First, the fruit is reduced to a mash, usually with skins and seeds included, except for grapes. Then, the mash is fermented to total dryness. The third step is to load the fermented mass into the still, and distill off the ethyl alcohol along with other higher alcohols called congenerics. In the process, wood alcohol (methanol) is removed, as it is poisonous.

The still used in the Cognac region of France is the *alembic*. It is a single-stage still, and several passes though the still are usually required to achieve the desired end product purity. Each pass narrows the spectrum of constituents remaining in the product.

The other design of still is multi-stage. The best are made in Germany. It has plates at varying heights in the distillation column, so specific components can be selected or discarded. Usually, only one pass is needed.

Cognac style brandies are aged in oak barrels, the best of them for more than three years. Alsatian style eaux-de-vie are aged in neutral (old) wood, if at all. Eaux-de-vie are crystal clear.

Cognac-type brandies are usually consumed, undiluted, in a snifter (glass) designed for the purpose. The tradition of heating the glass is not needed for good-quality brandies. The practice was contrived to blow off the bad stuff, which is not present in the well-made versions.

In France, eaux-de-vie are served in a snifter, lying at about a 45° angle in a bowl of shaved ice. Sugar is added to the snifter, at one to three cubes depending on the preference of the consumer. Both of these actions are intended to reduce the fiery nature of the product, and they succeed in small measure.

Further reading

American Viticultural Area; *Wikipedia* website: http://en.wikipedia.org/wiki/American_Viticultural_Areas

Appellation America website: http://wine.appellationamerica.com

Capps, Eric R., Smith, Tony Kenneth Wolf, and B. Jerry Walker. *The Economics of Wine Production in Virginia.* Virginia Cooperative Extension, Virginia Tech University, 1998. Website: https://vtechworks.lib.vt.edu/bitstream/handle/10919/24688/VCE463_008_1998.pdf?sequence=1&isAllowed=y

ഇൻൽ

Winemaking and pivotal role of the winemaker

We've all heard winemakers humbly exclaim something like: "The wine makes itself. All I have to do is get out of the way."

In all likelihood, a winemaker who actually practices that philosophy probably turns out a lot of subpar wines.

In preceding chapters, we explored some realities of assuming winery ownership, and the importance of securing high quality grapes and other fruits. In this chapter, attention is focused on the winemaker, who has an unparalleled role in everything the winery and vineyard do to produce high-quality wine.

Evidence of intervention

If that claim about letting the wine make itself were true, why is so much money invested in *gentle* destemmer-crushers and presses, *temperature-controlled* crushing and fermentation equipment, *French* oak barrels, various types of *specific and high quality* fining materials and filters, *high-tech* bottling equipment, and *analytical laboratories*? Why do the good winemakers perpetually study, research, taste and meet in discussion groups with their peers here and abroad? Why has the quality of average wines risen so dramatically in the past thirty years?

Read a survey about winemaking equipment preferences and you'll learn about new destemmers to minimize maceration of the fruit, sorting tables and belts where workers can pick through the fruit before fermentation, and using a gravity feed for fruit from destemmer to fermentation vessel. This is "getting out of the way?"

Skilled winemaking is at the center of the process

Good winemakers control the winemaking process, shepherding their progeny through every step from vine bud to bottle, adjusting and shaping the product and process, measuring, testing, sniffing, tasting, intervening, controlling, and orchestrating. The winemaker's stylistic and quality control functions don't begin when the fruit hits the crush pad. They begin with oversight of vineyard operations, whether the grapes are grown by the winery or by independent growers.

Skill in winemaking is learned, earned, and most important of all, dependent on innate abilities. Like a great musician, a winemaker must acquire a large body of technical knowledge through experience and independent study. However, by itself, classroom time and books are not enough, nor is the simple possession of knowledge. Analogies with music, athletics, mathematics and a long list of talents are valid. Some people have good aptitude for winemaking, others do not. A good wine palette is a gift possessed by few; and so is the ability and skill to apply it to the winemaking process. This subject was pursued in greater detail in Chapter 1.

So, how does a new owner assemble capable winemaking staff? Hiring a full-time experienced winemaker is the best way, but that may prove to be too expensive or not practical (in terms of availability outside of the West Coast) for a small operation. Experienced California winemakers are expensive, and they may not have experience in dealing with the cool climate vinifera grape varieties grown outside most of California, nor with the American varieties, French hybrids and non-grape fruits grown in the Midwest, East Coast and the South.

In some regions, professional winemakers work part-time for several wineries. Or, a consulting winemaker may be available to guide a full-time but inexperienced winemaker, or to train an ambitious owner into the role. By and large, this is an industry where technical staffers share a lot of secrets with their peers. It is unlike most other businesses regarding isolation of staff from competitors.

Impact on value

Let's assume that the winery is successful in quality and profit, but the winemaker is leaving. The absence of winemaking continuity is a very serious consideration in determining the value of the operation as "a going business concern." The conventional method for determining the value of a business is simple capitalization of net income before depreciation, interest and income taxes. Absent some adjustments, this method assumes that the current management-production team will continue in place, or that it is easily replaced.

Seldom would that be the situation. The tangible values that accrue to the operation are facilities, inventory, distribution (i.e., reliable links with effective distributors in good markets) and an established label (read that "reputation for consistently high quality and a loyal customer base").

But, the most important element of the production process, the winemaker, is missing from most small winery purchases and will be difficult to replace. Accordingly, the winery's acquisition value should be discounted for the cost and risk attached to replacing the winemaking skill and of perpetuating a high reputation in the marketplace.

Winery sellers can avoid this detraction by contractually locking in a carry-over period for guidance from the departing winemaker, if that is possible.

But let's say the owner is the winemaker. He (or she) wants to cash out and continuing performance is not part of the deal. The buyer will have to replace the winemaking capability, a tall order for a new owner without advanced winemaking skills.

What does a winemaker cost?

It will cost a minimum of $85,000 in salary to hire a California-trained wine-maker with an enology degree. If that winemaker has experience as a lead winemaker (not just an assistant position) you can expect $90,000–105,000 for a 20,000+ case operation—depending on where your winery is located.

The primary source for winemaker pay is the 2012 Salary Survey Report of *Wine Business Monthly* magazine (October, 2012). As one might expect, California data is best because most of the wineries are there. The survey is biased; responses are voluntary, but it is the best data available, buttressed by interviews with placement agency representatives as to prevailing pay rates. California wineries offer a high degree of mobility for winemakers, leading to a very stratified pay scale in each region.

For wine-producing areas outside California, the survey reports regional rates. However, pay scales are relatively unstratified, depend more on nego-tiation, rates for related occupations, and cost-of-living considerations. *U.S. Bureau of Labor Statistics* surveys of food processing technical workers, managers, office support and marketing representatives were used for propor-tionality. BLS' *Consumer Price Index-All Consumers in Urban Areas* was used to adjust for cost of living.

Further complicating the situation is many winemaking jobs do not fit into *Wine Business Monthly's* classifications. Take Oregon, for example. Less than one-fourth of the lead winemakers graduated from enology degree programs such as UC-Davis and Fresno State. The others come from the ranks of doctors, engineers, home winemakers, and others who apprentice at an established winery or are self-taught through reading, short courses, winery technical visi-tations and the like.

Profit-based bonuses seem to be gaining popularity with eastern wineries.

Then, the resulting pay rates were inflated to mid-2014 values.

In the financial calculations of this book, 25 percent (including anticipation of the Affordable Care Act's effect on business costs) has been added for payroll taxes and fringe benefits.

California winemakers bridle at the suggestion of a pay cut to reflect a lower cost of living. They are accustomed to being treated like rockstars, and can bring big marketing success to your winery. But, negotiation will always be part of the equation for an astute businessman. The salary ranges shown in Table 30 take into consideration cost-of-living differences as documented from reliable government sources. Beware of free online cost-of-living calculators... the author has found many to be outdated, and they tend to overstate differences.

Perhaps a number two winemaker at a medium-to-large winery can satisfy your expectations. They are available at $60,000–75,000. A lot of puffery and blowing of smoke over capabilities and accomplishments may be expected. In general, no winemaker is too young to develop a large ego.

If you are located in a cool wine growing climate (less than 2,500 degree-days), you can expect a California-experienced winemaker to be learning about handling cool climate fruit on the crush pad and in the winery during the first year. Yes, there is a difference. For that matter, any winemaker who has just finished wine schooling will need to learn a lot more on the job, particularly about crushing and pressing operations. The author has employed proud owners of masters degrees in enology from the best schools, who had interned at famous California wineries during their program, but who didn't know how to set up or operate a simple plate-and-frame filter.

Alternatively, there are under qualified young aspirants looking for somewhere to get a toe-hold for $45,000–60,000. They may have taken some winemaking courses or have been a cellarmaster (i.e., "grunt") at a small-to-medium size winery. If the latter is your choice, it may be wise to employ a consulting winemaker part-time to oversee his/her work.

Of course, assistant winemakers can be recruited from small and medium size wineries in states other than California. Oregon and Washington are good places to start.

Other personnel and responsibilities

How many employees will be needed? That depends on what roles the winemaker and owner are qualified for and expect to play. So many variables exist, such as what the organization is trying to do and the abilities of the people

Table 30	**"Typical" Lead Winemaker Salaries - 2014**		
Area	*Salary Range*	*Area*	*Salary Range*
Columbia River, WA	105,700-116,800	Shawnee Hills, IL	70,200-77,600
N. Willamette Valley, OR	91,500-101,100	Leelanau Peninsula, MI	78,200-86,500
Southern Oregon	78,700-86,900	Ohio River Valley, IL-WV	87,800-97,000
Snake River Valley, ID	75,600-83,600	Lake Erie Shores, OH-NY	85,800-94,800
Sonoma Valley, CA	93,300-103,100	Finger Lakes, NY	64,700-71,500
Central Coast, CA	104,400-115,400	Lancaster Valley, PA	93,200-101,900
Southeastern Arizona	80,800-89,300	SE New England Coast	94,100-104,000
Grand Valley, CO	78,900-87,200	Piedmont Plateau, MD	110,800-122,500
Texas Hill Country	99,600-110,100	Blue Ridge, VA	99,600-110,100
Central Missouri	64,700-71,500	Yadkin Valley, NC	84,300-93,200

Notes: 1. "Lead Winemaker" is defined as top winemaking decision-maker with enology degree.
2. Consumer Price Index for All Urban Consumers taken into consideration.
Sources: LAMY Winery Consultants; U.S. Bureau of Labor Statistics; 2014.

Table 31	**Staffing**				
Function	*Winemaking*	*Vineyard Management*	*Marketing*	*Regulatory Recordkeeping & Reporting*	*Overall Management*
Winery Size (in gallons):					
Up to 6,000	winemaker/owner			winemaker/owner	
6,000-15,000	winemaker	winemaker/owner		winemaker/owner	
15,000-30,000	winemaker + 1	vyd.mgr./owner	sales mgr./brokers	winemaker/owner	
30,000-75,000	winemaker + 1	vineyard mgr.	sales mgr./brokers	winemkr/acc'tant	owner/gen.mgr.
75,000-125,000	winemaker +2	vyd.mgr. +1	sales mgr. +1	winemkr/acc'tant	owner/gen.mgr.

Notes: 1. Slash ( ) means "and/or"
2. Assignment of duties depends on qualifications of people involved.
3. Supervisory personnel does not include labor-level workers.

Source: LAMY Winery Consultants; 2014.

involved, that it is possible only to offer a very generalized staffing plan (see Table 31) and to suggest how it may change with winery size.

Constituents of the grape

There is no more amazing fruit in all of the world than the grape. It comes in a variety of colors, and develops into a wide array of flavors and aromas as wine. As a food product, its consumption also provides a number of health benefits. And, whole cultures have been built around it.

Water makes up 70–80 percent, by weight, of the grape's juice (see Figure 46).

The sugars–glucose, fructose and pentoses comprise 15–25 percent (150–250 g/L). They are carbohydrates. Glucose and fructose are the fermentable

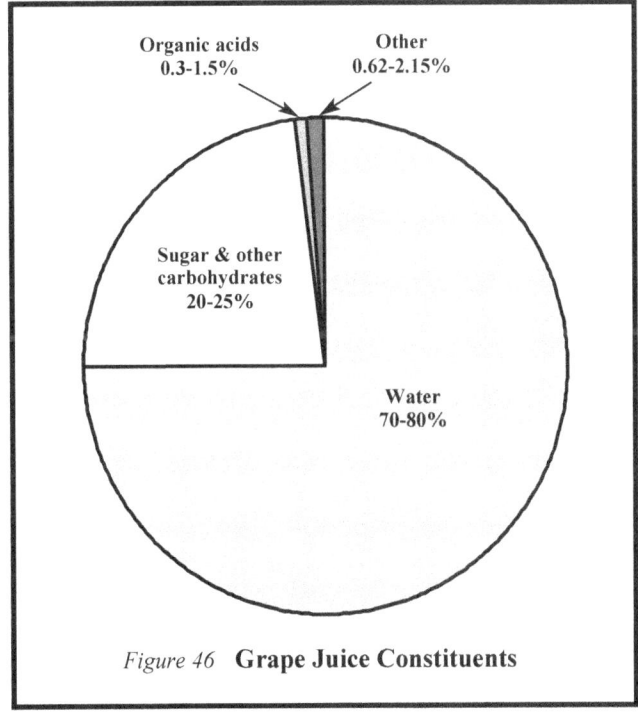

Figure 46 **Grape Juice Constituents**

sugars that are converted to ethyl alcohol (ethanol) by yeast-secreted enzymes. Pentoses are not fermentable, and they remain in the wine, usually at 0.2–0.4 percent by weight of the finished wine.

The sugars typically range from 16° to 25°Brix (equal to 16–25 percent by weight). Varieties differ in regard to the sugar content at full biological ripeness, with *Vitis vinifera* varieties toward the upper end of the range, and some French-American hybrids near the lower.

Further, grapes will be biologically ripe at a lower sugar content and higher acidity in cooler years than in warmer vintages. Hang time on the vine counts for something. Remember how photosynthesis depends on both ambient temperature and solar radiation received by the vine canopy? On cool, clear days, the sunlight keeps marching on. Even on overcast days, as much as 35 percent of the solar energy gets through.

Acceptable wine can be made from White Riesling grapes as low as 15°Brix, and wines from Germany's Mosel region frequently are made from 16–19°Brix grapes.

For sparkling wine production, sugar levels of 18°–18.5°Brix for Chardonnay and 19°–19.5°Brix for Pinot Noir are desired, because additional sugar will be added (the *dosage*) for the second fermentation in the bottle. In the Champagne Region of France, the grapes actually have some mature flavors at these lower sugars because of the cooler climate.

Usually, white grapes for still table wines will be harvested at 21°–23°Brix, the more aromatic varieties in the lower end of that range, Chardonnay closer to the upper end.

Red wine grapes tend to be picked relatively at high sugars, with Pinot Noir typically at 21.5°–23°Brix; Cabernet Sauvignon and its Bordeaux relatives at 22.5°–23.5°Brix; and Syrah, Nebiolo and Zinfandel at 23°–25°Brix. These are ranges that are characteristic of their respective growing areas, and the best ripeness level may vary elsewhere depending on local microclimate and topographical features.

Pectins and inositol, which are also carbohydrates, are each 0.1–1.0 percent (1–10 g/L).

Without making this into a dissertation, let's explore what happens during fermentation. What follows is abbreviated for understanding by the widest possible audience of new winery developers. Anyone who contemplates becoming a hands-on winemaker should acquire a much more detailed knowledge of the subject. It may be accomplished by taking a winemaking short course at UC-Davis or other qualified colleges, and reading authoritative texts like *Table Wines* by Amerine and Joslyn and *Knowing and Making Wine* by Peynaud. Valuable though they are, even those books are somewhat out of date (*Knowing and Making Wine* was published in 1984 and *Table Wines* in 1970). If you wish to spend a bit of money, you can invest in a more contemporary text, examples of which can be found denoted by asterisks in the bibliography of this chapter. To keep up with the rapidly-evolving science and art of enology, it is important to read *Practical Winery and Vineyard* and *Wine Business Monthly* regularly, and avail yourself of seminars and other current sources of winemaking information.

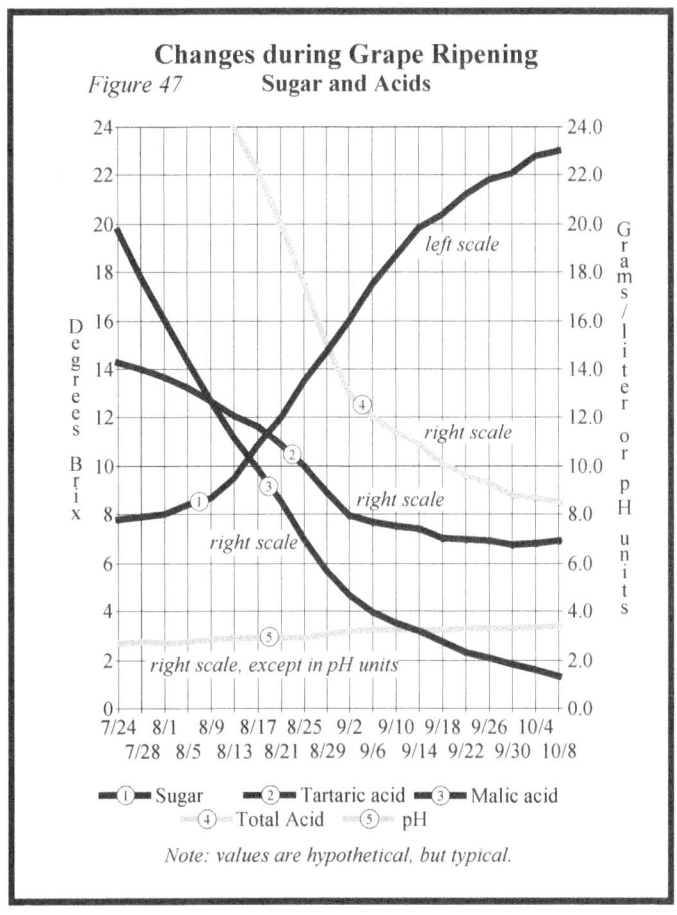

Changes during Grape Ripening

Figure 47   **Sugar and Acids**

Note: values are hypothetical, but typical.

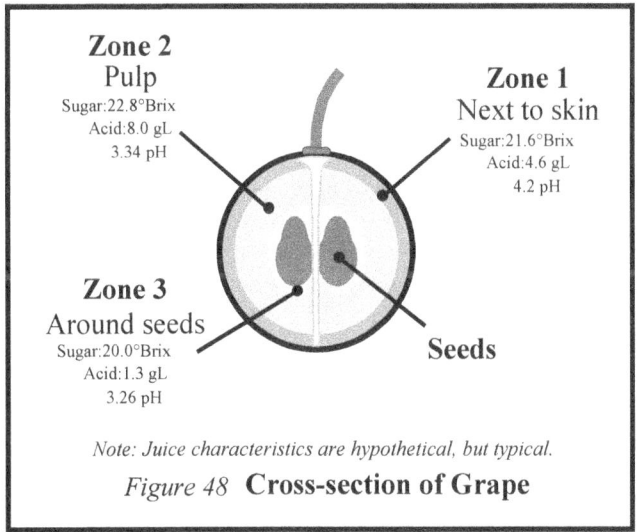

Zone 2
Pulp
Sugar:22.8°Brix
Acid:8.0 gL
3.34 pH

Zone 1
Next to skin
Sugar:21.6°Brix
Acid:4.6 gL
4.2 pH

Zone 3
Around seeds
Sugar:20.0°Brix
Acid:1.3 gL
3.26 pH

Seeds

Note: Juice characteristics are hypothetical, but typical.

Figure 48 **Cross-section of Grape**

This book is not intended to be a substitute for the books mentioned above, but to supplement them in practical issues, especially for those who plan to start a vineyard or winery.

Three kinds of fermentation are of interest to winemakers:

- **Yeast fermentation**—the process of converting sugar to CO_2 and alcohol. Yeast can be provided by selected laboratory-bred cultures or the wild yeast that comes from the vineyard on the grape skins' waxy bloom.

- **Malolactic fermentation**—a secondary fermentation carried out by bacteria in some wines, that converts malic acid to lactic acid and CO_2. This process is applied to almost all red wines, and to some white wines, particularly Chardonnay. Some winemakers in Champagne use the method to reduce acidity in a cool growing season. Some wineries rely on bacteria that reside on winery equipment, barrels, and walls and ceilings. Most, however, inoculate the wine with cultures propagated in a laboratory. The inoculation may be done early in the yeast fermentation or, a safer method, after yeast fermentation is complete.

- **Carbonic maceration** (or *macération carbonique*)—an intercellular fermentation caused by enzymes when the grapes are in an anaerobic environment (no oxygen). It produces an array of lesser acids and some ethyl alcohol by the reduction of both tartaric acid and malic acid, and CO_2. The reaction is caused by creating an oxygen-void environment (by a small yeast fermentation in the bottom of a tank filled with whole clusters, which drives off the oxygen) and sealing the tank with a relief valve to allow exhaust of the CO_2 generated. This method is used universally in Beaujolais, and to a lesser extent in other wine regions. For its softening effect on wine taste, carbonic maceration can also be implemented initially on a red wine. Whole clusters are blanketed with CO_2 to create the anaerobic environment for five to seven days. Then, the grapes are destemmed and crushed, and yeast fermentation is carried out as with a normal red wine (by inoculation with a yeast culture).

Some other secondary fermentations can occur under certain conditions, such as the reduction of alcohol to vinegar by *acetobacter ascendens* and the bacterial reduction of tartrates to volatile acidity (tourne disease), but winemakers seek to avoid them because they seriously degrade wine quality.

Inasmuch as a number of processes are occurring simultaneously, they need to be viewed together for their effects on the finished wine's composition. Table 32 steps through fermentation to illustrate this point.[1] An ideal juice composition is assumed for Pinot Noir grown in Oregon's northwest Willamette Valley.

Density of materials in juice and wine

This is a good time to explore the densities of water, sugar, acids and alcohol that are central to the winemaking process.

Water makes up most of the volume in juice and wine. In winemaking, and chemistry in general, water is used as the standard to which the densities of most other materials are expressed. The density of water varies with temperature. We all know that ice at 32°F is less dense than liquid water at 32°F. The standard of 1.0 grams per cubic centimeter (133.523 oz/gal) is the density of

---

1. Calculations for Table 32 and all of the other fermentations illustrated in this chapter were made using Wineplanner II Computer Model developed by LAMY Winery Consultants.

TABLE 32   Fermentation Changes, Ideal Pinot Noir—NW Willamette Valley, Oregon

Juice: Sugar: 22.6°Brix | TA: 8.4 g/L | pH: 3.33

Acid distribution: % Tartaric 54.0 | % Malic 44.0 | % Citric 2.0

Volume/weight: Juice (gal.): 1,000.0 | Gallons/ton: 168.50 | Tons: 5.93

Wine targets: Sugar: 0.4% wt. | TA: 6.2 g/L | Alcohol: 12.5% vol.

	Water	Sugar	Tartaric Acid	Malic Acid	Citric Acid	Lactic Acid	Total Acid	Alcohol	Other Constituents	Total
Juice:										
Density, oz/gal	133.284	211.796	235.003	214.840	222.318	160.229	225.878	—	176.280	146.283
% by weight	75.03%	22.60%	0.41	0.34%	0.02	0.00%	0.777%	0.00%	1.60%	100.00%
Gallons	823.51	156.09	2.58	2.30	0.10	0.00	4.96	0.00	13.28	1,000.00
% volume	82.35%	15.61%	0.26%	0.23%	0.01%	0.00%	0.50%	0.00%	1.33%	100.00%
Ounces	**109,761.3**	**33,060.0**	**605.6**	**493.5**	**22.4**	**0.0**	**1,121.5**	**0.0**	**2,340.5**	**146,283.4**
Additions:										
Chaptalization		0.0								0.0
Acid adjustment			0.0	0.0	0.0	0.0	0.0			0.0
Must before ferm	**109,761.3**	**33,060.0**	**605.6**	**493.5**	**22.4**	**0.0**	**1,121.5**	**0.0**	**2,340.5**	**146,283.4**
Changes in fermentation:										
Alcohol conversion		(32,621.2)				66.1	66.1	13,896.6	2,588.6	(16,069.8)
Acid			(27.3)	(138.2)	(1.0)	(0.0)	(166.4)	0.0	237.1	70.7
Evaporation	(19,757.0)		(109.0)	(88.8)	(4.0)		(201.9)	(3,376.9)		(23,335.8)
Extractions from solids									58.6	58.6
Loss of proteins									(0.7)	(0.7)
Must after ferm	**90,004.3**	**438.9**	**469.3**	**266.5**	**17.4**	**66.1**	**819.3**	**10,519.7**	**5,224.2**	**107,006.4**
Malolactic ferment				(266.5)		133.2	(133.2)			(133.2)
Detartration			(23.5)				(23.5)			(23.5)
Acid addition						0.0	0.0			0.0
Residual sugar addition	0.0	0.0								0.0
Finished wine, oz.	**90,004.3**	**438.9**	**445.9**	**0.0**	**17.4**	**199.4**	**662.6**	**10,519.7**	**5,224.2**	**106,849.7**
% by weight	84.23%	0.41%	0.42%	0.00%	0.02%	0.19%	0.62%	9.85%	4.89%	100.00%
Gallons	656.45	2.07	1.90	0.00	0.00	1.24	3.22	100.23	42.34	804.31
% by volume	81.62%	0.26%	0.24%	0.00%	0.01%	0.15%	0.40%	12.46%	5.26%	100.00%
Titratable acidity, g/L							6.17 g/L			

water when it is at its most dense state, which is at 4°C. However, our calculations for juice and wine apply to something closer to room temperature in the winery. Therefore, for grape juice, we will use the density of water at 20°C (68°F), which is 0.998203 g/cc. This equals to 133.284 ounces per U.S. gallon.

When water and ethanol are present together, however, their densities do not behave as when they are separate. The molecules nest together in a way that increases the densities of both. For calculation of wine composition, the two are calculated together, then separated after the combined volume is determined (see Figure 49).

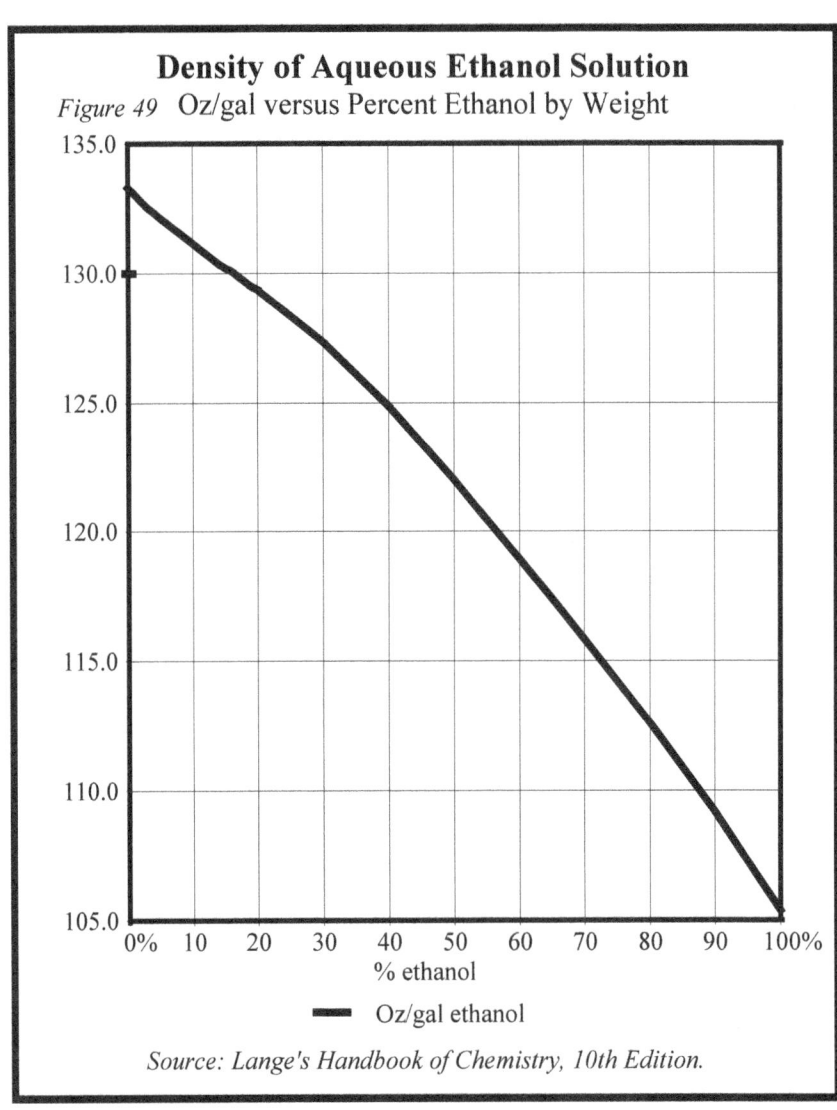

Density of Aqueous Ethanol Solution

Figure 49 Oz/gal versus Percent Ethanol by Weight

% ethanol

Oz/gal ethanol

Source: Lange's Handbook of Chemistry, 10th Edition.

Two equations were developed to approximate the density of the solution and percentage of ethanol by volume[2] (in the range of 10.0–15.0% ethanol by volume):

$$\frac{\text{Density of water}}{\text{Ethanol solution, in oz/gal}} = 131.087 + 0.177935 \left(\text{ethanol \% by weight} - 10.0 \right)$$

$$\frac{\text{Ethanol's percent of water}}{\text{Ethanol solution, in percent/volume}} = \left(\text{ethanol \% of solution by weight} * 1.48 \right) \left(-\frac{1}{4.549} \right)^{1.128}$$

Sugar is a substance of many densities. Pure sucrose has a density of 1.586.2 kg/m². Bulk white sugar is reported to be 880 kg/m², while bagged sugar is 700 kg/m.[3] Granulated sugar is rated at 849 kg/m.[4] These last three figures must apply to the whole volume occupied by crystalline sugar and air space.

To resolve the confusion, TTB requires in *CFR 24.181 Use of sugar*: "The quantity of sugar used will be determined either by measuring the increase in volume or by considering that each 13.5 pounds of pure dry sugar results in a volumetric increase of one gallon." Sugar is defined in *CFR 24.10* as "pure dry sugar, liquid sugar, and invert sugar syrup."

Those figures are converted to oz/gal, which is commonly used by winemakers, as follows:

	kg/m	oz/gal
Sucrose	1,586.2	211.796
Bulk white sugar	880.0	117.501
Bagged white sugar	700.0	93.467
Granulated sugar	849.0	113.362
TTB Standard	—	216.000

The density for pure sucrose used in our calculations is 211.796 oz/gal.

Densities of the acids are assumed to be as follows. (In addition, an estimated weighted average density for other substances in wine extracted from solids is also provided.)

	g/c³	oz/gal
Tartaric acid	1.760	235.003
Malic acid	1.609	214.840
Citric acid	1.665	222.318
Lactic acid	1.200	160.229
Other extracts from solids	—	176.280

---

2. Data on aqueous ethanol solutions from Lange's *Handbook of Chemistry*, 10th Edition; and Wikipedia.
3. Sugartech Co.
4. Simetric Co., UK.

Yeast fermentation

Many reactions and conversions occur during fermentation. The dominant one is conducted by yeast enzymes. The fermentation process is not performed by the yeast cells themselves, but by enzymes secreted by those yeast cells.

Alcohol conversion

In an ideal world, yeast fermentation of glucose to ethyl alcohol and CO_2 would be a simple one-step process. This is not a perfect world. The process of sugar's conversion is extremely complex. Amerine and Joslyn illustrate the conversion as a twelve-stage process (Figure 50).[5] At each stage, an intermediate compound is formed before it, in turn, is taken through the next step by another enzyme.

Along the way, some of the intermediate compounds can fail to be fully converted, but are left in the wine to contribute to complexity or cause problems. Acetaldehyde is one of them.

During fermentation, some of the alcohol is metabolized or boiled off with the CO_2. Additionally, some sugar, pentoses and heptoses (with five or six carbon atoms per molecule, respectively) do not ferment but remain in the wine. Their content is typically 0.2–0.4 percent by weight, and these levels are not taste-detectable by most people.

Other compounds resulting from yeast fermentation include: glycerin (as much as 2.2 percent of sucrose); acetaldehyde (trace); acetic acid (~0.3–0.5 percent of sucrose); and esters, the carbohydrates that give the wine its characteristic aromas and flavors (~1.7–3.6 g/L). Very small amounts of lactic acid, succinic acid and higher alcohols are also produced.[6]

Therefore, conversion is not 100 percent efficient, and the conversion rate varies with temperature. A typical alcohol conversion rate for an ideal, tightly controlled fermentation, is 47.4 percent. That is, 1,000 grams of sugar will result in 474 grams of alcohol by weight. The conversion rate can be lower for higher temperatures, and slightly higher for cold fermentations. Further, vigorous fermentation in an open-topped container will boil off a considerable amount of alcohol with the CO_2. It can drop the conversion rate to something like 45.0 percent.

Changes in acids

Three organic acids dominate grape juice. Citric acid is typically low, around 2–3 percent by weight. The White Riesling family (including Ehrenfelzer, Scheurebe, and Müller-Thurgau) have slightly more. The rest is tartaric acid and malic acid—divided about equally, though in some varieties as skewed as 60:40 between former and latter. Tartaric acid is unique to grapes; no other fruit produces it. Malic acid is the acid of apples. Citric acid is produced in citrus fruit.

> **Note:** *Be aware that **all juice and wine acids are expressed as tartaric acid equivalents in America**. In Europe, they are expressed as* sulfuric

---

5. Table Wines. See Further Reading section at end of Chapter.

6. Amerine and Joslyn, 349.

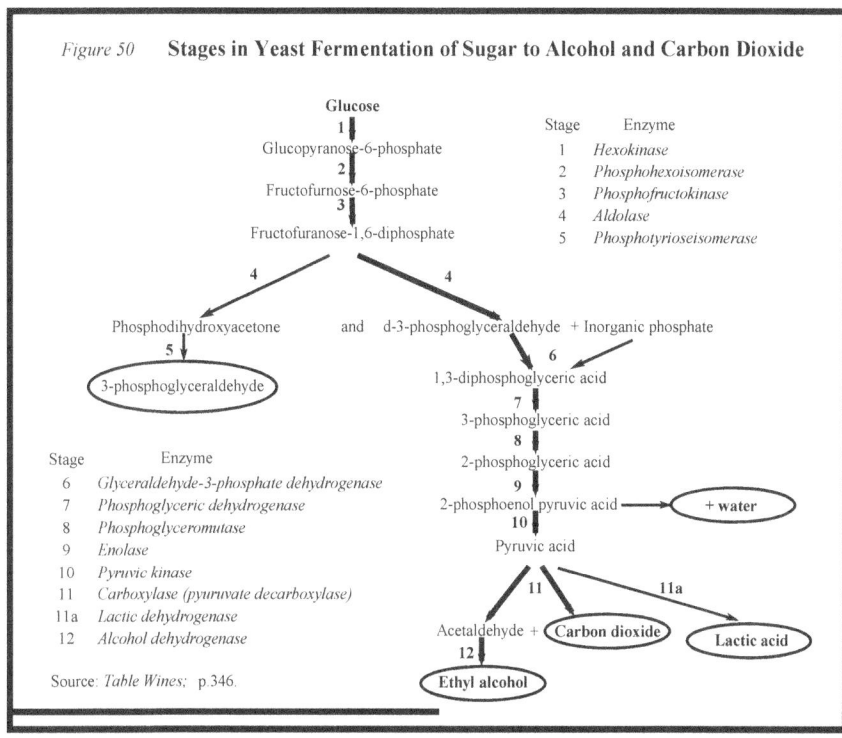

Figure 50   **Stages in Yeast Fermentation of Sugar to Alcohol and Carbon Dioxide**

acid. *So, when you see acid figures stated in Peynaud's text, for example, you will have to convert them to tartaric equivalents by multiplying by 1.53.*

During fermentation approximately ten percent of the acids are lost due to metabolism, detartration or destruction. Some potassium bitartrate is formed near the inside of the tank walls where the cooling jackets reduce the temperature. Potassium bitartrate's solubility varies directly with temperature: must at higher temperature holds more in solution, while at lower temperatures cause supersaturation (which induces some to precipitate). It either sticks to the tank walls or falls with the lees.

Organic acids are composed of large hydrocarbon chains, which is why they are called *carbohydrates*. Other constituents are also carbohydrates, including tannins and alcohols. At all stages of the wine—during fermentation and afterward in barrel and bottle—some of these chains break off and recombine with other unstable chains. Together, they form new compounds, including many of the esters that give the wine its characteristic flavors and aromas. Since much of this activity is part of the aging process after the wine is bottled, the aroma it adds is referred to as "bottle bouquet."

So, how do we estimate the titratable acidity of the finished wine? The calculation is complex, as illustrated in Table 33. Consider 1,000 gallons of Pinot Gris whose juice measures 7.0 grams/liter of titratable acidity (0.64 percent by weight) and is produced without a malolactic secondary fermentation. During fermentation, about 16–17 percent of that acid can be lost to various reactions. Then, cold stabilization will wring out as much as 10 percent more by detartration. The overall reduction in acid content is 24.3 percent in ounces. However,

TABLE 33   Fermentation Changes, Pinot Gris—NW Willamette Valley, Oregon

Juice: Sugar: 22.0°Brix | TA: 7.0 g/L | pH: 3.28

Acid distribution: % Tartaric 53.0 | % Malic 45.0 | % Citric 2.0

Volume/weight: Juice (gal.): 1,000.0 | Gallons/ton: 168.00 | Tons: 5.95

Wine targets: Sugar: 0.4.% wt. | TA: 6.4 g/L | Alcohol: 12.5% vol.

	Water	Sugar	Tartaric Acid	Malic Acid	Citric Acid	Lactic Acid	Total Acid	Alcohol	Other Constituents	Total
Juice:										
Density, oz/gal	133.284	211.796	235.003	214.840	222.318	160.229	226.684	105.351	176.280	145.957
% by weight	75.36%	22.00%	0.34%	0.29%	0.01%	0.00%	0.64%	0.00%	2.00%	100.00%
Gallons	825.25	151.61	2.11	1.96	0.08	0.00	4.14	0.00	16.56	1,000.0
% volume	82.51%	15.16%	0.21%	0.20%	0.01%	0.00%	0.41%	0.00%	1.66%	100.00%
Ounces	**109,992.5**	**32,110.5**	**495.3**	**420.6**	**18.7**	**0.0**	**934.6**	**0.0**	**2,919.1**	**145,956.7**
Additions:										
Chaptalization		0.0								0.0
Acid adjustment			0.0	0.0	0.0	0.0	0.0			0.0
Must before ferm	**109,992.5**	**32,110.5**	**495.3**	**420.6**	**18.7**	**0.0**	**934.6**	**0.0**	**2,919.1**	**145,956.7**
Changes in fermentation:										
Alcohol conversion		(31,672.6)				64.2	64.2	12,669.0	3,265.6	(15,673.7)
Acid conversions	(19,798.7)		(22.3)	(117.8)	(0.8)	0.0	(140.9)	0.0	230.2	89.3
Evaporation			(52.0)	(44.2)	(2.0)	0.0	(98.1)	(1,795.8)	(21,692.6)	(21,692.6)
Extractions from solids									39.0	39.0
Loss of proteins									(0.7)	(0.7)
Must after ferm	**90,193.9**	**437.9**	**421.0**	**258.6**	**15.9**	**64.2**	**789.4**	**10,873.2**	**6,453.3**	**108,718.0**
Malolactic ferment			0.0	0.0		0.0	0.0		0.0	0.0
Detartration			(52.6)				(52.6)		(52.6)	(52.6)
Lactic acid addition	0.0					0.0	0.0	0.0	0.0	0.0
Residual sugar addition		0.0								0.0
Finished wine, oz.	**90,193.9**	**437.9**	**368.4**	**258.6**	**15.9**	**64.2**	**707.1**	**10,873.2**	**6,453.3**	**108,665.4**
% by weight	83.00%	0.40%	0.34%	0.24%	0.01%	0.06%	0.65%	10.01%	5.94%	100.00%
Gallons	658.37	2.07	1.57	1.20	0.07	0.40	3.24	102.40	56.32	822.40
% by volume	80.06%	0.25%	0.19%	0.15%	0.01%	0.05%	0.39%	12.45%	6.85%	100.00%
Titratable acidity, g/L							6.44 g/L			

because of volumetric changes the decrease in titratable acidity (measured in g/L) is 8.0 percent.

	Tartaric Acid	Malic Acid	Citric Acid	Lactic Acid	Titratable Acidity	g/L	Gallons
Juice:							
Ounces	495.3	420.6	18.7	0.00	934.6	7.0	1,000.0
Finished wine:							
Ounces	368.4	258.6	15.9	64.2	707.1	6.44	822.4
Percent change	*−25.6%*	*−38.5%*	*−15.0%*	*Inf.*	*−24.3%*	*−8.0%*	*−17.8%*

Determination of titratable acidity

The procedure for measuring the titratable acidity of juice and wine is detailed in Appendix C.

On the other hand, let's calculate the acid loss for 1,000 gallons of Chardonnay, whose juice starts with 7.5 grams/liter total acidity and 22.6°Brix sugar (Table 34). Malolactic fermentation is conducted in the barrel. The tartaric:malic acid ratio of the juice is assumed at 58:40, with 2.0 percent citric acid. In addition to the 10 percent acid loss during yeast fermentation, the malolactic fermentation converts all (in this case) or most of the malic acid to lactic acid and CO_2. The overall reduction in ounces of acidity is 34.5 percent. However, if we take the volumetric effects of fermentation into consideration, the acidity of the finished wine is 5.51 grams per liter—a decrease of 26.5 percent.

	Tartaric Acid	Malic Acid	Citric Acid	Lactic Acid	Titratable Acidity	g/L	Gallons
Juice:							
Ounces	580.8	400.5	20.0	0.00	1,001.3	7.5	1,000.0
Finished wine:							
Ounces	446.9	0.0	17.1	191.5	655.5	5.51	891.43
Percent change	*−23.1%*	*−100.0%*	*−14.5%*	*Inf.*	*−34.5%*	*−26.5%*	*−10.9%*

Because the final titratable acidity is so low (5.51 g/L) this wine would be somewhat "flabby," and would benefit from addition of some tartaric acid before fermentation. With an addition of 0.7 g/L (or 93.5 ounces) the finished titratable acidity in this example would be 6.27 g/L.

Evaporation

Of course, there is some evaporation during fermentation. The amount lost varies with the fermentation procedures, equipment, temperature and vigor of fermentation. Small amounts of water and alcohol are evaporated during a cool fermentation (48–52ºF) in a closed tank (approximately 2–4 percent). It is unavoidable, as some of both are entrained in carbon dioxide vented to the outside.

TABLE 34   Changes with Malolactic Fermentation, Chardonnay—Willamette Valley, Oregon

Juice			Acid distribution			Volume/weight			Wine targets		
Sugar:	22.6°Brix		% Tartaric	58.0		Juice (gal.):	1,000.0		Sugar:	0.4% wt.	
TA:	7.5 g/L		% Malic	40.0		Gallons/ton:	168.50		TA:	6.4 g/L	
pH:	3.34		% Citric	2.0		Tons:	5.93		Alcohol:	13.1% vol.	

	Water	Sugar	Tartaric Acid	Malic Acid	Citric Acid	Lactic Acid	Total Acid	Alcohol	Other Constituents	Total
Juice:										
Density, oz/gal	133.284	211.796	235.003	214.840	222.318	160.229	227.894	105.351	176.280	146.492
% by weight	74.81%	23.00%	0.38%	0.20%	0.01%	0.00%	0.59%	0.00%	1.60%	100.00%
Gallons	822.21	159.08	2.36	1.37	0.08	0.00	3.81	0.00	13.30	1,000.0
% volume	82.22%	15.91%	0.24%	0.14%	0.01%	0.00%	0.38%	0.00%	1.33%	100.00%
Ounces	**110,086.3**	**33,060.0**	**580.8**	**400.5**	**20.0**	**0.0**	**1,001.3**	**0.0**	**2,135.7**	**146,283.4**
Additions:										
Chaptalization		0.0								0.0
Acid adjustment			0.0	0.0	0.0	0.0	0.0			0.0
Must before ferm	**110,086.3**	**33,060.0**	**580.8**	**400.5**	**20.0**	**0.0**	**1,001.3**	**0.0**	**2,135.7**	**146,283.4**
Changes in fermentation:										
Alcohol conversion	(10,958.7)	(32,621.2)						15,406.0	1,243.1	(15,906.0)
Acid conversions			(26.1)	(109.7)	(0.9)	66.1	(136.8)	(20.8)	(116.0)	(252.8)
Evaporation			(58.1)	(40.1)	(2.0)	0.0	(100.1)	(2,310.9)		(13,419.7)
Extractions from solids									39.1	39.1
Must after ferm	**99,077.6**	**438.9**	**496.6**	**250.7**	**17.1**	**66.1**	**830.5**	**13,073.4**	**3,301.2**	**116,743.3**
Malolactic ferment				(250.7)		125.4	(125.4)		(125.4)	
Detartration			(49.7)				(49.7)		(49.7)	
Lactic acid addition						0.0	0.0			
Residual sugar addition		0.0							0.0	
Finished wine, oz.	**99,077.6**	**438.9**	**446.9**	**0.0**	**17.1**	**191.5**	**655.5**	**13,074.3**	**3,301.2**	**116,568.3**
% by weight	85.00%	0.38%	0.38%	0.00%	0.01%	0.16%	0.56%	11.22%	2.83%	100.00%
Gallons	743.36	2.07	1.90	0.00	0.08	1.20	3.17	124.10	18.73	891.43
% by volume	83.39%	0.23%	0.21%	0.00%	0.01%	0.13%	0.36%	13.92%	2.10%	100.00%
Titratable acidity, g/L							**5.51 g/L**			

A Chardonnay, which may be fermented at a warmer temperature (60–65ºF) in a closed tank could lose 4–6 percent of its volume in tank, then another 4–8 percent in barrel aging. Losses in barrel will be greater for alcohol than for water, because the molecule size of water is smaller than that of alcohol, so water makes its way more easily through wood pores and between staves. That is why a wine can lose overall volume, but increase in alcohol percentage by volume while in barrel.

The warm, open fermentation of red wines induces an even larger volume loss by evaporation. Depending on temperature, punch-down or pumpover routine (and effervescing vigor allowed) evaporation losses can run 10 percent and even higher. And then, there still would be a considerable evaporation loss while in barrel for 10–24 months, depending on the humidity and temperature maintained in the barrel cellar.

Extractions from solids

Some constituents are extracted from grape solids during fermentation. Among them are esters, tannins (from the seeds and stems) and anthocyanins (from the skins). Almost all of the esters that make up the wine's flavors and aromas originate in the skins.

During a normal red wine fermentation, as much as 0.14–0.20 percent of the pulp solids may be extracted and remain in the finished wine. That amounts to approximately 0.035–0.05 percent of the total juice weight.

An extended fermentation of red wine extracts more from the skin and seeds. The extraction weight can run 0.05–0.08 percent of total juice weight.

Because white wines are not fermented "on the skin," the extraction is much smaller, but still occurs during pressing and from the small amount of grape debris remaining in the juice after settling. The amount may run 0.01–0.02 percent of the total juice volume.

Malolactic fermentation (MLF)

MLF is a bacterial fermentation, separate from the yeast fermentation. It is done mostly on red wines (Chardonnay is an exception) to reduce malic acid to the softer lactic acid and CO_2. MLF gives the wine the fat mouthfeel and buttery flavor that is appealing.

By removing nutrients necessary for bacterial spoilage, MLF also stabilizes the wine by removing nutrients that other bacteria need to ferment after bottling. MLF is carried out by a wide range of bacteria and each strain brings its own characteristics to the resulting wine. MLF can be conducted simultaneously with the yeast fermentation or after it. If inoculation is done at the start of the yeast fermentation, the bacteria will build to a preliminary population, then go dormant until the yeast fermentation begins winding down. Then, it will resume and go to completion.

There are three basic types of lactobacillus that are important to winemaking:

> *Oenococcus oeni*—one strain (also called Leuconostoc oenos)
>
> *Pediococcus*—four strains
>
> *Lactobacillus*—eleven primary strains (but there are more)

According to UC-Davis' Linda Bisson, only *Oenococcus oeni* is found in wines with a pH less than 3.5, while *Pediococcus* and *Lactobacillus* grow in wines over 3.5 pH. Sulfur dioxide inhibits MLF. If any SO_2 is added prior to fermentation, it will be gone by the end of fermentation. Further SO_2 additions must be delayed until after MLF is complete. The best temperature for MLF to thrive is in the range of 68–98°F. The low end of that range is preferred to avoid degradation of the wine.

Inoculation *after* the yeast fermentation is complete is the most common method. The reason is that lactobacillus can attack unfermented sugar and cause off-flavors and aromas.

Certain conditions favor development of a healthy MLF. First, the process requires nutrients and performs better while the wine is still on its lees. Then, there is the wine's pH. At a pH lower than 3.0, MLF is extremely unlikely to occur. At 3.0–3.2, MLF may not start or complete, at least with cool climate grapes. So, it may be necessary to adjust the wine's pH to 3.3 or higher if MLF is desired.

Several cultured bacterial strains are popular:

Strain number	Application	Source
Viniflora Oenos	red or white, low VA	Gusmer
Viniflora CH-35	fruity whites, low pH, high SO_2	Gusmer
Viniflora CH-16	reds, high alcohol, low VA	Gusmer
Viniflora CH-11	red or white, low temperature, low pH, high alcohol	Gusmer

Carbonic maceration

The French call it *macération carbonique* and it is always used on Beaujolais wines.

When whole grape berries are deprived of oxygen, an intercellular fermentation occurs which produces lactic acid, ethanol and carbon dioxide. The usual procedure is to fill a tank with whole clusters and seal it up except for a relief valve. The weight of the grapes crushes some at the bottom of the tank. Yeast fermentation starts spontaneously in the juice from the native yeast on the grapeskins. CO_2 production drives the air up and out, so intercellular fermentation can begin.

After eight to ten days, the grapes are sent to the destemmer-crusher and the resulting must is pumped to a tank—skins and all. Like a normal red wine, the yeast fermentation that is already underway, continues to completion.

The process metabolizes some of the malic acid, softens the wine's tannic edge, gives it a fat mouthfeel and imparts a taste dimension that distinguishes Beaujolais wines.

Fermentation management

Winemakers can manage key aspects of fermentation. Among these controllables are: yeast strain selection, preparation of yeast starters, addition of nutrients, acid and sugar adjustments, cap management, fermentation temperature, carbonic maceration, malolactic fermentation, seed removal and length of fermentation. We begin with skin contact issues.

Skin contact

Most white varieties will benefit from some skin contact time. This means the grapes are destemmed and crushed, then pumped to a tank for a brief period. If you have a leisurely period in crush pad activity and the grapes are cold, you can just leave them in the press with all the free-run juice still in the mass. Contact of the juice with the ruptured skins enables extraction of flavor and aroma constituents from the skins. The temperature should be cool (around 50°F) for this process. That will minimize the amount of tannins extracted, but allow the other extractions to occur.

Skin contact in tank means you will have to design some tanks specifically for the task. A cone-shaped bottom with a large-bore knife gate valve will expedite the transfer back to the press.

Cold soak

Cold soak is the red wine version of pre-fermentation skin contact. It requires a variable capacity tank. Over the past twenty years, cold soaking the must has become increasingly popular for some red wines, particularly for Pinot Noir. The method consists of preparing the must by destemming and crushing, then adding some whole clusters. The mass is treated with SO_2 (25 ppm of total SO_2 is mixed into the mass). Then, the top 3–4 inches are protected from invasion by bacteria by adding total SO_2 of 250–300 ppm for that top volume only. The must is blanketed with CO_2 to remove air. Then the tank is sealed, cooled to about 48°F and left to soak for four to eight days.

The process permits extraction of color pigments and fruity esters. Tannins, whose extraction is accelerated by heat and alcohol, are not extracted during this period. There are some who allege that wines processed by cold soaking all tend to taste alike. Others deny the claim. The practice, begun in Burgundy, just duplicates what Côte d'Or wineries used to experience naturally before the advent of winery heating.

What about the outrageously high level of sulfites in the upper 3–4 inches? Before inoculation, the must is punched down to mix it. For a must depth of 85 inches, the average total SO_2 content for the must is 37.9 ppm after mixing. At a must pH of 3.3, the free SO_2 content would be about 30 ppm.

The cold soak period can last four to eight days, depending on the condition of the grapes and the winemaker's stylistic preferences.

At the end of cold soak, the tank lid is removed and the contents are punched down to mix the high SO_2 layer at the top into the rest of the wine. The must is warmed to over 60°F and inoculated with the selected yeast starters. Warming can be accomplished by closing off the glycol inlet and outlet valves, thus isolating the tank from the refrigeration system. Then hot water can be run down the outside of the tank. The glycol/water solution in the cooling jacket works equally well as a heat transfer mechanism. However, this approach is not very energy efficient.

Alternatively, portable units are made that can be used for heating the coolant in the jacket. The tank is usually equipped for the task by installing "Y" adapters on both coolant inlet and outlet ports with shutoff valves on both sides of the "Y." That way, the heating unit can be connected and the coolant system disconnected from the tank. Some units can do either heating or cooling: a very attractive feature for small wineries.

Juice clarification

Pre-fermentation clarification procedures are performed only on white juice. The temperature is reduced to the low 50s Fahrenheit.

- For **Chardonnay** (and most other white grape varieties), typically no settling aid is used. The juice may be sufited to 25 ppm total SO_2 to kill off wild bacteria. If more SO_2 is added at this point, it will fix the harsh polyphenolics and they will stay in the wine. Otherwise the polyphenolics will degrade and disappear during fermentation.

    Settling should be adequate after 12–36 hours, depending on the variety and where it is grown. Germany's Geisenheim Institute has tested centrifuging versus settling and found that settling was superior. The objective is to reduce the suspended solids down to 2–3 percent by weight. This level adds some character to the wine: anything less would deprive yeast of nutrients.

    Some very large wineries employ vacuum separators to recover juice from the lees. Any operation like this should be blanketed from air to avoid excessive oxidation.

- For **White Riesling**, a settling aid has to be employed because of the presence of sticky pectins. It is best to add the enzyme *beta glucanase* which will break up the gummy pectins that interfere with settling, and would later plug up the filters at bottling. Then, bentonite should be added (at 2–3 lbs./1,000 gallons of wine) to remove some proteins along with grape solids, so the juice will be nitrogen-deficient. DAP needs to be added before fermentation.

Yeast selection

Selection of yeasts is also a complex subject. A detailed discussion of it certainly is beyond the scope of this book, except for several important considerations explored here.

Modern laboratories have isolated and commercially propagate a multitude of yeast strains. Some strains of yeast will work in most applications. But, specific yeast strains have special properties that may be used to advantage in commercial winemaking (Table 35).

Some strains have physical properties, or more appropriately, have *fermentation behavior characteristics* that are useful and/or produce unique attributes in the wine. The several examples presented in Table 34 are by no means the only selections available for each purpose.

Yeast strains that have been isolated from the yeast flora of specific European wine-producing areas and propagated commercially are called *cultured yeast*. Use of cultured strains enables the winemaker to achieve a predictable start, exercise tight control over fermentation and avoid the possible production of

TABLE 35   **Distinctive Yeast Properties**

Yeast strain	Desirable property
Assmanshausen (Lalvin AMH)	Accentuates spicy, peppery character in some red wines, particularly Pinot Noir and Zinfandel
Côte des Blancs (Epernay II)	Good all-purpose yeast for red and white wines
	Easy to stop fermentation before dryness by cooling must
Flor sherry	High alcohol tolerance
Pasteur Champagne	Persistent enough to carry fermentation to total dryness
	Good for restarting a stuck fermentation
Prise de Mousse (EC 1118)	Generates little foam, very useful in barrel fermentation
Steinberger (DGI 228)	Aromatic Germanic style White Rieslings, cold tolerant
VIN 13	Influences formation of certain aromatic fruit esters, yielding enhanced fruity aromas
	Good for restarting a stuck fermentation
58W3 (Vinquiry)	Enhances aromatic ester production
	From Alsace, it is beneficial to Pinot Gris and fruity, aromatic wines like Chenin Blanc, Gewürztraminer and White Riesling

off-odors and off-flavors owing to undesirable properties of some wild yeast strains.

Yeast that exists in the flora of a vineyard is *native*, or *wild yeast*. Traditionally, native yeast has been used by European winemakers producing the highest quality wines. Some American winemakers employ the practice. French winemakers feel that the use of native yeast allows wines to be produced that express the uniqueness and distinctiveness of the specific vineyard, or *climat*. Many yeast strains exist in the typical vineyard. Some have desirable properties and some do not. Some produce unpleasant aromas and flavors in wine. Some are unable to carry fermentation to conclusion because they have low alcohol tolerance.

Some yeast strains, called *killer yeast*, dominate fermentation. Most do it by monopolizing the nutrient supply, thus starving out the weaker strains. Undesirable strains that exist in the vineyard flora may be crowded out of fermentation by the laboratory cultures, enabling the stronger laboratory strains to take over.

Vineyards and growing areas that have existed for many years tend to have a desirable yeast flora because the wineries dispose of their pomace in the vineyard. It is loaded with the desirable yeast strains that survived fermentation and/or were not subjected to the government distiller (which would have killed them). A winery in a new growing area would be taking a big chance on jumping to native yeast methods before the source vineyard has had a chance to be "seeded" with desirable yeast strains.

Some winemaking practices recognize the challenges of working with yeast. In a *multiple-strain fermentation*, it is essential to inoculate the must in different locations, e.g., diametrically opposite sites, then allow the yeast populations to grow separately at first. There is no need to stir the must after inoculation. The strains eventually will be mixed together by the effervescing action of fermentation and by punching down if it's a red wine. This method allows all yeast strains to build a large cell count before mixing, thus enhancing the probability that all of them will survive to the end.

Truncated inoculation is another fermentation strategy. Say, for example, that the yeast strain first inoculated is selected for its ability to enhance fruitiness, but that strain is a weak finisher. Here is a more specific example: Côtes des Blancs (Epernay II) enhances fruitiness, but has a habit of not finishing to dryness in Pinot Gris. The must can be "swamped" with a sure-finisher like Pasteur Champagne at, say, a hydrometer reading of 1.015–1.020. Then, the Pasteur will take over and finish the fermentation to dryness.

Or, use the 58W3 strain.

Yeast starters

Many California winemakers prefer to inoculate the must by seeding it with freeze-dried granules of the selected yeast strain. That practice uses a large quantity of dried yeast.

The traditional method utilizes a winery-made starter culture. This method starts with some of the same freeze-dried granules (about one cup), rehydrated in perhaps a quart of warm water (100–104°F: temperatures over 105°F will kill the yeast). Then, the volume is doubled by adding a like volume of diluted apple juice or fresh grape juice and allowing that to reach vigorous fermentation. Finally, the volume is successively doubled up in steps, each time waiting until vigorous fermentation is reached before the next doubling. A starter volume of about 5–10 gallons is usually enough to inoculate a batch of 2,500 gallons.

Because you'll want to develop the starter before you've pressed the grapes on which it will be used, you'll have to use the apple juice, or fresh grape juice from another batch of white wine you've already pressed. The reason for diluting frozen apple juice (2:1 water to juice concentrate) is to reduce the concentration of its preservatives to a level that won't prevent the yeast from propagating.

Keep the unused dried yeast in its original bag, taped shut and refrigerated. That will keep the yeast viable for at least the needs of one season.

Nutrients

Grapes that are dead-ripe are probably deficient in nitrogen. So, also, are grapes infected with *botrytis cinerea*—the mold that is beneficial to most late harvest wines. Yeasts absolutely require adequate nitrogen and other nutrients to propagate and carry out a problem-free fermentation. Otherwise, the yeast cells will break down proteins in order to obtain nitrogen. Protein molecules contain a sulfur atom, which would be released to form hydrogen sulfide.

The most basic of nutrients is DAP, diamonium phosphate, $(NH_4)_2HPO_4$. It is basically a phosphate salt of ammonia, NH_3, in a crystalline form. This granular product is dissolved in water before adding it to the wine. Federal regulations permit addition to a maximum of 20 grams of N (nitrogen) per hectoliter. Nitrogen accounts for 21.2 percent of DAP's total weight.[7]

Unless the juice is drastically deficient in nitrogen, 8 grams of N per hectoliter is a good place to start. More can be added later if necessary.

If bentonite has been added before fermentation to expedite juice extraction, it will reduce the must's nitrogen content significantly. See the section on "Fining" for more details.

One of the consequences of attempting a fermentation with inadequate nitrogen is the production of hydrogen sulfide, H_2S, which has a rotten-eggs odor. The presence of H_2S will be obvious throughout the winery by its odor, and it needs to be removed immediately with a dose of copper sulfate, $CuSO_4$, and the addition of DAP.

Federal regulations allow up to a maximum of 6 milligrams of copper per liter to be added for removal of H_2S. Because copper comprises 37.662 percent of the $CuSO_4$ molecule, the maximum amount of $CuSO_4$ that may be added is 15.93 mg/L. It would be prudent to add 30 percent of the maximum dose initially (4.8 mg/L), then repeat the dose if necessary. The amount of $CuSO_4$ that combines with H_2S precipitates out, but an excess of $CuSO_4$ will leave copper ions in the wine. By regulation, finished wine may contain no more than 0.5 mg/L of copper, so do not overtreat.

> **Warning!** *Do **not** combine DAP with an acid adjustment, if one is needed! The release of ammonia to the gaseous state is accelerated by high acidity (or low pH), and you will find yourself gagging seriously, or worse. Add the DAP solution separately.*

Some vitamins are also important for fermentation. Vitamin B1 (thiamine) can be provided by adding yeast "ghost cells," which are freeze-dried hulls of yeast cells. Pantothenic acid and biotin likewise are among yeast's needs. Some proprietary nutrient blends are available. It is always critical to add nutrients to yeast starter batches and to any other musts that are considered nutrient deficient. Many winemakers do it as a standard practice.

Other adjustments

Harvesting grapes that are perfectly balanced is not as common as one might think, based on the hype promoted by some wineries. Good winemakers are accustomed to tweaking such constituents as sugar, acids and even extract.

The best rule to follow is to make most necessary adjustments to the grape juice *before* beginning fermentation. The best wine will be made with a balanced must. Further, the yeast will perform better if the must pH is below 3.5. Fermenting with a pH higher than 3.5 is an invitation to development of unwanted microbial infections that bring foul aromas and off flavors.

---

7. The two nitrogen atoms are a molecular weight of 28, divided by the molecule's total molecular weight of 132.

Chaptalization

The addition of sugar to musts has a long history. The practice was conceived and first published by French chemist Comte Jean-Antoine Chaptal in 1800. It was intended to help wine producers in cool regions and cool vintages. The practice has been regulated in France since 1907, when producers in the better growing areas conducted violent protests to protect their market shares. Chaptalization in the poorer growing areas was actually making competitive wines. In America, the addition of sugar or concentrated juice of the same fruit, before or after fermentation, is limited, depending on the acidity of the juice.

The federal regulations that apply in America are stated in CFR 24.177–179. An effort is made to clarify them in Table 36. The author makes no representations as to the table's accuracy. The federal government must have a school where they send people from the IRS and TTB to learn how to write regulations in a convoluted style.

The calculation of sugar addition uses simple algebra. Assume that we have a Pinot Noir harvested in a cool year at 21.0°Brix. It is decided to raise the sugar content: to raise the sugar content to 23.0°Brix, 235.54 lbs of sugar is added.

Assumptions
S = sugar addition, in ounces
W = Initial weight of the juice before capitalization
Specific gravity of raw juice = 1.08858
Juice volume = 1,000 gallons
Target sugar content = 23°Brix

Calculation
W = 1,000 gallons × 1.08858 × 133.284 oz/gal
= 145,090.3 ounces
0.21W + S = 0.23(W + S)
= 0.23W + 0.23S
0.02W = 0.77S
S = 0.02W / 0.77
S = 3,768.6 ounces = 235.54 lbs.

To avoid retention of sugar in its crystalline state, sugar should be dissolved in a minimal amount of warm water prior to adding it to juice or wine.

Winemakers in Burgundy consider it best to make sugar additions in increments. The addition illustrated above, of 2°Brix, is best made in four 0.5°Brix installments, each one when the hydrometer reaches 1.010–1.020. The advantage in doing it this way is that it avoids a sudden increase in temperature, avoids a "stuck" fermentation and lengthens the fermentation period (which enables greater extraction from the skins).

In the production of high alcohol wines—like port and sherry—the installment approach is needed as well as using a yeast strain of high alcohol tolerance (i.e., Madeira). The sugar is added in as many as ten stages, each one when the hydrometer reaches 1.005. This procedure avoids a stuck fermentation,

TABLE 36   Addition of Sugar and Concentrate, Federal Regulations

All Natural Wines

	Chaptalization 27CFR 24.177	Amelioration 27CFR 24.178	Sweetening 27CFR 24.179
Added when?	Before ferment	Before, during, or after ferment	After ferment
Materials	Dry sugar or concentrated grape juice from same kind of fruit	Water, sugar, or both	Sugar, juice, or concentrated juice
Limitation	May not increase density of juice to more than 25°Brix	Fixed acid must exceed 5.0 g/L as tartaric before & after amelioration	

All Natural Wines

If starting fixed acid exceeds 7.69 g/L:	Maximum of 538.4 gallons may be added per 1,000 gallons of wine or juice
	Solids of sweetened wine may not exceed 21% by weight
If natural fixed acid exceeds 12.5 g/L:	1,500 gallons per 1,000 gallons of wine (60% of ameliorated juice volume)

Grape Wine

If alcohol is not more than 14% by volume	Maximum of 21% solids by weight
If alcohol exceeds 14% by volume	Maximum of 17% solids by weight

All Fruit Wines

	May not reduce fixed acid to less than 5.0 g/L
If fixed acid is below 7.69 g/L	Maximum of 538.4 gallons may be added per 1,000 gallons of wine or juice
If fixed acid is 7.69 g/L and 20 g/L	Addition may not exceed 35% of total volume
If fixed acid exceeds 20 g/L	Addition may not exceed 60% of total volume
If fixed acid exceeds 12.5 g/L	Maximum of 1,500 gallons may be added per 1,000 gallons of wine or juice
	Finished total solids content may net exceed 21.0% and alcohol content is no more than 14% by volume

Specially Sweetened Natural Wine	Finished wine must be between 17% and 35% total solids by weight and no more than 14% alcohol by volume

enabling achievement of a high alcohol content as much as 17–18 percent by volume.

La saignée

In French, the verb saigner means "to bleed." Some winemakers use la saignée (la **sahn'**-yay) to increase the intensity of red wines. Simply, the practice is to draw off a portion of the free-run juice after crushing, so as to increase the ratio between skin solids and juice volume. The amount varies with the variety and fruit ripeness, up to 10 percent of the juice. Usually, the drawn-off juice is processed as a blush or blanc wine.

A negative effect of bleeding off free-run juice is that some of the very best juice is removed while all of the poorest quality juice is retained. The result is an overall downgrade of juice quality. If you've tried your hand at making sparkling wine, you'll know what that means. With each successive squeeze of the press, the juice quality diminishes. When you get to the last of it, the press juice, its attributes are thin, harsh, acidic and tannic. That's the part that isn't included in the sparkling wine cuvée.

On the opposite side of the argument is that removal of some of the lowest-quality juice would require pressing some of the grapes before fermentation. To reduce juice volume 10 percent by removing only lowest-quality juice, you would have to press about 40 percent of the grapes prior to fermentation. That kind of rough handling of the grapes increases harshness and tannin content of the wine. In order to minimize harshness for Pinot Noir, and some other red grape wines, winemakers leave as many grapes uncrushed as possible.

So, while this procedure for removing lowest-quality juice might be considered heretical by some and rejected out of hand, it has shown some promise and probably deserves more exploration.

Amelioration

In order to reduce acidity, the federal regulations allow for the amelioration (dilution) of grape musts by addition of sugar and/or water to bring them into *balance*—whatever "balance" means in the context of the regulations. Although this practice is common to fruit and berry wines, it is not usually deemed desirable for varietal grape wines. Winemakers exert many efforts to maintain or increase the wine's intensity, and "dilution" is not in their vocabulary.

Sweetening after fermentation

Addition of sugar, juice, or concentrated juice *after* fermentation to sweeten the wine is called "sweetening." The resulting unfermented sugar content of the finished wine is called "residual sugar," expressed in percent by weight. If the addition is made with juice or concentrate, either one has to be of the same fruit as the wine being adjusted. For grapes, that means **grapes**, not necessarily of the same grape *variety*.

Stopping fermentation

Of course, residual sugar may be achieved by stopping fermentation prior to completion. Use of a yeast variety such as Côte des Blanc makes this feat possible by cooling to 48°F. Precision is most difficult to achieve with this method, because of *fermentation overrun*. Chilling may shut down the yeast cells quickly, but the enzymes that have already been secreted will continue to convert sugar to alcohol until those enzymes are exhausted. Anticipating the amount of such an overrun with any degree of precision is impossible.

Sweet reserve

Sweet reserve provides a more reliable degree of precision in hitting a desired sugar content than stopping fermentation. Simply, the method involves setting

TABLE 37   Fermentation Changes, Normal Fermentation of White Riesling

Juice			Acid distribution			Volume/weight			Wine targets		
Sugar:	21.0°Brix		% Tartaric	54.0		Juice (gal.):	1,000.0		Sugar:	0.4% wt.	
TA:	7.2 g/L		% Malic	42.0		Gallons/ton:	170.0		TA:	6.6 g/L	
pH:	3.30		% Citric	4.0		Tons:	5.88		Alcohol:	12.8% vol.	

	Water	Sugar	Tartaric Acid	Malic Acid	Citric Acid	Lactic Acid	Total Acid	Alcohol	Other Constituents	Total
Juice:										
Density, oz/gal	133.284	211.796	235.003	214.840	222.318	160.229	226.027	----	176.280	145.374
% by weight	75.34%	21.00%	0.36%	0.28%	0.03%	0.00%	0.66%	0.00%	3.00%	100.00%
Gallons	821.73	144.14	2.21	1.88	0.17	0.00	4.25	0.00	24.74	1,000.0
% volume	82.17%	14.41%	0.22%	0.19%	0.02%	0.00%	0.43%	0.00%	2.47%	100.00%
Ounces	**109,523.3**	**30,528.6**	**519.1**	**403.7**	**38.5**	**0.0**	**961.3**	**0.0**	**4,361.2**	**145,374.5**
Additions:										
Chaptalization		0.0								0.0
Acid adjustment			0.0	0.0	0.0	0.0	0.0			0.0
Must before ferm	**109,523.3**	**30,528.6**	**519.1**	**403.7**	**38.5**	**0.0**	**961.3**	**0.0**	**4,361.2**	**145,374.5**
Changes in fermentation:										
Alcohol conversion		(30,092.5)				61.1	61.1	11,709.3	3,724.5	(14,597.6)
Acid conversions			(23.4)	(113.0)	(1.7)	0.0	(138.1)	0.0	237.6	99.4
Evaporation	(19,714.2)		(41.5)	(32.3)	(3.1)	0.0	(76.9)	(1,264.6)		(21,055.7)
Extractions from solids									38.8	38.8
Loss of proteins									(0.7)	(0.7)
Must after ferm	**89,809.1**	**436.1**	**454.2**	**258.4**	**33.6**	**61.1**	**807.3**	**10,444.7**	**8,361.5**	**109,858.7**
Malolactic ferment				0.0		0.0	0.0		0.0	0.0
Detartration			(68.1)				(68.1)			(68.1)
Lactic acid addition						0.0	0.0			0.0
Residual sugar addition	0.0	0.0								0.0
Finished wine, oz.	**89,809.1**	**436.1**	**386.1**	**258.4**	**33.6**	**61.1**	**739.2**	**10,444.7**	**8,361.5**	**109,790.6**
% by weight	81.80%	0.40%	0.35%	0.24%	0.03%	0.06%	0.67%	9.51%	7.62%	100.00%
Gallons	658.01	2.06	1.64	1.20	0.15	0.38	3.38	96.63	72.97	833.05
% by volume	78.99%	0.25%	0.20%	0.14%	0.02%	0.05%	0.41%	11.60%	8.76%	100.00%
Titratable acidity, g/L							6.65 g/L			

aside and refrigerating a portion of the raw juice at pressing, then blending it with the main body of wine after the latter has been fermented to total dryness. (See Figure 51). The most prominent use of sweet reserve is in Germany.

The calculation follows for White Riesling juice that is 21.0°Brix and has 7.2 g/L of titratable acidity (Table 37). It is assumed that the unfermentable sugar content after fermentation will be 0.40 percent by weight, and the desired finished wine's residual sugar content is 2.5 percent by weight. Further, it is estimated (by calculation) that one gallon of juice ferments to 0.83305 gallon of unfinished wine in this example.

Assumptions:
Starting juice = 1,000 gallons @21.0°Brix
J = sweet reserve juice, gallons, @21.0°Brix
(1,000 − J) = volume of juice fermented
Volume of wine after ferment = 833.05 gallons
Weight of fermented wine = 109,790.6 ounces
Sugar of fermented wine = 0.040% by weight

Target:
Finished wine residual sugar = 2.5% by weight

Calculations:
$0.21 J + 0.004 (1 − J) = 0.025$
$0.21 J + 0.004 − 0.004 J = 0.025$
$0.206 J = 0.0210$
$J = 0.10194$
Volume of sweet reserve, J = 10.194% of finished wine @21.0°Brix
Volume of fermented wine, (1 − J) = 89.806% of finished wine @0.40% by weight sugar

But in this example, one gallon of juice yields 0.83305 gallon of wine, so the proportional volumes for producing 1,000 gallons of finished wine are:

	For 1,000 gals. starting juice	For 1,000 gals. finished wine	Percent of starting juice (gallons)
Juice volume	**1,000.0**	1,180.0	100.00
Sweet reserve volume	94.6	101.9	8.64
Finished wine volume	927.6	**1,000.0**	84.75

It is interesting to view the changes that occur as the juice ferments to wine, and then when the sweet reserve juice is added to it:

	Unfermented Juice	Fermented Wine	Finished Wine
Sugar, °Brix or % weight	21.00	0.40	2.50
Tartaric acid, % weight	0.36	0.35	0.35
Malic acid, % weight	0.28	0.24	0.24
Citric acid, % weight	0.03	0.03	0.03

Lactic acid, % weight	0.00	0.06	0.05
Total acidity: % weight	0.66	0.67	0.67
grams/liter	7.20	6.65	6.71
Alcohol, % volume	0.00	11.60	10.42
Specific gravity	1.0907	0.9888	0.9992
Density, oz/gallon	145.37	131.79	133.17

Cryoextraction

Cryoextraction is the concentration of juice by freezing. It affords a way to intensify taste and aroma-producing constituents. The natural process, freezing on the vine, is used to produce *Eisweins* in Germany, and *ice wines* in Michigan, New York and a few other states. But, industrial cryoextraction may also be employed to produce ice wines and sweet reserve concentrate for white wines.

A cold room can be partitioned off in the winery, a refrigeration-equipped shipping container can be acquired or a commercial cold storage warehouse serves the purpose as well. Whether freezing whole grape clusters or juice, it is necessary to drop the temperature to below 15°–16°F. Cold storage warehouses frequently have a zero-degree room, which will do the job. It is *not* advisable to use plastic bin liners or plastic bins for the purpose. The plastic becomes too brittle at the low temperatures and will probably shatter the next time some weight is put in the bins. It is better to use wood picking bins (4′ × 4′ × 4′), and line them with two thicknesses of clear heavy-duty vinyl sheet. Leave enough

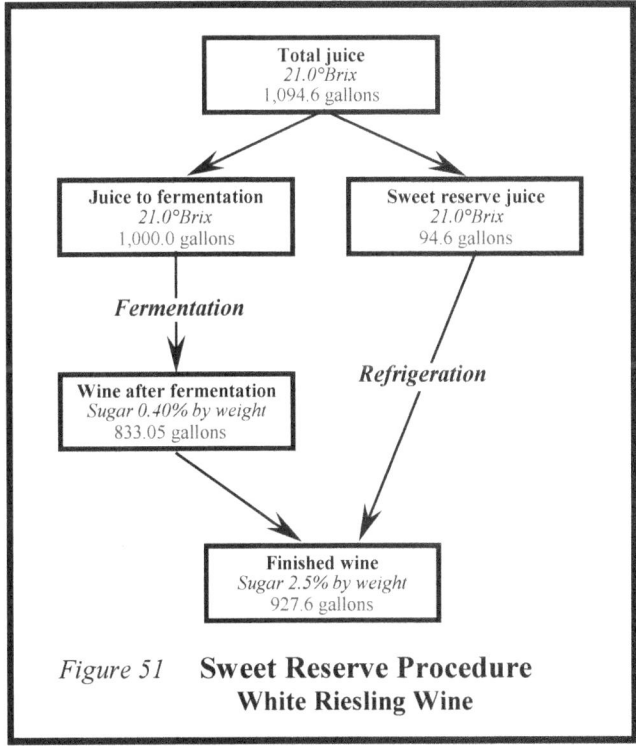

Figure 51 **Sweet Reserve Procedure**
White Riesling Wine

extra sheet material so the sheets can be folded over the top of the load and secured with duct tape.

If you've used a zero-degree room, you'll need to warm the mass up to 18°–19°F before pressing, or you won't get any liquid. The procedure is different for whole grapes versus juice, so we'll deal with whole grapes first.

Frozen whole grapes

For frozen whole grapes, load them into the press and begin pressing. Even membrane presses have been used for the task. Rolling the press cylinder will work to break up the mass and redistribute it for just so long. Eventually, the whole mass will be stuck together by ice. When that point is reached, it is best to rest the press for a while to allow warming, then press again without rotating. Keep vacuum operations to a minimum. There will be ice crystals in the air being sucked out of the press and it will put some wear on the compressor impellor.

The first juice can be extracted with a sugar content up to 70°Brix. It will push the hydrometer shuttle right out of the cylinder. The pressure applied to the mass of grapes puts some heat energy into it, so the temperature increases slowly. With each successive squeeze of the press, the sugar level will drop, as the temperature increase raises the melting point of the sugar-ice solution. If you collect juice until the sugar content of the latest extraction reaches about 30°Brix, you will end up with an overall concentrate content of 38–40°Brix. That's ideal for making ice wine. It can also be used for the sweet reserve addition to table wines and dessert wines.

One might think that freezing concentrates the acid content, the same as it does the sugar content. Wrong! There will be a massive detartration, both because the cold temperature decreases the solubility of potassium bitartrate in aqueous solution and ice crystals will encapsulate more of the acid. Experience indicates that grapes that have 7–8 g/L total acid at harvest will end up with 4–5 g/L total acidity after cryoextraction. Therefore, it is essential to measure the total acidity of juice promptly and adjust it upwards. For sweet reserve, an adjusted acidity of 7–8 g/L may be satisfactory. For ice wine, it will have to be closer to 10–11 g/L. Sulfiting is needed, too, as high as 80–100 ppm total SO_2 at this stage to protect the juice during storage and/or fermentation.

Frozen juice

A slightly different procedure is used for frozen grape juice. Freezing will drive the concentrated juice toward the center of the frozen mass. The basketball-size volume of syrup can be scooped out after chopping into the ice with an axe. The rest of the mass can then be broken up and loaded into the press, where it simply can be allowed to drip out as the mass warms. The drip period is ended at about 30°Brix with one hard press squeeze.

Juice settling is expedited by addition of *beta-glucanase* enzyme and 2–3 lbs. of bentonite per 1,000 gallons of juice.

Eiswein

Cryoextraction may also be used to produce *Eiswein*, or ice wine. We can't call it *Eiswein* in America by government agreement with Germany. According to German wine laws, the grapes have to be frozen on the vine, after being declared candidates for *Eiswein* in advance and after the local authority gives the green light to pick. Under those restrictions, a winery might be able to pick on one or two days before the grapes begin to rot with the daytime warming by the sun. Total annual production might run 150–200 gallons in an average of only four years per century. Rare wine, indeed!

This is not Germany. Using a cold storage warehouse, American wineries can produce a lot of ice wine (although German winemakers get upset about Americans deviating from their rules). Further, a controlled production method like cryoextraction enables achievement of very high quality consistently, taking some of the uniqueness out of the product.

The effects of botrytis are very becoming to all late harvest White Rieslings, even ice wine. It is possible to induce a strong botrytis infection in the vineyard. If botrytis occurs naturally in your growing area, all you have to do is avoid a botrytis-killing fungicide application at end of the growing season and maintain a high humidity level in the vineyard. That can be accomplished by running the air blast sprayers through the vineyard every 45–60 minutes during daylight hours and spraying clean water for three to four days (depending on the temperature profile). If botrytis isn't native to your area, it is possible to obtain a laboratory culture for seeding the vineyard.

It is also necessary to execute a strong bird control program: use canons and/or electronic devices to keep the birds away.

Within five to seven days, depending on temperature, there should be a relatively uniform botrytis infection throughout the treated area. It isn't necessary to spend all of that labor on cluster or berry selection. Everything is pretty good. Experience in Oregon's Willamette Valley indicates that the botrytis infection dominates and other late season molds (white, black and green) don't get started.

Harvest can commence at 25–26°Brix.

Use the same cryoextraction procedures as discussed above for sweet reserve.

A day's pressings of juice are accumulated in a tank. A 200-gallon plastic tank serves well. Each day's pressings are then adjusted to a total acidity of 10–11 g/L, and 80 ppm TSO_2 and bentonite are added. After settling overnight, the clear *supernatant* juice is racked off and added to the main batch that is already fermenting. DAP and yeast hulls are added, the amount appropriate for the new juice addition. The loose juice lees can be moved to smaller vessels for further separation.

Because the grapes are so ripe, they are nutrient deficient. Settling with bentonite has also removed some nitrogen-rich proteins. Add DAP and yeast hulls. You'll need to obtain the *Beerenauslese* yeast strain to cope with the high sugar content. Keep the fermentation around 52–55°F. It may take three to four months to complete. Daily inspection is necessary to detect any VA generation (most likely acetic acid). If detected take prompt corrective action with DAP and $CuSO_4$.

Acid reduction

If grapes are not fully ripe, it is necessary to adjust the total acidity downwards. Reduction is accomplished by treatment with *calcium carbonate*. And, it is best to use the *double-salt reduction* method. The procedure is to draw off a portion of the juice equal to the desired percentage acid reduction and remove *all* of the acid from it. For example, to reduce the total acidity of 1,000 gallons of juice from 9.0 g/L to 8.0 g/L, the acid reduction is 11.1 percent of the beginning 9.0 g/L. Therefore, draw off 11.1 percent of the juice and apply all of the necessary $CaCO_3$ to it.

	Total Acid	Gallons of Juice
Beginning total acidity	9.0 g/L	1,000
Target acidity	8.0 g/L	
Reduction:		
Amount	1.0 g/L	
Percent of total	**11.1%**	**111**
		(treated gallons)

The treated portion will turn gray and stink, but don't worry. Then, add the 111 treated gallons back to the main volume and mix it up.

Ahhh . . . it smells great again!

The reason for the convoluted procedure is that if you were to treat the whole volume, the $CaCO_3$ would attack the tartaric acid first, until it is almost gone. Then, it would move on to the malic acid, until all of the $CaCO_3$ has been precipitated out. The result would be an unbalanced must and wine with no tartaric acid. By taking all of the acid out of the proportional amount, 111 gallons, all three acids are removed. When combined with the main juice volume, the acids are present in the same proportions in which they existed in the raw juice. The amount of $CaCO_3$ needed for the above adjustment is calculated at 0.667 grams per liter of wine per gram of acid reduction.

$$= 1,000 \text{ gals. of wine} \times 3.784 \text{ liters/gal.}$$
$$\times 1.0 \text{ gms/liter reduction}$$
$$\times 0.667 \text{ gms } CaCO_3 \text{/liter}$$
$$= \textbf{2,523.9 grams (89.0 ounces)}$$

If an acid reduction is needed for the wine after fermentation, potassium bicarbonate, K_2CO_3, would be used instead of calcium carbonate $CaCO_3$. If $CaCO_3$ were used on a fermented wine, it would leave a significant amount of calcium in the wine that could cause an unwanted tartrate precipitation later in the bottle. The application rate is 0.9 grams of K_2CO_3 per liter for each 1.0 g/L acid reduction, instead of the 0.667 grams of $CaCO_3$ per liter.

TABLE 38   Fermentation Changes with Chaptalization, Severely Underripe White Riesling

Juice		Acid distribution		Volume/weight		Wine targets	
Sugar:	18.2°Brix	% Tartaric	50.0	Juice (gal):	1,000.0	Sugar:	0.4% wt.
TA:	13.3 g/L	% Malic	48.0	Gallons/ton:	165.0	TA:	6.4 g/L
pH:	3.05	% Citric	4.0	Tons:	6.06	Alcohol:	12.5% vol.

	Water	Sugar	Tartaric Acid	Malic Acid	Citric Acid	Lactic Acid	Total Acid	Alcohol	Other Constituents	Total
Juice:										
Density, oz/gal	133.284	211.796	235.003	214.840	222.318	160.229	226.684	—	176.280	145.398
% by weight	78.61%	18.15%	0.62%	0.59%	0.05%	0.00%	1.24%	0.00%	2.00%	100.00%
Gallons	845.77	122.89	3.78	3.97	0.32	0.00	7.74	0.00	16.27	1,000.0
% volume	84.58%	12.29%	0.38%	0.40%	0.03%	0.00%	0.77%	0.00%	1.63%	100.00%
Ounces	112,727.9	26,026.8	887.8	852.3	71.0	0.0	1,775.7	0.0	2,868.0	143,398.4
Additions:										
Chaptalization		333.8								333.8
Acid adjustment			(734.3)	0.0	0.0	0.0	(734.3)	0.0		(734.3)
Must before ferm	112,729.9	26,360.6	153.5	852.3	71.0	0.0	1,041.4	0.0	2,868.0	142,997.9
Changes in fermentation:										
Alcohol conversion		(25,924.9)				52.7	52.7	10,260.3	2,993.1	(12,618.8)
Acid conversions			(6.9)	(238.7)	(3.2)	0.0	(248.8)	37.8	341.1	54.5
Evaporation	(20,291.0)		(12.3)	(68.2)	(5.7)	0.0	(83.3)	(1,108.1)		(21,482.5)
Extractions from solids									38.3	38.3
Loss of proteins									(0.7)	(0.7)
Must after ferm	92,436.9	435.7	134.3	545.5	62.1	52.7	762.0	9,114.3	6,239.8	108,988.8
Malolactic ferment			0.0	0.0		0.0	0.0	0.0	0.0	0.0
Detartration			(13.4)				(13.4)			(13.4)
Lactic acid addition						0.0	0.0			0.0
Residual sugar addition		2,288.8								2,288.8
Finished wine, oz.	92,436.9	2,724.5	120.9	545.5	62.1	52.7	748.6	9,114.3	6,239.8	111,264.1
% by weight	83.08%	2.45%	0.11%	0.49%	0.06%	0.05%	0.70%	8.19%	5.61%	100.00%
Gallons	679.95	12.86	0.51	2.54	0.28	0.33	3.66	84.44	54.46	835.38
% by volume	81.39%	1.54%	0.06%	0.30%	0.03%	0.04%	0.44%	10.11%	6.52%	100.00%
Titratable acidity, g/L							6.71 g/L			

The effects on fermentation produced by reducing acidity are illustrated in Table 38, which depicts a White Riesling wine whose grapes were picked at a low sugar content.

Acid addition

Acidity may also be adjusted upwards. In the past, the addition of only tartaric acid was permitted. Now, it is permissible to use any of the acids that occur naturally in grapes. Tartaric acid and malic acid can be added before fermentation, but their addition may not increase the total acidity of the juice to more than 9 g/L. After fermentation, the wine's acidity can be adjusted by the addition of tartaric, malic, citric, lactic and fumaric acid, in any combination (provided the finished wine's total acidity does not exceed 9 g/L).

However, for late harvest wines whose total solids content after fermentation is more than 8 grams per 100 milliliters (8 percent by weight), any combination of those same five acids may be added, up to a total acidity of 11 g/L. The result is that winemakers can now *legally* restore the juice and wine to ideal acid distributions. For winemakers, it's almost like the monk taking off his hairshirt.

The calculations can be complicated. And, we are tempered in the following effort by Emile Peynaud's admonition to not bother trying to calculate fermentation with precision. That warning only serves to raise the curiosity of some who have spent years constructing mathematical models.

Table 39 details fermentation changes for a Pinot Noir juice that is very ripe and needs some upward acid adjustment.

Let's say we have 1,000 gallons of Pinot Noir juice that has 6.5 g/L of total acidity. If you put this juice through both yeast and ML fermentations, the finished wine's total acidity will be too low (about 5.3 g/L). That would be one flabby Pinot Noir!

Your experience tells you the ideal acid level for Pinot Noir grown in this climate will be produced if the grapes come in from the vineyard at 8.4 g/L total acidity. Your challenge is to adjust the acid so as to end up with about 6.2 g/L after fermentation.

It is decided to make the acid addition in equal parts of tartaric and malic acid. We can add the tartaric before yeast fermentation. That will drop the pH some and assist a problem-free fermentation. But, there's no point adding the malic acid before fermentation, because about ten percent of the addition will be lost during yeast fermentation and half of the rest of the addition will be converted to CO_2 during malolactic fermentation. So, the malic acid addition is made after both fermentations. Doing it then provides another element of control: you can measure the wine's acidity and make a more precise malic adjustment. The additions are 0.5 g/L of tartaric before yeast fermentation and 0.5 g/L of malic after MLF. The result, with wine acidity calculated at 6.26 g/L, should be a lively wine.

For wines not subjected to malolactic fermentation, the calculation is fairly simple. Let's say you have a Pinot Gris that is harvested at 6.5 g/L titratable acidity and you want to raise the pre-fermentation TA to 7.0 g/L. Simply add the

TABLE 39   Fermentation Changes, "Advanced Ripe" Pinot Noir—NW Willamette Valley, Oregon

Juice:		Acid distribution:		Volume/weight:		Wine targets:	
Sugar:	23.0°Brix	% Tartaric	64.0	Juice (gal):	1,000.0	Sugar:	0.4% wt.
TA:	6.5 g/L	% Malic	34.0	Gallons/ton:	168.5	TA:	6.4 g/L
pH:	3.45	% Citric	2.0	Tons:	5.93	Alcohol:	12.7% vol.

	Water	Sugar	Tartaric Acid	Malic Acid	Citric Acid	Lactic Acid	Total Acid	Alcohol	Other Constituents	Total
Juice:										
Density, oz/gal	133.284	211.796	235.003	214.840	222.318	160.229	227.894	105.351	176.280	146.492
% by weight	74.81%	23.00%	0.38%	0.20%	0.01%	0.00%	0.59%	0.00%	1.60%	100.00%
Gallons	822.21	159.08	2.36	1.37	0.08	0.00	3.81	0.00	13.30	1,000.0
% volume	82.22%	15.91%	0.24%	0.14%	0.01%	0.00%	0.38%	0.00%	1.33%	100.00%
Ounces	109,587.5	33,693.3	555.4	295.1	17.4	0.0	867.8	0.0	2,343.9	146,492.4
Additions:										
Chaptalization		0.0								0.0
Acid adjustment			66.8				66.8			66.8
Must before ferm	109,587.5	33,693.3	622.2	295.1	17.4	0.0	934.6	0.0	2,343.9	146,559.2
Changes in fermentation:										
Alcohol conversion		(33,253.8)						14,166.1	2,638.2	(16,382.1)
Acid conversions			(28.6)	(82.6)	(0.8)	67.4	67.4	0.0	182.5	71.1
Evaporation	(19,725.7)		(112.0)	(53.1)	(3.1)	0.0	(168.2)	(3,442.4)		(23,336.3)
Extractions from solids									58.7	58.7
Loss of proteins									(0.7)	(0.7)
Must after ferm	89,861.7	439.5	482.2	159.3	13.5	67.4	722.3	10,723.7	5,222.6	106,969.9
Malolactic ferment				(159.3)		79.7	(79.7)		(79.7)	(79.7)
Detartration			(24.1)				(24.1)		(24.1)	(24.1)
Lactic acid addition						53.8	53.8		53.8	53.8
Residual sugar addition		0.0								0.0
Finished wine, oz.	89,861.7	439.5	458.1	0.0	13.5	200.9	672.4	10,723.7	5,222.6	106,920.0
% by weight	84.05%	0.41%	0.43%	0.00%	0.01%	0.19%	0.63%	10.03%	4.88%	100.00%
Gallons	655.0	2.08	1.95	0.00	0.06	1.25	3.26	102.15	42.32	804.81
% by volume	81.39%	0.26%	0.24%	0.00%	0.01%	0.16%	0.41%	12.69%	5.26%	100.00%
Titratable acidity, g/L							6.26 g/L			

difference in weight—0.5 g/L of granular tartaric acid. Divide grams by 28.35 to convert to ounces, then multiply liters by 3.785 to convert to gallons.

Dessert wines

Wines with alcohol content of 14.0 percent or more by volume are classified as *dessert wines*. The two dessert wines most frequently encountered are port and sherry.

Port is made in Portugal. Red grapes are harvested at advanced ripeness, 26–28°Brix for example, crushed and fermented initially the same as table wines. When the alcohol content reaches about 8 percent by volume the must is swamped with ethanol to bring alcohol content to 16–18 percent by volume. This stops fermentation, leaving residual (unfermented) sugars. The wine is aged in barrel for a number of years—depending on the style desired, ruby or tawny. It is then bottle aged for an extended period.

Some very good port-style wines have been made in America. Widmer Winery (Finger Lakes, NY) has a rich history. Beringer Winery (St. Helena, CA) makes one from Cabernet Sauvignon. Kramer Winery and Shafer Vineyard Cellars in Oregon (near Forest Grove) have made them from Pinot Noir.

Sherry-style wines made in America are rare. The wine is fermented with *flor* yeast, a strain that causes the typical oxidized flavor. The wine is aged in a stack of barrels called a *solara* at relatively high temperature for many years. Wine to be bottled is removed from the bottom barrels, the rest of the older wine racked down a level, then the new wine is added to the top level.

Fruit & berry wines

Because federal regulations allow addition of substantial amounts of sugar, water and acid to fruit and berry wines, juice adjustments in the winery are far more complex than for grape wines. Here is the pertinent section of the ATTTB regulations:

> *Section 24.178. Ameleoration.*
> *. . . (b)(3) For all wine, except for wine described in paragraph (b)(4) of this section, the volume of ameliorating material added to juice or wine may not exceed 35 percent of the total volume of ameliorated juice or wine (calculated exclusive of pulp). Where the starting fixed acid level is or exceeds 7.69 grams per liter, a maximum of 538.4 gallons of ameliorating material may be added to each 1,000 gallons of wine or juice.*

What that means is that you can add sugar and water sufficient to make the raw juice equal to 65 percent by volume of the finished wine. The calculations are fairly complex because of the sugar-to-alcohol conversion and because any residual sugar added to the finished wine is part of the 35 percent addition. The regulation requires that *fixed acid* be measured as parts per thousand of citric acid.

We're going to use tartaric acid equivalent in this discussion, because

1. Everything else winemakers do with grape wines is measured as *tartaric acid*; and
2. Using tartaric acid equivalent will not change the example calculations. The citric acid standard is only used to determine whether the sugar-water addition falls under (b)(3)—35 percent of finished wine . . . or under (b)(4)—60 percent.

Section (b)(4) pertains to juice with fixed acid of 20 grams per liter and over, as *citric*.

As an example, let's walk through the adjustment process for a marionberry wine (Table 39). Assume that we receive two tons of fruit. A total of 39.2 gallons of hot water is added to the fruit to aid breakdown and extraction of juice. After pressing, the juice analysis is 17.90 grams/liter total acidity (as tartaric), 9.6°Brix of sugar, and 3.18 pH.

First, we have to calculate the properties of the raw juice prior to dilution with the hot water:

	Diluted Juice after Pressing	Juice before Dilution
Total acidity, grams/liter	17.90	=17.90 × 458/418.8
		=19.58
PH	3.18	3.11
Fermentable sugar,°Brix	9.60	=9.60 × 458/418.8
		= 10.50
Volumes (in gallons):		
After pressing	458.00	
H2O added	−39.20	
Raw juice	418.80	
Spillage	−0.00	
Net juice gallons to production	**458.00**	**418.80**

Laboratory analysis of raw juice and targets for finished wine gives these figures:

	Raw Juice Analysis	Finished Wine Targets
Sugar, degrees,°Brix	10.50	6.0
Total acidity, grams/liter	19.57	10.00
pH	3.11	3.16
Juice yield:		
lbs/gallon	9.6	
gallons/ton	209.4	
Production gallons of finished wine		= 418.80/0.65
		= 644.3

The detailed calculations are presented in Table 40. The finished wine volume permitted by regulation is 644.3 gallons, *including* the finishing dose of sugar after fermentation. There are substantial volume losses because of CO_2

and evaporation, however. So, the actual volume of the adjusted must *before* fermentation (and *before* the addition of residual sugar) will be 769.44 gallons, summarized here:

	Gallons	Percent of Volume	Ounces	Percent of Weight
Raw juice gallons	418.80	65.0	55,970.8	63.9
Must before fermentation	769.44	119.4	110,972.7	126.7
Wine after fermentation	627.81	97.4	82,919.7	94.7
Finished wine after residual sugar addition	644.30	100.0	87,563.8	100.0

As Table 40 illustrates, the calculations for ameliorating fruit and berry wines can be complex. In practice, winemakers develop simple ratios that come close most of the time. For this wine, it might be satisfactory to calculate the final volume at 100/65 = 1.539 times the raw juice volume. Then, figure the adjusted must before fermentation at 119 percent of the final volume, adjusted to 19°Brix sugar.

Every maker of grape wines should make some fruit and berry wines early in his/her career. It would take the fear out of making adjustments to sugar and acid in the winery. These days, young winemakers are so intimidated by the purist and pious talk of the old hands they get the idea that if you can't get the desired balance in the vineyard it's time to put on the hairshirt and suffer with the imbalance in the winery. That, of course, is unnecessary.

With fruit and berry wines, remember to add pectic enzyme to the must before pressing. Fruits and berries contain pectins that have to be degraded before juice separation. If hot water is added to the pomace to aid in extraction, make sure to cool the mass before adding the enzyme, or the heat will denature the enzyme and it won't work.

Temperature control

Must temperature during fermentation affects the types of compounds that are generated. Generally, aromatic white wines, like Chenin Blanc, Gewürztraminer, Müller-Thurgau and White Riesling, are fermented cold, at 52–55°F. At these temperatures, fermentation is slow, and very little of the aromatic esters are boiled off with the CO_2. Such cool fermentations can take three to five weeks.

Some white wines, including Chardonnay and Pinot Gris, are typically fermented at 60–65°F. Chardonnay fermented in the barrel may reach as high as 90°F, because wood is a poor transmitter of heat.

Most red wines are fermented hotter, because heat aids in color and tannin extraction. Pinot Noir is relatively low in color pigments, so a longer fermentation is usually desirable.

One popular regimen for Pinot Noir is to:

- Warm the must to 60°F (if cold soak is used);
- Inoculate; allow yeast fermentation to take the must temperature up to 86°F, keeping it there for 24 hours;

TABLE 40   Marionberry Wine, Additions and Changes

	Water	Sugar	Acid	Alcohol	Other Constituents	Batch Total
Effective density, oz/gal.	133.28	211.8	160.23	119.44	176.28	
% of juice weight	86.08%	10.50%	1.96%	—	1.46%	100.00%
Gallons	361.50	27.75	5.01	—	4.64	418.80
% by volume	86.32%	6.63%	1.20%	—	1.20%	100.00%
Juice Ounces	**48,182.5**	**5,876.9**	**1,094.2**	**—**	**817.2**	**55,970.8**
Additions b/ferm						
Chaptalization	39,850.0[1]	15,300.0	—	—	—	55,150.0
Acid adjustment	—	—	(148.2)[2]	—	—	(148.2)
Must, before ferment	**88,032.5**	**21,176.9**	**946.1**	**—**	**817.2**	**110,972.7**
% by weight	79.33%	19.08%	0.85%	—	0.74%	100.00%
Changes in fermentation:						
Alcohol conversion[3]	—	(20,571.9)	—	9,463.1	280.3	(10,828.5)
Evaporation	(15,845.8)	—	(99.3)	(1,341.4)	—	(17,286.6)
Other[4]	—	—	(97.0)	—	171.5	62.0
Must after fermentation	**72,186.6**	**605.1**	**737.3**	**8,121.7**	**1,269.0**	**82,919.7**
Residual sugar addition	—	4,650.0	—	—	—	4,650.0
Finished wine, oz:	**72,186.6**	**5,255.1**	**731.4**	**8,121.7**	**1,269.0**	**87,563.8**
% by weight	82.44%	6.00%	0.99%	9.28%	1.45%	100.00%
Gallons	529.01[5]	24.81	3.92	75.495	11.08	644.31
% by volume				11.72%		100.00%
Grams/liter			8.50 g/L			

Notes:

1. Hot water added before pressing is included.

2. Deacidified by 98.8 oz $CaCO_3$ in double salt precipitation.

3. Effective alcohol conversion from sugar at 46.0%.

4. Acid respiration and conversion, extractions from solids and loss of proteins to yeast assimilation.

5. Water and alcohol content calculated together as aqueous solution, then separated.

- Then reduce the temperature to a maximum of 80°F for the rest of the fermentation. Cooling jackets, coupled with gentle punching down, enables such control;

- When fermentation can no longer raise a cap (capfall), punch down one last time, blanket the wine with CO_2 and seal it up for another 3–4 days;

- Then, the tank can be opened, free-run wine pumped to another tank and the pomace loaded into the press and pressed. Total skin contact time can be 23–28 days: 6–8 days in cold soak; 14–16 days in fermentation; 3–4 days of hot soak;

- After 10 days of fermentation in contact with the solids, extended contact allows some gross tannins to attach themselves to the stems, seeds and skins, making the wine softer.

Red grape varieties like Cabernet Sauvignon and Syrah are very rich in color and tannins. Their wines are usually fermented on the skins for a much shorter period (eight to ten days). The free-run is transferred to another tank and the pomace loaded into the press. The now pomace-free wine finishes fermentation without the solids. Total time of skin contact may be nine to twelve days.

Cap management

Before leaving the subject of tanks, a brief discussion of cap management is in order. Cap management is what you do to break up the cap and keep it wet, thus enhancing extraction and cooling the cap and protecting it from developing volatile acidity.[8]

The most gentle tactic is *punching down*. In the past, winemakers would climb into the tank and do the punching down with their feet and legs. Then, we progressed to a pole with a foot attached, so the winemaker didn't have to get into the tank. That is a physically demanding method, but it avoids getting into the tank, which carries a risk of asphyxiation and drowning. Then, California wineries discovered that the winemaker could *pump over* the fermenting must by drawing it through the racking valve and pumping it onto the cap. Some used a gentle flooding method, but many advanced to "blasting" the cap with the help of a fire hose nozzle. Blasting pumpover worked for sturdy varieties like Cabernet Sauvignon, but it greatly reduced the quality of Pinot Noir.

Some creative wineries developed pneumatically-powered punch down devices, which significantly reduced the physical burden of punching down. The rigs worked pretty well.

Then, deFrancesci (Italy) developed an automated punchdown tank, in which vertical rams are mounted in the tank lid. Rams have feet with louvers that close on the downstroke and open on the upstroke so pomace can drop through. Several U.S. tank fabricators also make this type of tank.

---

8. Volatile acidity (abbreviated "VA") is the term used for three compounds that can occur in a troubled fermentation. The most offensive of the three is hydrogen sulfide, a very small amount of which smells like rotten eggs. The second is acetic acid, commonly known as vinegar. It gives a sour taste and smell to the wine. The third is ethyl acetate, a solvent that smells like nail polish. In most cases, these three compounds generate together from a variety of causes. A deficiency of nitrogen is one, an overheated cap or hot fermentation is another.

Now, we have Ganimede® and Pneumatage®, which use bubbles of carbon dioxide generated by fermentation or filtered air to break up the cap and mix it with the must.

Which of these methods is best for high quality wines?

It is commonly accepted that fermenting white wines at cold temperatures, (48–52°F) avoids a "boiloff" of the aromatic compounds in the wine. The esters that are responsible for aroma are volatile under warm temperature and/or otherwise vigorous fermentation. Why wouldn't it be the same for red wines?

Now, we also have scientific evidence of the mechanism by which aromatic compound molecules get trapped in the CO_2 bubbles of sparkling wine.[9]

That's what gives Champagne its intense aroma and, as a result, its flavor, since aroma contributes to flavor. The finding also means that the aroma will be gone quickly.

So, if extremely vigorous fermentation or cap management procedures take something out of white wines and Pinot Noir through accelerated CO_2 activity, then why would it not also be true that they remove something from Cabernet Sauvignon, Syrah and other sturdy reds?

Punching down helps avoid high cap temperatures. Manual punching down is the most gentle method, with the possible exception of a slow flood-type pumpover.

It stands to reason that exuberant use of the bubble method would tend to promote a loss of aromatic constituents because of its vigor, and the large bubbles no doubt promote volatilization of the aromatic esters as they rise through the must. Some winemakers have eagerly embraced the method, because it reduces the onerous physicality of punching down. The author's experience in analyzing wines produced with this method indicates that those wines have lost some distinctiveness. There seems to be a reduction of aroma and flavor, and a blurring of differences among vineyard sources. That is an important consideration in this era of single vineyard bottlings.

There are supporters for this new technology, though, and some of them are very successful winemakers.[10]

Comparison test data that would prove that the method is better or worse than punching down is sorely lacking, however. Perhaps that is the next great challenge for academic research coordinated with commercial wine producers.

Barrel aging

Time in barrel can have a profound effect on wine. The size of the barrel and length of time the wine spends in it vary greatly for different grape varieties and wine styles. Almost all wine made in America uses the barrel sizes discussed in the Chapter 1. Figure 52 presents a general guideline for time in barrel.

---

9. Bryner, Jeanna. "Secret to Champagne Flavor Is Right Under Your Nose," *LiveScience* (September 28, 2009).

10. Danehower, Cole. "New Technologies Offer Promise for Cap Management," *Wines & Vines;* 38–43. (March 2007).

Red wines

All red wines are aged in oak barrels. Virtually all red wine is aged in barrels of approximately 60 gallons. Time in barrel is related to where the grapes are grown, the richness of the new wine's tannin content, its intensity and the winemaker's stylistic preferences. Time in barrel varies widely (Figure 52). Two examples that illustrate the extremes follow.

- Really hot temperatures are rare on Michigan's Leelanau Peninsula. Temperatures are moderated by adjacent Lake Michigan on the west and Grand Traverse Bay on the east. The area enjoys endless 80°F days in July and August. Annual degree-days run about 2,250, comparable to Burgundy and Oregon's Willamette Valley. But, they occur in a growing season that is one month shorter. Consequently, there are less polyphenolics in the grapes. Even for Cabernet Sauvignon, the time in barrel runs only three to four months and a supplement of oak chips is added to extract enough oak flavor in the shorter time frame. The wine goes to market less than one year after harvest.

- The other extreme is Domaine de La Romanée Conti, the top quality producer in Burgundy. The red wines there (all Pinot Noir) are so concentrated and full of tannins, they are barreled for eighteen months in new Allier oak.

Chardonnays

Most Chardonnays have some time in oak, but 100 percent barrel fermentation is reserved for the best. And, some Chardonnays are fermented in stainless steel (SS) tanks and never see oak. But, the great majority are some combination of fermented in oak and in SS and running at least a portion of the SS wines through barrels to pick up vanilla and other oak flavors, as well as some enhanced softness. French barrels of Nevers and Center of France wood, and

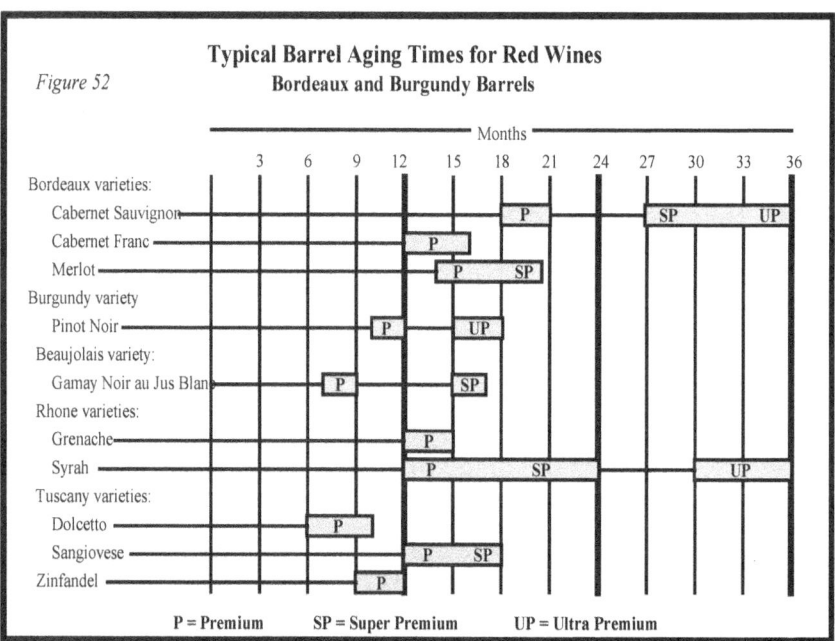

Figure 52 — Typical Barrel Aging Times for Red Wines — Bordeaux and Burgundy Barrels

P = Premium　　SP = Super Premium　　UP = Ultra Premium

American oak barrels, are very popular because of their higher vanillin extract, particularly the oak from American forests.

If the wine is fermented in barrels, it is usually left on the fermentation lees for several months and the lees are stirred up every two to three weeks to avoid microbial degradation.

A fairly normal regimen for premium quality Chardonnays has the wines being rotated through the barrels for periods of three to four months.

Other white wines

Some other white wines are either fermented in oak or aged briefly in it. Sauvignon Blanc may be the most prominent, and it is frequently fermented in 500-liter puncheons. A few wineries employ oak aging on Pinot Gris and Viognier to enhance body and softness. In Alsace, it is conventional to ferment Pinot Gris and White Riesling in neutral oak that may still have tartrate encrustations left over from previous vintages.

Rieslings

In Germany, many high-quality White Rieslings used to be aged in neutral oak ovals (or fuders) of 500 liters. The practice is being phased out and replaced by stainless steel ovals with cooling jackets. One advantage of the oval shape would be a greater separation of lees during settling. The romantic old oak ovals, measuring up to several thousands of liters, are disappearing from the scene also. If you have been to Rüdesheim, you've seen how some have been put to use as entries to wine shops and motel room doors.

Rough filtration

As soon as possible after yeast fermentation, white wines are rough filtered. Most wineries accomplish this step with a diatomaceous earth (DE) filter. DE is fossilized miniature seashells, and it is available in several grades. First, a bed of fibrous material is built up on the fine mesh stainless steel screen. Then the wine is injected with a DE slurry coming into the filter. The DE builds up on the screen, forming a filter bed which traps particles. The constant build up of the filtration bed avoids *sliming over* which would plug the filter.

White wines are allowed to settle for a few days after fermentation is complete, then DE filtered to remove yeast cells and other debris. Various grades of DE and filter sheets are shown in Figure 53. DE filters must be precoated with a cellulose fiber such as Fibra-Cel®.

Small wineries can acquire a plate-and-frame filter with interchangeable frames: thin ones for paper sheets, and thick ones with canvas sheets for use with DE. A disadvantage of them is that they use a mohno pump to generate the high pressure, and the rubber stator wears out rapidly. DE is very abrasive. An air diaphragm pump may be better for this application.

Alternatively, a plate-and-frame filter can be used with very coarse filter sheets, although they will slime over with gummy constituents and seal off, unlike DE, whose filter bed builds in depth as more wine is filtered.

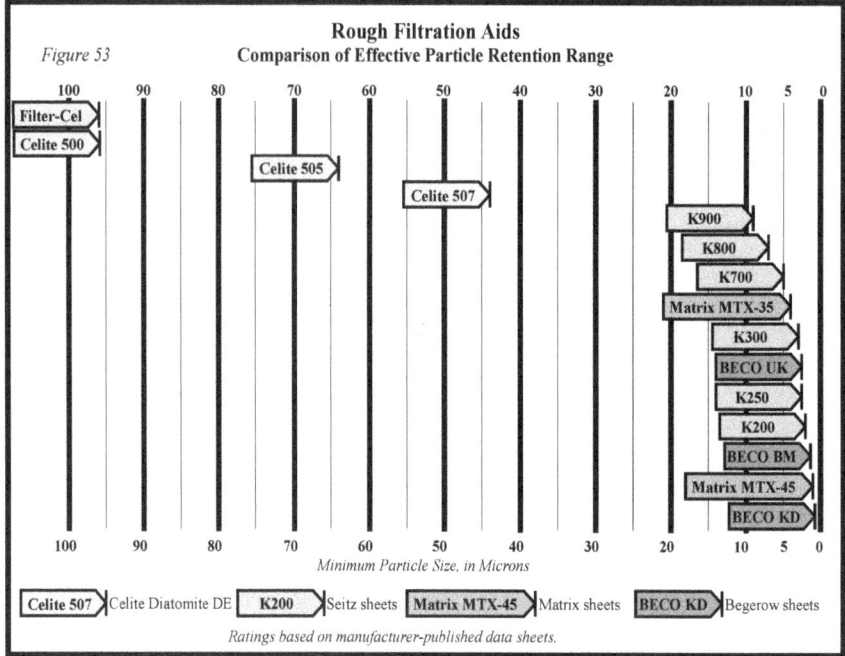

Figure 53
Rough Filtration Aids
Comparison of Effective Particle Retention Range
Minimum Particle Size, in Microns
Ratings based on manufacturer-published data sheets.

Barrel-fermented Chardonnay is filtered after removal from barrels. Steel-fermented Chardonnays are rough filtered the same as any other white wine.

Red wines are usually rough filtered after barrel aging *and* egg white fining. The latest trend for high-end reds is no filtration or fining. Clarification is accomplished by several rackings during barrel aging, and the wine must be stable with respect to MLF and tartrates before bottling.

Cross-flow filtration

A new method of wine filtration is rapidly replacing the use of both DE and plate-and-frame filtration. It is called *cross-flow*, or *tangential flow, filtration*.

The technology is not new. It has been used in the food processing and pharmaceutical industries for years. Until recently, however, it was unsuitable for use on wine because it removed tannins and other flavor constituents, thus reducing the wine's quality. Advances in membrane materials and manufacturing processes have resolved those problems and cross-flow is now regarded as a way to save significant production time and costs, as well as yield high-quality finished wine.

In traditional filtration methods, the flow of the unfiltered wine is directed perpendicular to the filter medium. The particles and molecules being removed stack up on the surface of the medium and eventually plug it up. This result is less troublesome with DE filtration because the filter bed is built up as more unfiltered wine is submitted to it. In plate-and-frame filters though, larger particles, including gummy pectins, slime over the surface of the paper sheet and close off all flow. The remedy is to break down the assembly and change out all of the sheets with new ones.

Conversely, the unfiltered wine flow in cross-flow filtration runs parallel to the medium's surface, scouring from the surface all of the material that didn't go through the membrane. There is no build-up. The rejected material is cycled back into the incoming wine stream. The effluent becomes thicker, and then the equipment automatically backflushes the membrane and removes the effluent to a holding tank. The timing of the backflush cycle is adjustable.

Two types of membrane material are suitable for wine. The most favored is *hollow fiber tubes* made from polysulfone. The other is *ceramic tubes* made of an aluminum/titanium compound. Both are utilized in the pore size, 0.20 μm (microns). Cross-flow has proven suitable for red wines, too, even at the tighter pore size. For reference, the standard membrane pore size for traditional sterile filtration is 0.45 μm.

Ease of use, time savings and substantial cost savings are the reasons why cross-flow is meeting with such popularity. Further, by replacing DE filtration, a winery eliminates airborne DE dust—a health hazard that can cause *silicosis*.

Setup time is less than one-half hour. The equipment does not have to be attended. It can be left to perform the batch's entire clarification in one pass, with scheduled backflushes—even overnight—and shut off automatically.

Cost savings are substantial. Setup, DE or sheet replacement and multiple filtration passes add up. A quick cost analysis for a typical 50,000-gallon winery show a filtration cost savings by cross-flow of 70.2 percent. The payback period is 8.5 years.

	Traditional DE/P&F	Cross-Flow
Labor	$3,690.00	$375.00
Materials	$1,566.98	
Depreciation	$812.35	$1,435.00
Total Filtration Cost	$6,069.33	$1,810.00
Savings from Cross-Flow		$4,259.33
Percent Savings		70.2%

For comparison, the cost for using a mobile cross-flow service would be $4,497 at 38.22¢/gallon plus five hours of the winemaker's time. In this situation (a 50,000-gallon winery) the purchase of the cross-flow equipment clearly is the superior alternative. (All values are in mid-2014 dollars.)

Protection with sulfur dioxide

The use of sulfur dioxide for protection of wines has come under fire from food purists. They misunderstand. First, some sulfur dioxide is produced naturally by yeast fermentation. So, all wines have some SO_2—although these small amounts are inadequate for protection against microbial activity. Second, the wine industry experienced a big change in knowledge and practices in the late 1970s that greatly reduced the amount of SO_2 added to wines for protection.

The first treatment with SO_2 is usually made at the crush pad. A minimal dose of 25–50 ppm SO_2 (TSO_2) is made either at the crusher or when the juice is first in tank (more will be needed if some of the grapes are moldy). This dose suppresses wild yeast and bacteria that came in with the grapes until yeast begins protecting the must with its CO_2. This initial dose is rapidly dissipated during yeast fermentation.

After fermentation is completed (including MLF if that is desired) the wine should be sulfited to achieve a free SO_2 (FSO_2) of 25–35 ppm (see Figure 54).

Attention must be paid to SO_2 levels all through the processing of wine after fermentation is completed. The level should be checked at regular intervals and adjusted as needed. But, what is the appropriate level of FSO_2? First, *free sulfur dioxide* exists in several molecular forms in wine and juice: SO_2, HSO_3 and SO_3. The rest of the total SO_2 is *bound* to other wine constituents, a state in which it is not available to protect the wine.

The distribution of free SO_2 among its three forms depends on the wine's pH level. The most important of them in providing microbial protection is the molecular portion of free SO_2. It has been demonstrated that 0.8 ppm of molecular SO_2 is adequate to protect white wine. The minimum FSO_2 level that provides the necessary 0.8 ppm of molecular SO_2 according to the wine's pH is shown graphically in Figure 54.

Each time potassium metabisulfite (PMB) is added to the wine, it increases the FSO_2 level. With time, some of the addition becomes bound, leaving less FSO_2 to protect the wine. A rough rule of thumb used for anticipating this loss is that two-thirds of the addition remains FSO_2, and one-third becomes bound to other constituents. This ratio is not precise, but serves the purpose.

Always check the FSO_2 level after additions to verify that the desired level has been achieved. It may be necessary to add more PMB. And, always write down the results of PMB additions in your wine record book. The reference will enable you to be more precise in making future PMB additions.

Use Table 41 to determine the amount of PMB to add. Theoretically, $TSO_2 = 57.6\%$ of PMB weight.

TABLE 41   **Potassium Metabisulfite Addition**

To increase FSO, ppm	Grams per 100 gallons	Oz. per 100 gallons
5	3.3	0.1
10	6.6	0.2
15	9.9	0.3
20	13.1	0.5
25	16.4	0.6
30	19.7	0.7
35	23.0	0.8
40	26.3	0.9
45	29.6	1.0
50	32.9	1.2
60	39.4	1.4
70	46.0	1.6
80	52.6	1.9
90	59.1	2.1
100	65.7	2.3
200	131.4	4.6
300	197.1	7.0

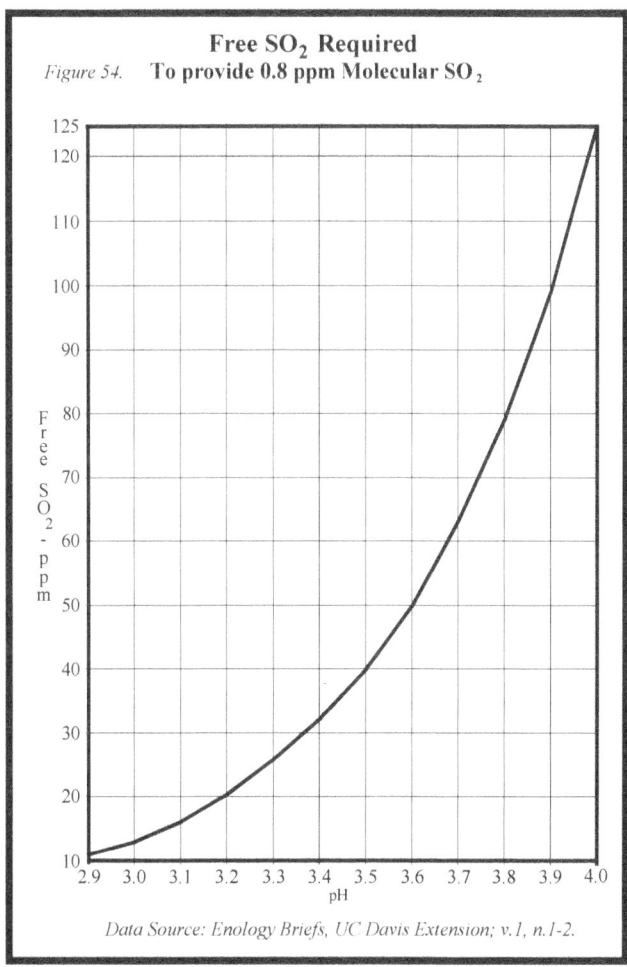

Free SO₂ Required

Figure 54.   **To provide 0.8 ppm Molecular SO₂**

Data Source: Enology Briefs, UC Davis Extension; v.1, n.1-2.

Experience has provided guidelines for the appropriate FSO_2 levels needed for wine in its different processing stages and for the various types of wine. See Figure 55 for the amounts recommended by Peynaud.

Larger wineries use a more efficient method of making SO_2 additions: liquid SO_2 from pressurized cylinders. Metering devices can be used to inject the SO_2 into the wine during racking. Liquid SO_2 is dangerous in the hands of a winemaker who is not trained in its use.

Additionally, some other materials are utilized for protection against microbial activity, notably sorbic acid (as potassium sorbate). Its use is more common to fruit wines and other very sweet wines than to grape wines. They will not be discussed further here, except to note that treatment with sorbic acid can leave undesirable odors in the wine.

Finishing operations

Before a wine can be bottled it must be clarified by fining and filtration and rendered stable with respect to changes that might occur in the bottle.

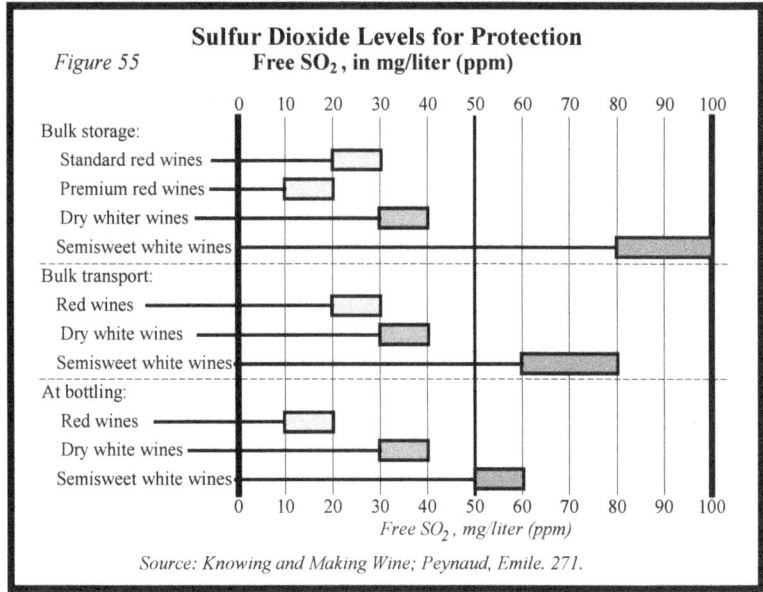

Sulfur Dioxide Levels for Protection
Free SO$_2$, in mg/liter (ppm)

Figure 55

Source: Knowing and Making Wine; Peynaud, Emile. 271.

Fining

In fining, a material is added to the wine which binds with undesirable constituents so the latter may be removed. The fining agent does not remain in the wine.

A wide range of fining agents is used by wineries in America and Europe. Application rates and methods of implementation are very complex and will not be dealt with here, beyond a general classification as to their effectiveness and use (see Table 42).

Fining is not an exact science. Grape variety, ripeness of the grapes, growing conditions and other factors determine the presence of constituents to be fined. It is always a good idea to conduct bench trials to determine the appropriate dosage for each juice or wine. For example, let's say you think a dose of 2 lbs/1,000 gallons is about right. You would set up test batches at 1-½, 2, 2-½ and 3 lbs/1,000 gallons. If further fine tuning is indicated, you could test applications in a narrower range. Trial batches should be at least one gallon in volume, as it is extremely difficult to measure fining materials for smaller volumes. It is important, also, to make your test applications in as close a manner as possible to the way you will treat the full volume.

Pay attention to temperatures and avoid aeration as much as possible. Be sure to review TTTB's regulations on approved additives for wine at §24.246. Some items have been added in recent years to catch up with winery practices, including use of malic acid to balance the wine, fining with milk (smooths out Chardonnay) and filtration by reverse osmosis to remove volatile acidity and excess alcohol.

Always consult the manufacturer's information for the fining material before proceeding. The most common types of fining are discussed in greater detail in the following sections.

TABLE 42 Fining Materials

Material	Type	Used for	Dose Range
Bentonite	montmorillonite clay	assist settling of juice lees remove heat unstable proteins	1–4 lbs/1,000 gals. typically, more for warm climate grapes
Carbon, decolorizing	KBB	remove brown color from white wines	¼–1 lbs/1,000 gals. for browning, (max: 3.0 g/L)
Carbon, deodorizing	AAA	remove off-odors & -flavors	¼–4 lbs/1,000 gals. For most odors
Casein	protein	remove color, bitterness, reduce oakiness	$\frac{1}{16}$–2 lbs/gal. may be used with tannin, kieselsol
Copper Sulfate		remove H2S, mercaptans	maximum of 6 parts copper per million parts wine. Finished wine must not exceed 0.5 mg/L of copper
Cufex	ferrous sulfate & potassium ferrocyanide	remove copper and iron	see ferrocyanide below
Egg albumin	protein	remove phenolics, soften red wines	1–6 whites per 228L barrel (max: 3 lbs/1,000 gals.) fresh twice as effective as frozen
Ferrocyanide		remove trace metallics, H2S, mercaptans	max. one part/million in finished wine
Gelatin	protein, 75–100 bloom	remove tannins, clarification, settle juice lees	¼–½ lbs/gal. for tannins $\frac{1}{8}$–¾ lbs/1,000 gals. for clarification may be used with kieselsol or tannins
Isinglass	protein, from sturgeon air bladders	clarify white wines, unmask fruit flavors	$\frac{1}{8}$–$\frac{1}{4}$ lbs/1,000 gals. may be used with tannin or gelatin
Kieselsol	silica collagen	clarification of white wines, remove bitterness from white wines	varies, used with bentonite and/or gelatin to aid settling , 1 liter/1,000 gals. wine for gelatin
Pectic enzymes		break down pectins, enable settling & clarification	½–2 lbs/1,000 gals.
PVPP (nylon)		remove browning/pinking precursors, color	1–6 lbs/1,000 gals. (max 60 lbs/1,000gal. requires filtration to remove
Sparkolloid	Seaweed	clarifying wines	1–2 lbs/1,000 gals. as a 2.4% solution in hot water
Tannins			less than ¼ lb/1,000 gals. (max: 3.0 g/L) may be used with casein or gelatin

Sources: Several. Always consult manufacturer data before using fining agents. See CFR Title 27, §24.246 Materials authorized for the treatment of wine and juice for further details.

Bentonite

We have already covered the use of bentonite in expediting the settling of juice lees. Typically, 2–4 lbs/1,000 gallons are used for that purpose. Warm climate grapes may need more. You will have a second chance at removing heat-unstable proteins during finishing procedures, so it is not necessary to use large doses at the juice stage. Remember, using bentonite pulls nitrogen-rich proteins out of the juice, so the deficit will have to be made up by adding DAP before fermentation.

Heat stabilization

The second chance for treatment with bentonite occurs during finishing procedures. Every white wine needs to have heat-unstable proteins removed for clarity. So do all blush wines and red wines produced by carbonic maceration. The tannin content of most red wines assures protein stability.

Let's say you buy a bottle of white wine, then leave the wine in your car while you make another shopping stop. The temperature in the car rises to 110°F. When you get home, you place the wine in the refrigerator to chill it for the night's dinner. When you take the bottle out of the refrigerator—much to your horror—there is copious white flocculent in the wine. It looks like one of those snow scenes inside a glass ball. What you have experienced is what happens to a white wine that has not been adequately treated for removal of heat-unstable proteins.

During finishing of the wine, the winemaker tests for the presence of such proteins by heating a sample (usually in an incubator or oven) to a temperature of 122°F for 48 hours (or 140°F for 24 hours). The sample is then placed in a refrigerator. If unstable proteins are present, they will make their presence known. You will have to treat with bentonite, then repeat the heat test until clarity is achieved.

Bentonite comes in two forms. The conventional product must be rehydrated in hot water, then added to the wine as a slurry with constant agitation to mix it well. It helps to rehydrate then age the slurry for a few days before adding to the wine. For small quantities (up to a couple of pounds of bentonite) rehydration is quickly accomplished with a blender. Fill the blender about halfway with hot water, turn it on, then sprinkle the bentonite into it a little at a time. If you get too much bentonite in the mix, the slurry will seize up in a muddy mass, so be careful not to add too much. The slurry can be dumped into a plastic bucket, then another small batch prepared.

The KWK form (or agglomerated bentonite) may be added directly to the wine without rehydration. Follow the manufacturer's instructions for the bentonite you buy.

Cold stabilization

All wine contains tartaric acid salts commonly known as *cream of tartar*. The solubility of tartrates depends on the wine's temperature. So, if a wine with tartrates is chilled below the temperature at which the wine is able to hold all of its tartrates in solution, the excess tartrates will precipitate in clear needle-like crystals. The result is a cloudy wine.

Let's use the wine buyer example again. Suppose you buy a white wine that has been cold stabilized down to 50°F. You chill the wine to 40°F in your refrigerator. When you serve the wine it is cloudy, or at least it shimmers in the light. If the wine was in the refrigerator long enough, the crystals would drop to the bottom of the bottle. They are called *argols*. Such precipitates used to be common in red wines, present both as a sediment and also attached to the underside of the cork.

Tartrate precipitants are not harmful. They are the same material called cream of tartar used in cooking. But, they are not pleasing to the wine's appearance and are now considered commercially unacceptable.

The usual winery procedure used to remove tartrates from white and blush wines is chilling the wine to 29°F for two weeks. Some winemakers expedite the process by seeding the wine with tartrate crystals.

Red wines aged in barrels in cool cellars are usually sufficiently tartrate stable, so extended chilling is not needed. It is *not* a good idea to refrigerate red wines below 60°F prior to serving!

Filtration

Filtration is an important part of finishing operations for all wines, except for some super-premium reds. Usually, the process begins with a plate-and-frame filter and paper filter sheets. Selection of the sheets' pore size depends on the grape variety and condition of the wine. The first pass is typically made with 1.0–1.5 micron pore size. (See Figure 56)

Filter sheets function by trapping particulates within their network of fibers. They are not perfect. For example, a filter sheet rated at 1.0 micron will trap about 98 percent of the particles larger than 1.0 micron. Not only do some larger particles get through the filter, but cells that can cause trouble in the bottle are smaller than 1.0 micron. The latter would be the acetic and lactic bacteria that produce vinegar and unwanted MLF in the bottle. That's why sheet filtration is usually followed with sterile filtration at bottling for white wines.

Sterile filtration uses cylindrical filter elements that have a constant pore size. No particles or cells larger than the rating get through. To use these filters, it is necessary to acquire a stainless steel filter shell equipped with pressure gauges, fittings and a tripod to hold the assembly. Shells are available for 10-inch, 20-inch and 30-inch lengths of filter element. The elements come in 10-inch lengths and can be screwed together end-to-end. A longer element enables faster filtration flow-through. Setup includes a test called *bubble point* to check for the element's integrity. The objective is to determine the pressure at which the test gas begins to pass through the filter.

Wine is considered sterile filtered after it passes through a 0.45 micron filter element. That level will remove *all* of the bacteria that can cause problems later in the bottle. Elements are also available at 0.22 microns, but that severity is seldom used in commercial wine production.

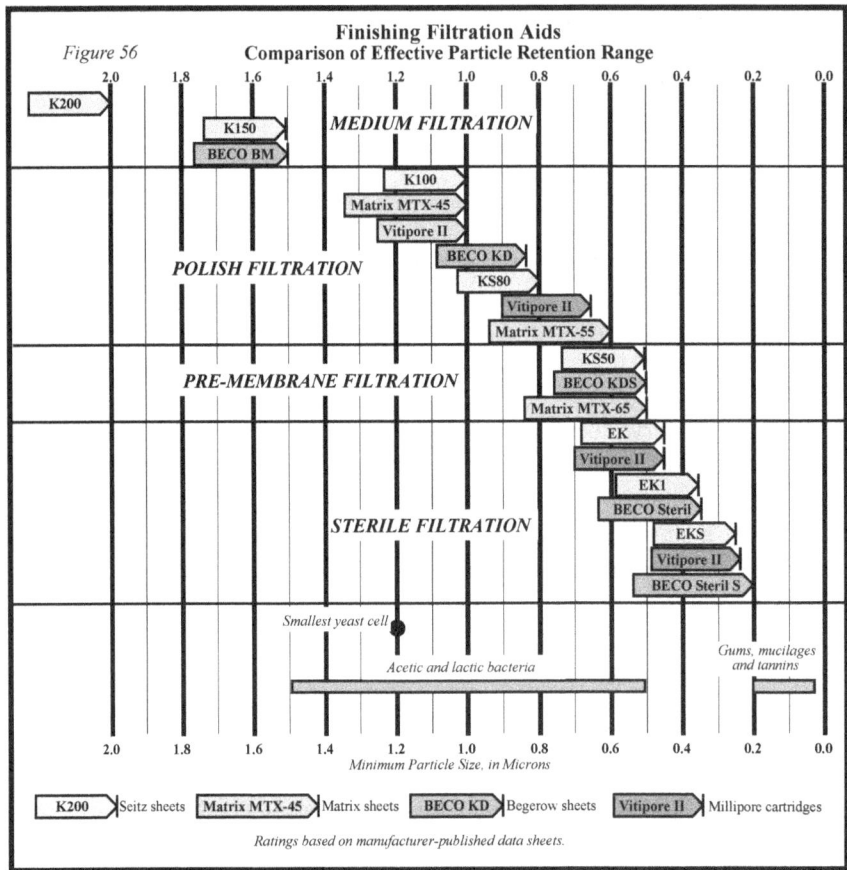

Finishing Filtration Aids
Comparison of Effective Particle Retention Range

Figure 56

Usually, winemakers fabricate a PVC cylinder to store the filter element in SO$_2$ solution when not in use. It is a simple task. Use 4-inch I.D. PVC pipe. Glue an end cap on one end, and a threaded adapter for a threaded end cap on the other.

Bottles

Wine bottles come in a wide variety of sizes and shapes. Selection of bottles involves the image the winery is seeking to portray and the expectations of the marketplace. Some shapes (Figure 57 and Table 43) are traditional to European growing areas and have been adopted by American wine producers.

American wineries have departed from the European traditions in many ways, while making some concessions to appearing similar to their European counterparts on the shelf. Examples include making several styles the same height, so as to reduce adjustments of bottling equipment and to be able to deal with a standardized case height in stacking and shipping. Some European shapes do not fit very well on supermarket shelves. Hence, German Hock bottles and Burgundy bottles have replaced the taller Alsatian bottles for wines like Gewürztraminer and Pinot Gris.

Wines from the Rhône Valley in France use a bottle shape similar to Bordeaux, as do most Italian and Spanish still wines.

TABLE 43   **Use of Bottle Shapes, Europe and America**

	Bordeaux	Burgundy	Hock	Alsatian	Champagne	Port
Color	Medium green	Dead leaf green	Amber or dark green*	Dark green	Dark green	Dark brown
France	Bordeaux reds Bordeaux whites Sauternes	Chardonnay Pinot Noir Pinot Blanc	White Riesling Müller-Thurgau	Pinot Gris White Riesling Gewürztraminer	Most sparkling wines	Port Sherry
America	Cab.Sauvignon Merlot Sauvignon Blanc Pinot Grigio	Chardonnay Pinot Gris Pinot Noir Pinot Blanc Syrah	White Riesling Müller-Thurgau Gewürztraminer	Seldom used	Most sparkling wines	High-alcohol dessert wines

*Dark green in Mosel Valley, amber in all other German winegrowing areas.

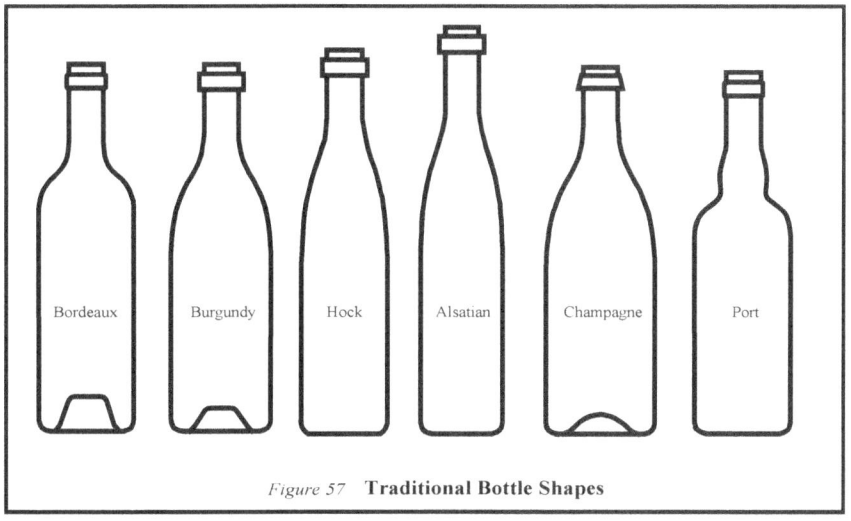

Figure 57   **Traditional Bottle Shapes**

Many American wineries use flat bottom (no punt) Burgundy bottles for White Riesling and other German and Alsatian grape varieties.

A wide array of bottle shapes and sizes (Table 44) are available on the market today. California wineries in particular have led the way in designing more appealing packaging in terms of bottles, labels and closures. Bottle manufacturers—especially those in Italy—have been very creative in bottle designs.

Reverse taper is a design feature that is gaining in popularity for upscale wines. The diameter at the bottom is smaller than at the shoulder. These bottles present a label design challenge, however. In order for the lines of print to appear level in the horizontal dimension, they must be printed in a concave downwards arc. To illustrate this point, attach a blank label to the bottle, then hold a pencil point against the label at a fixed height from the base while rotating the bottle.

Several colors are used for wine bottles. Here, again, the French and German practices are traditional and regulated. Dead leaf green is used for all Burgundy wines. Medium green dominates Bordeaux wines. In Germany,

TABLE 44   **Wine Bottle Sizes**

Name	Volume (in liters)	Equal to Std. 750-ml bottles
Demi	0.375	0.5
Standard	0.750	1
Magnum	1.5	2
Jeroboam	3 or 4.5	4 or 6
Rehoboam	4.5	6
Methuselah or Imperial	6	8
Salamanazar or Mordechai	9	12
Balthezar	12	16
Nebuchadnezzar	15	20
Melchior	18	24
Solomon	20	26.67
Sovereign	25	33.33
Primat	27	36
Melchizadek	30	40

dark, or champagne green is used for all wines of the Mosel Valley. Elsewhere in Germany, the color is amber.

A few adventurous American wineries have employed cobalt blue bottles for some white wines, White Riesling for example. It is very bright, and an attention-getter for consumers who look for such things . . . but definitely a novelty.

Closures

The traditional wine bottle closure is *natural cork*, made from the bark of the cork oak tree. Even today, a natural cork relates to high wine quality all over the world. However, there are some modern innovations that are gaining popularity.

First, let's discuss natural corks. The standard cork closure size is #9, which means it has an uncompressed diameter of 24 mm. The same size is used for Bordeaux, Burgundy and Hock bottles of 375ml, 750 ml and 1.5 liters. Some bottles use size #8 (notably dessert wine bottles for port and sherry). See Table 45 for cork dimension standards.

In general, the length of the cork determines how long it will last, and the perception of value. Corks that are 1.75 inch are the standard for grape wines. Many of the highest quality wines use a 1.88 inch cork. In the hands of a sommelier, the longer cork seems to be coming out of the bottle forever. There is not a lot of different in service life between the two.

Much more important to achieving a reliable seal of the bottle is the quality of the cork material. The highest quality designation is given to corks that have very few occlusions and other imperfections.

It is now commonplace for wineries to have their winery logos branded on their corks. A few wineries have even gone so far as eliminating the capsule, and using the cork brand as part of the visual package.

TABLE 45   **Standard Cork Specifications**

	Short	Medium	Long
Natural cork:			
Length of service		7–20 yrs	
Diameter	24mm	24mm	24mm
Length, mm	38	44	47
inches	1.5"	1.75"	1.87"
Agglomerated:			
Length of service		1-½ yrs	2 yrs
Diameter	23mm	23mm	44mm
Length, mm	1-½	2	
inches	1.5"	1.75"	
Synthetic:			
Length of service	3 yrs	5 yrs	
Diameter	22mm	22mm	
Length, mm	38	42	

Historically, *TCA* (or *2,4,6-tyrichloroanisole*)—a chemical derivative of chlorine that gives the wine a "corky" or "wet newspaper" aroma—posed a large problem. The wines were said to be "corked." Some wineries experienced losses of 2–4 percent of their wines to the defect. Most TCA entered the wine from corks that were treated with chlorine, but some also came from other sources in the winery. Thanks to research by the cork manufacturers, a treatment process has been developed that eliminates the problem. Corks are sanitized in a hydrogen peroxide bath and dried before being packaged in sealed plastic bags of 1,000 blanketed in SO_2 gas.

Corks are expensive. After the corks have been punched from the slab of oak, the remaining web of material is ground, coated with an adhesive and pressed into cork shapes. These are called *agglomerated corks*. Agglomerated corks offer a shorter storage life for the wine, lower cost and a perception of lower wine quality. In addition, they are harder than 100 percent natural cork and more difficult to remove from the bottle.

Beginning in the late 1980s, *plastic corks* have been available. Manufacturers have improved materials and molding technique, resulting in a much better closure. Again, they are harder to remove and carry the perception of low-quality wine. Some fairly large wineries now use them on their lowest-priced wines and have found good consumer acceptance. Among the advantages are lower cost and freedom from TCA. Of course, plastic closures can be branded (just like natural and agglomerated corks) and the range of colors is large.

Corks that are 1.5-inch provide short-term protection up to three years. Their use is pretty well limited to fruit and berry wines, which are consumed quickly.

The truth be told, most grape wines are consumed shortly after purchase. There is a standing joke in the wine industry that the average cellaring time at home is 45 minutes from the time of purchase. However, plenty of wine consumers still age wines for several years, particularly red wines. European producers are more likely to age a wine longer before sending it to market. In America, cash flow is king, so many wines are marketed before they are ready to consume. Those who go the extra measure to cellar their wines at a cool temperature for two to four years are usually richly rewarded for their patience.

By the way, the best cork puller is the double-tang gizmo called "ah-so." It adds the least compression to the cork, therefore making it easier to pull the cork out. The secret to success with its use is to move one tang at a time and alternate sides.

Corkscrew types pale in comparison, including the universally-used *waiter's lift.* They add a lot of volume to the cork, press the cork tight against the inside of the bottle's neck and make it very difficult to extract. Besides, if you get good at the ah-so, you can reinsert the cork without leaving a hole through the cork's center for seepage of oxygen into the wine. And, the impressions left on the sides of the cork by the ah-so quickly disappear, leaving a good seal. Coupled with an inert gas blanket—like CO_2 or nitrogen—you have a reliable method for saving the bottle's contents for another day's enjoyment.

This method is used in many tasting rooms to carry partial bottles over to the next day's tastings. Oh yes, refrigeration is a good idea, too.

A recent innovation for wines in America is the *screw-top closure*, also known as *ROPP*. An increasing number of wineries are using screw tops on their lowest-priced wines. Improvements in materials have enabled the manufacture of metal closures that are impermeable to air. Remember the previous observation about the average cellaring time for wines between the retail shelf and table. For lower-priced wines, the ability to cellar for a long time is not an issue. So, regardless of the "chateau le screw-top" stigma that continues to be associated with screw-tops, the innovation is very likely to increase dramatically in use. In both France and Germany, the method is very common for the everyday wines sold in one liter reusable bottles.

Label design

The label is the most important element of the wine package. It conveys the image the winery seeks to impress on consumers' minds. For many wine consumers—especially those who are not intensely loyal to certain brands—the label is what draws attention on the shelf.

For many new wineries, label design can be one of the most contentious issues encountered. Most winery owners are very particular about how their image is represented by the label. Label design costs of upwards of $50,000 have been experienced. Some commercial artists refuse to accept assignments to design labels because of the stresses involved. Through all of this task, it is important to keep in mind that *the primary objective of the label is to sell the wine, not the owner's ego.*

Just any old paper will not do. The information on the label has to be readable and the label must remain attached when it is soaked in an ice bucket. The glue shouldn't turn the label pink. It may be necessary to varnish coat the label to prevent scuffing and provide some waterproofing.

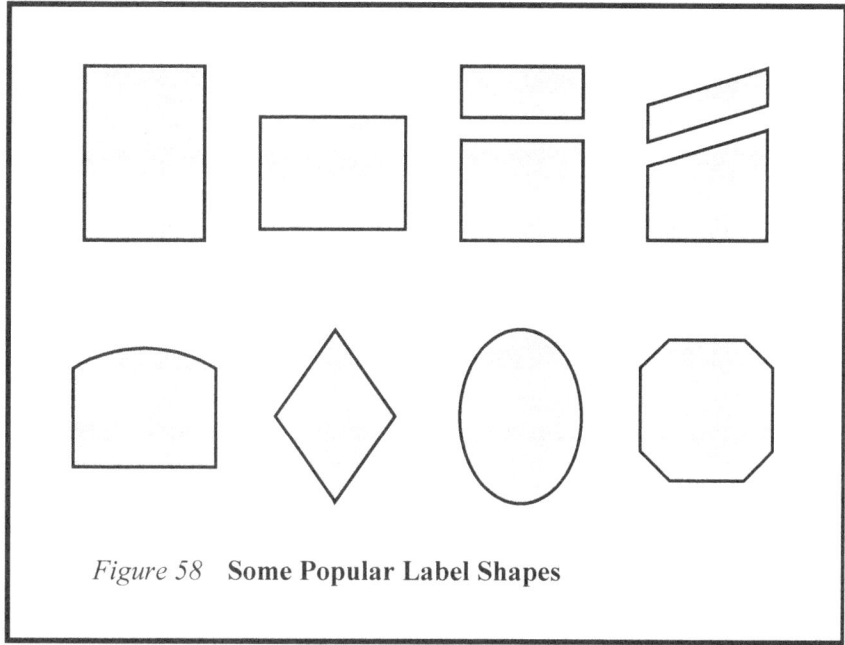

Figure 58   **Some Popular Label Shapes**

Labels can be attached with wet glue or by contact adhesive. It makes a big difference. Different labeling equipment is needed and the method chosen will probably affect which printers are able to print the labels. In the past twenty years, contact adhesive has become the preferred method.

Many people (in addition to the artists and owners) get excited about wine label design. To save yourself a lot of grief and mistakes, it pays to employ someone who knows wine labels and has experience in designing them. The artist who just did a magnificent pen-and-ink portrait of your house is probably not the best person to design your wine label.

Labels come in many sizes and shapes, but only a handful are most common. By far, most labels are rectangular in shape. In general, a vertical label looks best on Bordeaux and Hock bottles because the bottles are tall and thin. A horizontal label appears best on the Burgundy bottle because the bottle is more short and squat. Beyond those commonalities, the sky seems to be the limit as to shape. Some wineries have divided the front label into two parts vertically. A few have divided the label into two stripes. Circles, ovals, octagon and diamond shapes have also been used (Figure 58). Recently, some adventurous types have torn the top edge of the label (why they would do that is anyone's guess).

A helpful exercise in label design is to visit a wine shop with a large selection of American and European wines with your designer in tow. Take a look at the way the best wineries present themselves in the label and the rest of the package. It doesn't hurt to emulate success.

Typically, wine bottles have front and back labels. The back label is commonly used to describe the wine and to display the mandated Government Health Warning statement. Nothing in the regulations prevents putting all of the mandatory information on the real front label and using the back label for artwork. The back label is really intended to be the front label in terms of its positioning on the shelf. One creative winery glued the label to the bottle with all of the information on the side attached to the glass. You had to read the label through the wine, which was a pale rosé.

The front and back labels can be printed in one piece. It can be done with contact adhesive labels and the practical limit on label length is about nine inches.

One further point (and one of the most important!): do **not** change your design unless you have a really unappealing label. We've all heard the advice about advertising: always run the ad at least three times. Repetition builds memory. If you change the label, your loyal customers may not be able to find your wine on the shelf. There may just be too many good-looking alternatives beckoning to them.

Many wine consumers dread the possibility of serving an unacceptable wine to their dinner guests. They develop trust in a label. Change the label and you lose the customer.

The key elements of a label are illustrated in Figure 59.

Single vineyard designations

Another trend has appeared in America's wine industry: single vineyard bottling. The trend is a natural outgrowth of the attempt to produce wines that truly reflect the microclimate where they were grown, just the way they do in Europe. Some of the label designations are justified by the distinctiveness of the wines consistently, year after year.

Sorry to say, many of the single vineyard wines do not deserve to be singled out this way. Wineries have been tempted to use the practice to inflate prices unjustifiably. Outstanding wines previously achieved by blending the characteristics of several sites have been pulled apart, and the single vineyard wines are not as good as the previous blend. The folly of jumping into this trend for

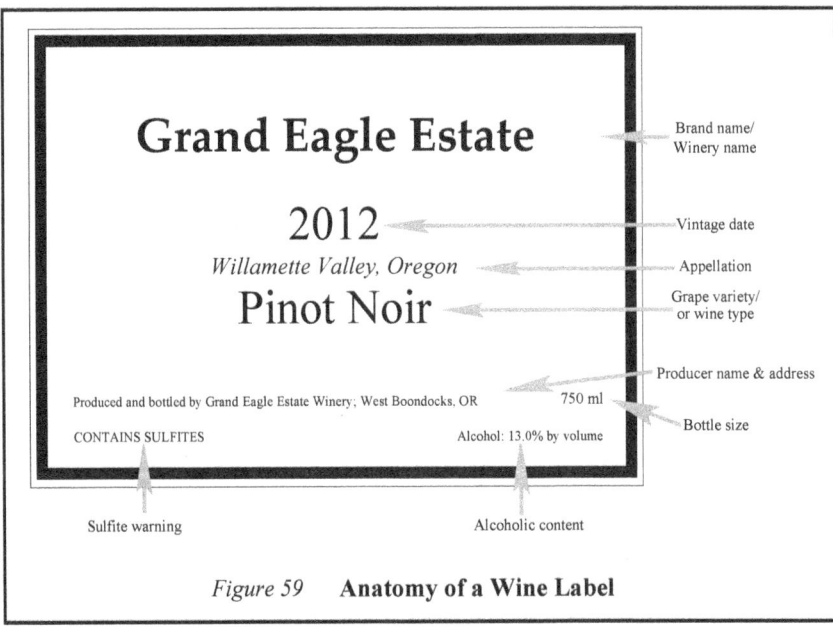

Figure 59 **Anatomy of a Wine Label**

many wines will prove out in the marketplace's reaction to them. Meanwhile, distributors and retailers are plagued with a blizzard of additional labels to deal with and not enough shelf facings to accommodate them.

Mandatory label information

Federal regulations require certain information to be displayed in the label (Table 46).

TABLE 46   **TTB Wine Label Requirements**
From Title 27; Part 4—Labeling and Advertising of Wine

Information	Conditions		
Brand name	§4.33		
Class, type or other designation	Table wine, sparkling wine, etc. or name of grape variety §4.23, §4.34		
Alcoholic content	% by volume, stated level allows range of +/−1.5% by volume. Naming as "Table Wine" implies alcohol is 12% by volume. §4.36		
Blends	§4.32(4)		
Name & post office address	Where bottled. Grower permit wines show location where the wine was bottled, and the grower identity is adopted as a DBA by the bottling winery. §4.35		
Net contents	If >1 liter, stated in liters to two decimal places. If <1 liters, in milliliters. Not needed if molded into bottle. §4.37		
FD&C Yellow No. 5	If it is used §4.32(2(c)		
Declaration of sulfites	"Contains sulfites" sufficient, but if 10 ppm or more at time of bottling, content must be stated		
Year of harvest	§4.27		
"Bottled, produced, blended by"	§4.35		
Size of print—bottles >187ml	For mandatory information on all sizes over 187 ml, at least 2 mm in height. If there is descriptive or explanatory information, type for mandatory statements must be substantially larger than such information.		
Size of print—bottles =/<187ml	At least 1 mm in height. If there is descriptive or explanatory information, type for mandatory statements must be substantially larger than such information.		
Size of print—alcoholic content	No larger than 3 mm or smaller than 1 mm on bottles smaller than 5 liters. Shall not be set off with border or otherwise accentuated.		
Information on cases	Most wineries glue a label of the wine to the end of the case.		
Prohibited statements	§4.39		
Government Health Warning	Bottle Size	Minimum type height	Maximum characters/inch
	<238 ml	1 mm	40
	237 ml–3 liters	2 mm	25
	>3 liters	3 mm	12

The official Alcoholic Beverage Health Warning Statement is imposed in Title 27; Part 16; § 16.21 Mandatory label information. The standards for type size and spacing shown above are found in TTB's Industry Circular Number 93-9 dated 12/3/93:

GOVERNMENT WARNING: (1) ACCORDING TO THE SURGEON GENERAL, WOMEN SHOULD NOT DRINK ALCOHOLIC BEVERAGES DURING PREGNANCY BECAUSE OF THE RISK OF BIRTH DEFECTS. (2) CONSUMPTION OF ALCOHOLIC BEVERAGES IMPAIRS YOUR ABILITY TO DRIVE A CAR OR OPERATE MACHINERY, AND MAY CAUSE HEALTH PROBLEMS.

All capital letters and narrow spacing are used for the Government Warning by many wineries for a reason. It enables you to meet the type height requirement while using the least space—a desirable objective in label design.

Virtually all wine labels have a bar code. Supermarket chains rely on it to provide price and inventory information at checkout. If you want to keep your wine out of supermarkets, don't put a bar code on the label. You probably won't be able to obtain a distributor, either.

Bar codes (or the Universal Product Code [UPC]) are issued by GS1 US. The barcodes used by wineries and all other food products are twelve digits. Digits 2-6 are issued by GS1 US and are the winery's identification number. Digits 7–11 can be used by the winery to identify separate products. A winery can adopt its own codification scheme. The first of the five digits can designate the grape variety. The second can indicate the lot, if more than one wine of a variety is produced. Digit 3 might stand for the bottle size. Digits 4 and 5 would be the vintage year.

The concept was developed by contractors including NCR, RCA and IBM for the National Association of Food Chains.

Information prohibited on labels

Title 27; Part 4 §4.39 prohibits many kinds of information on wine labels. Because the following summary has been rewritten in the interest of clarity and brevity, make sure you read TTB's actual wording before you launch your label design. Here are the prohibitions:

- False or untrue claims;
- Disparaging of a competitor's product;
- Anything obscene or indecent;
- Misleading claims about wine's attributes;
- Misleading statements regarding guarantees;
- Names of individuals or public prominences misleading as endorsements;
- Claims distilled spirits content, compares to distilled spirits or claims intoxicating properties;
- A brand name that falsely implies wine is entitled to a permitted designation;

- A brand name or class that implies the wine is distilled spirits;

- Any statement of the wine's age other than the vintage date;

- Any statement that the bottling date is indicative of age;

- Date of winery's founding larger than 2mm;

- Simulation of any government stamp;

- Bonded Wine Cellar and bonded winery numbers must be stated together; e.g., "Bonded Winery No. 10";

- If wine is imported with certification of origin or vintage, the certification may be cited without further embellishment;

- Domestic wines my not bear the word importer or similar words;

- Flags and coats-of-arms may not imply that the wine is endorsed by the government, any of its services, an organization, family or individual;

- Health benefits, or nutritional content;

- Referral to a third party for information about health benefits;

- Use of the name of an area of viticulture significance unless all of the wines under that brand name meet the requirements of the named appellation;

- Use of an appellation name unless the wine meets all of the requirements of that appellation;

- A state, county or viticulture area name if the brand name bears a state name;

- Names that mislead as to the wine's origin;

- Foreign names that indicate the area of origin or quality level of foreign wines;

- If the brand name contains the name of the ranch, vineyard, etc. that has viticulture significance, 95 percent of the wine must originate in the significant area;

- Use of a grape varietal name or geographic designation in the brand name, product name or fanciful name is considered misleading unless the wine meets all of the criteria for the variety named.

Neck bands are sometimes used to hide the dividing line between head space and wine or cork.

Capsules

The origin of the capsule was to protect the cork from insects like the cork borer. Capsules also kept the cork from drying out. Capsules were made exclusively of lead foil until the 1970s. Then, environmental awareness caused an industry response and motivated TTF (then BATF) to ban lead and the race for a substitute material was on. First, tin was preferred because it looked like the traditional lead on the bottle. But, tin leaves sharp edges when it tears resulting in cuts. Then, a sandwich of aluminum foil with a plastic laminate became popular. Then there were heat-shrinkable plastics. A foil spinner was required in the bottling line for the first three. A heat shrink tunnel is needed for the fourth.

Capsules are now available in a wide range of colors, and with artwork or logos printed or embossed on them.

Then, Robert Mondavi Winery once again showed why is an industry leader. Mondavi did away with capsules altogether. First, they had their bottles made with a flare at the top of the neck. The artwork on the cork was upgraded, so it was artistically pleasing. A wax disc was glued on top of the cork (it had Mondavi's initials embossed on it), to prevent drying out of the cork and just in case there were any insects around. The label was redesigned to make a very attractive package.

Pallets

The standard size wood pallet used by wineries is commonly called a *grocery pallet* according to specifications of the Grocery Manufacturers' Association (GMA). It measures 48" × 40", and is lift truck accessible from two sides. The standard pack for wines is fourteen cases per tier, and four tiers, for a total of 54 cases per pallet.

Wine cases have to be aligned in a certain way (illustrated in Figure 60) to best fit the pallet dimensions. The assembly has to be film wrapped to prevent horizontal shifting and otherwise provide stability. Also called *stretch wrap*, the plastic film usually is applied using a hand dispenser and 12"–15" wide rolls of film. Very large wineries can acquire a machine that automatically stretch-wraps pallets.

Bottling

Wineries perform bottling with a wide variety of equipment. Illustrated in Figure 60 is a bottling line typical for producing 25,000 cases. The core of the line is a monobloc, which is an enclosed assembly of rinser, sparger, filler and vacuum corker along a chain-driven conveyor belt. Additional modules (monobloc or not enclosed) are attached to the same chain drive for applying and spinning the capsules and labeling. Rotating tables are located at both ends of the line to get empty bottles on and filled bottles off.

Bottling equipment can be adjusted for size and shape of the bottles. Star wheels to accommodate different diameters are changed out on the filler. Heights of the filler heads and other pieces of equipment are adjusted for bottle height. And the lines are usually adjustable for speed. The illustrated mono-bloc can typically operate at 10–50 bottles per minute. Including the foreman, this setup requires seven to eight workers, depending on the capabilities of the workers.

Final filtration

Final filtration is integrated with the bottling operation (see Figure 61). First is the positive displacement pump. It is usually a gear pump (never a centrifugal) equipped with electronic controls that conduct a smooth ramping-up and slowing down of flow as the pump is turned on and off. A feedback wire connects the pump's controls to a float sensor in the bottling filler's bowl, so operation is automatically adjusted to the bottling line's speed.

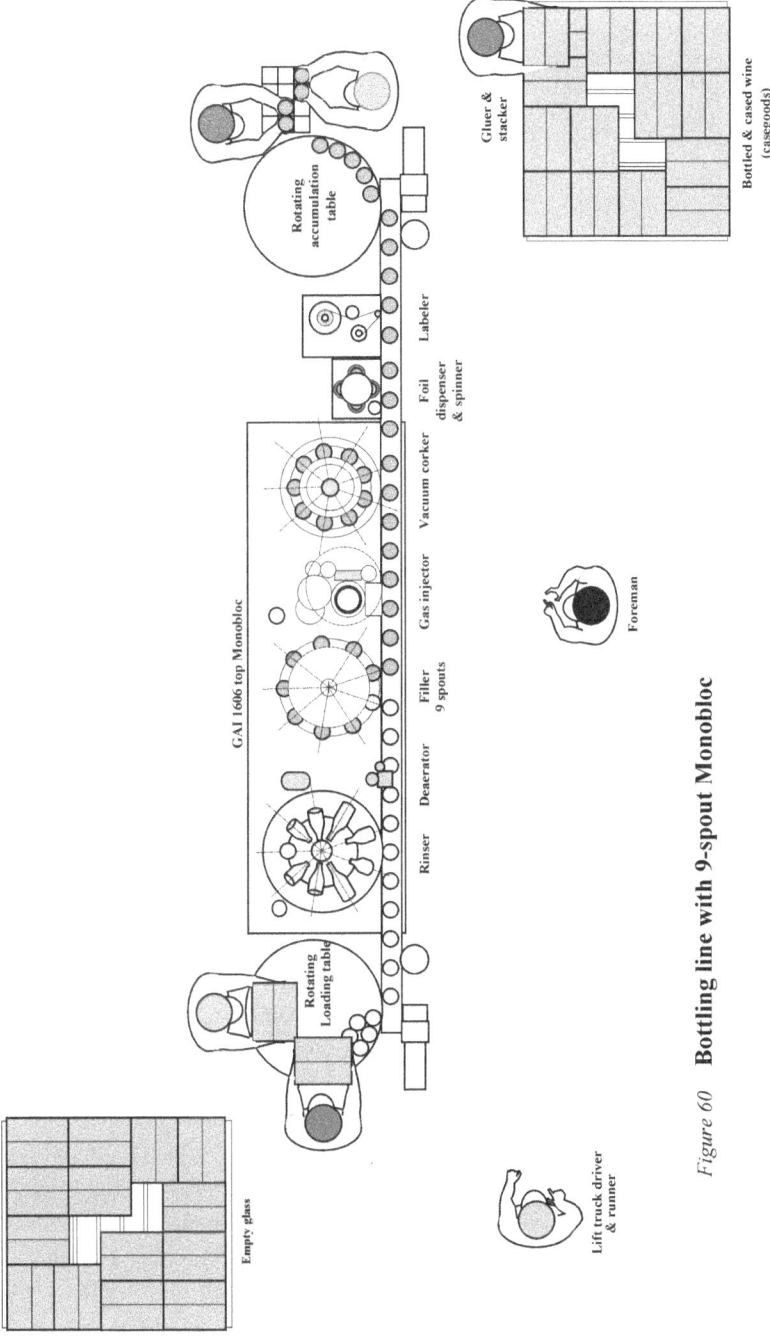

Figure 60 **Bottling line with 9-spout Monobloc**

A *plate-and-frame filter* is next. It is set up with polishing grade filter sheets rated at 0.50–0.70 microns. The purpose of this filter is to protect the membrane filter which follows and to minimize the buildup of particulates on the membrane filter element. Membrane filter elements are much more expensive than paper filter sheets.

The third and last component of the final filtration pass is the *membrane filter*, also called a *sterile filter*. As pointed out previously, the pore size is

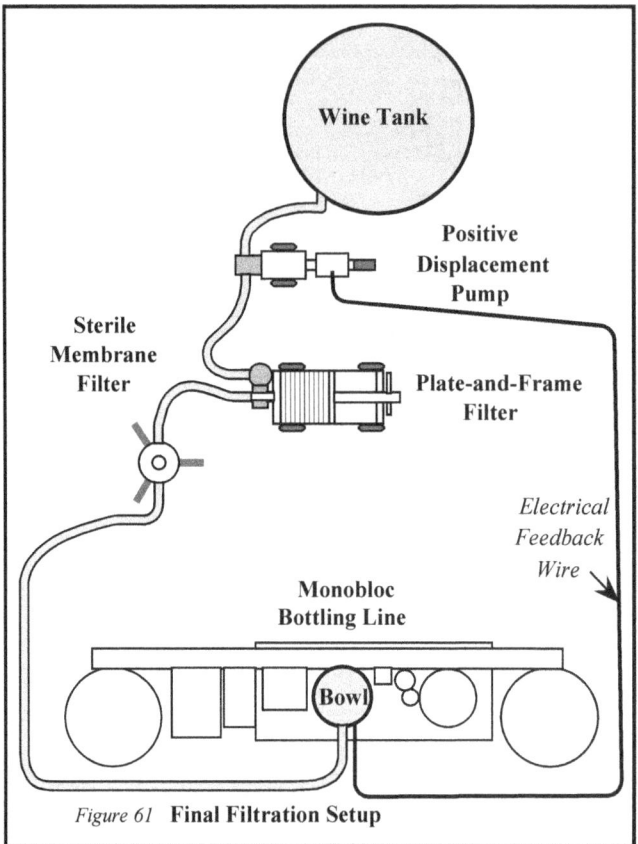

Figure 61 **Final Filtration Setup**

absolutely uniform, which means nothing larger than the pore size passes through. Membrane filters are unlike sheet filters that trap particles in a maze of criss-crossed fibers, but allow a very small percentage of particles larger than the size rating to get through.

The most commonly used membrane filter is 0.45μ (micron) pore size. This is sufficiently tight to remove all cells that might cause problems later in the bottle. Because some of the larger polyphenolic molecules responsible for flavor and color in red wines are larger than 0.45μ, most of the higher-quality reds are not subjected to either of the tight sheet or membrane filtrations depicted here. But, for white wines—particularly those that have some residual sugar—sterile filtration is essential. In the case of Chardonnays that have completed MLF (verified by paper chromatography or equivalent) and have no fermentable sugar, sterile filtration may be passed up.

Membrane filters must be subjected to a procedure called a bubble point test prior to use to verify the element's integrity. Follow the manufacturer's instructions for this test.

Membrane filters can be backwashed during an interruption in bottling if the buildup of particulates is slowing the flow. It is a good idea to repeat the bubble point test before resuming bottling. The element it is also backwashed before storing to remove particulates.

Further reading

Amerine, M.A., and M.A. Joslyn. *Table Wines: The Technology of Their Production.* 2nd ed. Berkeley, University of California Press, 1970.

Amerine, Maynard A., and Edward B. Roessler. *Wines: Their Sensory Evaluation.* San Francisco: W.H. Freeman and Company, 1976.

Bisson, Linda. *Section 4—The Malolactic Fermentation, Lesson 12.* Davis, CA: University of California at Davis, 2001.
Website: http://lfbisson.ucdavis.edu/?PDF/VEN124%20SEction$204.pdf

*Bolton, R.B., V.L. Singleton, L.F. Bisson, and R.E. Kunkee. *Principles and Practices of Winemaking.* New York: Chapman & Hall, 1996.

*Margalit, Yair. *Concepts in Wine Chemistry.* San Francisco: Board and Bench Publishing, 2013.

*Margalit, Yair, *Concepts in Wine Technology.* San Francisco: Board and Bench Publishing, 2013.

Peynaud, Emile. *Knowing and Making Wine.* New York: John Wiley & Sons, 1981.

Practical Winery and Vineyard: Technical Resource for Growers and Wineries. (Journal) San Rafael, CA: PWV, Inc. Website: http://www.practicalwinery.com

TTB. *Wine Laws and Regulations.* Website: http://www.ttb.gov/wine/wine_regs.shtml

Wine Business Monthly. Santa Rosa, CA: Wine Communications Group, Inc.
Website: http://www.winebusiness.com/wbm/

Winkler, A.J., J.A. Cook, W.M. Kliewer, and L.A. Lider. *General Viticulture.* Rev. and enlarged ed. Berkeley: University of California Press, 1974.

ॐ౮ॐ

—9—

Aptitudes for winemaking

Can anyone listen to Itzak Perlman play the violin, Celine Dion sing, or watch the "Flying Tomato," Shaun White, ride the snowboard down the halfpipe, without realizing that these megastars possess something very special? Sure, they have worked years to learn, practice and hone their skills. But, there is something else at play here. In each case, the person is endowed with physical gifts that make such performances possible. Perlman has his hands, coordination and the ability to become one with the violin. Dion has the voice, ability to control it and creativity of style. Shaun White has the athletic ability and courage.

Well, experience teaches that winemakers are no different. Underlying the performance are a cluster of aptitudes that enable the making of good wines. Yes, winemakers can study the process extensively, taste wines broadly, and work, work, work at the skill. In the end, hard work alone will not make a good winemaker.

- **Good wine palate**. Good tasting equipment is the key to everything else. A good wine palate is a gift. Some people have it, and others don't. Literally defined, a wine palate is *the sense of taste as related to wine*. Taste and aroma are interlinked, and both are important.

  Taste is detected by the tongue's taste buds. Aroma is detected by the olfactory sensors in the sinuses. A quick exercise will illustrate how the two work together. With one hand, pinch your nose to close it off. Place a pinch of grated Parmesan cheese on your tongue and rub it against the roof of your mouth with your tongue. What do you taste? It's pretty tasteless, isn't it? And, it feels like sawdust. Now release the nose and take a big sniff. Now what do you taste? Parmesan cheese, right? The only difference is whether or not you're smelling it while tasting it.

A good palate is important, not just to identify grape varieties and to enjoy wine, but also to detect wine problems that will need to be dealt with in the winery. Constituents like hydrogen sulfide, ethyl acetate, acetic acid, oxidation and excessive sulfur dioxide are among the problems to be avoided or corrected.

Possession of a good wine palate does not necessarily mean every taste and aroma is sensed equally. Frequently, people with an otherwise good wine palate are "blind" to one or more tastes or aromas. Some are hypersensitive to one or more tastes or aromas. Experienced winemakers recognize such shortcomings by participating in extensive tastings with other skilled winemakers. Once a shortcoming is acknowledged, the wise winemaker will include other practitioners in important tastings in order to compensate for his/her own deficiencies.

This is not a place to let a strong ego get in the way of making good wine.

- **Physical strength**. Winemaking is a physically demanding profession. If you operate a small winery, you will have to do most of the heavy lifting yourself. If you have a medium-to-large winery, you can afford to hire help to take care of the physical tasks.

  Equipment is available to help with the heavy lifting, but the size of your winery operation will determine whether or not you can afford to buy it.

- **Willingness to learn**. Winemaking requires heavy learning, too. The intensity may taper off with time, but the effort to learn should be intense until you become facile in far more than the basics. Thereafter, the learning process continues throughout a career.

  Even graduates of established enology programs will have to learn new things. Probably the most important of them will be how to handle the fruit on the crush pad. Different grape varieties, and where they are grown, require different methods. The methods you choose also will play a significant role in the wine style you produce. The kind of equipment you have may alter what you have to do to accomplish the desired results. This is "on-the-job" training, and it may take more than a few vintages to get it right.

  If you are lucky, your state's land grant university, or the local community college, has an enology seminar or workshop program addressing winemaking. Few states have them, but the number is growing along with local interest in winemaking. If all else fails, University of California at Davis has an excellent offering of seminars and short courses. In those states with many established wineries, the winemakers sponsor wine tech meetings where participating wineries' wines are blind-tasted and a wide variety of winemaking-related subjects are discussed.

  Winemakers are willing to do this for each other because they feel that "a rotten apple will spoil the barrel in the marketplace." They don't want substandard wines on the market that would detract from the reputations of all wineries in their producing area.

- **Commitment, or dedication**. Winemaking requires a strong commitment to producing quality wines. Relentless pursuit of this goal is a must.

Activities like monitoring fermentations, checking sulfur dioxide levels and racking of barrels must be done correctly and done on time.

- **Professional discipline**. In some ways interrelated with the preceding aptitude, professional discipline is simply an unswerving allegiance to doing what needs to be done in the vineyard and winery, come what may. No shortcuts. No postponements. No deletions for convenience's sake. It means being a self-starter when the winemaker doesn't feel like getting started.

- **Facility with numbers**. Winemaking requires working with numbers all of the time. Conversions from metric to Imperial (US) systems are frequent and must be accurate. Your life will be full of conversions from grams to ounces, liters to gallons and gallons to cases. Compounding the challenge is the use of different number systems depending on where you are in the winery process. On the crush pad, grapes are logged in by ton and pound. During winemaking, juice and must are measured in US gallons. Additions of sulfur dioxide, nutrients, diammonium phosphate (DAP) and yeast hulls; adjustments with tartaric acid, calcium carbonate, potassium bicarbonate or sugar; and finings like pectic enzymes, PVPP, tartrate seed crystals, isinglass, carbon powder and Sparkeloid may be measured in mg/L, g/L, oz/1,000 gals or lbs/1,000 gals. Once the wine is bottled, it is measured in 9-liter cases (12 bottles of 750 ml each), from bottling and storage at the winery, through distributors and on to retailers.

  If you aren't good with numbers, it is probably wise to choose a different career.

- **Knowledge of basic chemistry**. Winemaking is full of chemistry terms and materials identified by chemical names. The most respected winemaking texts were written by wine chemists. A high school course in chemistry is enough to understand what you need to know. If you didn't like chemistry or did poorly in chemistry class, you'd better pursue a different career path.

- **Willingness to work long hours**. Stamina is also essential. Particularly during the crush, it is not unusual to work several 80–100 hr weeks. In the first crush at one new winery, this writer averaged 104 hours weekly over two weeks. And that was with two full-time helpers who themselves worked about 60 hours per week. Even though all of the appropriate arrangements had been made, tanks and equipment were not in place to receive grapes. The winery wasn't ready to go on time because of financial and turf machinations by the owners and their accountants. Unfortunately, this kind of stuff happens, and you can see who ends up paying the price for it.

  Consider, too, the tasting room operation at the winery. The most effective hours for it to be open are on the weekend. Of course, the winery may choose its hours to be open to visitors, and a small winery can be open a few afternoon hours when the winemaker is otherwise doing paperwork. Being open when the wine-touring public is on the move can be crucial to establishing a new winery's reputation in the marketplace. Your banker will like tasting room sales, too. Sales at the winery bring twice the price of sales through normal distribution channels, and as much as three or four times the profit.

  Marketing events can force long hours, too. Day of 12–16 hr are common, as aggressive winemakers seek to maximize the payout from travel expenditures by participating in the tasting event, then visiting as many wine shops as possible. The distributor may set up a winemaker's dinner at a good restaurant in order to seek a position on the wine list or reward a good customer.

- **Commitment to cleanliness**. Wine is a food product. Cleanliness is essential to maintaining product quality. Federal and state regulations mandate cleanliness. Hoses, pumps and filters have to be cleaned after every use, and prior to most operations. Floors and drains have to be washed and flushed regularly with bleach solution or other cleaner.

  The only area that is subject to some argument is the development of yeast and malolactic bacterial flora on walls and in barrels. The mold will have to be at a height of more than 8 ft on the walls, though. Food regulations in most states require walls to be "smooth and scrubbable" (government word that means "able to be scrubbed") up to 8 ft above the floor. If you have concrete block walls, the surface pits should be filled to make a smooth surface.

- **Tolerance for regulations**. Winemaking is a heavily regulated business. Most regulations were adopted by the federal government to promote the production of marketable wines. The Fed's primary interest is in protecting its revenues, i.e., the excise tax.

  Almost all of the regulations pertaining to wine production are based on California conditions. After all, California was, and is, the overwhelmingly largest producing area. And, with the exception of Upper New York State, California was the nation's only wine-producing area coming out of Prohibition when the regulations were written. Some regulations pertaining to allowable adjustments to wine may not make sense in cooler growing areas. **The primary goal of all winemakers is to make good wines**, so follow the regulations and your conscience. Alcohol and Tobacco Tax and Trade Bureau (TTB) has a procedure for obtaining exceptions to the regulations.

  Cooperation with regulatory authorities is absolutely essential. Several winery owners of the author's acquaintance chose to defy regulations, and they were brought to heel in spectacular fashion. Most regulators are very helpful people to work with, if your heart is in the right place and you are trying to do right. But, if you choose to resist, they can be downright unpleasant.

- **Willingness to fill out government reports**. Since winemaking is heavily regulated, one should expect a lot of reporting. Production must be recorded and reported monthly at both federal and state levels. Of course, there is an annual summary report. See Chapter 11 for more specifics.

- **Patience**. Winemakers have to be patient. So do owners, if they are separate people. Things do **not** happen overnight in the wine production business. It takes years for a lot of things to happen, including the realization of real profits and the achievement of vineyard potentials. If you are a person who expects quick payouts, in spite of the warning that wines will require some time to convert to dollars, don't get involved in ownership or operation of a winery. It will result only in repetitive frustration. You might try becoming a distributor or retailer of fine wines instead.

- **Ego**. As a general rule, winemaker egos come in two sizes: large and larger. This condition is not necessarily a problem, as evidence shows that egos of all magnitudes have succeeded in the winemaking business. True humility can be a very becoming trait in a winemaker, but those people also tend to "get less ink" in the wine media, and that can be detrimental to the winery's marketing efforts.[1]

---

1. Overpowering winemaker egos are not universal, however. The author counts many truly humble winemakers among his friends and clients. Barney, Bill, Bob, Brent, Dick, Don, Harvey, Jacques, Jake, Jim, Phillipe, Sara and Scott know who they are. There are many more among the independent growers.

Large egos can become a problem, if they are possessed by both
the owner and winemaker, assuming they are not the same person.
Unfortunately, that combination ends most frequently in a parting of the
ways for the winemaker.

The foregoing psychological and physical profile narrows the field a bit
doesn't it?

೮೦೪

—10—

Does the wine sell itself?

Anyone entering commercial winemaking needs to understand what drives preferences of the American wine consumer. Among the motivators are the highly influential wine publications, such as *Wine Spectator Magazine* and Robert Parker's *Wine Advocate*. Their reviews and ratings prompt the better restaurants and wine shops to sell certain wines. Those wine publications, in turn, are influenced by the chatter coming out of California and European wineries. Wine stories are romantic and compelling.

Most wines do **not** sell themselves. Only a few exceptions come to mind where the wines are so popular that the biggest marketing challenge is allocating the scarce supply so as not to alienate the entire marketplace. Ponzi (Oregon), Ken Wright Cellars (Oregon), Leonetti Cellars (Washington) and Williams-Selyem (California) are four such operations.

Marketing savvy

For all wineries, marketing success must be earned. Personal selling, motivating distributor sales personnel, encouraging positive press coverage, emphasis on specialty wine shops and restaurants, and a well-directed tasting room program are all keys to success.

There are only a few good books dealing with wine marketing. Heretofore, the best book appears to be *Blood and Wine*,[1] the book about the Gallo empire

---

1. Hawkes , Ellen. *Blood & Wine*; See "Further Reading" at chapter end.

and how it developed, and it's a good read, and valuable to every wine marketer in understanding how a big player works in the marketplace.

Heavy emphasis on chain supermarkets and volume discounters can be harmful to your bottom line. These volume-oriented retailers play the discount game, and a very large portion of the wine sold through them moves at discounted prices. Small wineries simply cannot make a reasonable profit by selling at the same prices as million-gallon operations. At the other end of the spectrum, tasting room sales and direct shipment can bring the winery over four times as much profit as sales through distributors.

Wine Spectator Magazine is a treasure trove of meaningful and meaningless wine facts, but it will give you a full dose of how the best wineries in the world present themselves to the trade and public. *Practical Winery & Vineyard Magazine* is the best technical publication structured for the industry. A relatively new source with enlightening articles about wine marketing and, increasingly, about vineyard and winery technical issues, is *Wine Business Monthly*.

Marketing wines is very different from most other products. So, if your marketing experience is not in a regulated beverage industry, forget about your previous successes and get ready to learn a lot and change your approach to marketing.

Some of the important elements of a successful marketing program are:

- A **quality reputation**, promoted by delivering consistently high product quality, appealing packaging (not just labels) and letting wine consumers know about it through the wine press.

- **Visible presence** in the marketplace, meaning product on retail shelves and restaurant wine lists, which is achieved by the distributor and winery working together. Additional high profile activities that enhance visibility are participation in wine judgings, charity wine events and local wine festivals. In some states, these functions include in-store wine tastings.

- **Imaginative promotional events** that spotlight the winery and its key people.

- Winery **support of distributor efforts** by providing point-of-sale materials, sales incentives (in states where they're allowed), informational briefings, field appearances by key winery personnel (such as winemaker dinners in trend-setting restaurants) and maybe, even field sales representatives and/or wine brokers. It is also productive, in your key metropolitan markets, to have winery-employed people visiting stores and helping the distributor's staff with merchandising tasks like installing shelf stickers, putting neck hangers on bottles, cleaning up your shelf space and reminding the store manager what to reorder.

- **Cultivation of a loyal following**, by communicating effectively with consumers through winery events, wine clubs and newsletters, for example.

- Systematic efforts at **wine media relations**, by issuing press releases and offering wine column suggestions.

- A **direct shipping program** plus, perhaps, a winery-operated wine club, to access new markets, cater to loyal customers, and expand those high-margin tasting room sales.

Did you notice that all of these marketing functions require effort and expenditures by the winery?

A winery owner will get used to idea that the winery has to carry a large part of the marketing burden, even though distributors and retailers take about fifty percent of the wine's retail shelf price. This concept is the regrettable marketplace reality that government regulation has allowed to develop, by virtue of the wholesale oligopoly.

Channels of distribution

Most wine is sold through the three-tiered distribution system (Figure 62). Under that system, instituted following the repeal of Prohibition, the federal government has sought to separate: (1) manufacturing; (2) distribution and wholesale functions; and, (3) retailing, in hopes of preventing monopolies and keeping criminal money out of the system.

In the three-tiered system, wineries sell wines to wholesalers/distributors, who transport the wine into a local market, warehouse the wines temporarily, and then sell them to retailers. In most states, each operator in the system has to sell at the same price to every company at the next level. This provision is intended to prevent favoritism and encourage competition.

In many states, wineries enjoy a special privilege: they can sell at all levels, to wholesalers, to retailers and to retail consumers.

In some states, like Pennsylvania, and in the Canadian provinces, the government is the wholesaler **and** retailer (except for restaurants) of all wines coming into the state. The differences among states in regard to channels of distribution are so numerous, the subject will not be pursued further here. Let us just say that the discrepancies among states—channels, licensing, fees, reporting—present a chaotic and expensive world for the small local winery to cope with.

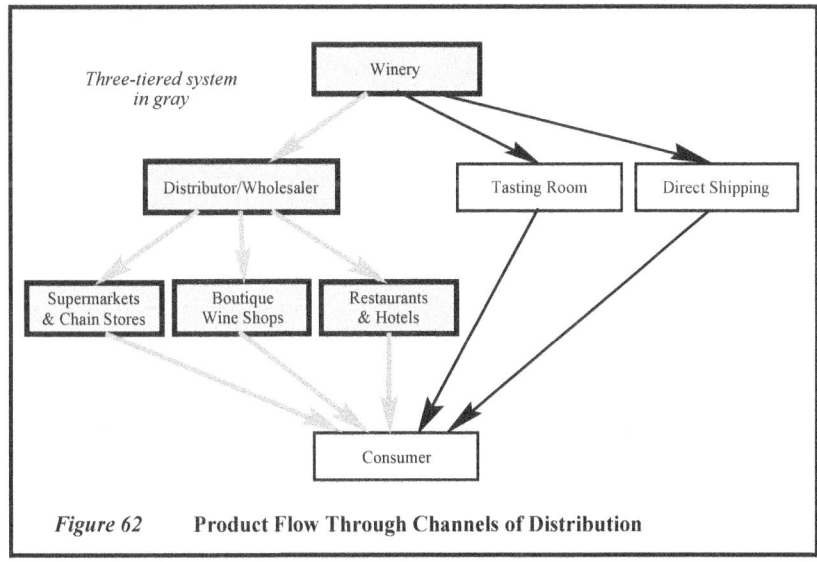

Figure 62   **Product Flow Through Channels of Distribution**

Distributors control your marketing destiny

Distributors control almost every winery's marketing success.

Distributors fill their wine portfolios with the wines their customers want. That should come as no surprise, since what the restaurants and wine shops want is what the wholesalers should be expected to provide to them. It has become common practice for distributors to have their senior sales staff taste new wine offerings and vote as to whether or not they want to sell those wines.

In general, there has been a substantial consolidation of companies at the wholesale level, with larger distributors buying smaller ones. Each of these mergers reduces the number of wines available in the service area, as the surviving operation discards its weakest lines. Consolidation also creates opportunities for new distributorships to get started, because there are plenty of wineries who want distribution, and there are many consumers who seek new wine experiences.

In rapidly growing areas (Atlanta and suburban Washington, DC were good examples in the early 1990s) wine consumption is expanding fast enough for distributors to take on more wineries. The flip side of that coin is the otherwise population-stagnant East Coast markets, where many distributors have to drop a winery to take on a new one.

Making the task more difficult, some states forbid winery representatives from calling on retail accounts unless accompanied by a distributor representative.

Most states allow their wineries to function as wholesalers by selling their own wines direct to retail outlets inside the state. But government monopoly states (Pennsylvania and the Canadian provinces are good examples) require all wine to be bought and sold by the government, except in restaurants, and the government does not allow freely competitive access to their jurisdictions. Some states, like Oregon and California, allow wineries located within their states to function as wholesalers by selling direct to retail outlets in the same state. However, many distributors do not tolerate direct winery-to-retailer sales in their areas by the wineries they distribute.

You have the choice in your own state: utilize the broader sales coverage and efficient distribution provided by a distributor, if you are fortunate enough to convince a good one to carry your wines, or distribute you own wine within the state.

Most states permit their wineries to sell direct to consumers in their own states through winery tasting rooms and at wine festivals.

Supermarkets and large chain stores

Supermarkets count, too. But supermarkets are less venturesome when it comes to pioneering the marketing of new wines. Their decisions regarding which wines to place on their shelves are driven by looking in the rear-view mirror. They base most of their shelf placements, or *facings,* on how well a wine already has been selling, and psychological studies of which shelf positions sell the best

Here is how the seasonal *shelf-setting* exercises are conducted. Nowadays, there are computer programs for the task. Consultants, distributors and some of the chain stores themselves have the programs. In goes the sales history of each wine, and out comes a plan, indeed a map of the shelves and where each wine is to be placed. Price is considered because the store's profit is determined by it. The best profit-producers get eye height and center of the row. Jug wines and the slowest sellers go to the bottom shelf. The distributors' sales people and some winery representatives volunteer to do the physical labor. Every now and then, there's a tossup or vacancy in the shelf assignment; it pays to have your winery's representative present.

Oh, didn't we mention? These "shelf-setting" exercises begin at 3 or 4 am. There's no point in disrupting the customers' shopping efforts.

To be sold in supermarkets, wines have to have *barcodes*, so they can be scanned for identification (SKU number) and price. Supermarkets don't like to update their check stand computers more than annually. Many would prefer that wineries use the same barcode for a specific wine, say, Chardonnay, from year-to-year. That way, the vintage can change without updating the computer.

One supermarket chain threatened a $500 service charge, for corrections and changes made between the annual updates.

Some states allow supermarket chains to charge rent to the wineries for shelf space, the same as they do for non-alcohol products. Other states forbid the practice as unfair to competition. We will not go into identifying those states here.

During special promotions, supermarkets may utilize *end stacks* and/or *free-standing stacks*, or *islands*. It usually requires supernormal sales efforts to get one of these. An advertising campaign can help. Your sales through this store must already be substantial, or you'll have to put some advertising muscle behind the promotion.

Some states allow *cooperative advertising*. You've seen them. The store's weekly print ads feature selected wines, and the wineries share the advertising cost.

In-store wine tastings

Some states allow wineries to conduct promotional tastings inside retail stores. The winery rep brings a card table and, in some states, the wines to be used for tastings (rather than draw on the shelf inventory). It may also be necessary to arrange with the distributor and store manager to have extra cases of wine delivered to meet the sales generated. The tasting table is set up in the wine department. A good wine salesman can move ten to twelve cases of wine a day this way. Oregon allows each winery to conduct two of these tastings in each store per year, one in the spring at the release of white wines, and one in the fall for reds, although the law does not specify which wines may be poured at either. An off-premise Special Events License is required each time. Of course, the store manager has to approve these events.

Boutique wine shops

If yours is a small winery, boutique wine shops can be a winery's best friend. Not only do they support a higher price structure and a greater tolerance for a wide variety of wine labels, but they will also help by hand-selling the wine, and by conducting in-store tastings to help introduce each wine. Boutique, or specialty, wine shops cater to a highly knowledgeable and loyal customer base. Store employees need to know about the winery and wines, so they can discuss them intelligently with their customers.

Winemaker dinners

To establish and maintain a strong base of sales in restaurants, a winery needs to do winemaker dinners. The restaurant builds a menu around the wines, and sells the event at $75–100 a plate. **The diners expect to meet the winemaker.** Owners and sales representatives are not acceptable, unless they are the winemaker, or have achieved superstar status on their own, **and** have a strong command of wine knowledge. See Chapter 18 for further discussion of this point.

Consider the plight of one winery owner whose confidence far exceeded his meager wine knowledge. He tried to fill in at the scheduled dinners after he fired his winemaker. Besides making a fool of himself, he learned a tough lesson the hard way. Within days, the distributor told him to send a truck to pick up his wines because the distributor had, expressed in industry jargon, "resigned the account" (as in *terminated*).

Winemaker dinners present an opportunity to solidify the winery's position on the wine list and a nice way to reward a restaurateur for featuring the wines. A winery can double up on the benefits by inviting the local paper's wine writer to attend the dinner.

Robert Mondavi maintained a prodigious schedule of winemaker dinners. His wines were very strong in the restaurant trade.

Direct shipment and wine clubs

That brings us to the subject of direct, or reciprocal, shipment of wines across state lines by wineries direct to consumers.

Direct shipment is a new wrinkle over the past twenty years that has brought some success. Difficulty in getting acceptable sales effort from distributors, or failure to secure a distributor at all, has driven wineries to this alternative. The thinking is, if you can establish a beachhead with consumers, that success will convince a distributor to carry your wines. The system has worked that way.

Orders for wine can be placed in the tasting room, by mail, by telephone or online. Generally, the winery is allowed to keep a signed authorization on file, as an aid to circumvent purchases by minors over the telephone.

Under this system, states agree among themselves to consider the shipping winery to be the point of sale, thus avoiding collection of taxes at the recipient's address and the requirement for the wine to pass through local distributors. But, regulators have demonstrated their genius for imposing requirements on verifying that the recipient is 21 and sober. The direct shipment system is called "reciprocal," because the states have to agree to "reciprocate" with the other states in regard to what can be done and how it will be reported and/or regulated.

However, the strong lobbies of the distillers, coupled with support and political influence of the big city distributors, have been successful in repealing direct shipping laws in some states, and prevented them from ever being adopted in others.

At this writing, fifteen states prohibit direct shipping outright. Thirty-four states, including Washington, DC, permit direct shipping subject to some kind of limitation. Two states, Iowa and New Mexico, allow full reciprocal shipping. That means, they will allow whatever shipments the other state in the transaction allows.

Many wineries have been very successful in developing a loyal customer following through wine clubs. Many of them feature automatic monthly shipments direct to consumers, with the winery selecting the specific wines in each shipment. The winery secures the credit card number and a standing advance authorization through a signed agreement with the member. Of course, each shipment carries the opportunity to put promotional information and an order form in the customers' hands.

Many wine clubs offer their members admission to exclusive special events and discounts at the winery.

Tasting rooms

The winery tasting room is an important element in any winery's distribution system.

It's amazing how many people are swept up in the wine-touring scene. In some parts of our society, it's entertaining and almost a way of life. Uncle Joe and Aunt Lynne come to visit and what will we do? . . . why, pile them into cars with the kids (if they're old enough) and friends, or even rent a stretch limousine, and take them on a winery tour, of course.

Winery visitors seem to find magic in the experience. To most, it matters little whether the winery is a Taj Mahal, Disneyland, a utilitarian industrial building, or just a well-kept rustic building. They seem to get a kick out of all of them. What matters is **the product**, **the process** and **the people,** not the building. Many wine tourists come back, again and again. Wine touring has become commonplace in wine-producing areas.

Tasting room businesses are very attractive, profit-wise. Wineries usually sell in the tasting room at the same list prices as specialty wine shops. That's a little higher than the supermarket, who make their money on volume. But typically, the winery will capture the wholesale and retail markups in tasting room sales, bringing the winery a much larger profit than selling through a distributor. This subject is discussed in detail in the chapter on winery costs and revenues.

Winery tasting rooms also help create demand through usual distribution channels. Where better to imprint customer loyalty than where the wine is made? The ambiance smells great. The barrels are quaint. The winemaker is a rock star.

Consumers, and not just those of wine, have found winery tours to be an entertaining social event. Tours to Napa Valley wineries became so popular that wineries instituted tasting room fees so as to discourage young people in pursuit of a cheap date. Wineries in many states have now adopted the same practice, although many of them will waive the fee if you buy something. Others will let you keep the nice monogrammed wine glass you use for tasting.

Some states allow a winery to have off-premise tasting rooms in addition to the one at the winery. Oregon allows two off-premise tasting rooms. This practice enables a winery to do its own retailing in places like metropolitan downtowns and vacation/tourist areas.

Related merchandise

Cork pullers, foil cutters, wine glasses, carafes, gas injectors, gift boxes, serving baskets and trays, coolers, crackers, Pinot Noir chocolate sauce and other similar items can legitimately be called "wine-related." Printed shirts, monogrammed sweaters, jogging suits, trivets, posters, calendars, stationery, napkins, placemats, art, sculptures, aprons, hats, umbrellas, cheeses, sausages, roasted hazelnuts, jerky, honey, jelly, coffee, tea and a seemingly endless array of stuff are sold in tasting rooms. It seems no effort is spared in the effort to separate customers from their money.

Some states look unkindly to this kind of tasting room product proliferation. Take Oregon, for example . . . folks are pretty persnickety there. Neighbor complaints about winery-sponsored rock concerts spurred the legislature and state planning agency to clamp down on "non-wine" activities and impose a "farm stand" concept. After all, vineyards are "exclusive farm use" land, and the government is going the extra step to allow a winery, which is a food processing facility (of the crop grown on the property), as a "non-conforming" use. Restaurants are not agriculture-related, nor are retail stores or theaters. Oregon statutes limit revenues derived from sales and fees for everything other than wine to 25 percent of total on-premise retail revenues. Not only that, every item sold at retail must be considered to be agriculturally related and necessary for the sale of wine.

As of this writing, there is no evidence that the state or counties have audited or otherwise uniformly enforced these statutory limitations.

In some other states, it seems that almost anything goes.

Wedding and conference facilities

As an adjunct to tasting room activities, some wineries build additional facilities to host meetings, weddings and occasional winemaker dinners. In particular, some quaint wineries provide a romantic backdrop for a wedding. These activities can prove to be large money-makers. Usually, local chefs are used to cater food, and the tasting room staff takes care of the wine. Beer and mixed drinks are excluded under the winery license.

The support cost for such activities is not cheap. The winery has to be careful to recover all costs for personnel and equipment rentals or use charges, as well as added insurance premiums to cover third party liquor liability. Fees can range upwards from $2,000 per event.

Some states have not taken too kindly to these "non-agricultural" commercial activities either. In Oregon, for example again, the 25 percent limitation on non-wine revenues may preclude space rentals. Can you imagine a wedding party consuming enough wine to account for three times the rental fees for the facility? Does the winery already sell more than 25 percent of its total on-site revenues in non-wine merchandise?

But then, Oregon allows development of destination resorts in exclusive farm or forestry zones. Such facilities can operate restaurants, provide lodging, do unlimited weddings and conferences and conduct other non-agricultural activities. The reason for this permissiveness is economic development.

Let's get this straight: it's illegal if a winery does it, but it's legal if a destination resort does it?

That's Oregon.

Quality and the product line

We cannot leave the subject of marketing without discussing the products being marketed.

There is a turf battle for control of the products being offered. Winemakers feel that **they** should control the types and qualities of wines produced. In other words, the company should be "production driven." This is only right, they feel, because the quality and quantity of the wines vary from year-to-year according to the weather. And besides, isn't it true that wine consumers have made the winemakers the center of adulation as the creative artists who craft the wine's style? Therefore, the winemakers are crucial to creating demand for the wine.

Marketing people counter that they are the operatives out in the trenches who have to move the wine, and they know better than the cellar rats back at the winery what it is that consumers want to buy. Therefore, the winery operation should be "market driven."

So, what is the right answer to this classic struggle that occurs in many industries? The right answer is that neither end of the spectrum is correct; the best situation is a combination of inputs somewhere between the poles. Each winery has to find the balance that is right for them.

As a general rule, the smaller and more specialized a winery is, the closer to the "production driven" end of the spectrum it will find success. Smaller wineries tend to have loyal customers who follow the vintages and don't mind year-to-year variations, just so long as they can be traced back to climatic conditions. With these smaller producers, season-to-season variations are a large part of the appeal, or "romance" of the wine product. And, the unique character of an occasional 95-point wine is what makes the winemaker a superstar. But, the winery is in for real difficulty if it doesn't pay attention to what is going on out there in the marketplace.

Conversely, the larger a winery is, the greater is the need to standardize the product for acceptance by the overwhelmingly largest segment of the wine market. Under these conditions, it is very important to understand what kind of product the market wants to put on the table, day-in and day-out, without unexpected variations in quality. Reliance in a consistent product is important to consumer confidence. This part of the market doesn't follow the wine press closely, or at all. It wants to be able to buy a label, and not be adversely surprised by the product behind the label. Of course, the larger wineries are better equipped to control wine characteristics. They have more blending options, better equipment, better quality control laboratories, more and higher-paid personnel. They are able to follow the pulse of the market better because they have more people working "out there" in the marketplace.

Therefore, the largest wineries will find success closer to the "market driven" extreme, but they should not ignore what the production people have to say. After all, most wine is not made from off-the-shelf ingredients that are the same year after year. Unless the producer wants to get into the spices and extracts formulation of wine, the product still has to be made from grapes.

Quality of "reserve" wines

It seems that every winery feels compelled to have reserve wines which go by the label declarations "winemaker's reserve," vintner's reserve," "proprietor's reserve," "barrel select," etc. Some of them deserve the designation, and some don't. When a winery chooses to use this practice, some sort of threshold is usually established for quality and other characteristics, then the winemaking staff tries to replicate that standard each year. Sometimes the standard is simple: the best barrels of the vintage. Sometimes it is more profound: selected from the best barrels bearing desired flavor and aroma characteristics from a specific vineyard site.

Regardless of what the standards are, it is usually the winemaking staff that is best qualified to make the judgment. The reasons are simple. The winemaker is closest to the wine as it develops in barrel or tank and, if he/she is skilled, has some knowledge of how the wine is likely to evolve once it is blended and bottled. Marketing people don't spend enough time in the cellar, tasting the wines throughout their development, nor do they receive the technical training, to acquire such skills.

Once a winery gets into the "reserve" game, it is of paramount importance to maintain that high standard of quality and characteristics. Wine consumers who care enough to pay for the "reserve" designation expect continuity of the wine, if not in intensity, at least in varietal and site characteristics.

The author has seen marketing managers and consultants try to plan future winery production of the various types and qualities of wine. Then, they go to the distributors and make promises that the production volume will be there, so it's worth committing the effort to establish and maintain the brand. Maybe highly repeatable weather patterns enable California wineries to come close to this ideal. The Pacific Northwest's weather conditions, and those in most other marginal climate areas across America, do not.

Then, in a poor weather year, the pressure is on to relax the standards, so enough wine will qualify for "reserve" status. The result, more often than not, is that good customers transfer their loyalties to another winery. In like manner, so do the distributors' sales staffs; they don't like to hear customer complaints.

How much "reserve" wine to bottle each year? A good rule is to set your minimum threshold of quality high . . . and stick to it! That may mean that there will be no reserve wine in off years. It also means that there may be more reserve wine in excellent vintages. Imagine that! Or, the excess reserve-quality wine can be used to upgrade the regular label for that variety. Price and/or allocation may be used to spread out the availability of an outstanding wine from an excellent vintage.

How much of a given "reserve" wine is available each year, and the price fluctuation relating to demand and supply, are all part of the mystery that makes wine so interesting to high-end wine consumers.

Vintage predictions

Wineries have to be careful about how they tout the quality expectations for an outstanding year. If they talk too much about the quality coming next year, it has a depressing effect on demand for the wine currently on the shelves. Some wine buyers will defer present purchases and wait for the new vintage. Tactics including post-offs and other promotional efforts may be necessary to clear the current wine from the marketplace.

Single vineyard wines

A trend swept across American wineries over the past fifteen years: the single vineyard label designation. It was related to European wine-producing regions, most of them in France, where identity with the growing site is a significant element in a wine's market value. Once the trend got started in America, wineries discovered that they could command a higher price for such wines. Reserve blendings were ripped apart and the component parts sold under different vineyard names. In some cases, the practice revealed some distinctive wines that were worth the price. In most cases, it did not. In too many cases, none of the single vineyard wines were as good as the reserve blend had been. But, it was sort of like "keeping up with the Joneses."

The proliferation of single vineyard wines butted up against distributor and retailer tolerance for the number of labels from a single winery. Every label has to have a separate barcode and shelf facing. Distributors and retailers reacted by limiting the number of labels they would carry for a winery and/or wine variety. A lot of new labels failed to make it to the shelf.

It has always been difficult to get distributors and retailers to carry both a regular and a reserve label for a variety, say Merlot. Single vineyard wines have crowded the field even more.

Setting prices

The prices of your wines do two things. They determine the revenue side of your income statement. But, they serve an equally important function: they have a strong influence on how wine consumers perceive the quality and desirability of your wines.

Allocation

Wineries whose products are in high demand frequently find that it is necessary to "allocate" the supply by consumer market. The practice limits the amount of a wine that is available to each distributor. It is something of a compromise: alienate everybody the same amount, in order to avoid making a few really mad. Besides, it helps support a higher price structure.

Linking varieties

Sometimes one wine is highly sought-after, and others are not. By linking sales, requiring that the distributor take a case of White Riesling as a condition of buying a case of Pinot Noir, for example, the winery assures sales of the weaker product.

Advertising

Media advertising

Advertising is another area of wine uniqueness. In general, print and radio/television advertising are of marginal effectiveness in creating wine sales, except for stimulating sales for standard quality and jug wines in chain outlets by very large wineries during the Thanksgiving-Christmas holiday season. It is true that large and prestigious wineries use print advertising in highly selected publications primarily to burnish their image.

Television

Buying time on television is a very expensive proposition. It doesn't make economic sense to commit part of the winery's advertising budget to it. On the other hand, any exposure you can achieve through news stories and feature shows is golden, especially in advance of regional wine touring events.

Watch out for offers of low-priced TV ad packages. One owner was very proud that he had scored a coup, even bragging to his friends about it. His exuberance changed when he saw the schedule for the commercials . . . all between midnight and 5 am. Who is watching TV during those hours?

The author also has had experience with an NBA team sponsorship, a package which brought television ads during home games and exclusive rights to listing on the menu for the sponsor's dining room and sky boxes. It didn't sell wine . . . beer, yes, wine no.

Radio

Advertising messages on radio reach a limited market, say, a metropolitan area. You are spending a lot of money on reaching a lot of people who don't drink wine. To enhance your effectiveness, it is smart to ask the radio sales rep for a copy of their **Arbitron Rating** versus other radio stations in the same market area. Arbitron surveys a shopping basket of purchases, even wine. In a major metropolitan market, which would have many radio stations, you can prioritize your budget according to wine-buying listenership.

If the rep won't give it to you, it probably means his station doesn't do well. Hard rock and country-western stations are probably not a good bet.

Newspaper

The most effective place in the newspaper is the wine writer's column saying good things about your wine. Second best is a space ad adjacent to the wine column, if you can get the editor to position it so it looks like your wine is being featured. That is not always possible.

Another possibility is to talk a supermarket chain into cooperative advertising. Usually, this is done by the distributor's salesman, and it features a group of wines carried by the same distributor. Your wine gets exposure in the weekly food ad, where a lot of people look for bargains. That is the problem. Cooperative ads always feature big discounts, which means you are posting off the wine's price for the whole month to everybody in the state

State laws do not permit discount coupons or rebates on alcoholic beverages.

Internet website

This is the computer age. Wine consumers are heavy computer users. Establish your own website to advertise the wines, give directions to the winery, introduce your key personnel, build your mailing list and wine club, and advertise your wines for sale by direct shipping.

Wine media

Now, here's the vehicle to present your advertising message to the very people you want to receive it. As wine regions grow, wine-related tabloids have a habit of developing. This is the best place to put your advertising dollars to reach the customer base within your region. Such papers usually carry listings of winery events and feature stories about individual wineries. What could be better? The cost is probably very reasonable, too.

America's top wine consumer publication is *Wine Spectator* magazine. Others of note are: *Food & Wine*, *Wine Enthusiast*, *The Wine Advocate*.

Direct mail

A much more effective avenue of advertising is direct mail to a wine-related mailing list. A winery can compile such a list from the visitors' log in the tasting room, and perhaps buy membership rosters of wine-related organizations. In some areas, wineries have pooled their mailing lists to promote area-wide winery touring events.

Wine marketing is largely a game of personal selling at the wholesale and retail levels, and word-of-mouth.

Point-of-sale materials

Printed materials that are used in the retail store to draw attention to a wine are called **point-of-sale materials** (POS). The most common are: shelf talkers, neck hangers, posters and highlight stickers:

> **Shelf talkers** are cards carrying a glowing review and score by a wine magazine or wine columnist, or reporting an award in competition. They are usually taped on the shelf edge, below the store's price sticker.
>
> **Neck hangers** are collar-style pieces placed on the bottle's neck.

Posters are useful in boutique wine shops. They are rarely allowed in supermarkets, unless placed with an end stack or island display.

Highlight stickers are usually metallic foil medallions touting an award won in competition. Market research demonstrates that stickered bottles will sell before unstickered bottles, even if they are the same wine, adjacent to each other on the shelf, and the only difference is the medallion.

It is good practice for the winery to include an envelope with the relevant shelf talkers or neck hangers when the wine is put in the case, right off the bottling line. Medallions are almost always added well after the wine is bottled, so they have to be applied in the store.

Technically, anything attached to a wine bottle is part of the label, and requires TTB label approval along with front label, back label and neck band. State control agencies may have to approve them, too. In practice, most wineries do not bother with this State triviality.

Who places point-of-sale materials on the shelf and bottle? In boutique wine shops, it is usually done by the store employees. Supermarkets are different. In them, winery field representatives or the **distributor's merchandisers** do the job. The way wine is delivered to supermarkets shelves makes the difference. The distributor's truck delivers the wine, in case, to the wine department aisle. Merchandisers come along separately to place the wine on the shelf and apply the POP materials. Some distributors are good about this task, others are not. Store employees usually do not put the wine on the shelves. Nowadays, retailers do not maintain back-room inventory. What's on the shelf is what's in the store.

An effective tactic is for a winery field representative to visit the best supermarkets on a regular schedule, prior to the distributor's designated delivery day. In addition to dusting the winery's shelf inventory, the winery rep fills out a duplicate order form, indicating the wines that need to be brought in. One copy of the order goes to the store manager to expedite his/her reorder process, and the other copy goes to the distributor to make sure the order is received.

Does it seem like the winery has to do a lot of the distributor's work? Do you want your wines to sell? *C'est la vie!*

Charity auction events

There are times when winery people feel that whoever invented the concept of wine donations to charity auctions should be taken out at sunrise and summarily shot. Well, fortunately, it's not quite that bad.

But, a belief exists that wineries make wine for the purpose of donating it to any and every charitable cause there is. Wineries are repeatedly subjected to requests that they cannot afford to grant. In particular, fledgling wineries are not in a position to squander product. And then, every time a winery turns down such a request, it runs the risk of alienating customers. So, how do you handle this delicate situation?

Of course, there are charitable events for which the winery owner wishes to be a philanthropist.

Some wineries establish a budget each year for donations. When it's gone, it's gone. Others propose to donate a bottle for every bottle purchased at retail price, essentially selling the wine at winery FOB price. Most wineries try to set some rational guidelines for granting donation requests.

Focus on the needs of your wine business rather than the needs of the charity. Adopt a *business-based* guideline policy: treat charitable donations as advertising expenditures under these considerations:

- Every donation request must be submitted in writing, with the applicant stating the purpose of the charity, how the wine will be used and exposed and how its patrons relate to wine consumption.

- The requesting group or its event audience has to be comprised of people who consume wines at your quality and price levels.

- Make sure that your wine will receive the best exposure to event patrons. That means getting it into the oral auction rather than the silent auction.

- If you donate wine to be served with the dinner, make sure it is clear to everyone that you donated the wine, rather than letting them conclude that the wine is being donated by the hotel, which is charging full rates for the room and the meal.

- The patrons attracted to a specific charity auction usually repeat year-after-year. Your objective is to expose your wines to potential new customers. So, adopt a rule that you will participate in a specific charity event no more than two consecutive years in a row. By that time, you will have reached almost all of their patrons and it is time to move on.

Community celebrations

Many communities stage celebration events to promote the local economy and civic pride. To the winery tempted to participate, the considerations are similar to those for charity fundraisers. These events require staffing, licensing, transportation and other costs. The winery should be asking itself these questions:

- What kind of people will come to the event? Are they likely to be wine consumers, or beer fans?

- Will we sell enough wine by the glass to make our appearance worthwhile?

- How can we promote sales by the bottle and case?

- Can we use the event to promote customer traffic to our tasting room?

- Can we use the event to sign up more people for our wine club and/or direct shipments?

- Is our staff's time better spent doing something else?

Joint market promotion tours

The state's wineries, or those of a region, can band together for market promotion tours. A very effective format offers two main events. First, in the morning, there is a seminar about pairing the region's wines with food. Arrangements are made with local chefs in the target city, New York for example, to prepare the food in hors d'oeuvre-size servings. Wine writers and other chefs are invited.

Careful . . . there are jealousies. Presentations on the wines are integrated with presentations on the food items.

The afternoon session is a tasting for the trade. Wineries set up Tables to present their wines. Invitees include wine writers, restaurant beverage managers, wine retailers and distributors. The distributors can help by sending invitations to their good customers.

Several cities can be included in such a tour, allowing one or two days between cities for travel and individual winery promotional efforts. The tour can be funded by wineries picking up their own travel expenses and paying a fee for common costs. In some states, additional support can be provided by the State and/or USDA marketing grants.

Whether or not you allow wineries to participate who don't already have distribution in a market, it is advisable to have some kind of wine screening program. This can be done in an annual event where wineries submit wines in advance, then the participating winemakers evaluate the wines blind, i.e., brown-bagged.

Fish where the fish are

It has been said: "If you want to catch a fish, it helps to fish where the fish are."[2] Over the years, many wineries have labored unsuccessfully to market their wines in areas of intense competition or that don't buy much wine. So, it helps to quantify wine market demand by major metropolitan areas.

For analysis, wine purchases can be placed in two categories:

- **Resident purchases.** These are purchases made by local people though retail stores, restaurants, tasting rooms, and now, direct shipment.

- **Visitor purchases.** These are wines sold to tourists, business travelers, sports fans, conventions and other group events to customers who don't live in the area.

In the mid-1970s, Dr. Ray Folwell, agricultural economist at Washington State University, conducted a national market survey aimed at identifying the markets for a "market basket" of food products. Table wine was included in the study. Dr. Folwell found that most purchasers of wine, at that time, could be described by these characteristics: income over $35,000, 35–55 years of age, some college education, and frequent travel.

In 35 years, things have changed considerably. Let's review those four demographic indicators of wine demand.

- **Household income.** Female participation in the labor force has increased so dramatically (in 2008, 59.3 percent compared to males at 73.2 percent), it is now more appropriate to consider *household income* rather than individual personal income. If Dr. Folwell's findings were correct, they would indicate that wine consumption was a truly elitist phenomenon in the 1970s. While that may have been true in some parts of the country, it was not true on the West Coast.

---

2. This observation is attributable to Ken Hicks, who was Regional Marketing Director for the author at Montinore Vineyards. Hicks had held the same position with Inglenook Winery.

In the following analysis, households with incomes exceeding $60,000 will be used as the basis for calculations. Income distribution curves constructed according to HUD housing analytical techniques are used to estimate the quintiles.

- **Prime wine consuming age.** On the young end, many young adults have grown up in families with wine-consuming parents, the age spectrum of wine consumers now begins effectively at the legal age of drinking. At the other end, middle age wine consumers have progressed into their retirement years. They haven't left their preferences for wine behind. Figure 63 depicts the continued growth expected of the most important age groups, 20–34 and 35–64 years. The trend suggests that the number of households likely to consume wine will continue to increase for twenty or more years, until the shrinking birth rate and increasing immigration assert a decreasing effect. The trend warns of a shrinking market for teachers and products marketed to teenagers in the near term. The impact of wine consumers lies further in the future.

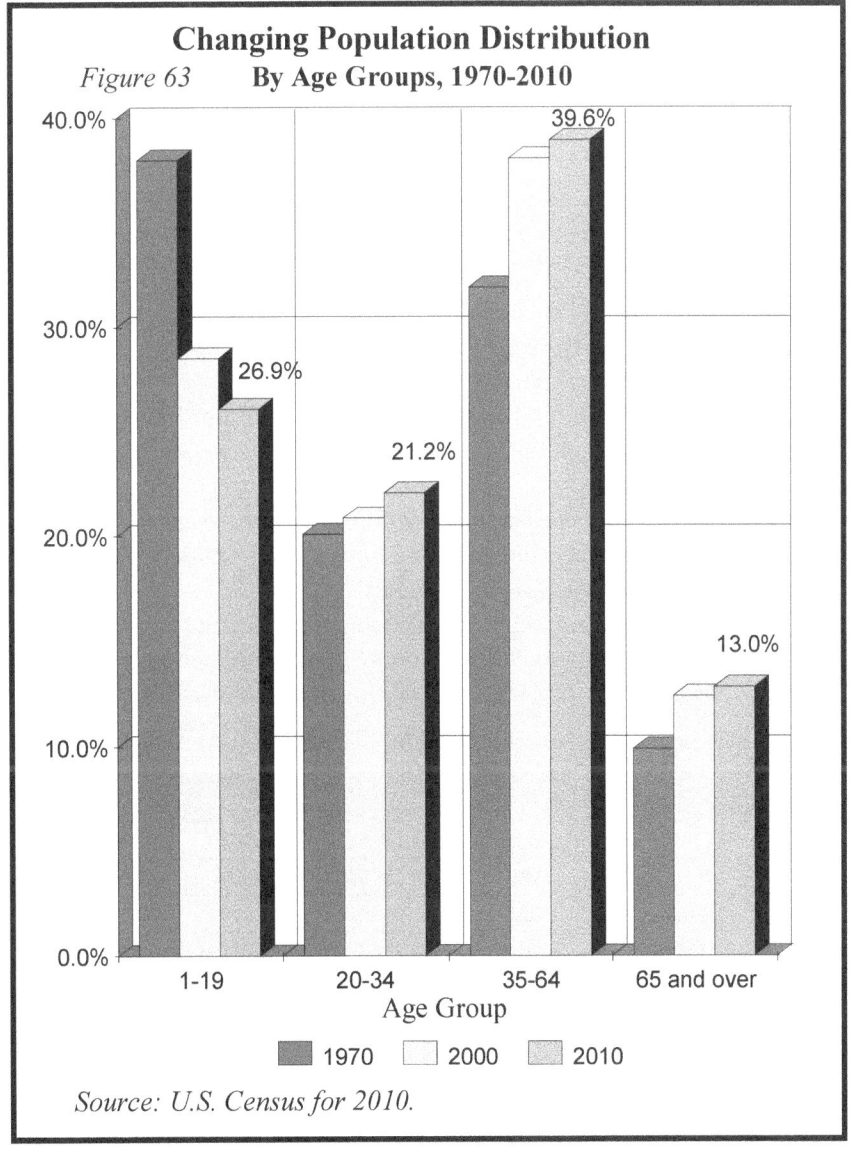

Changing Population Distribution

Figure 63   **By Age Groups, 1970-2010**

Age Group

1970   2000   2010

Source: U.S. Census for 2010.

- Some college education. The educational attainment of the American people has grown dramatically since 1970. The percentage of persons 25 years of age and older who have completed some college education almost tripled between 1970 and 2012:

1970	21.3%
1990	45.2%
2000	51.8%
2010	55.4%
2012	57.3%

The wine-consuming portion of the population cannot be taken as directly proportional to attainment of some college education. There has been a proliferation of community colleges, whose enrollment has been swollen by vocational course offerings that used to be provided in high schools, by continuing education of persons beyond college age, and by "recreational" programs. In other words, "some college education" does not mean the same thing today in terms of economic and social standing as it did forty years ago. The growth history does indicate a significant increase of interest in lifestyle and cultural behaviors, which is reflected in wine consumption.

- **Frequent travel**. Frequent travel is still a positive characteristic, and it applies to many more people. The best indicator of public travel activity is the volume of passengers on air carriers operating out of U.S. airports. These days, who can say, "I haven't been on an airplane?" Between 1975 and 2008, the number of revenue-producing enplaned passengers using air carriers at American airports increased by 268.9 percent (Table 47 and Figure 64).

The September 11, 2001 airline hijackings had a major impact on air travel that lasted four years. High fuel prices and a lengthy recession dropped air travel in 2006 and 2008.

The best market research relating to defining the purchasers of wine is no longer done by agricultural economists. It is done by anti-alcohol zealots in the public health departments of medical schools.

Statistics for wine consumption within regional and local areas are not available. It is possible, though, to construct a model that uses demographic data and consumer expenditure patterns to approximate purchases by residents

TABLE 47   Airline Passengers, 1990–2014 (in 000s)

Year	Passengers	Year	Passengers	Year	Passengers
1990	499,070,988	1999	684,163,592	2008	736,470,443
1991	488,666,536	2000	710,299,349	2009	698,003,078
1992	514,051,065	2001	661,069,429	2010	713,776,556
1993	528,920,496	2002	644,594,329	2011	726,007,934
1994	573,575,959	2003	651,728,887	2012	742,822
1995	586,326,851	2004	706,424,048	2013	748,537
1996	621,613,161	2005	737,186,780	2014	767,931
1997	641,563,706	2006	739,308,556		
1998	656,688,855	2007	763,513,050		

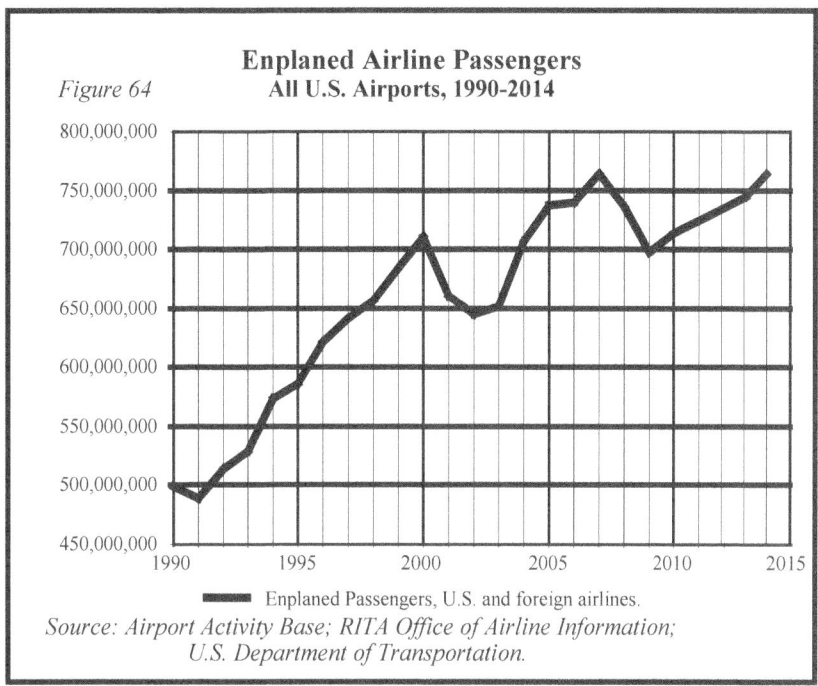

Figure 64

Enplaned Airline Passengers
All U.S. Airports, 1990-2014

━━━ Enplaned Passengers, U.S. and foreign airlines.

Source: Airport Activity Base; RITA Office of Airline Information;
U.S. Department of Transportation.

of an area. Records of wine excise tax receipts might be helpful, but they do not pick up direct shipments in the purchaser's area, and they are distorted by transferring the wine in bond to an intermediate bonded warehouse. Visitor wine consumption can be estimated using revenues from hotel bookings and airport passenger enplanements (i.e., boardings) with a handful of adjustments.

It is debatable whether constructing an econometric model or using the usual method of market basket surveys based on sampling is more accurate. Both are estimates. But, unless one is prepared to conduct 25,000 interviews for 50 metropolitan areas, the survey method is probably not more accurate in this instance than a model based on demographic and other available data.

Exactitude is not critically important for this application anyway. The important objective is to approximate the relative magnitude of wine consumption in the various metropolitan areas, so that the information may be used to prioritize marketing efforts.

Wine consumption is driven by population, households, spendable income and cultural norms in each market area. Factors such as religious behavior (i.e., the "Bible Belt" states) and state dominance by large distillers and breweries have a damping effect on wine consumption.

Selecting and prioritizing your target markets

Where you choose to market your wines, i.e., get good distributors, is a key strategic decision that must be made by every winery.

1. The **winery tasting room** provides an influential basic element in the marketing strategy. Its relative importance depends on the presence of other wineries in the area, and prospects for a significant potential for tourist flow.

2. The **nearest large metropolitan area**, preferably in the winery's home state. This is where a winery can establish significant patronage awareness, and cultivate attention by the news media. One influencing factor is the amount of home state pride that has developed. Another is the shipping distance from the winery, which may or may not outweigh the home state factor. Is the distributor confined to certain counties, or is it licensed statewide, an advantage when there are two or more major metropolitan areas in the same state?

Examples serve to illustrate the considerations. Say your winery is near Carbondale, Illinois. The nearest major metropolitan area is St. Louis, Missouri. Would it be better to go after a distributor in Chicago or St. Louis? A base in St. Louis might encourage more visitor traffic to the winery. Chicago offers a much larger market.

Where do other wineries in your growing area have distribution?

If your winery is in Grand Junction, Colorado, the obvious choice is Denver. There, a strong interest in Colorado wines has already been established.

Now we deal with the distant metropolitan wine markets.

1. A **direct shipping program**, with or without a wine club, comes next. Of course, your winery has to have a way of building a mailing list for such a program. The Internet has proven valuable for this purpose. It is a low-cost way to get the winery's message out to a lot of people.

2. **Out-of-state distribution**. In how many distant cities should you seek distribution? That depends on your winery's size. Most wineries peg their wine production to their own vineyard production, so there will be a ramping up of wine volume over four to seven years. One distant metropolitan market may be sufficient. If you have large growth plans, then you may want to start with two or three.

See Table 48 and Figure 65 to identify America's top wine markets.

In aggregate, the largest 25 metropolitan markets account for 72.5 percent of national table wine consumption, according to these calculations.

But, the size of a market area is not the last word. Notice that many of the largest markets are in Eastern and Midwestern states where population growth has slowed significantly, if not declined because of America's migration to the south and west. Experience reveals that distributors in the slower-growing states are coping with a zero sum game. In order to add your winery to their portfolio, it is likely they will have to drop one of their present wineries. That's a tough sell.

So, to look at it another way, the shelf facings a distributor may expect to fill in any given store or supermarket chain is a finite number.

On the other hand, entrepreneurs in the faster-growing markets are forming new distributorships and expanding the lines of existing distributors. There should be easier opportunities for your wines in those markets.

Therefore, it is instructive to view the largest 25 markets in terms of table wine consumption growth, which is done in Table 49.

Securing good distributors is the difficult part of marketing wine. Distributors pay attention to the wine magazine ratings, too. It's almost a "Catch-22" situation. Good wine press coverage is necessary, but the national wine magazines

TABLE 48   Estimated 2014 Table Wine Consumption, Largest 25 Metropolitan Areas Ranked by Wine Volume

Metropolitan Statistical Area	Projected Mid-2014 Population	Gallons per Capita All Wines	Estimated Gallons Table Wines	Rank
Los Angeles-Long Beach-Riverside	17,717,967	5.25	81,391,900	1
New York N.-New Jersey-Long Island	20,036,767	4.44	76,508,400	2
San Francisco-Oakland	4,574,408	7.68	30,213,100	3
Miami-Ft. Lauderdale-Pompano Beach	5,914,303	6.22	32,188,600	4
Chicago-Naperville-Joliet	9,576,014	3.87	31,870,900	5
Washington, DC-Arlington-Bethesda	6,041,353	5.24	27,066,500	6
Boston-Cambridge-Quincy	4,716,328	6.36	25,946,400	7
Seattle-Tacoma-Bellevue	3,662,521	6.70	21,471,500	8
Dallas-Fort Worth-Arlington	6,970,044	3.40	20,617,400	9
San Diego-Carlsbad-San Marcos	3,255,786	6.04	17,206,800	10
Phoenix-Mesa-Scottsdale	4,487,268	4.04	15,861,500	11
Atlanta-Marietta	5,626,710	3.04	14,967,000	12
Houston-Sugarland-Baytown	6,432,584	2.22	12,495,300	13
Portland-Vancouver-Hillsboro	2,348,281	5.80	11,917,500	14
Denver-Aurora-Broomfield	2,740,315	4.80	11,509,300	15
Tampa-St. Petersburg-Clearwater	2,875,949	4.42	11,122,700	16
Philadelphia-Camden-Wilmington	6,061,604	2.08	10,906,000	17
Detroit-Warren-Livonia	4,300,256	2.90	10,849,500	18
Minneapolis-St. Paul-Bloomington	3,489,345	3.40	10,380,800	19
Charlotte-Gastonia-Concord, NC	2,376,817	4.58	9,525,100	20
St. Louis	2,800,636	3.83	9,278,400	21
Orlando-Kissimmee	2,323,192	4.42	8,984,900	22
Baltimore-Towson	2,792,368	3.25	7,850,000	23
San Jose-Sunnyvale-Santa Clara	1,947,942	4.60	7,840,500	24
Las Vegas-Paradise	2,067,521	5.76	7,556,800	25
United States	318,308,837	2.39	665,812,700	—

Sources: U.S. Bureau of Census; U.S. Bureau of Labor Statistics; "American Housing Surveys," U.S. Department of Housing and Urban Development; Federal National Mortgage Association (Fannie Mae); U.S. Bureau of Economic Analysis; CCRI; National Flight Data Center, FAA, U.S. Department of Transportation; WineAmerica; The Wine Institute; various trade magazine articles regarding wine consumption. Analysis by LAMY Winery Consultants, May, 2013.

do not want to review wines unless they are readily available to a large part of their readership. Direct shipment has provided an important way to achieve that on a relatively small scale.

If you call on a distributor in New York and say, "Hi! My winery is in Carbondale, Illinois," he is likely to look at you like you have three heads and just arrived from Pluto.

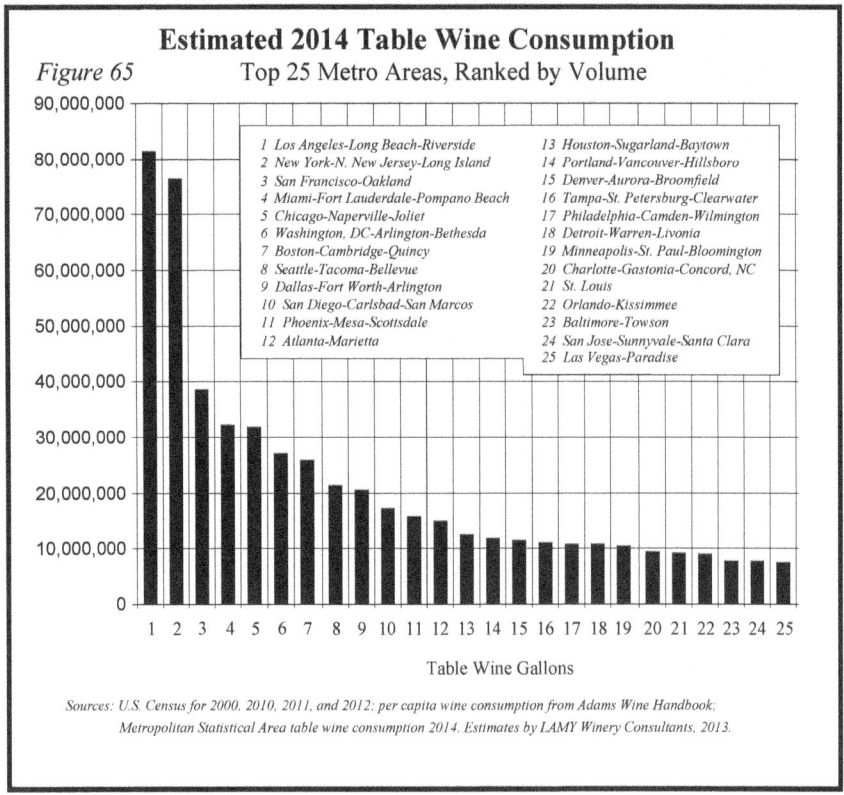

Estimated 2014 Table Wine Consumption
Figure 65   Top 25 Metro Areas, Ranked by Volume

1 Los Angeles-Long Beach-Riverside
2 New York-N. New Jersey-Long Island
3 San Francisco-Oakland
4 Miami-Fort Lauderdale-Pompano Beach
5 Chicago-Naperville-Joliet
6 Washington, DC-Arlington-Bethesda
7 Boston-Cambridge-Quincy
8 Seattle-Tacoma-Bellevue
9 Dallas-Fort Worth-Arlington
10 San Diego-Carlsbad-San Marcos
11 Phoenix-Mesa-Scottsdale
12 Atlanta-Marietta
13 Houston-Sugarland-Baytown
14 Portland-Vancouver-Hillsboro
15 Denver-Aurora-Broomfield
16 Tampa-St. Petersburg-Clearwater
17 Philadelphia-Camden-Wilmington
18 Detroit-Warren-Livonia
19 Minneapolis-St. Paul-Bloomington
20 Charlotte-Gastonia-Concord, NC
21 St. Louis
22 Orlando-Kissimmee
23 Baltimore-Towson
24 San Jose-Sunnyvale-Santa Clara
25 Las Vegas-Paradise

Table Wine Gallons

Sources: U.S. Census for 2000, 2010, 2011, and 2012; per capita wine consumption from Adams Wine Handbook; Metropolitan Statistical Area table wine consumption 2014. Estimates by LAMY Winery Consultants, 2013.

If you are fortunate enough to hit it off with a distributor who already carries several wineries from your growing area, the job will be easier. But, it is important to keep in mind always the amount of promotional effort the winery will have to make to succeed. Among them will be visits with the distributor's sales staff to stimulate sales effort, calls on key accounts (with or without the distributor sales rep), advertising, schmoozing wine writers, and winemaker dinners. You may even have to employ an area sales representative or the services of a local wine broker.

It is advisable to take on only one or two additional distributors each year because of this intensive support effort.

Most popular cities

Look at Figure 65. Is there any wonder why most wineries want to get into the New York-New Jersey Metropolitan Area? Not only is it the second largest market for wines, but it's where trend-setting is done. Most wine writers base in New York, as do influential wine publications. It's "where the action is." It's also where the competition for distributors is the most intense, with the possible exception of San Francisco.

The five most sought-after wine markets are as follows, in descending order:

1. New York–Northern New Jersey
2. San Francisco
3. Washington, DC

4. Los Angeles

5. Boston

In the Washington, DC Metropolitan area, the real household growth is occurring in the suburban areas of Bethesda, Maryland and Arlington-Alexandria, Virginia. However, much of that demand is realized through stores in the District of Columbia, where there is no wine excise tax, and where most of the entertaining and influence-peddling takes place.

Miami comes next, particularly because some distributors also bring access to the large markets in Jacksonville, Orlando and Tampa. Restaurant and resort sales are very large in Florida, and that market segment requires a strong, ongoing promotional program by the winery.

Chicago still is not hotly contested by wineries other than those in California.

Several states have statewide distributors who can service several large metropolitan areas. In Texas, you can access Dallas-Fort Worth, Houston, San Antonio and Austin through a single distributor. It's up to you to determine if you will sell more wine with a statewide distributor such as Glazers, or by focusing on a distributor who serves only one area.

Then, there are plenty of significantly large and relatively young wine markets. Atlanta, Raleigh-Durham, Memphis, Denver and Phoenix come to mind among others. Las Vegas is no longer just casino hotels. A huge retirement community has developed owing to Nevada's weather, entertainment offerings and absence of an income tax on retirement benefits.

Pooling transportation

Distributors do not want to send a truck all over the countryside picking up wine for their warehouses. At least three solutions are available for this challenge.

- Set up a cooperative bonded wine warehouse in your growing area. Individual wineries can transfer their wines, in bond, to that warehouse. Then, a distributor-ordered truck, or one working with the bonded warehouse, can deliver from that warehouse to distant distributors.

- On the West Coast, bonded wine warehouses already exist in Napa and Santa Rosa. Wineries in other areas (or states) can maintain an inventory at those warehouses, and trucks ordered by distant distributors can pick up for several wineries on the same trip.

- Arrange with your distant distributor to function as a master distributor. Then, you can ship all of the wines intended for a region full of distributors, and your master distributor will take care of shipment to the other distributors.

Under all of these options, the federal wine excise tax is payable when the bonded warehouse removes the wine from bond and loads it onto the truck bound for a distributor. Any state wine excise taxes are collected as the wine passes through the distant distributor. This explains why it is misleading to use wine excise taxes for tracking winery shipments.

In any of the options, your winery will have to pay fees for services rendered, of course.

TABLE 49   **Estimated 2014 Table Wine Consumption, Largest 25 Metropolitan Markets Ranked by Growth**

Metropolitan Statistical Area	2014 Table Wine Gallons	Rank by Size	Percent Table Wine Growth 2010–2014	Table Wines Gallons	Rank*
Los Angeles-Long Beach-Riverside	81,391,900	1	14.6	5,207,985	1
Washington, DC-Arlington-Bethesda	27,066,500	6	20.8	4,651,217	2
New York-N. New Jersey-Long Island	76,508,400	2	20.4	4,039,911	3
Seattle-Tacoma-Bellevue	21,471,500	8	31.3	3,494,252	4
Miami-Ft. Lauderdale-Pompano Beach	32,188,600	4	19.9	2,813,644	5
Dallas-Forth Worth-Arlington	20,617,400	9	16.0	2,794,527	6
Charlotte-Gastonia-Concord, NC	9,525,100	20	28.2	2,550,449	7
San Francisco-Oakland	30,213,100	3	17.4	2,393,695	8
Boston-Cambridge-Quincy	25,946,400	7	17.6	1,936,116	9
Chicago-Naperville-Joliet	31,870,900	5	16.2	1,869,227	10
Phoenix-Mesa-Scottsdale	15,861,500	11	17.5	1,780,417	11
Denver-Aurora-Broomfield	11,509,300	15	16.8	1,658,128	12
San Diego-Carlsbad-San Marcos	17,206,800	10	19.6	1,286,594	13
Altanta-Marietta	14,967,000	12	11.9	1,185,675	14
Minneapolis-St. Paul	11,863,773	20	22.0	1,072,007	15
Houston-Sugarland-Baytown	12,495,300	13	19.7	1,069,479	16
Detroit-Warren-Livonia	10,849,500	18	12.0	1,010,062	17
Orlando-Kissimmee	8,984,900	22	23.5	989,846	18
Portland-Vancouver-Hillsboro	11,917,500	14	24.3	740,899	20
Tampa-St. Petersburg-Clearwater	11,122,700	16	17.4	704,249	22
Las Vegas-Paradise	7,556,800	25	−44.3	681,936	23
San Jose-Sunnyvale-Santa Clara	7,840,500	24	18.1	638,158	24
Baltimore-Towson	7,850,000	23	17.3	551,526	25
Philadelphia-Camden-Wilmington	10,906,000	17	4.7	492,960	27
St. Louis	9,278,400	21	10.2	268,442	32

*Includes only top 25 metro areas by total table wine volume.

(For Sources, see Table 48) Analysis by LAMY Winery Consultants, May, 2013.

Lessons in strategy

The current wine market situation offers many lessons in marketing strategy. Interest in red wines has grown significantly since the late 1990s. In its wake, distributors were eager to handle Cabernet Sauvignon, Merlot, Cabernet Franc, Syrah and, particularly Pinot Noir. Why not? The wines offered high unit value and they were flying off the shelves. This situation, as previously discussed, has typified Pinot Noir, whether made in Oregon or California. Wineries were quick to jump on the $30+ bandwagon. The high prices led to an unhealthy focus on restaurant and resort sales.

Now, with the economy just coming out of a multi-year recession, wine consumers have changed their buying habits. They are dining out less, and dining and entertaining more at home, in order to spend less. The result is predictable: restaurant sales down, supermarket sales up. Costco Wholesale, the nation's largest retailer of wines, recently doubled the floor space devoted to wines in some of its stores.

Further, with the high-flying days over, many distributors are pruning their wine portfolios. Many of those Pinot Noir makers whose income statements looked so good have lost the magic. Suddenly, a lot of new wineries found themselves without distribution in some markets.

During the $30+ days, a lot of wineries were raking in the profits. They should have set aside a rainy day fund while times were good. A lot of small wineries, born of the frenzy after the movie *Sideways*, relied too heavily on the high prices to get their wineries into production, and now find themselves in financial difficulty.

The moral of the story is: don't put all of your eggs in one basket:

- **Diversify into several market sectors**. That includes direct shipping and marketing on the Internet plus building a strong following at the tasting room.

- **Don't rely too heavily on a single variety**. If you're coining money with one of your wines, set a fund aside for the lean days that are sure to come. And, promote your other wines.

Government actions influence industry growth
Industry growth versus protectionism

There is a tendency for wine producers of a new area to band together to adopt standards for wine production. The practice can yield good and bad consequences, the latter not always unintended.

First, such standards may provide the wine-consuming public with assurances that a wine made under the rules is of good quality. Frankly, the author doesn't know how you can legislate the quality of a wine. It seems that poor quality wines can be made under any set of winemaking or labeling standards. It depends on the winemaker and the fruit he/she must deal with. But, adopted quality standards sound good to wine writers and sommeliers.

The federal government already has fairly extensive regulations in place for making wine. They are administered by the Alcohol and Tobacco Tax and Trade Bureau (TTB). Beyond those, wine quality is determined by fruit quality and the many processing choices a winemaker makes.

The appellation laws of France have some upward effect on wine quality, but, down and dirty, those laws are protectionist. They amount to institutionalized price fixing.

Here is how they work. If your vineyard is inside the appellation's delimited area, and your wine passes the appellation's tasting panel, you are entitled to place the appellation's name on the label. The presence of that name admits the wine to a price structure that is already determined. In Burgundy, the structure is set by the prices bid at the Hospice de Beaune wine auction. If your vineyard has the poor fortune of being located outside the delimited area, it makes no difference how good the wine is. It will never achieve the price levels of a wine grown on the other side of the line. Winegrowers outside the top appellations have responded by acquiescing to lower vine density and higher yields, in order to succeed economically with their lower wine prices.

Because each appellation specifies the variables of vine spacing, buds left at pruning, yields and varieties to be grown, the appellation laws effectively place a maximum on the wine produced within the appellation, thus preventing the entry of new competition. The basic economic relationship between supply and demand prevails: when supply remains constant in the presence of increasing demand, the price increases.

Hopefully, America's burgeoning AVA system will not degenerate into such a restrictive morass.

There are some messages here for the legislatures and alcoholic-beverage-regulating agencies of states who are new to winemaking. When wineries in a new producing area demonstrate that they can grow special wines, the state has a new proven resource. Now, the people of the state have a stake in the future of the new wine industry. It represents a source of economic growth (jobs) for the state, a new image of quality, and also a platform for wonderful cultural enhancements.

It is preposterous to think that the first handful of winemakers in an area already have all the answers relating to best growing sites and best varieties to grow on them. Those answers will be found only through trial and error over many years, by more new producers exploring more new areas and varietal matches.

It is beguiling to be lobbied by the wine industry. The wines are so good. The receptions the wine lobby throws are so much fun and it's so easy to be agreeable after a glass or two. And then, what politician doesn't like to cozy up with the rockstar winemakers hoping some of it will rub off on them? It is better to think big picture on these issues.

We owe the wine pioneers of an area a tremendous debt of gratitude for having had the courage and determination to challenge the unknown and come out a winner, for having proven that it could be done. What we don't owe them is protection from competition. That, they should have to earn continuously through performance, and not resting on laurels.

Critical mass and market recognition

And then, there is the marketplace fact of life: an area's wine production has to reach a certain *critical mass* before the area's wineries can truly penetrate the nation's major metropolitan wine markets. Stated more simply, the local wine industry must grow in order to achieve a reputation in national markets.

Otherwise, the growing area will remain a local curiosity, its wineries mostly dependent on their tasting rooms and the tourist trade. How large is that "critical mass"? It is impossible to specify a universal number, but it is large enough to earn the respect of wine writers, distributors and the wine-buying public. Look to Washington and Oregon for examples of how much size is enough to achieve the desired status.[3]

Oregon's success has been attributed to many factors. They deserve to be examined.

Washington was led by huge Chateau Ste. Michelle/Columbia Crest. Oregon, without the benefit of such a large winery and achieved national acceptance during the 1985–1990 period. As Figure 66 shows, two major events appear to have had little to do with the growth in number of Oregon wineries, even though both provided major boosts to winery sales. The Burgundy Challenge wine tasting at New York's International Wine Center, in which Oregon took the first five places, woke up many wine writers. The movie *Sideways* generated unbelievable demand for Pinot Noir. But, no jump in new winery licensees followed either event.

Those two events, plus the annual International Pinot Noir Celebration (started in 1987), aggressive and repeated annual cooperative trade tasting events in major metropolitan markets, systematic wooing of wine writers, and production of outstanding wines contributed to the success of the Oregon wine industry. And then in 1987, prominent Burgundy négociant and winemaker Robert Drouhin purchased 225 acres of land near Dayton, Oregon and began planting a vineyard. All seem to have had the collective effect of national recognition, but not of accelerated winery growth.

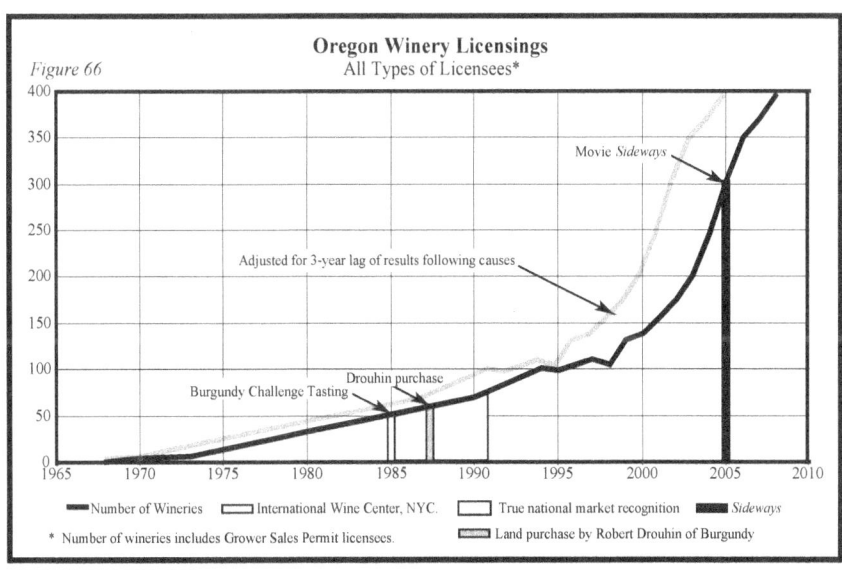

Figure 66

Oregon Winery Licensings
All Types of Licensees*

* Number of wineries includes Grower Sales Permit licensees.

---

3   Oregon is singled out for examination not because of a pro-Oregon bias, but because it is an impressive story. Oregon's industry, now 400 wineries strong, developed without the help of a giant winery, as was the case in Washington. Oregon's wine industry is still a collection of relatively small wineries. Along the way some brilliant actions were taken, as well as some protectionist schemes that were not well advised.

If we consider that new winery licenses tend to lag about an average of three years behind the decisions to enter the business, it does not help us clarify the cause and effect relationship any better. In Figure 66, the gray curve is the red curve moved three years to the left to simulate the lag time. Like everything else in this winemaking business, it takes a lot of time for results.

But, was Oregon's winery growth unique? No, it wasn't. New winery licensings for California and Washington, as well as for the nation as a whole, experienced almost identical growth patterns. The three Pacific Coast states, accounting for about 75 percent of national growth, clearly led the way during a period that saw winery operations spread to all fifty states. To use a cliche, it was "a rising tide that lifted all boats."

For national wine recognition, think about wineries approaching one hundred in number, production over a million gallons. It's a big wine market out there.

Government actions with negative effects

Here are some efforts that can assert a depressing effect on wine industry growth in a new wine state:

- **Land use restrictions.** Arbitrarily placing a restriction on building a residence on a vineyard parcel of 10, 20 or 40 acres works a hardship on new growers. They need to be at the vineyard, especially in the early establishment years. Sure, some people will use development of a small vineyard to leverage a residence in the country. But, who is to say that their vineyards won't achieve super quality? Furthermore, isn't a ten-acre vineyard a farm use that is likely to be around for a long time? Ask the proposers of such limitations if their vineyards would be large enough to qualify the house they are living in. Oh yes . . . you're likely to find that they would be "grandfathered in" under their proposal.

- **Ban on off-premise tasting rooms.** Only for new wineries, of course. Existing facilities will be "grandfathered in." Such a limitation would be welcomed by distributors and retailers because it would restrict competition. However, it would limit the wineries' opportunities for exposure in the marketplace.

- **Truncated tax schedules.** Lower rates that appear to help small, struggling new operations survive seem a worthy cause. But, higher tax rates based on production volume can act as a deterrent to expansion and establishment of larger wineries. They are born of paranoia and an animosity towards business, as if "small is good, big is bad." All wineries provide jobs, state tax revenues and secondary economic benefits. Moreover, large wineries are more likely to be "export" industries. That is, they bring revenues into the state, which is the objective of most states' industrial development programs.

- **Restriction of direct shipment.** As this book goes to print, trade associations for winery competitors seek legislation that would take direct shipment of wine out from under the interstate commerce clause. That means that states that have huge breweries and distilleries would be able to hamstring direct shipment of wines into their states. Their states would be free to discriminate between in-state and out-of-state wine shipments crossing their borders. This kind of legal assault is nothing new. Major distillers have tried for years to derail direct shipment of wines, while wine distributors have sought to force all wines through distributors. From the wineries' perspective, direct shipping is essential to economic survival. As already discussed, obtaining a good distributor is not easy and certainly not possible for all wineries. Direct shipment has provided a means for new and small wineries to get their wines into many out-of-state markets.

State support programs for the wine industry

Government's role should be one of support and encouragement for expansion and free market competition. There are two areas where government can really help the new operations. They are:

- Fund and establish **research and instructional programs** at the college level that pay more attention to the needs of the industry than the academic wishes of the researchers; and,

- **Help new operations get established in the marketplace**, both inside **and** outside the state.

- **Highlight your wine industry in the state tourism advertising**, particularly the television spots.

- **Encourage cross-marketing** in promotions of other food commodity commissions.

Take a hard look at these functions and it is apparent that they benefit every producer in the state. Even help for the established wineries with out-of-state marketing promotions helps the small local wineries by taking some pressure off the local marketplace.

Several states new to the premium wine industry appear to have gotten off to a strong start by establishing vineyard and/or winery support programs, some within their extension services. Oregon (Oregon State University, Southern Oregon Community College and the Northwest Viticultural Center), Iowa, Ohio, Indiana (Purdue University), Kentucky, Tennessee, Texas, North Carolina (Surrey Community College) and Pennsylvania are among those setting good examples.

Industry cooperative market promotions

Cooperative marketing forays into major metropolitan markets have become relatively ineffective primarily because everybody's doing it. The first use of this technique was made by the California Wine Institute (CWI) and leading California wineries in the early 1960s. CWI provided the format in the form of a structured wine tasting. The events included an opportunity to sign up for a mail order short course on wines. Consumers all over America took advantage of the opportunity to gain some wine knowledge. Distributors conducted each event within their local market areas.

A local charity was selected to co-sponsor each event. That accomplished two things. First, it provided a vehicle that the local press could embrace without reservations about making profits for a handful of wineries. (Recall that old saw, "If you want an ad, pay for it.") Second, the charitable organization offered a sales force to sell tickets to the event, virtually guaranteeing that the patrons would be of socio-economic stature likely to be wine consumers.

The next major effort was conducted by Sonoma County wineries during the early 1980s, in an attempt to differentiate themselves from Napa Valley, which at that time, totally dominated public awareness of California wine.

It is important to know that most distributors these days hold their own tasting events for the trade. Wineries in that distributor's portfolio set up tasting booths. Frequently, the distributor partners with specialty foods distributors, in order to make the event more appealing to chefs and wine managers for restaurants. These events do not utilize charitable organizations. There is no charge for admission, but attendance is limited to wine writers and trade accounts: restaurants, wine shops and chain retailers.

Now comes the industry-sponsored tasting events. These events are organized by winery trade organizations, and may enjoy some funding from USDA and/or their states. But, for the most part, they are funded by the participating wineries with some money coming from the sponsoring trade organization (which also comes from the wineries, through an excise tax on wines.) Distributors in the area send out the invitations to their trade accounts. Attendance is limited to those trade accounts and wine writers.

The trade tasting event may be coupled with a public tasting event, co-sponsored with a local charity to sell the tickets and make press coverage possible.

A critical element is missing from such tasting events: helping new wineries secure good distributors in targeted market areas. There are reasons why this has not happened. Wineries who already have distribution in an area are usually not eager to share the market with other wineries. It is those established wineries who usually dominate and control how the trade tours are constructed. It is usually those established wineries who monopolize the opportunities for exposure at the events. Put together a panel presentation on pairing of wines with foods, or focus attention on where the best growing areas are. Who gets the prominent panel positions and the wine writer columns resulting therefrom? . . . the established wineries. The practice even makes the established wineries look like the best of the growing area. Everyone else is left trying to coattail on the leaders and pick up a few crumbs.

So, the events fail to help new wineries find good distributors.

It may take a separate committee, with a separate budget, to conduct activities that help emerging new producers this way. How about a tasting event by wineries seeking distribution, and inviting the distributors' senior sales staffers? Consider a direct mail advertising program aimed at distributors?

Funding sources

There are regional differences in how the various states have chosen to go about funding their wine industry support programs. States in the West look to a portion of wine excise taxes, but far more often to commodity commission-imposed assessments on producers. States in the Midwest and East like to finance those activities with part of their alcoholic beverage excise taxes and other business taxes already collected by the state, thus relieving wineries from some of the tax burden.

U.S. Department of Agriculture has provided grant money to assist in marketing agricultural products, both domestically and internationally.

Further reading

Hall, C. Michael, and Richard Mitchell. *Swine Marketing: A Practical Guide*. London: Elsevier, Ltd., 2008.

Hawkes, Ellen. Blood and Wine: *The Unauthorized Story of the Gallo Wine Empire*. New York: Simon & Schuster, 1993. The story of Ernest and Julio Gallo, and the development of the world's largest winery. Insightful information on marketing.

Lapsey, James, and Kirby Moulton. *Successful Wine Marketing*. Berkeley: University of California Press, 2001.

Wagner, P., J. Olsen, and L. Thach. *Wine Marketing and Sales: Successful Strategies for a Saturated Market*. San Francisco: Wine Appreciation Guild, 2009.

The Wine Institute. *State Shipping Laws*.
Website: http://www.wineinstitute.org/initiatives/stateshippinglaws

–11–

Recordkeeping and accounting in a regulated industry

The maintenance of good records by a winery is at once a helpful tool and a heavy burden. The weight of the latter can be minimized by setting up a recordkeeping system that is straightforward, non-duplicative and yields data useful for future winemaking decisions and production cost management.

This will nevertheless be the dreary chapter for most readers, who most likely would prefer to focus on the romantic aspects of wine. So, pour yourself a glass of wine, find a comfortable chair and kick off your shoes.

In this chapter, attention is focused upon the recordkeeping function essential to the operation.

Gallons or cases?

What units do you use to measure wine volume? American grape growers use *tons per acre* to measure vineyard output. European producers talk hectoliters of wine per hectare of vineyard area.

Once the grapes are on the crush pad, interest turns from tons to *gallons*. Grapes start out as tons, are destemmed and crushed in tons per hour and are pressed as tons. But, the juice gets pumped to tanks in *gallons per minute*. There's the first transition.

In the tank room, winery equipment is generally rated in *gallon capacity* (tanks) or *gallons per minute* (pumps and filters). But then, the bottling line processes *bottles per minute* (second transition), and its output is measured in *cases* (third transition). Whew! Did you follow that confusing ride?

The federal Alcohol and Tobacco Tax and Trade Bureau (TTB) bi-weekly winery production reports are stated in gallons. That's because everything is measured in the winery as gallons, and the conversion to cases doesn't occur until the wine is "tax paid." Even the wine excise tax, paid on finished case goods at time of release, is figured in dollars per gallon, not cases. The TTB reports require that case goods inventory be stated in gallons for the sake of continuity.

So, vineyardists talk in tons. Winemakers think in gallons. Everybody else down the line, from wine marketing people through distributors to retailers, even bankers, talks in terms of cases.

The conversion is:

one case = twelve 750 ml bottles = 9 liters = 2.37753 gallons.

This last is the official number adopted by TTB, regardless of what other conversion rates may be calculated:

> 1 liter = 0.26417 gallons
> 1 gallon = 3.78544 liters
> 1 case = 9 liters = 2.37753 gallons

To convert grapes from tons to gallons of juice or wine is a much more complicated matter. It depends on the grape variety, growing season, vine culture methods, press efficiency and winemaker choices as to severity of pressing.

Reference database of experience

Each year's harvest presents different phenological data for such things as sugar, acidity, pH, average cluster weight, clusters per vine, harvest date, etc. Keeping these numbers improves future crop estimates and the purchase of a variety of winemaking materials (yeast, enzymes, acid, sugar, acid-reducing and fining agents, filters, tanks, barrels, etc.) These records also enable accurate label descriptions and winemaker notes.

Recording of production data is mandated by federal regulations that bear the force of law. Recording of weights, volumes, and all materials used, as well as transfers among vessels, blendings, additions, chemical adjustments, lab test results, and production methods are all required. Some data are needed for calculation of federal and state taxes at the production level.

Detailed inventory records have to be kept for all materials used in the winemaking process: grapes, chemicals, filter sheets glass, corks, etc. The records have to show when and where the materials were acquired, when and where they were applied, i.e., batch number and tank number.

When TTB performs an audit of your winery, they will have to be able to track a wine from the vineyard through the winery to the case. They will even check the validity of individual vineyard appellations on the label.

Oregon has the nations' strictest label regulations, adopted at the request of its own producers and administered by Oregon Liquor Control Commission (OLCC). Wineries in all other states have to conform to the federal label regulation, administered by TTB. Oregon wineries have to satisfy both TTB and OLCC label approval procedures, but the former is required only if the wine is to be sold outside Oregon.

Not all of this recordkeeping has to be government-imposed drudgery. Processing records can also permit back-checking to correlate finished wine quality with the methods that were employed in production, and to expedite calculation of treatment materials. Production records can also provide for retrieval of production costs that guide future pricing, vendor selection, cost control, and product mix decisions.

Tracking production

Figure 67 is an example of how production facts can be recorded by the winemaking staff.

Two ring binders are set up. One is a chronological record, and it has two sections, one for the vineyard, the other for the winery. Items are recorded in the order in which they occur.

The other ring binder also has two sections: vineyard and winery. This binder has a page (or more) for each vineyard block (in the vineyard section), and each wine batch (in the winery) section. Actions are entered in the order in which they occur, but all of the records pertaining to each batch are in one place. Thus it is easy to view everything that has been done to the batch.

Every action is entered in two places, but that is the price of good recordkeeping. Personal computers can be set up to do this, making the records accessible from several locations.

The curse of the accountant

There is no doubt that cries of anguish will flow from this characterization. The mantle is not intended for independent CPAs. Many of them are good friends and valuable resources. The target of this derision is employee staff accountants who drive a wedge between owners and managers

Accounting is essential to a winery's operation. The industry's high capitalization needs, long lead time from harvest to market and government regulation, ensure that the accountant's craft is important to the operation, if not critical to its success. It's just that this is not among the fun aspects of winery operation, like winemaking and marketing are.

For wineries large enough to have middle management (i.e., winemaker and vineyard, marketing and tasting room managers), staff accountants have to walk a fine line between protecting proprietary information from disclosure, and divulging operating cost data needed by line managers. If staff accountants are too tightfisted with internal information or oppressive in cost control

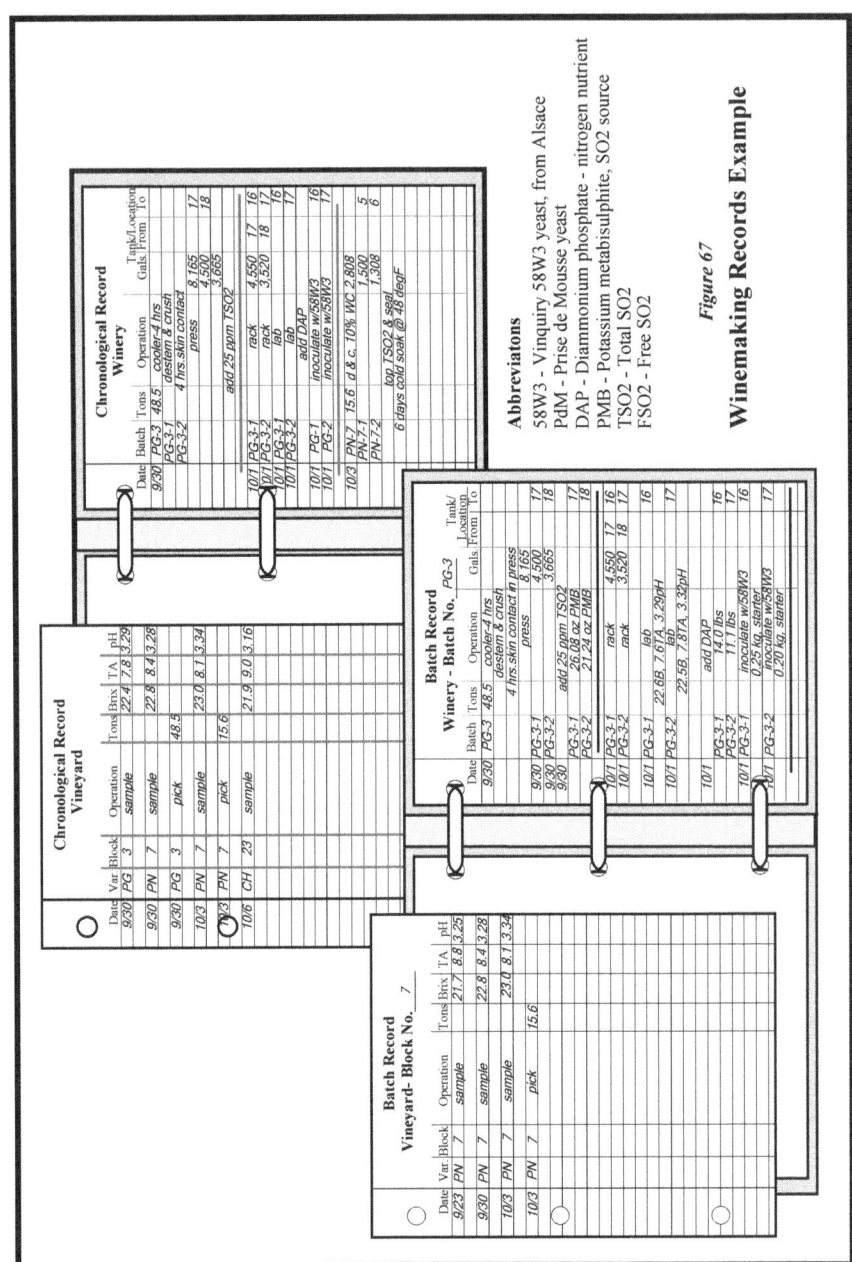

Figure 67

Winemaking Records Example

efforts, they risk being viewed as "gestapo," or a divisive force between owner-ship and fellow employees. If allowed to fester, such conditions can defeat any attempt at efficiency through team effort.

What do you mean by accounting?

There are four types of accounting that are required of, or valuable to, a winery, presented here according to the uses to which each is applied:

- **Financial accounting**, which measures the profitability of the business in terms of return on invested dollars and profit earned per dollar of revenues received. This type is very important to the owners or shareholders of the winery.

- **Tax accounting**, which follows government-imposed methods for figuring depreciation and handling of inventory and certain other expenses, some based on social engineering objectives. (Expensing of selling costs like entertainment is a good place to start.) It is used to calculate the net profit subject to income and capital gains taxes.

- **Production accounting** for regulated production of alcoholic beverages. This recordkeeping task is imposed on wineries by TTB and state agencies. Its primary purpose is stated clearly in the Code of Federal Regulations: "to protect the revenues." Wineries participate in this protective process every two weeks by sending production reports to TTB and state agencies. The reports detail all materials entering the process, losses during production, contents of vessels, finished wine inventories and wine transferred to tax paid status. These reports establish the gallons of wine subject to federal and state wine excise taxes.

- **Managerial accounting**, in which cost and other production and marketing data are collected, analyzed and presented in such a way that it may be used by line managers to control costs, set prices and determine product mix. "Operations research," the broader science of the economics of production, is another name appropriate to some of this activity.

Small and medium-sized wineries can be helped in management by doing an effective job of "managerial accounting." Its effectiveness depends on structuring the data capture to include "meaningful" information (in the sense that it is capable of leading to something that is useful to management actions), allowing its regurgitation in forms that can be used by the people who are managing the production process, and then making the information available in understandable form to those line managers. The task has been simplified greatly by the personal computer.

What is "meaningful"? It doesn't help much to holler that tartaric acid expenses are abnormally high in an abnormally hot year. That expenditure is needed to make acceptable wine. On the other hand, it is really meaningful to management's product mix decisions to work out charge rates for overhead items that more accurately reflect the use of those "indirect" expenses for specific wine types. It requires a little more effort at "job cost accounting" rather than "process cost accounting," but it's usually well worth the effort.

And then, there is the issue of the time-sensitivity of monetary values, the economist's realm. Because of the length of time between grape harvest and the sale of wine, the present worth concept is particularly appropriate. What it entails is discounting each cost and revenue item to its value at some point in time, usually today.

Many wineries don't have a clear picture of how much it costs to produce a bottle of, say, Pinot Noir, as compared with one of White Riesling, except for the cost of the grapes. And they don't have a handle on the difference in marketing costs it takes to establish acceptable market demand for Müller-Thurgau, as opposed to the "slam dunk" of Chardonnay. Their accounting system is not structured to provide such information.

Sounds simple and just like common sense, doesn't it? In practice, such an approach is seldom implemented in all but the huge wineries. If this subject is interesting, be sure to read Chapters 12, 13 and 14.

Depreciation

The IRS considers wineries to be manufacturers, and thus federal regulations require them to use accrual accounting *and* the UNICAP (uniform capitalization) method of determining indirectly, depreciation. Under this system, all cost incurred in production, and some costs incurred indirectly, have to be capitalized and held on the books until the wine they produced is sold. It's really just *job costing* as differentiated from *process costing*. (See Chapter 14 for a more detailed discussion of this issue.)

An independent vineyard may use the *cash accounting* method to figure its taxable income. Under this method, revenues are realized when payment is received, and costs are expensed as they are paid for. If you are under a calendar fiscal year, it is possible, even probable, that some revenues will be matched against the next year's production costs because of the widespread practice of deferring some of the payment for grapes to the next calendar year.

If the winery owns the vineyard, then vineyard production costs relating to a specific vintage will be treated as any other production cost. They will have to be capitalized under UNICAP, and expensed when the wine is sold.

Inventory valuation

At the time this book goes to print, a great debate rages in the wine industry regarding the use of LIFO inventory valuation. Under *LIFO* (last-in, first-out), the first items going into the year-end calculation of *cost of goods sold* are the last items produced during the year. Essentially, the year-end inventory is valued at last year's cost rates. The result is an overstatement of *cost of goods sold* and an understatement of taxable income.

In general, the accounting profession seeks to match revenues received to the costs incurred to produce those revenues. For wines that are released three years after harvest, the accounting ideal would have the revenues received upon sale of the wine to be matched with the actual costs incurred over a three-year period to produce it. There are two reasons why such a precise method of taxable income determination would be undesirable. First, it would require a lot of recordkeeping, reporting and accounting costs to accomplish, so there is an issue of justifying the extra costs versus the benefits gained. Second, the producer would be taxed on the inflation in sales prices.

Other methods of valuing year-end inventory are: *FIFO* (first-in, first-out), average cost, and replacement cost. Under FIFO, items are charged to *cost of goods sold* beginning with the cost of the first ones to enter inventory. *Average cost* allows all costs to be entered in one account, then items are charged to *cost of goods sold* at the arithmetic average unit cost of all items in inventory. *Replacement cost* is what it would cost at year-end to produce the item, regardless of what it really cost when it was produced. Replacement cost differs from

LIFO in that **all** items are valued at year-end costs, rather than some valued at cost rates incurred during the year and others valued at year-end cost.

LIFO has been allowed for calculating taxable income because it enables the company to avoid, to some extent, being taxed for inflation.

The IRS is conducting detailed audits of some twenty-eight wineries in Napa and Sonoma Counties to determine the effects of LIFO on taxable income. Specifically at issue is the use of only two categories for accumulating production costs: bulk wine and case goods. Because of greatly differing production periods, generally from one to three years for different wine types, it is alleged that taxable income is distorted to the government's disadvantage.

Accounting firms are warning their clients that, if the LIFO inventory method is ultimately abolished by IRS, then many wineries will face a very large tax bill, which the government will generously allow them to pay over four years.

Wineries are not being singled out for special treatment by the IRS. The LIFO issue is not unique to the wine industry. The use of LIFO is widespread among most businesses, manufacturing and other kinds. To further complicate the issue is the reality that many businesses use LIFO to determine taxable income, but also use other accounting methods in their shareholder reporting. Yes, it is possible to understate income for the tax collector, while at the same time overstating it for investors.

Our Financial Accounting Standards Board (FASB, under the SEC) is following standards set by the International Financial Accounting Standards Board (IFASB) in trying to get America to comply with the same accounting practices as are used in almost every other country. It appears that only the U.S. allows the use of the LIFO inventory method. So, the LIFO method is going to disappear, according the CPA-firm advisory letters. Here is the way cost of goods sold is determined using LIFO:

> Last year's ending inventory
>
> + This year's purchases and additions by production
>
> − This year's ending inventory
>
> = Cost of goods sold

The IRS argues that the practice leads to a large overstatement of cost of goods sold, rather than matching costs with the revenues that relate to them.

Accounting for other "indirect" costs

In addition to capitalizing direct production costs, some indirect costs directly related to production must also be allocated and capitalized to inventory. The IRS lists them as

> Administration expenses;
>
> Taxes (excise and property);
>
> Depreciation;
>
> Insurance (production-related only);

Compensation to officers (allocated by time devoted to production management);

Rework labor (repackaging or rebottling);

Contributions to pension stock bonus, certain profit-sharing, annuity or deferred compensation plans.

On-site residence

It is common for a winery's owner or employee to live in a house located on the vineyard or winery property. If that residence is owned by the business entity, it is possible for the business to deduct depreciation and operating expenses for the home. The resident does not have to pay income taxes on the benefit, under several conditions:

- The residence has to be located on the vineyard or winery property and owned by the entity;
- Residence by the owner or employee has to be beneficial to the business for business-related reasons;
- The owner or employee must be required to live in the residence as a condition of employment.

Fiscal year

Vineyards have a natural business year beginning December 1 or January 1. The calendar year suffices.

A winery, even as a Subchapter S corporation, can elect to use a calendar year, or other fiscal year if it better relates to the business year. The winery that buys all of its grapes from other sources has a business year that begins with the crush; September 1 is good.

For an integrated vineyard-winery operation and entity, on the other hand, the business year should begin January 1 with the winter pruning in the vineyard.

Further reading

Alcohol and Tobacco Tax and Trade Bureau. *TTB Regulations.* Website: http://www.ttb.gov/other/regulations.shtml

IRS. *Publication 946 (2013), How To Depreciate Property.* Website: http://www.irs.gov/publications/p946/

Stoel Rives, Attorneys at Law, LLP. *Selected Federal Tax Issues Facing Vineyard and Winery Owners.* 2010. Website: http://www.stoel.com/webfiles/OregonWine/federaltax.pdf

৪০ ০৪

–12–

Winery equipment

The most important factor in winemaking success is human: the wine-maker. Winemakers will detest me for saying this: a good winemaker can make good wine with crude or sophisticated equipment. It is also true that crude equipment is woefully inefficient, particularly with wine volumes greater than a few thousand gallons. Even though this writer has seen wineries handle up to 6,000 gallons annually with little more than some modified home winemaker equipment, it takes a very good winemaker to maintain high quality standards with substandard equipment.

The largest equipment categories, in terms of cost, are the crush pad, tanks, barrels and bottling line. Together, they account for 80–85 percent of total winery equipment. After the winemaker, crush pad equipment is the factor next in importance in regard to its impact on wine quality.

Crush pad equipment

Equipment used on the crush pad includes a bin rotator on tractor or fork lift, the destemmer-crusher, pomace pump, press, transfer pump and pressure washer. Some sticklers for gentle fruit handling may have a sorting belt to hand remove moldy fruit. Larger operations may have a conveyor to carry uncrushed fruit up to the press door, and an auger or conveyor to help move pomace from the press to dump wagon. Some wineries are able to substitute plastic buckets or a gravity chute for the pomace pump if the operation is on two floor levels.

Europe still makes the best. The best destemmer-crushers and presses are made in Germany, France, Switzerland and Italy. This enables you to have some investment fun, because you get to play arbitrage with fluctuating currency exchange rates. You will pay for the equipment either in the currency of the manufacturer's country, or the exchange rate will be fixed on the date the shipment lands at a U.S. port. The same will be true for French barrel purchases.

Destemmer-Crusher. It is imperative that the fruit be crushed gently *after* it is destemmed, not before. If you're a small winery, don't fall for those cheap, small-scale Italian crusher-stemmers (which crush first); they will give you very poor wine quality because too many harsh constituents are extracted from the peduncle and stem pieces that they create. Make sure it is a destemmer-crusher, and the gap between the crusher rollers is adjustable.

On the other hand, if your labor of love is a very small winery, you may be able to remove one of that Italian unit's crusher rollers, thus using the unit only as a destemmer. Then, a separate crusher (with hopper) can be mounted beneath, and you will have a destemmer-crusher for a few bucks over $1,000. But why bother? Relatively low-cost destemmers, that do not also crush, are now available from Italy.

The volume at which a winery advances to two destemmer-crushers depends on how compressed the harvest season is, and how many varieties and batches have to be kept separated through fermentation. Thus it is advisable to walk through the harvest on paper (or spreadsheet) first, before deciding the size and capacity of crush pad equipment.

For years, Amos (Heilbron, Germany) destemmer-crushers were considered the best destemmer-crushers (Figure 68). Amos has been acquired by Defranceschi, the Italian maker of high-quality presses, tanks and other equipment, and this writer sees no reason why there would be any drop in quality owing to the acquisition.

Pomace pump. The pomace pump moves the crushed fruit to the press or, in the case of red wines, to the fermenting vessel. Several pump designs are suitable for moving juice or wine containing seeds and skins. They are presented in order of suitability, in Figure 69, beginning with the best.

- **Piston pump**. A piston drives the head through a cylinder equipped with inlet and outlet valves.

- **Peristaltic pump**. Operates by rollers moving axially along a flexible hose and squeezing. Pomace touches only the inside of the hose. This is the most gentle pomace pump.

- **Lobe pump**. Two lobed heads rotate like gears, creating alternating expanding and contracting volumes, assisted by valves. The material being pumped travels between the rotor and the pump casing. It does not move between the two rotors.

- **Progressive cavity pump**, also called a Moyno, mohno or mono pump. A spiral-shaped rotor turns within a flexible boot, creating spaces that move in an axial direction. No valving is required.

- **Air diaphragm pump**. One or two flexible diaphragms are moved by a reciprocating piston, creating expanding and contracting volumes. Inlet and outlet are equipped by ball check valves. A large pump size, with

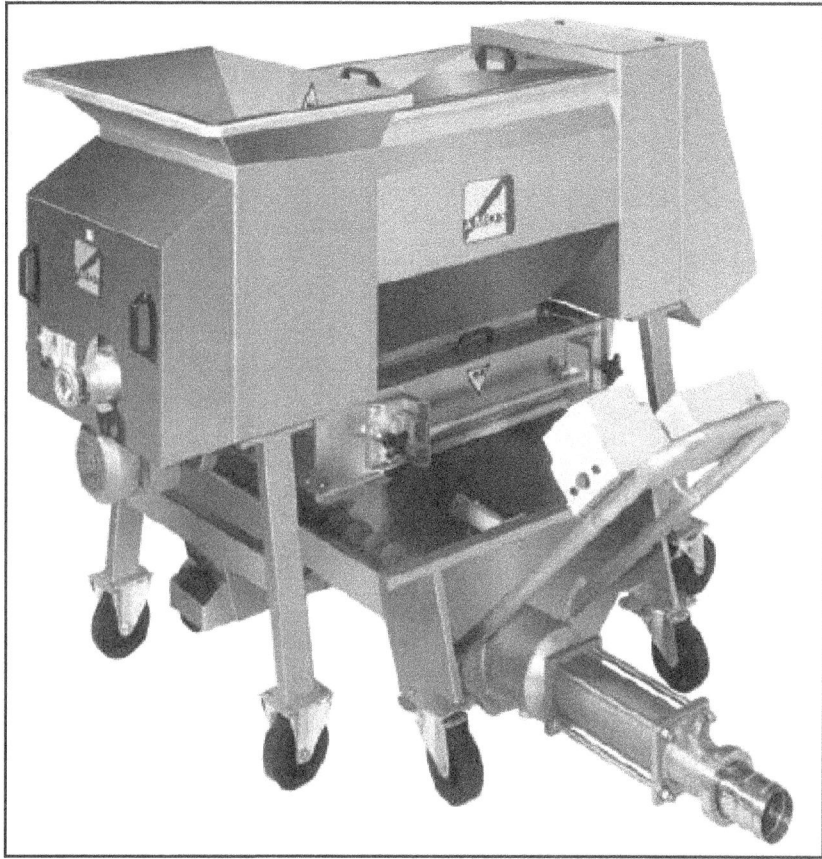

Figure 68 **Amos Destemmer-Crusher Kiessel Pomace Pump underneath**

Photo Courtesy of Valley Pipe & Supply

around a 3-inch diameter inlet and outlet, is required in order to pass through an acceptable volume of whole berries, so this pump design is a poorer choice for small wineries on the crush pad. Its use will more appropriate to the tank and barrel rooms.

Of course, the need for a pomace pump can be eliminated in several ways:

- The destemmer-crusher can be mounted above the press so pomace falls directly into the press.

- A conveyor can carry the pomace up to the press door.

- A bin can catch the pomace, then be lifted up to the press door by the fork lift and dumped.

- A very small producer can use buckets.

Sorting belts and conveyors

Following French traditions, American wineries are increasingly employing sorting belts and conveyor mechanisms to transport the grapes to the destemmer-crusher, and then to the press. The purpose of conveyors is to

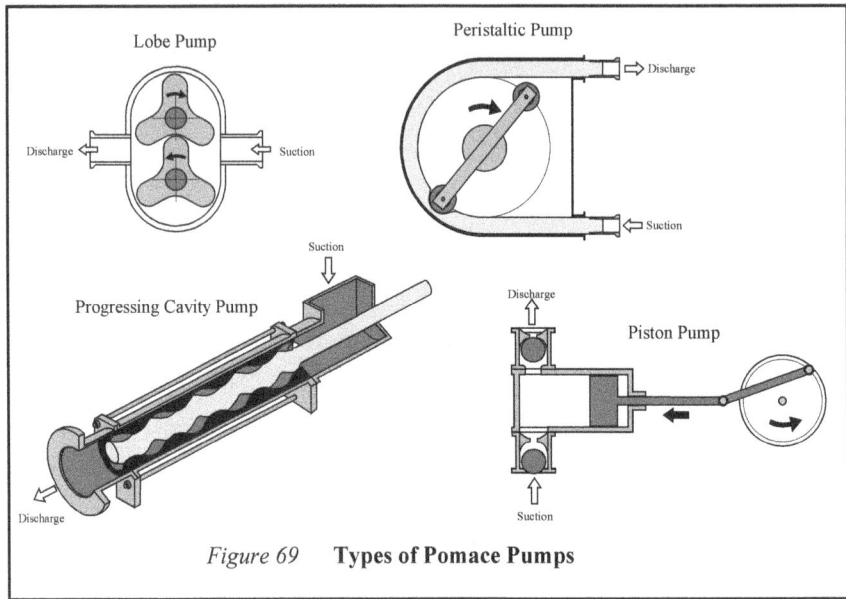

Figure 69   **Types of Pomace Pumps**

eliminate rough handling of the fruit. Workers along the sorting belt remove moldy and underripe fruit from the crush.

A sorting table and elevating conveyor are depicted in Figure 70.

The cost of a typical sorting-conveyor system can run $30,000–40,000, and it can vary widely depending on the chosen features.

Press

On a small scale, say up to 8,000 gallons annual production, two or three relatively inexpensive bladder-basket presses may be used (about $2,800 each, see Figure 74). At greater volumes, it pays to step up to a good membrane press.

Figure 70   **DeJonge Shaker Table & Conveyor**

Photo courtesy of Joseph H. Lamy

For production over 50,000 gallons and a typical product mix, two membrane presses will be needed, say 50 hectoliter and 25 hl.

For production above 10,000–12,000 gallons of wine annually, much more sophisticated presses are needed. Several design alternatives are available: tank press, bladder press and ram press (Figure 71).

First in ability and popularity is the tank press (Figure 72). The shell, or outer wall, is solid, and has a removable door, or doors, through which fruit may be loaded manually. All of the larger models have an axial port at one end through which crushed fruit can be loaded by a pomace pump. An internal flexible membrane presses inward toward the axial center, powered by compressed air. Juice exits by way of slotted channels in the center of the press, to a juice pan below the press.

Most tank presses are controlled by a built-in computerized system that has up to a dozen pre-programmed sequences in addition to the ability to be controlled manually. In general, the tank press makes the highest quality wine.

Next is the *membrane press*, sometimes called a *bladder press*. The pressing action is from the inside out, again powered by compressed air. The membrane is made of rubber or a rubberized canvas. There are narrow slits in the outside shell wall that permit the juice to exit, and then flow by gravity to a juice pan

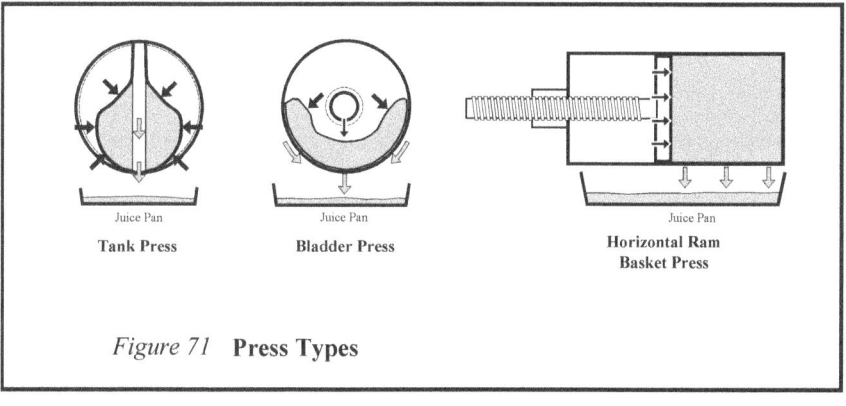

Figure 71 **Press Types**

Figure 72   **Willmes Sigma 4 Tank Press**
Photo courtesy of Scott Laboratories

underneath. Most new membrane presses now have computer-controlled programming, just like tank presses.

Built-in press programs bring simplicity to the job. One of the tank presses has twelve built-in programs for the winemaker to use. It's kind of like the menu in an Oriental restaurant. You don't have to order *Kung Pao Chicken*, you can just say "number sixteen!" Of course, the manufacturers of these presses have surveyed the practices used by various winemakers to handle specific grape varieties, and have come up with standardized procedures. It's like winemaking by committee.

Well, grapes grown in different microclimates have different characteristics, and good winemakers will always find special ways to process certain grapes that don't conform to the standards. Fortunately, these presses allow for the winemaker to fly them "by the seat of the pants."

> **Tip!** *Here's a little tip you won't find in a textbook or manufacturer's operating manual: the press cycle time for a tank press or bladder press can be shortened as much as 40–50 percent by plumbing a compressed air nurse tank between the air compressor and press. That is, you can get the same job done in half the time with no sacrifice in quality, unless you enjoy staying up all night. It all has to do with how rapidly you can inflate the membrane. Efficiency is gained because the compressor is compressing the air supply while the press is dwelling at full (for the cycle) pressure (see Figure 73). You can make this modification with some presses, but not with others.*

Ram presses, also called **basket presses**, be they horizontal or vertical, have been largely obsoleted by the advent of membrane presses. Some are still in use in Champagne, and some wineries still use them to press red wine pomace. Whether that is due to stubbornness or romantic public relations is a subject for further debate. However, the newer facilities have membrane presses, as do the U.S. operations of French Champagne houses like Moët et Chandon. A membrane press can handle pomace just as well as a ram press, and the juice/wine quality will be much better.

Small scale crush pad

For very small wineries, say 3,000–6,000 gallons annually, the crush equipment shown above is out of the question because of cost. It is necessary to shift gears into a different scale entirely.

Two options are depicted in Figure 74. An alternative would be to invest in the more expensive machine, which destems and crushes in one pass, in the proper order. This method will save you a lot of bucket work and, most assuredly, enable you to make much better quality wine.

In either case, it would be best to mount the machines one above the other by means of a tubular steel frame so the grapes are delivered by gravity to the next machine. Hoppers can be made cheaply of welded PVC sheet.

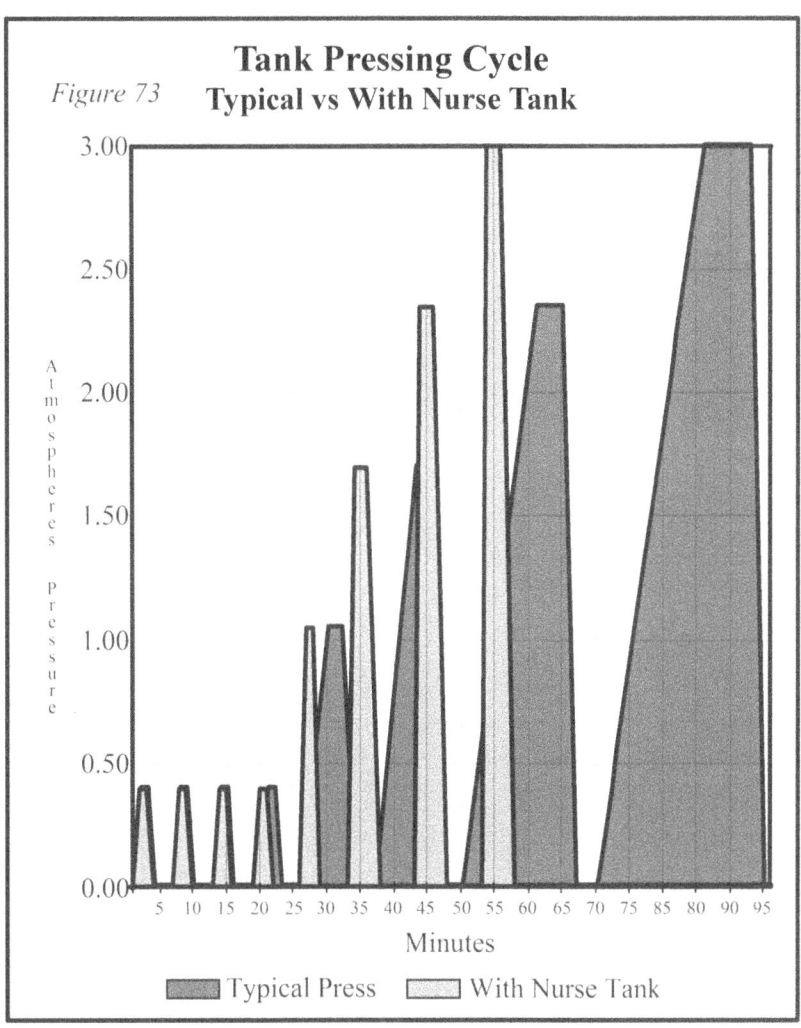

Figure 73

Tank Pressing Cycle
Typical vs With Nurse Tank

The next step up, say to 10,000 gallons of wine, would be a destemmer-crusher which processes 3–4 tons per hour (See Figure 75).

To speed up pressing, two wood basket rubber bladder presses can be used, so as to fill one while the other is pressing. This is a hybrid press. It uses a rubber membrane instead of a ram and presses outward toward the basket. These presses can be operated with water or compressed air. Most winemakers use water, providing the water supply is around 40 psi. The disadvantage to working with this design is that the press has to be opened and the pomace stirred manually between press cycles. It is a physically demanding and time-consuming task.

Juice transfer pump. A flexible impeller pump (rubber impeller) is common, and least expensive, for transferring juice from the press pan to tank. Alternatively, an air diaphragm pump (driven by compressed air) can be used here (Figure 76). Either pump can be used to transfer juice or wine from tank to tank, or to/from barrels. The air diaphragm pump is the gentler of the two. However, gentleness is less important for juice, whereas non-turbulent flow is

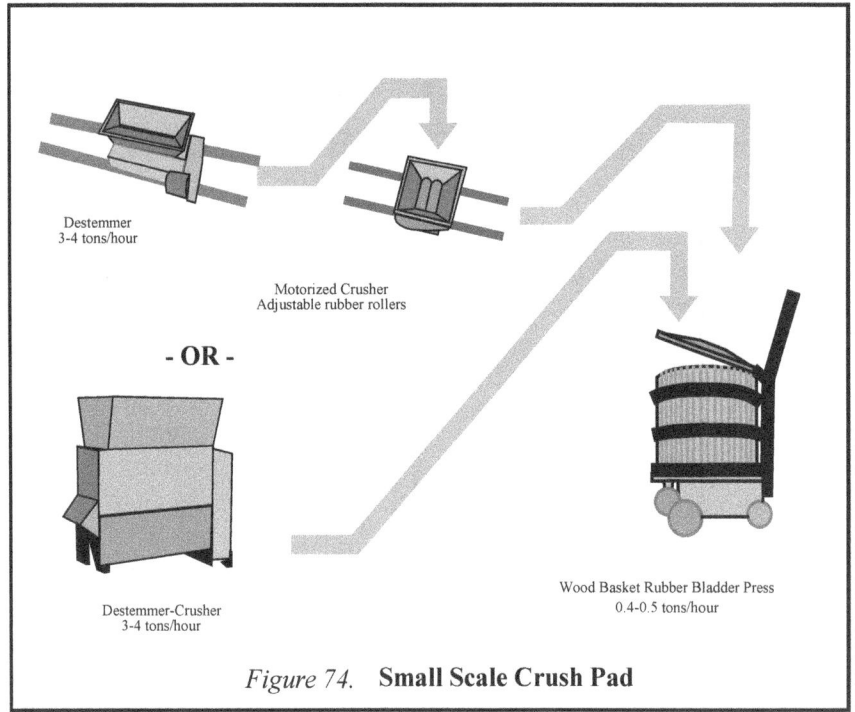

Figure 74. **Small Scale Crush Pad**

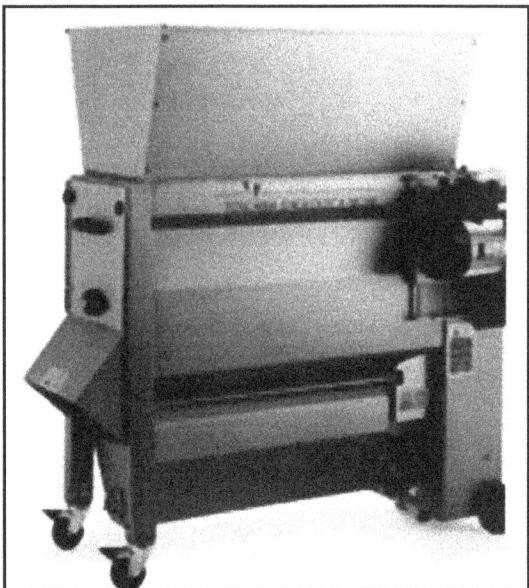

Figure 75 **Delta 30-R Destemmer-crusher**

very important for wine quality. Juice transfer pumps are available in a wide range of sizes to accommodate any scale of operation.

The initial cost of all crush pad-related equipment is summed in Table 50 for all five production volumes.

Figure 76   Liverani Transfer Pump

Photo courtesy of Prospero Equipment Corp.

TABLE 50   **Crush Pad Equipment Investment**

	Winery Production				
Cases	2,500	5,000	10,000	20,000	50,000
Gallons	5,946	11,893	23,785	47,570	118,925
Low	**$10,000**	**$29,000**	**$84,000**	**$103,500**	**$195,000**
High	**$11,500**	**$30,500**	**$86,000**	**$107,500**	**$205,000**

Tank room

Tanks. With the possible exception of some highly specialized stainless steel and fiberglass containers routinely made in Europe, the best-known tank suppliers for American wineries are JVNW, Inc. (Canby, OR), Santa Rosa Stainless Steel (Santa Rosa, CA) and Paul Mueller Company (Springfield, MO). Other good tank makers have emerged over the past fifteen years.

Tank prices depend on size, ratio of height to diameter, cooling jacket or not, number of openings and ports, polish of finish, shipping cost to the winery, number of accessories and other factors. One should bear in mind that gallons of tank capacity needed are likely to run 1.2–1.5 times annual wine production volume.

Two basic types of tanks are in use. The photo (Figure 77) depicts a line of *fixed-top tanks*. The volume is constant. Wine in less-than-full tanks has to be blanketed with inert gas, i.e., nitrogen, argon or carbon dioxide, to prevent development of oxygen-dependent organisms.

Figure 77   **JVNW Red Wine Fermenter Tanks**

Photo courtesy of JVNW.

Figure 78 **JVNW Variable Capacity Wine Tanks**

Photo courtesy of JVNW.

The other kind of tank (Figure 78) is called *variable capacity* because it has a removable lid that can be set at any level or volume. Obviously, an open-top tank is needed for red wine fermentation unless the tank has a built-in punch-down device. The lid is sealed against the tank walls by an inflatable boot similar to a bicycle balloon tire innertube.

The most popular optional accessories for both of these common wine tank configurations include: a cooling jacket; an extra manway at the bottom for removal of red grape pomace; racking and drain valve ports; a thermometer well; a temperature controller that controls the inlet solenoid valve for the cooling jacket; a sampling valve; flat, conical or sloping floor; and legs to elevate the tanks so equipment can be placed beneath the manways and racking ports.

An additional feature favored by the author for large tanks is a valve port just below the tank wall shoulder, for pumping over during fermentation of medium quality red wines, and for better vertical circulation of wines during cold stabilization and mixing with such additions as sugar, bentonite and other fining materials.

Specialized tank features that are now available include

- **Rotating horizontal tanks**, used for red wine fermentation. Rotation breaks up the cap and keeps it wet.

- **Automatic punch-down tanks** for red wine fermentation. Ram plungers are built into the tops with louvered "feet" that close on the down stroke and open on retraction to allow pomace to fall through.

- **Ganimede® tanks** with a funnel-shaped barrier in the midsection that captures CO_2, then releases it in large bubbles to rock the cap and break it up.

- **"Pneumatage" tanks**, made by Pulsair, which are equipped with a mechanism for injecting large bubbles of gas (air or nitrogen) at the bottom of the tank which do pretty much the same thing as Ganimede® tanks.

- Tanks with a built-in **automatic pumpover** mechanism.

- **Mixing tanks**, equipped with a Guth mixer.

- Tanks that allow **removal of grape seeds** during fermentation, thus reducing the amount of harsh tannins extracted.

- **Transportable fermentation tanks** that can be moved, by forklift or rail track, to the press and dumped into the press with help from an overhead crane. JVNW makes a stainless steel model for small lots (1 and 2 tons), that has a cooling jacket, drain valve port and feet that allow movement with a forklift or hand truck. Some wineries have designed larger fermentation tanks that move on rail.

- **Small stackable tanks**, to economize on floor space.

- Tanks outfitted with an "ox box" for **micro-oxygenization** of the wine.

The most recent innovation for red wines is to ferment in open-top barrels. This method reportedly yields softer wines, better integration of oak flavors and earlier bottling date. The use of oak powder or chips during fermentation claims similar effects.

None of these innovations are incorporated in the tanks used for the following cost analyses. All of the tanks have cooling jackets, though, and red wine tanks have variable capacity lids.

The tank shapes that are used in the analyses respect the principle that the lowest manufacturing cost is achieved when the ratio of tank diameter to tank height is 1.0. Those tall, skinny tanks used in some wineries have a much higher manufacturing cost in $/gallon, which should be considered, along with the stratification of wines in them, within the context of the greater floor space efficiency they permit.

Plastic wine tanks

Pasco Poly, Inc. (Weiser, ID), makes excellent food quality polyethylene tanks. Plastic tanks are not the best for every purpose, but they have proven completely acceptable for wines with a short crush-to-bottling time. They are extremely portable (when empty) and handy for overflows and temporary holding capacity. Plan on getting white wines out of them within three months.

Plastic tanks are also appropriate for red wines that spend most of their time between fermentation and bottling in barrels. Tank time is very short, one to three months. It may be necessary, however, to maintain a higher free SO_2 level and occasionally sparge with nitrogen, in order to prevent oxygen-dependent organisms from growing in the wine.

Most plastic tanks can be refrigerated. Their cost advantage over stainless steel is very attractive. There is a size limitation: 4,500 gallons at last check. Not all polyethylene material is suitable for use with wine, especially the type called "cross link" that is used in water tanks. Wines are prone to leaching plasticizers out of non-food quality plastics, and the plastic taste comes with them. Stick with Pasco Poly Tank, or check out other fabricators making "food quality polyethylene" tanks suitable for winemaking. (See Figure 79)

Some plastic tanks are included in the cost estimates in Table 51, particularly for lower production volumes, and as standbys and small lot storage.

Barrels

The process of aging wine in wood has become very complex. Twenty-five years ago, the equipment choices were limited to French oak barrels, and an occasional puncheon or oval, also of French oak. Some California wineries were still fermenting and storing red wines in redwood tanks.

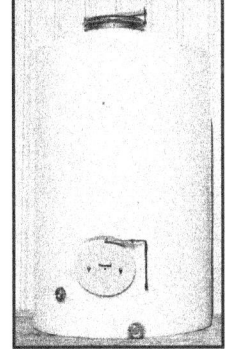

Figure 79 **Pasco Poly 1,000-gallon Wine Tank**

Photo courtesy of Pasco Polytank, Inc.

TABLE 51   **Tank Investment (in Dollars)**

	Winery Production				
Cases	2,500	5,000	10,000	20,000	50,000
Gallons	5,946	11,893	23,785	47,570	118,925
Plastic Bins	6,280	8,790	12,500	5,020	12,560
Stainless Steel Tanks	0	32,550	115,750	245,950	569,070
Plastic Tanks	30,160	45,950	50,270	48,890	73,280
Low	**34,600**	**82,000**	**169,700**	**284,900**	**622,200**
High	**38,300**	**91,700**	**187,500**	**314,900**	**687,700**

Then, along came Innerstave® and American whiskey barrels. The industry has not been the same since.

Most of the best wines are still made using barrels made of French oak. The wood available to American winemakers comes from six forests: Allier, Bourgogne, Limousin, Nevers, Tronçais, and Vosges. Each has its distinctive flavors and aromas, which can be modified by the "toast," or amount of firing applied to the inside of the barrel.

The use of American oak (Missouri, Minnesota, Tennessee, Kentucky, North Carolina) has gained acceptance in America, especially for Chardonnay, Merlot and other wines where a strong vanilla characteristic is attractive.

Barrels made from Hungarian and Romanian oak now offer a lower-cost alternative to French wood, although they are not generally considered to be as distinctive as the prominent French forests.

Barrels are also now made from Oregon white oak. Their aroma is more "herbal" than the French barrels most commonly used in Pinot Noir production. (Figure 80).

Some winemakers view the use of forest and toast like a rack of spices. Desirable aromas and flavors are selected to compliment other characteristics of the wine and to establish a "house style" in their wines.

Figure 80   **Barrels on Western Square 7" SS Barrel Pallet**

Extensive research into the aromas and flavors of wines aged in these different woods and "toast" levels has been done by ETS Laboratories, St. Helena, CA, working with Vincent Bouchard, owner of Bouchard International Cooperages.

ETS Laboratories has designed a spider diagram, Figure 81, to depict the aroma/flavor profiles of barrels. They can apply the method to any maker's barrels. The makers shown in the illustration are distributed by Bouchard Cooperages.

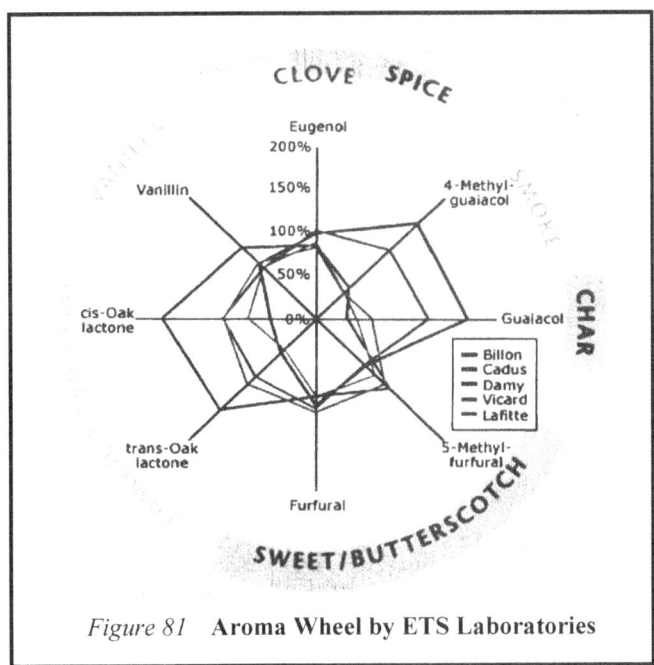

Figure 81   **Aroma Wheel by ETS Laboratories**

Barrels (and tanks) come in many sizes. Those in most frequent use by wineries are:

Configuration	Liters	Gallons
Barrels:		
Bordeaux	225	59.4
Burgundy	228	60.2
American wine		60.0
American whiskey		52.0
Puncheons:		
350L puncheon	350	92.5
500L puncheon	500	132.1
Ovals:		
German fuder	1,000	264.2

It should be noted that French barrels always sell out. That is because, under France's socialist system, the national government owns the entire forest resource and limits the cut. Therefore, the price of French barrels is much higher than for those of other countries (more than double the price). Quantity discounts are small, limited to full container loads where there are some savings in handling costs. To obtain French barrels, it is usually necessary to place your order early in the production year. You will be asked to pay a deposit with the order, usually around 20 percent.

Further, these cost projections are *startup* costs. Startup year costs will be higher than for a steady-state operation, which produces its own used barrels. Also, it is not necessary to buy all new barrels at startup. Used barrels, reconditioned or not, are readily available from existing wineries at appropriate prices. In reconditioning, they are put on a lathe and about 3/16" of the inside surface removed before toasting. Otherwise, the wine left in that 3/16" will be burned and impart unpleasant odors and flavors to the next filling.

Choices as to what wines to make, and which country's wood to employ, result in widely differing barrel costs. The point is illustrated in Table 52.

Assumptions made in estimating the Table 52 costs for specific barrel programs include:

- The winery's production is entirely within the cited barrel program, e.g., all production is red wine with French barrels on that line.

- Useful extraction life of barrels without replacement or "alternative" rejuvenation is three years. Thereafter, a barrel's useful life may be extended by using barrel alternatives.

- Time in barrel for white wines is three months.

- Time in barrel for red wines is ten months for Pinot Noir, twelve months for all other red varieties.

- "White wines—50 percent American" means 50 percent of volume in American barrels, 50 percent of volume in French barrels.

- "White wines—25 percent American" means 25 percent of volume in American barrels, 75 percent of volume in French barrels.

- "Red wines—20 percent Alternatives" means 60 percent of volume in French barrels, 20 percent of volume in American barrels, 10 percent of volume with French oak chips, and 10 percent of volume with American oak chips.

- "White wines—50 percent American" means 50 percent of volume in French barrels, 50 percent in American barrels.

- "White wines—50 percent Alternatives" means 25 percent of volume in French barrels, 25 percent of volume in American barrels, 25 percent of volume with French oak chips, and 25 percent of volume with American oak chips.

- All barrels are 60.2-gallon (228L) Burgundy Export or 60-gallon American barrels.

- There are no 350-liter or 500-liter puncheons.

- Estimates include steel barrel pallets, urethane bung plugs and plastic airlocks.

In Table 53, barrel costs are estimated for a winery producing 50 percent red wine, 25 percent Chardonnay (with barrel fermentation and six months in barrel), and 25 percent other white wine without the use of barrels. The production parameters for these estimates are:

- 50 percent of the wine is red wine aged in barrels (75 percent French, 25 percent American) for ten to twelve months.

- 25 percent of the volume is Chardonnay fermented and aged in barrel (50 percent French, 50 percent American) for six months.

- The other 25 percent is white wine made entirely in steel or plastic tanks.

- Estimates include steel barrel pallets, urethane bung plugs and plastic airlocks.

It should be obvious that estimating barrel costs is not a simple task.

TABLE 52   First-Year Investment for Various Barrel Programs (in Dollars)

Entire Production Devoted to Cited Barrel Program

		Winery Production				
	Cases	2,500	5,000	10,000	20,000	50,000
	Gallons	5,946	11,893	23,785	47,570	118,925
Red Wines						
24 Months	Low	48,000	98,000	198,000	389,000	945,000
	High	50,000	102,000	206,000	405,000	983,000
10–12 Months:						
100% French	Low	48,000	$98,000	198,000	389,000	945,000
	High	50,000	102,000	206,000	405,000	983,000
25% American	Low	34,000	90,000	180,000	354,000	859,000
	High	35,000	93,000	187,000	369,000	894,000
20% Alternatives	Low	19,000	72,000	145,000	285,000	692,000
	High	20,000	75,000	151,000	296,000	720,000
White Wines						
100% French	Low	15,000	32,000	65,000	127,000	311,000
	High	16,000	33,000	67,000	132,000	324,000
50% American	Low	10,000	25,000	52,000	82,000	255,000
	High	11,000	26,000	54,000	85,000	265,000
50% Alternatives	Low	4,000	12,500	27,000	55,000	294,000
	High	5,000	13,500	28,000	57,000	306,000

TABLE 53   First-Year Investment for Barrels (in Dollars)

Winery with Three Wines in Product Mix

		Winery Production				
	Cases	2,500	5,000	10,000	20,000	50,000
	Gallons	5,946	11,893	23,785	47,570	118,925
Red Wines	Low	25,000	34,000	74,000	132,000	353,000
	High	26,000	35,000	77,000	138,000	367,000
Chardonnay	Low	3,000	4,000	16,000	18,000	44,000
	High	3,200	4,200	16,400	19,000	46,000
Winery Total	Low	29,000	38,000	90,000	151,000	397,000
	High	30,000	40,000	94,000	157,000	414,000

Notes: 50% is red wine production with 75% French barrels, 25% American barrels, for twelve months. 25% is Chardonnay production with 50% French barrels, 50% American barrels, for three months. 25% is white wine production in steel.

Pumps

The **rubber impeller transfer pump**, specified in the crush pad discussion (Figure 76) can be used also for transferring wine in the tank room.

The specialized pumps that are usually needed in the tank room are shown in Figure 82.

Air diaphragm pumps (Figure 83) can be used for gentler movement of must and wine. They are gentler because they don't have rotors that chew up the wine. They work by a flexible diaphragm that expands and contracts the cavity. It is powered by compressed air, and the pump speed is adjustable by controlling the compressed air flow.

Variable speed positive displacement pumps (Figure 84) are used to move the wine through the final filtration and on to the bottle filler, an operation that is usually done in a series in one pass. They permit precise pumping speed by a timer or electrical feedback from a float control in the bottling bowl, and have

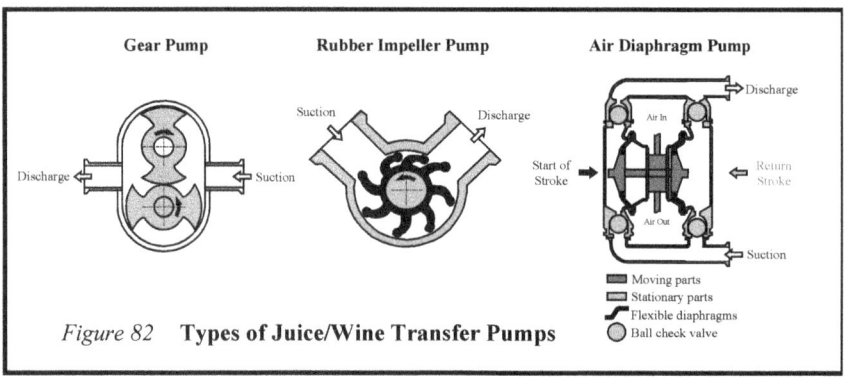

Figure 82   **Types of Juice/Wine Transfer Pumps**

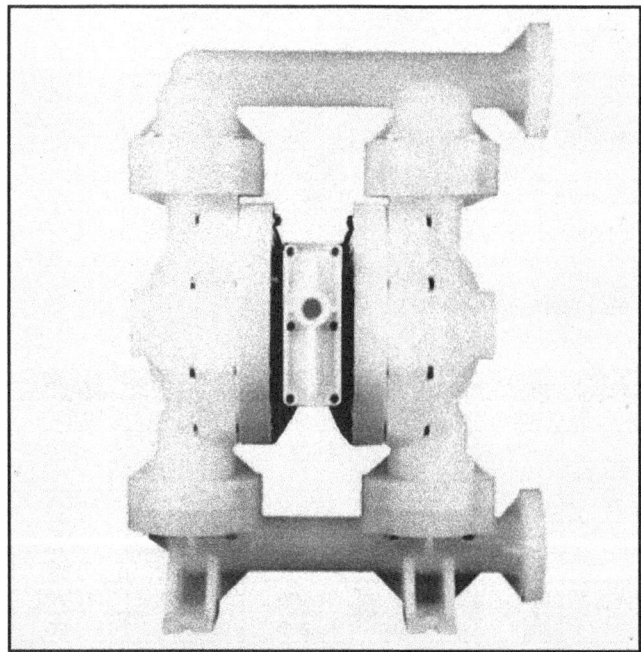

Figure 83   Wilden Diaphragm Pump

Figure 84   Carlsen/Waukesha Positive Displacement Pump with
Variable Speed Controls

an electronic controller that ramps the speed up and down so as to avoid slamming paper filtration sheets and splash in the filler bowl.

Bulldog Pup (Figure 85) is a racking wand powered by inert gas (typically nitrogen or argon), used to transfer wine from barrel to barrel and barrel to tank. It is the gentlest method of wine transfer, with the exception of gravity flow. It is most frequently used on high-end red wines.

Filters

There are several types of filters, including plate-and-frame, vacuum lees filter, diatomaceous earth (DE) filter, cross-flow, and sterile membrane filter. Each of them has its specific use in the winery, and some can be used for several operations.

Previously, the most important and most versatile filter was the plate-and-frame. This filter, illustrated in Figure 86, has a series of frames with either canvas cloths or paper pads between them.

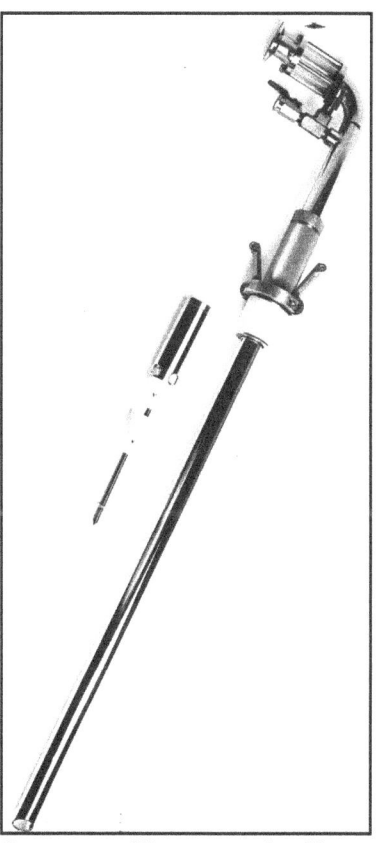

Figure 85   Bulldog Pup Barrel Racking
Wand

Thicker reinforced plastic plates are used with canvas cloths because the pressures are higher and more horizontal room is needed to accommodate the DE that is mixed with the lees or wine. Thinner plates are used with paper filter pads for cleaning up wines at several points between fermentation and bottling. Paper pads come in a range of densities suitable for rough through fine filtration.

Figure 86   ITAL Plate-and-Frame Filter

Plate-and-frame filters can even be used for sterile filtration at bottling, but paper pads are not as good as a membrane filter for this purpose. The reason is that paper pads don't necessarily remove all of the smallest harmful organisms, whereas the membrane filter (see below) has a uniform pore size that absolutely stops every particle larger than the filter's pore size.

DE filters (Figure 87) are used for initial rough filtration of wines coming out of fermentation.

Vacuum lees filters are used by large wineries to recover juice from the settling lees before fermentation. This operation is usually done instead by successive rackings of the juice lees in small- and medium-size wineries.

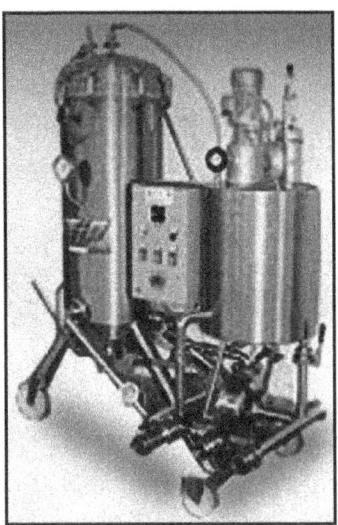

Figure 87   Velo Diatomaceous Earth Filter

Sterile membrane filters (five sizes are shown in Figure 88) have filter elements with a uniform pore size that block the passage of all particles or organisms larger than the pore size. Therefore, all yeast cells and bacteria that can harm wine in the bottle are eliminated. As general practice, 45 micron filters (that's 45 millionths of an inch) are used to render white wines "sterile." The practice is seldom applied to red wines anymore because it strips color, flavor and aroma from them.

Cross-flow filters (pictured in Figure 89). The new kid on the block is cross-flow. The principle is the flow of unfiltered wine across the surface of the surface of the filter element, or *tangential* to it. Thus, the surface is swept clean and excluded particles do not clog the filter pores. The "sludge" is recycled into the unfiltered wine.

The method was not feasible for use on wine until about 2008, when improvements in materials and manufacturing technique yielded the desired results.

Filter elements are available in two materials, polysulfone tubes and ceramic, the former favored at this time.

Cross-flow replaces both DE and plate-and-frame. For some wines, it even makes sterile filtration at bottling unnecessary. Respected winemakers report that the pore size of 0.2 microns is not injurious to high-quality red wines.

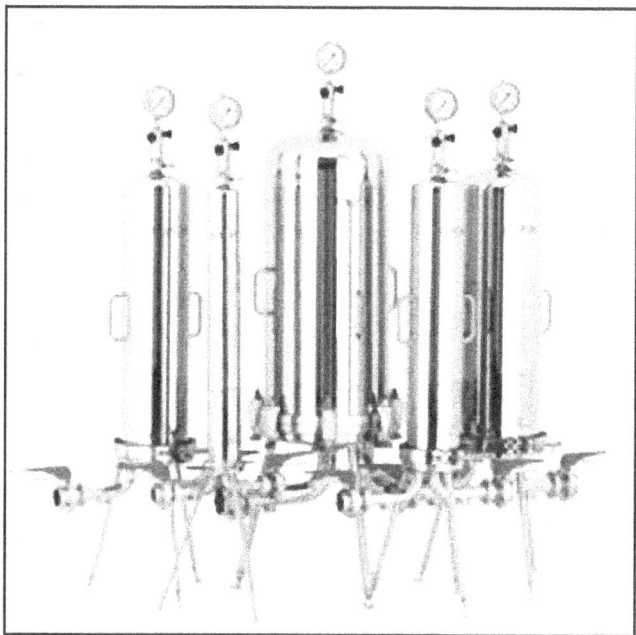

Figure 88   Millipore Sterile Membrane Filters

Figure 89   Koch WF-3 Cross-Flow Membrane Filter

The investment in pumps and filters is summed in Table 54. Two sets of figures are shown, the first using cross-flow filtration, the second utilizing the traditional DE (diatomaceous earth) and plate-and-frame methods. The equipment costs are almost the same for production over 10,000 cases. For smaller wineries, mobile cross-flow filtration may represent a viable economic alternative.

TABLE 54   **Pumps and Filters Investment (in Dollars)**

	Winery Production				
Cases	2,500	5,000	10,000	20,000	50,000
Gallons	5,946	11,893	23,785	47,570	118,925
With cross-flow filtration:					
Low	4,950	5,050	31,400	31,400	41,600
High	5,450	5,550	35,400	35,400	46,000
With DE and plate & frame filtration:					
Low	9,900	16,700	33,500	37,800	41,000
High	10,900	18,400	37,100	41,700	45,400

Bottling line

A good friend once offered to show me his new Italian bottling line. Then, he took me out into the winery and pointed at his wife—of Italian heritage—of course, hand bottling the wine. Many small wineries bottle by hand. It's cheap on equipment (you can get a six-spout filler for about $2,000), but long on labor, and may be hazardous to your marriage. Further, hand bottling is not very safe: it presents too many opportunities exist for oxygen and harmful organisms to get into the wine.

A representative monobloc bottling line for a winery around 20,000–25,000 gallons is pictured in Figure 90. The assembly includes bottle deaerator/sparger, 16-spout filler, pre-cork sparger, vacuum corker and capper. It will fill 10–50 bottles per minute.

The investment in bottling equipment is displayed in Table 55.

Mobile Bottling Line. Another alternative exists in place of buying a first-class bottling line. There are mobile bottling lines, with all the bells and whistles, mounted on truck trailers in the Northwest and California. You provide

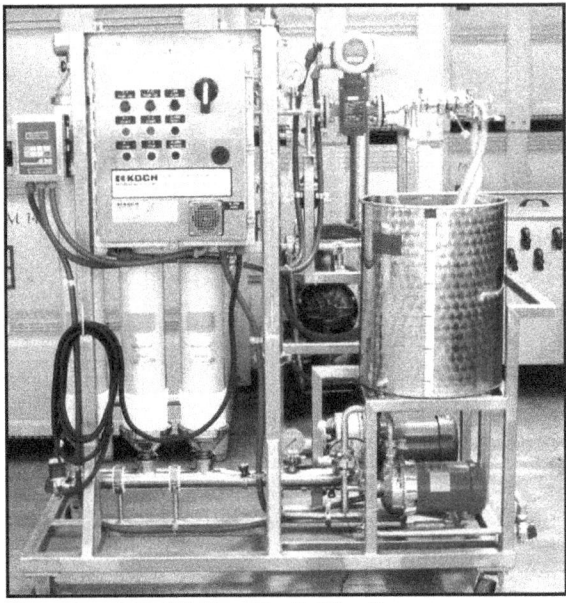

Figure 90   GAI 1603 Monobloc Bottling Line

TABLE 55 Bottling Line Investment (in Dollars)

	Winery Production				
Cases	2,500	5,000	10,000	20,000	50,000
Gallons	5,946	11,893	23,785	47,570	118,925
Low	4,900	69,100	96,300	129,000	139,900
High	5,400	76,400	106,500	142,500	154,600

the wine, bottles, corks, capsules, labels and crew. The bottling service pulls up to your door and hooks up for the day. You get pre-fill bottle rinse, sterile filtration, inert gas-blanketed fill, vacuum cork insertion, capsule spinning and labeling in one pass, just like the big guys. At about $2.45/case, it's expensive, but a good alternative for the small winery and definitely superior with respect to quality control.

There are some qualifications for a mobile bottling line. Typically, the winery has to bottle a minimum of 1,000 cases in a day to make it worth the mobile line operator's time to show up. Several wines can be bottled on the same day in order to meet the threshold volume.

Threshold for winery to invest in a monobloc bottling line

At what wine volume can a small winery justify the large investment in a mobile bottling line? It probably depends on what kind of value you put on your time. Just think, you could be out doing winemaker dinners instead. With your own monobloc bottling line, you'll need a smaller crew, and that 3,000 gallons will be done in three days, compared with hand bottling for about nine very long days.

There is no precise point at which this capital investment makes good business sense for all wineries. Among the key variables are differences in final filtration used (sterile versus pad versus none); the flow rate of the winery's filtering equipment; the winery's ability to schedule enough volume for one full day's bottling; bottle size; and the logistical costs of moving empty bottles to the mobile line and full bottles to case goods storage.

Using a typical situation, though, it is possible to calculate the threshold volume at which investment in a monobloc line makes sense. Those calculations are illustrated in Table 56.

The payback period of 6.41 years for the monobloc compared with hand bottling is very good. Any payback period up to eight years is generally considered acceptable for a capital investment in machinery. At 6.41 years, only 3,000 cases are needed to justify the investment.

We can't compare monobloc versus mobile bottling in the same way, because there is no investment with mobile. The observation we can make is that the mobile service offers a $2,043.30 savings versus hand bottling ($9,393.30–7,350.00).

Let's set the bar at a payback period of eight years. In comparison to hand bottling under the above assumptions, the monobloc investment achieves a payback period of eight years at 2,288 cases (5,442 gallons). The present worth

TABLE 56   **Threshold Investment Analysis for Monobloc Line**

Monobloc vs. Hand Botttling vs. Mobile Line

	Hand Bottle	Monobloc	Mobile Line
No. of laborers	7	5	5
Hourly wage	12.25	12.25	12.25
Plus 20% for fringes	14.70	14.70	14.70
Supervisor	1	1	1
Hourly wage	17.00	17.00	17.00
Plus 25% for fringes*	27.56	27.56	27.56
Total labor per hour	130.46	101.06	101.06
Total cases bottled	3,000	3,000	3,000
Bottles per hour	500	1,500	1,500
Cases per hour	41.7	125.0	150.0
Hours of bottling	72.0	24.0	20.0
Days of bottling/year	9.0	3.0	2.5
Bottling cost	$9,393.30	$2,425.50	$7,350.00**
Annual savings for monobloc	$6,967.80		
Less allowance for maintenance	−1,328.70		
Net annual savings for monobloc	**$8,296.50**		
Purchase price	$16,751		$66,435
Less salvage value @20%	3,350		13,287
Net investment	$13,401		$53,148
Payback period, years		**6.41**	
Capitalized value of savings (Capitalization rate of 8%)		**$103,706**	
Return on investment		195.1%	
Cumulative present worth of savings (ten years @8%)	**$55,670**	Exceeds Net Investment of $53,148	

* Includes 5% premium for federal healthcare.

** 3,000 cases @$2.45

of the cost savings over a ten-year period, plus present worth of salvage value, is $54,697 at 2,838 cases (6,750 gallons).

Viewed another way, the winery invests a net amount of $53,148 in the monobloc line and receives an asset worth a capitalized value of $99,003. The pre-tax return on investment is 186.3 percent. These are rather compelling arguments.

Of course, a well-maintained monobloc bottling line has an economic life of 20–25 years, much greater than the ten years used in this analysis. So, a case can be made that the monobloc investment is justified at a lower winery volume than has been illustrated here.

Hoses and fittings

All wine and juice is transferred from press-to-tank to tank-to-bottling by means of flexible plastic hoses. The most popular hose type is *Spiralite* or equivalent.

For the example winery, all hose in the tank and barrel rooms is 1-½" inside diameter and 20-foot lengths. The pomace hose transporting crushed must from the destemmer-crusher to press or fermentation tank is 4" inside diameter, same hose make.

All end fittings are Tri-Clamp barbed, secured by two stainless steel radiator clamps at both hose ends.

All of the wineries also have red rubber hot water hoses for sterilizing the final filter and bottling line. These costs are summed in Table 57.

TABLE 57   Hose and Fitting Investment (in Dollars)

	Winery Production				
Cases	2,500	5,000	10,000	20,000	50,000
Gallons	5,946	11,893	23,785	47,570	118,925
Low	750	1,200	2,100	3,500	6,400
High	850	1,300	2,200	3,600	6,700

Refrigeration system

Cooling is needed for red wine fermentation, cold stabilization, in-tank storage and cellar temperature control. The function is usually provided by a water-propylene glycol chiller and a plastic pipe distribution system. Very large wineries can benefit economically by using an ammonia coolant system, but all of the winery sizes in this analysis will find propylene glycol to be the safest and most efficient system.

The smallest wineries can use small package chillers. A portable must heater-cooler unit is available that connects to as many as four individual tank cooling jackets, allowing must heating for the start of red wine fermentations in addition to cooling for fermentation and storage.[1]

Because the coolant distribution system is usually made of Schedule 40 PVC pipe, many wineries can do the installation themselves without calling in a plumber. Check your building code to be sure.

Refrigeration system costs are totaled in Table 58.

Laboratory

To read the prominent texts on winemaking, one would think that laboratory tests performed on grape juice and wine are legion. Well, what happens in academic research labs is not indicative of common winery practices. There are a handful of tests that are essential to winemaking, and every winemaker should become proficient in performing them and incorporate them into his/her winemaking protocol.

The tests run most frequently are listed in Table 59.

Essential laboratory equipment for the tests listed in Table 60 and costs are detailed for the three example laboratories in Table 61. Some items of "Optional Equipment" are also referenced, although they are not included in Table 61 costs.

---

1. G&D Chillers; Eugene, Oregon.

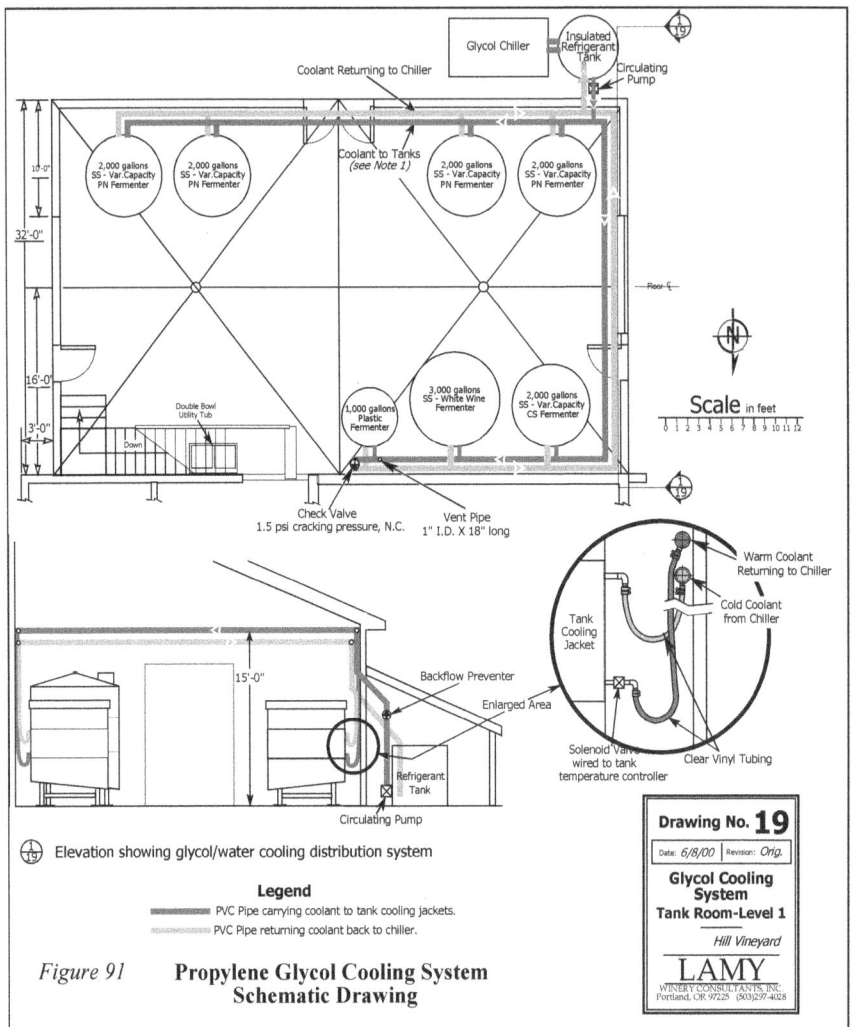

Figure 91   **Propylene Glycol Cooling System Schematic Drawing**

TABLE 58   Refrigeration System Investments (in Dollars)

		Winery Production				
	Cases	2,500	5,000	10,000	20,000	50,000
	Gallons	5,946	11,893	23,785	47,570	118,925
Glycol chillers		13,100	16,230	16,230	29,130	48,610
Controllers and solenoids		330	1,960	4,580	6,210	15,040
Tubing, pipes and connectors		6,420	13,910	23,530	29,950	69,520
Installation costs		750	1,030	2,000	2,440	4,150
Total refrigeration system						
	Low	**19,600**	**31,500**	**44,500**	**65,700**	**134,600**
	High	**21,600**	**34,800**	**48,200**	**69,800**	**140,100**

The cost of sophisticated optional laboratory equipment easily can add $8,000–20,000 to those totals.

Building costs for laboratory shelves, cabinets and counters are presented in Chapter 14, as are suggested floor plans for three different sizes of winery production.

TABLE 59   Common Laboratory Analyses

Stage	Attribute	Equipment
Fresh grapes and grape juice	sugar content	refractometer
	total acidity	titration with NaOH
	pH	pH meter
Must in fermentation	specific gravity	hydrometer
	residual sugar	Gold Coast or other
	malic & lactic acidity	paper chromatography
	yeast budding (sparkling)	microscope
Wine before bottling	tartrate stability	cold test
	protein stability	heat test
	alcohol content	ebulliometer
	total acidity	titration with NaOH
	pH	pH meter
	total and free SO_2	Merkel, Ripper, etc.

TABLE 60   Laboratory Equipment List

Essential Equipment		
Acid titration	SO_2 test (Fritz Merkel Sulfacor)	Digital cooking timer
Burettes & stand	Residual sugar test (Gold Coast)	375 ml glass bottles w/caps
Ceramic hotplate-stirrer	Ebulliometer	Bottle brushes
PH meter	Triple beam balance	Refrigerator
500 ml beakers	Digital scale	Dishwasher
Erlenmeyer flasks	Refractometer	Sink
Pipettes	Hydrometers & cylinders	Cabinets
Thermometer	Microscope	Tasting glasses
Jar for paper chromatography	Calculator/computer	Petri dish covers
Optional Equipment		
Ripper SO_2 test	Gas chromatograph	Lab centrifuge
Cash still	Liquid chromatograph (HPLC)	Petri dishes
Vacuum aspirator	Separate hotplate	Polyethylene juice bottles
Sulfide detector		

TABLE 61   Laboratory Equipment Investment (in Dollars)

		Winery Production				
	Cases	2,500	5,000	10,000	20,000	50,000
	Gallons	5,946	11,893	23,785	47,570	118,925
Total laboratory equipment						
	Low	3,600	3,600	5,300	5,300	6,600
	High	4,000	4,000	5,900	5,900	7,300

Other winery equipment

This catchall category includes most of the following items and costs $1,400–3,500 (Table 62), in addition to about $7,300–38,000 for the forklift truck, depending on whether it's new or used.

> **Winemaking**—punch-down device for red wine fermentation, portable stainless steel cooling plates, filter sheets of varying grades, diatomaceous earth and precoat powder for DE filtration, sterile membrane cartridges, cylinders of nitrogen, carbon dioxide and argon (with hand trucks), liquid SO_2 injection equipment, bung plugs and air locks for barrels and carboys.

> **Material handling**—forklift truck, pallet jack, plastic rakes, plastic scoop shovels, wood tote bins and plastic liners, 400-gallon plastic tote bins, 5-gallon plastic buckets, 5-gallon glass carboys, wood pallets, pallet jack, wine hoses, hose drying racks, vinyl siphon tubing, additional transfer pumps, plastic tubs and drums, plastic buckets, hand trucks, conveyors for grapes and cases, portable stairway, catwalks.

> **Packaging**—glue gun and sticks, tape dispenser and packaging tape, shrink wrap dispenser and shrink wrap, duct tape.

> **Maintenance**—tool box and tools (particularly in metric sizes), grease gun and food grade grease, maglites, utility knives, shop rags, push brooms.

> **Sanitation and safety**—tank cleaning balls, barrel cleaning spray ball, hot water hose (red rubber), garden hose, spray nozzles, bottle brushes, carboy brushes, Nitrile gloves, thick rubber gloves, non-metallic scrubber pads, sponges, spray bottles, paper towels, first aid kits, face shield, box fans for ventilation and cooling, portable flood lighting, rotating screen and NH_3-injector for winery wastewater.

Tasting rooms

There seems to be no correlation between winery size and the size/quality dimension of the tasting room. It all depends on how the winery management wishes to use tasting room activities in its overall marketing strategy. Therefore, the reader is referred to the previous chapter on marketing for a more thorough discussion.

Table 63 shows the initial capital investment is estimated for a typical tasting room setup, without any extraordinary functions performed. They include: cork pullers, refrigerator, sterile glass washer, cash register, credit card equipment, tasting glasses, display racks, shelving, hand truck (for case sales).

TABLE 62   Other Winery Equipment Investment (in Dollars)

		Winery Production				
	Cases	2,500	5,000	10,000	20,000	50,000
	Gallons	5,946	11,893	23,785	47,570	118,925
Winemaking		680	680	1,360	1,700	2,040
Material handling		7,750	7,750	14,500	39,440	39,620
Packaging		160	160	320	400	490
Maintenance		30	30	60	80	100
Sanitation and safety		170	170	340	420	520
	Low	**8,400**	**8,400**	**15,800**	**40,000**	**40,500**
	High	**9,200**	**9,200**	**17,400**	**44,200**	**44,900**

TABLE 63   Tasting Room Equipment Investment (in Dollars)

		Winery Production				
	Cases	2,500	5,000	10,000	20,000	50,000
	Gallons	5,946	11,893	23,785	47,570	118,925
Refrigerator, washer, cash register		2,170	2,170	5,910	5,910	5,910
Tasting glasses & cork pullers		160	290	580	600	1,150
Fixtures, folding tables, hand truck		590	760	1,290	1,890	3,280
	Low	**2,800**	**3,100**	**7,400**	**8,000**	**9,800**
	High	**3,100**	**3,400**	**8,200**	**8,800**	**10,900**

Total winery equipment costs

All of the equipment costs are summed in Table 64.

TABLE 64   Summary of Winery Equipment Investments (in Dollars)

		Winery Production				
	Cases	2,500	5,000	10,000	20,000	50,000
	Gallons	5,946	11,893	23,785	47,570	118,925
Crush Pad	*Low*	10,000	29,000	84,000	103,500	195,500
	High	11,500	30,500	86,000	107,500	205,000
Tanks	*Low*	34,600	82,900	169,700	284,900	622,200
	High	38,300	91,700	187,500	314,900	687,700
Barrels	*Low*	28,000	38,000	189,500	150,000	397,000
	High	29,500	39,500	93,500	157,000	413,000
Pumps & Filters	*Low*	4,950	5,050	31,400	31,400	41,600
	High	5,450	5,550	35,400	35,400	46,000
Bottling Line	*Low*	4,900	69,100	96,300	129,000	139,900
	High	5,400	76,400	106,500	142,500	154,600
Hoses & Fittings	*Low*	750	1,200	2,100	3,500	6,400
	High	850	1,300	2,200	3,600	6,700
Refrigeration System	*Low*	19,600	31,500	44,500	65,700	134,600
	High	21,600	34,800	48,200	69,800	140,100
Laboratory Equipment	*Low*	3,600	3,600	5,300	5,300	6,600
	High	4,000	4,000	5,900	5,900	7,300
Other Winery Equipment	*Low*	8,400	8,400	15,800	40,000	40,600
	High	9,200	9,200	17,400	44,200	44,900
Tasting Room	*Low*	2,800	3,100	7,400	8,000	9,800
	High	3,100	3,400	8,200	8,800	10,900
Total Winery Equipment						
	Low	**117,000**	**271,850**	**546,000**	**821,300**	**1,593,700**
	High	**128,900**	**296,350**	**590,800**	**889,600**	**1,716,200**

Notes: Based on all new equipment for over 5000 cases production. Under 5,000 cases, mix of new and used equipment is assumed. For crush pad sizing, use 170 gallons of juice per ton of grapes. Tank capacity runs 1.2–1.5 times gallonage bottled. "Pumps and filters" includes cross-flow option.

Further reading

Barrel Builders, Inc., Calistoga, CA. (Tonnelerie Marchive).
Website: http://www.barrelbuilders.com/

Bouchard Cooperages; Napa, CA and Beaune, FR. (Billon, Damy, Cadus, Vicard & Canadell). Website: http://www.bouchardcooperages.com

Canton Cooperage, Lebanon, KY & Windsor, CA. (American oak barrels).
Website: http://www.cantoncooperage.com/

Carlsen & Associates (Healdsburg, CA). Website: http://www.carlsenassociates.com

Cork Supply USA; Benicia, CA. Website: http://www.corksupply.com/

Criveller California Corp., Niagara Falls, Ontario and Windsor, CA. (Tanks, Enoveneta, Ganimede®). Website: http://www.criveller.com

Demptos Napa Cooperage, Napa, CA. Website: http://www.demptos.fr/en_v2/de_22.php

EuroMachines, Inc., Suisun City, CA. (Rausch, Kiessel, Europress).
Website: http://www.euromachinesusa.com

Forest Origin Comparisons; barrel wood characteristics by forest; Vincent Bouchard; 2013.
Website: http: //www.bouchardcooperages.com/usa/news/forest_origin.html

G.W. Kent, Inc. (Ann Arbor, MI). Website: http://www.gwkent.com

G&D Chillers, Inc. (Eugene, OR). Website: http://www.gdchillers.com/

Independent Stave Co.; Columbia, MO. (World Cooperage & Tonnelerie Quintessence, Missouri Kentucky wood). Website: http://www.independentstavecompany.com/sales

Lafitte Cork & Capsule, Inc.; Napa, CA. Website: http://www.lafitte-usa.com/

Mel Knox, Barrel Broker; San Francisco. (Francois Freres, Taransaud).
Website: http://www.knoxbarrels.com

PRO Refrigeration, Inc., Auburn, WA. Website: http://www.prorefrigeration.com/

"Product Review Update"; *Wine Business Monthly* magazine; September, 2010.
Website: http: //www.winebusiness.com/wbm/?go=getArticle&dataId=80416

Prospero Equipment Co., Pleasantville, NY & Windsor, CA. (GAI, ITAL OMAC).
Website: http://www.wineryequipment.com

RLS Equipment Co., Inc.; Egg Harbor, NJ. (Keissel, Magitek).
Website: http://www.rlsequipment.com

Scott Laboratories, Inc., Petaluma, CA. (Velo, Willmes). Website: http://www.scottlab.com

Seguin Moreau Napa Cooperage, Napa, CA. Website: http://seguinmoreaunapa.com/

St. Patrick's of Texas, Austin, TX. Website: http://www.stpats.com

StaVin, Inc., Sausalito, CA. (Tonnelerie Saint Jacques barrels, oak alternatives).
Website: http://www.stavin.com/

TCW Equipment, Santa Rosa, CA. Website: http://www.tcwequipment.com

Tonnelerie Mercier, Barbezieux, FR & Napa, CA.
Website: http://www.tonnellerie-mercier.com

Valley Pipe & Supply, Inc. Fresno, CA. (Amos, Defrancheschi).
Website: http://www.valleypipe.com

Western Square Industries (Stockton, CA).
Website: http://www.westernsquare.com/index.html

Wine Country Classifieds, St. Helena, CA. (used barrels and equipment listings).
Website: http://www.winerysite.com/images/pdf/classifieds.pdf

Photo credits

Figure 68	RLS Equipment Co., Inc. and Valley Pipe & Supply
Figure 70	Joseph H. Lamy and Kramer Vineyards
Figure 72	Scott Laboratories, Inc.
Figure 74	G.W. Kent and Prospero Equipment Co.
Figure 76	Prospero Equipment Co.
Figures 77–78	VNW, Inc.
Figure 79	Pasco Poly Co.
Figure 80	Roberta Manell Montero, Bouchard Cooperages
Figure 81	ETS Laboratories and Vincent Bouchard
Figure 83	Wilden Pump & Engineering, Pump Solutions Group, Dover Corporation
Figure 84	Carlsen Associates
Figure 85	Bulldog Manufacturing
Figure 86	Prospero Equipment Co.
Figure 87	Scott Laboratories, Inc.
Figure 88	Millipore Corporation
Figure 89	Corey Morris, Willamette Crossflow Mobile Filtration
Figure 90	Prospero Equipment Co.

13

Winery building

Winery building

Wineries come in all shapes, sizes and styles. Some winery buildings are utilitarian and functional. Some are exotic and functional. Some are exotic, but not very functional. And, a few are dumps. Fortunately, not many are in the last category.

Principles of winery design

Many design options are available to the new winery developer. But, there are a few guidelines that will prove helpful in the task of design.

1. **Operational objective**. Every winery should be committed to the objective of making *good* wine. This principle applies to the winery's design just as much as it does to production methods considered to reduce costs.

2. **Cleanliness**. This reality should always be born in mind: *the cleanliness of a winery speaks volumes to wine consumers about a trustworthy product.*

3. Layout of production floor. **Flexibility** is the key attribute. Why? Because all processing equipment except large tanks and the bottling line are mounted on wheels or are otherwise easily portable. Hoses are flexible. So, relative positioning of the major processing areas—crush pad, tanks room, barrel room, bottling line—are not critical for small and medium-size wineries. The longest dimension of production areas typically is shorter than 200 feet. Hoses can be made up of any length. The easiest to handle, particularly in hanging them up on drying racks, are

20–25 feet. But, a winemaker can also have a 50-foot hose in the repertoire. Many hoses may be linked together.

4. Sequences of operations for the major wine types are illustrated in the production flow chart of Figure 92.

5. Perusal of the flow chart shows that the dominant movement is from crush pad .. to tanks .. to bottling .. to casegoods storage. Red wines and wood-aged white wines make a side trip to the barrel area. Sparkling wines follow a uniquely tortuous path owing to the second fermentation in bottle.

6. Some working relationships among processing areas deserve consideration, though, and they increase in importance with winery size. The first is between the crush pad and tanks. All juice goes from the press to tanks. Even Chardonnay intended for barrel fermentation is transferred first to a tank for overnight settling in order to reduce suspended solids to less than 2–3 percent.

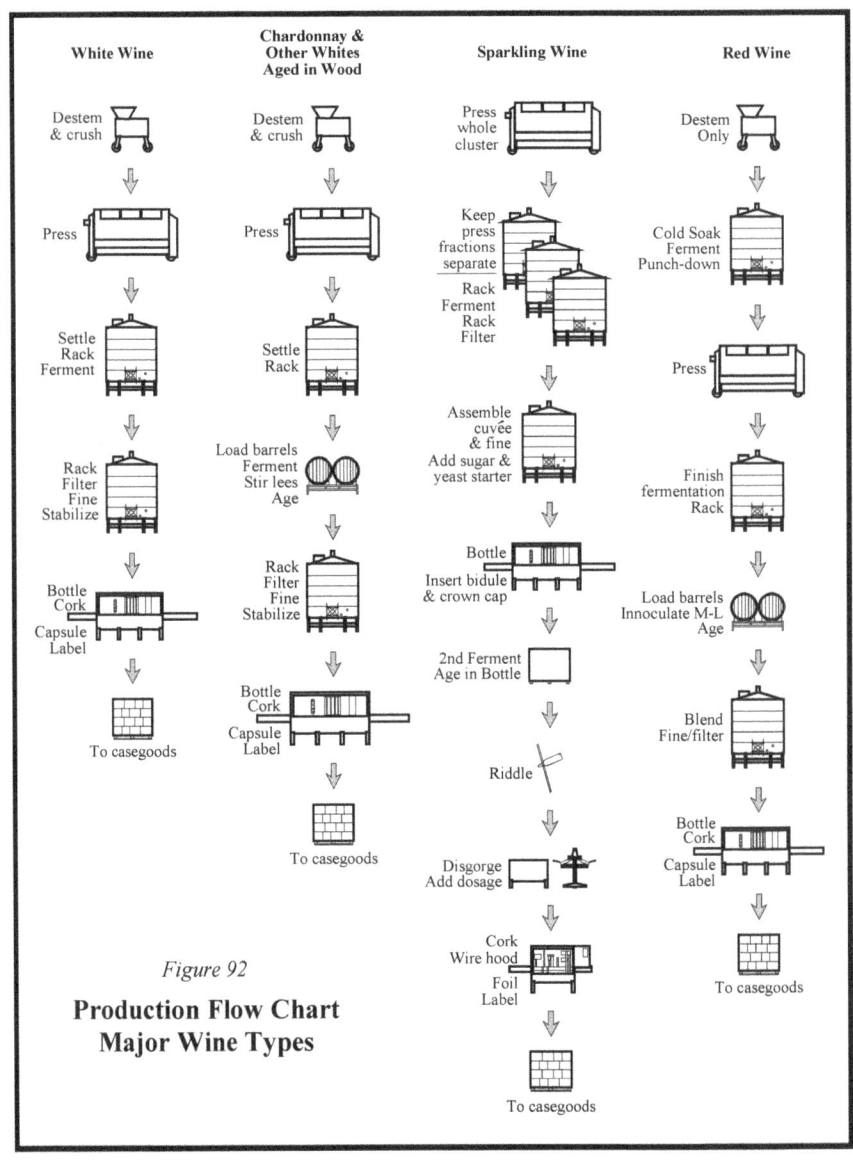

Figure 92

**Production Flow Chart
Major Wine Types**

7. Crushed but unpressed red grapes are usually pumped directly from the destemmer to a tank or bin for fermentation, then they are sent to the press after most of the yeast fermentation is complete. So, it makes sense to position tanks adjacent to the crush pad, especially the red wine fermentation tanks and bins.

8. **Barrels are loaded from tanks**. The task is accomplished by using a hose with a shutoff valve and nozzle or racking wand at the barrel end. Barrels are portable when mounted on barrel pallets and using a pallet jack or fork lift truck. Therefore, the barrels may be filled near the tanks and transported to their storage area, or the hose may be taken to the barrels.

9. It is common in small wineries that barrels are kept in the same room as the tanks, but larger wineries keep them in a partitioned room or separate building. Ideally, barrels are kept in a relatively humid environment to minimize evaporation losses, compared to the tank room which is cooler and drier.

10. A locational relationship that is far less important is the one between taxpaid storage and the tasting room. **Taxpaid storage** is a space separate from casegoods storage. When the winery declares some wine ready to go to marketing, it pays the federal and state excise taxes and either ships the wine or places it in taxpaid storage. Tasting room supplies are typically drawn from taxpaid storage.

11. **Ceiling clearance**. Height of the tanks defines the necessary ceiling height. Even in small wineries, a minimum of 16 feet is a good rule of thumb. For wineries producing more than 20,000 cases, 24 feet ceiling height is more appropriate.

12. **Door openings.** A winery requires at least one rollup door. A minimum for a small winery is 10 feet wide by 12 feet high. The main issue is getting tanks into the building.

13. Because most wineries grow, at least during the first ten years, it is of utmost importance to provide a door opening large enough to admit the largest tank anticipated. A 20,000-gallon tank will probably require a 16 feet wide by 18 feet high door. That's even sufficient to let in a semi-trailer truck for offloading of barrels and glass during inclement weather.

14. **Insulation.** Wall and ceiling insulation should be R-22 as a minimum. In warmer climates and colder climates, the rating should be higher. For tilt-up concrete wall panels, the concrete will provide adequate insulation by itself.

15. For wood frame and steel buildings, as well as the roof insulation on tilt-up concrete buildings, a new product is available, Radiant Foil. This new product uses dead airspace trapped between foil layers to provide superior insulating properties.

16. **Floor design.** Floor and drainage system design can yield a lifetime of satisfaction or grief. Floor slopes designed so liquids flow to the drains, and properly designed drains, can ease the task of keeping floors dry and clean. Getting juice and wine off the concrete floor promptly prevents erosion. Fruit acids are tough enough on concrete, but the sugar in juice is really destructive. And then, painful falls can occur on a wet or juice-slicked floor.

17. Extensive floor repair can present a major disruption to winery operations.

18. Proper floor design has to anticipate the eventual placement of tanks, barrels and bottling line; slope to floor drains; the wastewater drainage system itself; conduit access for electrical cables (unless you go overhead); plumbing for water supply; and fork lift traffic.

19. It is necessary to calculate the maximum expected load for full tanks in specifying slab thickness and concrete compression strength. Tanks on

legs assert much higher unit loads than tanks on pads. A structural engineer is needed for the task of drawing specifications for the floor slab.

20. Good wastewater drainage is a must for winery sanitation. That means the floor slab has to be pitched at least 1/4 inch per lateral foot to cause liquids to flow naturally to floor drains. Area drains may be used for the tank space of small wineries. Trench drains are appropriate for the tank rooms of larger wineries. In areas where relatively flat floors are needed and spills are seldom, casegoods storage for example, area drains may be used.

21. **Wastewater drainage system.** The best drainpipe system is designed to "daylight" on a hillside site, or into an open-air sump pit. Such a design enables the use of sweep elbows at the drains rather than "p-traps," thereby minimizing blockages and easing cleaning. The reason why building codes specify "p-traps" for drains is that they prevent sewer gasses from backing up into the building. If the drainpipe system empties to daylight outside the building, falling by gravity from the pipe end through a screen and deflected into a sump for stabilizing and pumping to the eventual disposal site, there is no sewer gas to back up through the drainpipe. Hence, there is no need for a "p-trap."

22. A winery has two kinds of waste to dispose of. One is sanitary waste that originates in bathrooms and sinks. That waste is routed either to a municipal sewer system, or to a septic tank with a leach field.

23. The other type, and usually the one of much larger volume, is **winery wastewater**. It is the liquids and debris that result from processing grapes and wine. It contains grape juice; a small amount of grape solids; wine; organic acids; bentonite and several protein-based fining agents; diatomaceous earth and screen-coating fiber; yeast lees; calcium carbonate; potassium metabisulfite; bleach, soda ash and some phosphate-based cleaners; and other materials. This waste, too, can be disposed of in a municipal sewer system or septic system, but its volume frequently justifies pH stabilization by ammonia injection, and then aeration in a lagoon to reduce its BOD (bio-oxygen demand) prior to running it out as irrigation water.

24. **Wall finish.** Typically sanitation specifications for food processing facilities require that walls be "smooth and scrubbable" up to 8 feet from the floor. On concrete and wood, such a surface can be provided by direct application of primer and an epoxy-based food-quality paint. Concrete block is more difficult. A trowel coat of filler is needed to smooth the pitted surface before applying primer and the epoxy-based food-quality paint.

25. Some winemakers fret that such sanitation measures prevent formation of a desirable yeast and malo-lactic bacteria flora on the walls. Well, we're leaving the wall areas above eight feet and the ceiling for that. Besides, it can be argued that such resident flora aren't important as in the old days. Inoculation with selected yeast strains and malo-lactic cultures is commonplace in today's winemaking protocols, rendering dependence in such flora unnecessary.

26. **Ventilation.** A critical ventilation need is encountered during fermentation, when the yeast produces large volumes of carbon dioxide. Gravity will move the gas outside if sufficient openings are provided near floor level and there are inlet vents up higher. Here, the use of sweep elbows at the floor joints and "daylighting" of the effluent will remove some of the CO_2 purely by gravity. Ventilation fans are usually employed in the roof (blowing down) and at doors and other vents near the floor (blowing out).

27. An ideal **CO2 ventilation system** would include a CO_2 sensing controller at 24–32" above the floor that automatically turns on ceiling fans (blowing down) and opens shuttered wall vents (at 12–18" above the floor).

28. Another danger is posed by using inert gas to sparge or blanket a tank of wine. The gas can overflow through the top manway or over the wall of an open-top tank, and flow down the outside of the tank wall. These gasses are heavier than air and can fill the lungs of an unsuspecting winemaker standing next to the tank, resulting in asphyxiation. Argon is the most dangerous of these because it is the heaviest, although CO_2 and nitrogen can cause a similar problem. Portable box fans are a simple fix for the problem.

29. A similar need for ventilation can be presented when a winemaker adds SO_2 in liquid form to a wine.

30. There are more considerations relating to building design. Does the building have heat and insulation in order to avoid frozen pipes in winter? Does it have an adequate hot water supply? Does the power supply have 230-volt three-phase service? 460-volt three-phase in a large winery? Do you want a constantly circulating hot water supply system that provides hot water to the work site instantly?

31. The **lowest construction cost** is achieved with a **square building footprint**. As a general rule, the most efficient movement of product also can be accomplished with a square building footprint.

Sizing the winery

Production level. Five production levels are chosen for the analysis of winery development costs. They are

	Winery Production				
Cases	2,500	5,000	10,000	20,000	50,000
Gallons	5,946	11,893	23,785	47,570	118,925

Each of the wineries is assumed to produce 50 percent red wines, 25 percent Chardonnay, and 25 percent other white wines.

Tanks. The first step in designing a winery is calculation of the required floor space. That task begins with calculating the number of tanks, fermentation bins and barrels required.

Let's say you wish to produce 10,000 gallons of white wine, fermented and stored only in tanks. So, we need four tanks at 2,500 gallons each, equals 10,000 gallons, right? . . . Nope, there are two factors that increase the total capacity needed. First, you will need some headspace in the tanks to accommodate the volume increase and foaming that occurs during fermentation. If you use a medium-foaming yeast strain and have glycol jacketing capable of maintaining a 52°F temperature, then a 10 percent allowance may be appropriate. Now, we have

$$10,000/0.9 = 11,111 \text{ gallons of needed capacity.}$$

The second factor is the reality that you will need one extra vessel of each size, so you have a place to put the wine when you fine, filter or rack it. Now we have

$$11,000/4 \times 1.25 = 13,889 \text{ gallons of capacity.}$$

The ratio between needed capacity and wine volume produced is 138.9 percent. If we stay with five tanks, the size of each tank is now 2,778 gallons.

Now let's consider red wines. Again, let's plan for 10,000 gallons of wine production. You've determined that 2,000 gallons is the optimum tank size for a variety of reasons. That means five tanks at 2,000 gallons each. But, if you apply the same reasoning as above, you will have to allow 25 percent of head space for fermentation, including about 15 percent of volume for skins and seeds as well as space for the cap to rise.

$$10,000/0.75 = 13,333 \text{ gallons of capacity.}$$

That's 13,333/2,000 = 6.67 tanks, or close enough for seven tanks. Add in the extra tank for racking, and you'll need eight tanks.

$$8 \times 2,000 = 16,000 \text{ gallons capacity.}$$

The ratio for this setup is $(8 \times 2,000)/10,000 = 160.0\%$, capacity to production. As an alternative, you could use seven (six plus the extra) tanks at 2,000 gallons each, plus four plastic fermenting bins at 400 gallons each. Each 400 gallon *bin* will handle 300 gallons of wine in fermentation.

$$6 \text{ tanks} \times 1,500 = 9,000 \text{ gallons in tanks;}$$
$$10,000 - 9,000 = 1,000 \text{ gallons in bins}$$
$$1,000/300 = 3.33 \text{ bins, or 4 bins}$$

Six tanks at 2,000 gallons plus 4 bins at 400 gallons gives us

$$(0.75 \times 2,000 \times 6) + (0.75 \times 400 \times 4) = 10,200 \text{ gallons may be processed.}$$

and we need that extra tank and bin for racking. In total, we have

$$2,000 \times 7 + 400 \times 5 = 16,000 \text{ gallons of capacity.}$$

This alternative yields a ratio of 16,000/10,000 = 160% capacity to production, again. However, you have replaced a $14,000+ tank with 5 bins at a cost of about $3,100.

Figure 93 shows the tank's footprint including clearances.

Calculations of floor space needed to accommodate tanks and bins are shown in Table 65.

Barrels. The same calculations are applied to the number of barrels needed. The results are displayed in Table 66. The barrel footprint used is shown in Figure 94.

The capacity/production ratio is constant at 63.8 percent, indicating that there are no economies of scale in barrels as there are in tanks. Greater efficiency, as winery size increases, is available by increasing the height of barrel stacks, as the floor space/production ratio shows.

Casegoods. Space required for casegoods storage also depends on the types of wine produced, as well as wine volume. Red wines typically require one to

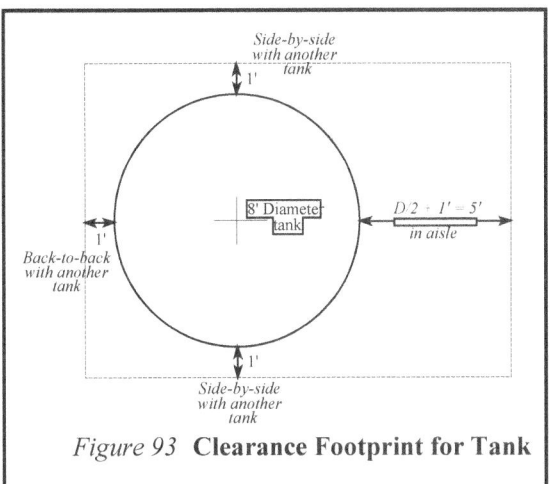

Figure 93 **Clearance Footprint for Tank**

TABLE 65   **Number of Tanks/Bins and Floor Space Required**

Five Example Winery Sizes

		Winery Production								
Cases		2,500		5,000		10,000		20,000		50,000
Gallons		5,946		11,893		23,785		47,570		118,925
		No.	SF	No.	SF	No.	SF	No.	SF	No.	SF
Plastic bins		10	400	14	560	20	800	8	320	20	800
500 gal. plastic tank		6	225	10	375	10	375	5	18	12	450
1,000 gal. plastic tank		3	162	4	216	5	270	8	432	9	486
2,000 gal. SS var. capacity		0	0	1	96	4	384	8	768	20	1,920
2,500 gal. SS tank		0	0	1	122	3	365	7	851	9	1,094
5,000 gal. SS tank		0	0	0	0	0	0	3	450	7	1,050
10,000 gal. .SS tank		0	0	0	0	0	0	0	0	3	648
Total Floor Space, SF			787		1,369		2,194		3,008		
Capacity, in gals.			10,000		19,100		33,500		62,200		150,500
Capacity/production ratio			168.2%		160.6%		140.8%		130.8%		126.6%
Floor space/production ratio			0.132		0.115		0.092		0.063		0.054

TABLE 66   **Number of Barrels and Floor Space Required**

Five Example Winery Sizes

		Winery Production								
Cases		2,500		5,000		10,000		20,000		50,000
Gallons		5,946		11,893		23,785		47,570		118,925
		No.	SF	No.	SF	No.	SF	No.	SF	No.	SF
Red wines		49	551	98	613	196	1,225	395	1,646	988	4,117
Chardonnay		14	88	27	169	54	338	109	454	272	1,133
Total Floor Space, SF			639		781		1,042		2,100		5,250
Pallet stack height			2		2		3		3		4
Capacity, in gals.			3,793		7,525		15,050		30,341		75,852
Capacity/production ratio			63.8%		63.8%		63.8%		63.8%		63.8%
Floor space/production ratio			0.107		0.066		0.044		0.044		0.044

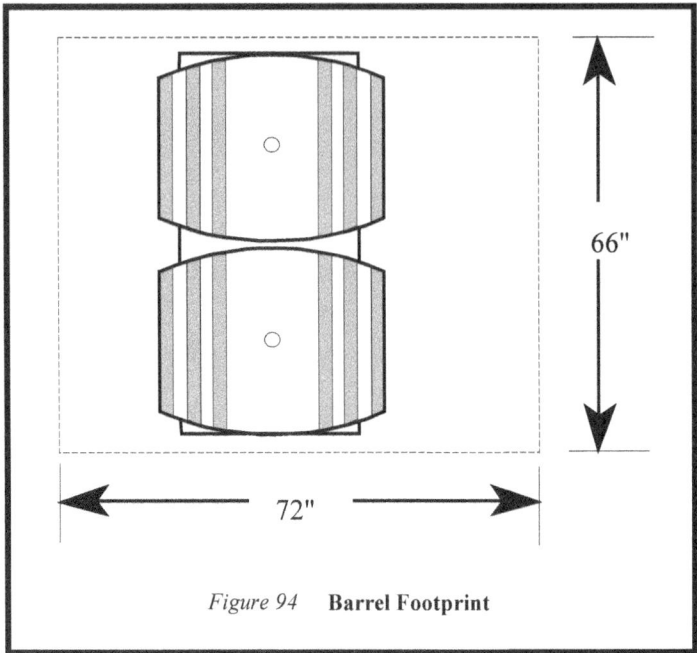

Figure 94   **Barrel Footprint**

two years in bottle before they are ready for release to marketing. Chardonnays also require a year in bottle. Other white wines may need a minimum of two to five months' bottle age in inventory.

Another variable is stack height. The number of pallets (of 56 cases) you can stack depends on the mast height of your forklift and ceiling clearance. Two-three pallets are common; larger wineries may go to five or six.

The amount of floor space needed for casegoods is presented in Table 67.

TABLE 67   **Number of Cases and Floor Space Required**

Five Example Winery Sizes

		Winery Production				
	Cases	2,500	5,000	10,000	20,000	50,000
	Gallons	5,946	11,893	23,785	47,570	118,925
Cases produced		2,500	5,000	10,000	20,000	50,000
Average years in inventory						
Red wine		2.75	2.75	2.75	2.75	2.75
Chardonnay		1.75	1.75	1.75	1.75	1.75
Other white wine		1.25	1.25	1.25	1.25	1.25
Maximum cases in inventory		5,313	10,625	21,250	42,500	106,250
Pallets of 56 cases		95	190	379	759	1,897
Pallet stack height		2	2	2	3	4
Rows		2	2	3	4	6
Number of stacks		47	95	190	253	474
Total Floor Space, SF		**1,897**	**3,036**	**6,071**	**6,476**	**10,435**
Floor space per pallet, SF		*20.0*	*16.0*	*16.0*	*8.5*	*5.5*

Tank inventory efficiency

It is revealing to review how the tank and barrel inventories are utilized during a typical production year. That is done graphically in Figure 95, where the vertical dimension of the bars is proportional to the gallons processed.

The greater amplitude of the bars during the harvest period is due to the need for headspace to accommodate fermentation. The red wine and Chardonnay move from tanks to barrels, and back again. What is glaringly obvious is the very low efficiency in the use of tanks. That is because the tank capacity is determined during crush and fermentation, when all of the wine volumes have to pass through tanks in a short period. We're dealing with an agricultural product, though, and the inefficiency's magnitude depends on how compressed the harvest is.

It does seem a shame to have all of those empty tanks doing nothing for so long a period. There are some countercyclical opportunities to put those tanks to use in the "off season," so to speak. High quality fruit and berry wines, as well as liqueurs and eau de vie (brandies), can be made from frozen material, if the winery can justify taking on the marketing challenges associated with them. Such opportunities may be geographically related; the products are more popular in Eastern and Midwestern states. Figure 96 illustrates the utilization of tank/bin capacity by a winery making 20,000 cases/year, divided into 50 percent Pinot Noir, 25 percent Chardonnay, and 25 percent other white wines such as Pinot Gris and White Riesling.

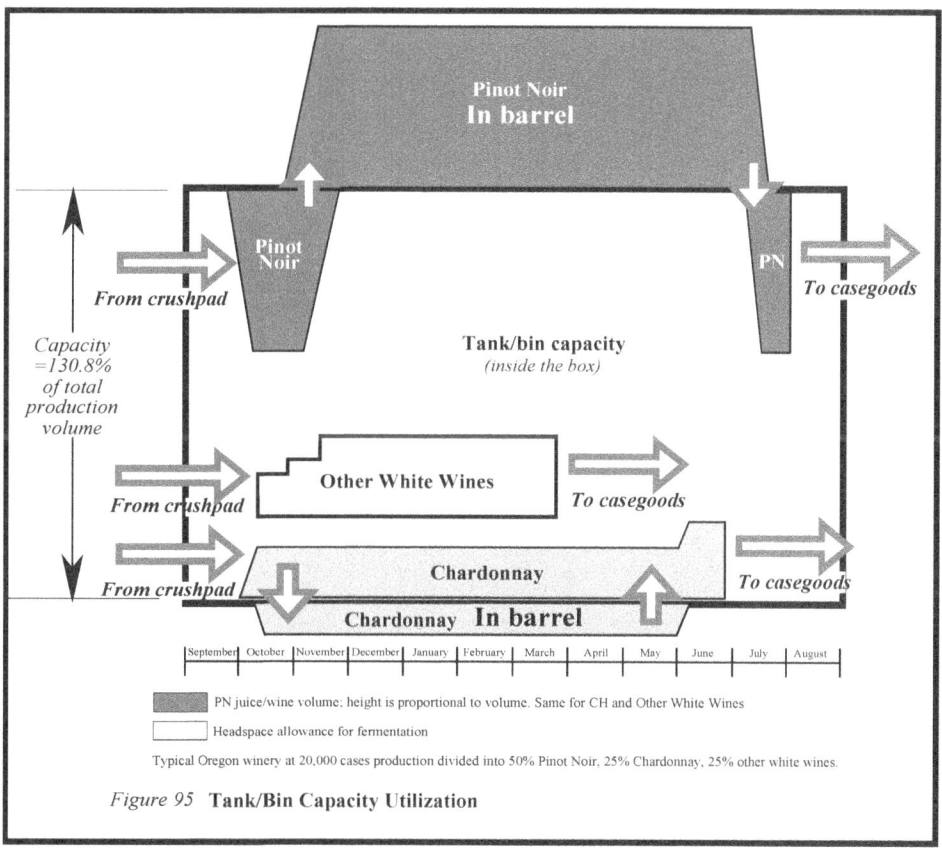

Figure 95 **Tank/Bin Capacity Utilization**

Laboratory floor plans

Three floor plans are suggested for the important laboratory function. Their size and complexity varies according to winery production. They are:

Figure No.	Winery production (gallons)
96	Up to 15,000 gallons
97	15,000–100,000
98	100,000–300,000

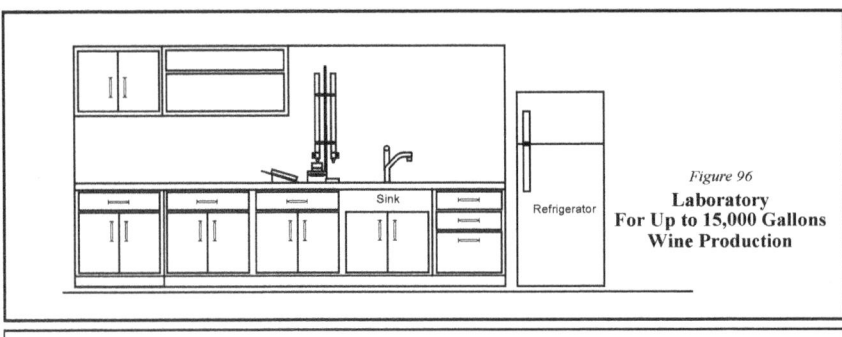

Figure 96
**Laboratory
For Up to 15,000 Gallons
Wine Production**

Side Elevation

Right End Elevation
Both ends the same

Side Elevation

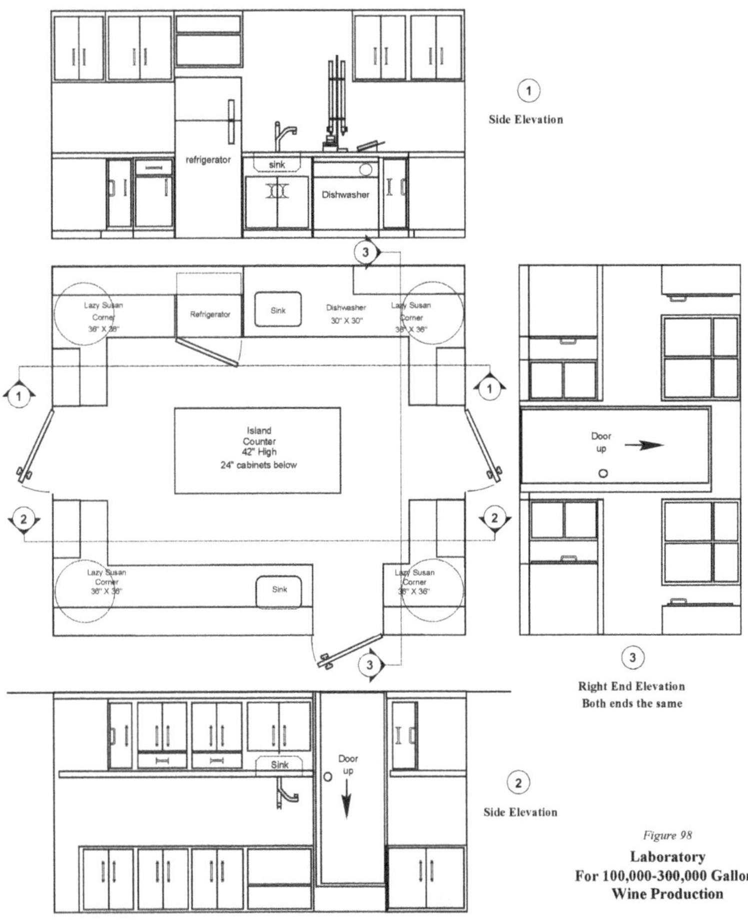

Figure 98
**Laboratory
For 100,000-300,000 Gallons
Wine Production**

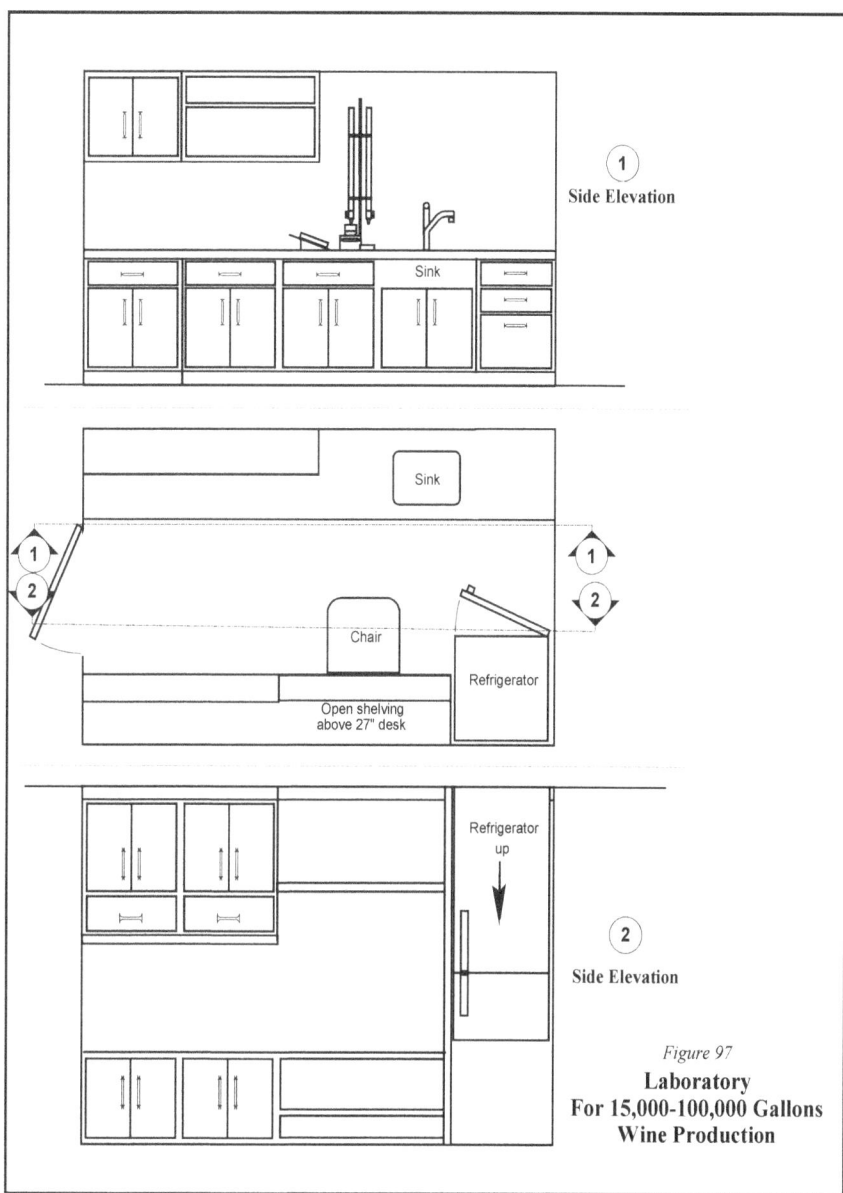

Side Elevation ①

Side Elevation ②

Figure 97
**Laboratory
For 15,000-100,000 Gallons
Wine Production**

Nothing is sacrosanct about these designs. They are based on experience. Some winemakers may want more laboratory facilities, others prefer less.

Total floor space requirements based on calculations

Adding all of the space requirements for the winery, Table 68 sums the total floor space to be used for preliminary design purposes.

TABLE 68   **Preliminary Summation of Floor Space Requirements**

Five Example Winery Sizes

		Winery Production				
	Cases	**2,500**	**5,000**	**10,000**	**20,000**	**50,000**
	Gallons	5,946	11,893	23,785	47,570	118,925
Crush pad		600*	800*	800*	1,200	1,200
Tanks		787	1,369	2,194	3,008	6,448
Red wine barrels		551	613	817	1,646	4,117
Chardonnay barrels		88	169	225	454	1,133
Bottling line		600	900	1,200	1,500	1,500
Casegoods storage		1,897	3,036	6,071	6,476	10,435
Taxpaid storage		200	200	300	400	500
Laboratory		112	112	126	126	210
Office		250	250	450	600	725
Utilities & bathrooms		112	150	180	372	480
Tasting room		240	300	400	1,000	1,400
Conference room		—	—	240	240	240
Hallways		100	120	180	300	450
Miscellaneous storage		160	160	200	240	300
Total Floor Space, SF		**5,987***	**8,177***	**13,383***	**17,562**	**29,138**

*Includes crush pad exterior to building.

Materials of construction

Construction costs vary widely for different materials and methods of construction. A comparison of materials costs (Figure 99) indicates, as of mid-2014, these characteristics:

- For a typical winery building of less than 5,500–6,000 square feet, concrete block is the least expensive, followed by wood frame, steel, then tilt-up concrete, in ascending order of cost.

- For winery buildings larger than 6,700 square feet, concrete block is still the least expensive, with tilt-up concrete emerging as a close competitor, then steel and wood, again in increasing order.

These cost relationships may vary, depending on regional climate and preponderance of local materials usage. But, by and large, the relationships are as stated in most wine-producing areas with moderate climate conditions.

Of course, construction costs are only part of the overall cost impact of choosing a method of construction. Energy costs are substantial for a winery. Temperature stability requires refrigeration in summer and heat in winter. Substantial insulation must be installed in steel and wood frame buildings to achieve temperature conditions necessary for wine. Humidity control is as important as temperature control for barrel storage. Building height limitations affect land cost and floor space efficiency. The ability to utilize subterranean concrete structures depends on opportunities presented by site topography and geology.

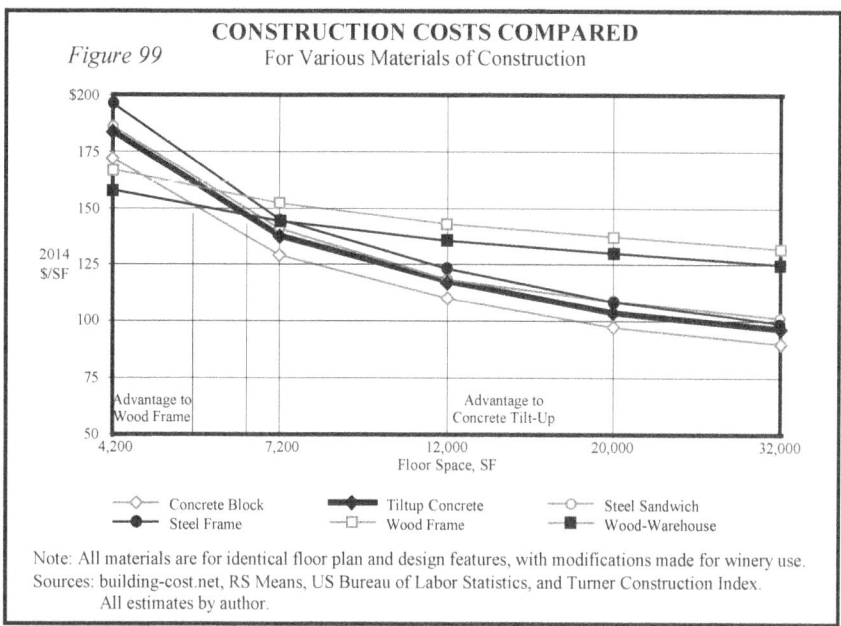

CONSTRUCTION COSTS COMPARED
Figure 99   For Various Materials of Construction

Note: All materials are for identical floor plan and design features, with modifications made for winery use.
Sources: building-cost.net, RS Means, US Bureau of Labor Statistics, and Turner Construction Index.
    All estimates by author.

Over time, tilt-up concrete appears to be the superior choice for a winery. It is energy efficient. The walls have a low thermal transmission rate. They function as a heat sink, storing heat from the outside air and solar radiation during the day, and giving it up to the interior at night during a large part of the year. It is durable compared with concrete block. And it has a very low maintenance cost.

Below-ground cellars enjoy the benefit of stable temperature (53–54°F), and of natural humidity favorable to barrel storage. There are two types: "cut-and-cover" and the bored tunnel. Cut-and-cover is essentially a box placed in an excavated hole, which is then covered with soil material and planted. Material choices are concrete block or "poured-in-place" concrete for the walls of the cut-and-cover design, and hollow-core concrete planks for the roof.

Bored tunnels are just that, possible only in rock hillsides. Bored tunnels are lined with "shotcrete" walls and ceilings, a type of sprayed-on concrete.

For many years, steel construction offered a low cost alternative in building construction. However, the escalation in steel prices recently forced by China (and discussed earlier) has driven up steel building costs. And then, the added cost of wall insulation must be considered.

Wood frame construction offers aesthetic features that are difficult to match with concrete or steel. However, because of the added bracing needed for strength as building size and ceiling height increase, wood frame does not enjoy the economies of scale offered by tilt-up concrete.

The only acceptable floor material is poured concrete. A relatively "dry mix" will probably be needed for high compression strength and to avoid cracking in the long spans between expansion joints.

Floor plans

Detailed floor plans for the five selected winery sizes are presented in Figures 100 through 104. All of them are designed for production that is 50 percent red wine, 25 percent Chardonnay, and 25 percent other white wines.

The smallest winery, 2,500 cases annually and Figure 100, is wood frame construction with gable roof. Ceiling clearance in the production areas is 16 feet. A staircase is included, in order to access additional light storage above the office space. The crush pad is exterior to the gable roof. In a spirit of keeping costs low, the crush pad is covered with a carport, and the miscellaneous storage is provided by a prefabricated garden shed. The fermentation bins (not tanks), as in all of the plans, are stackable when not in use, in order to increase open and access space.

A 5,000-case winery is shown in Figure 101. It, too, is of wood frame construction. As with the smaller facility, laboratory facilities are provided as a counter within the office room. Ceiling height is 16 feet. The crush pad is exterior, and it may be covered by two pre-fabricated carport units

Figure 102 is a 10,000-case winery. Because it is in the zone where the cost advantage shifts from wood frame to tilt-up concrete, the structure is comprised of two modules. The main building, containing the production functions, is tilt-up concrete and 10,560 square feet.

The winery in Figure 103 will produce 20,000 cases per year. It is all within one rectangular tilt-up concrete building with a flat roof. Ceiling clearance is 20 feet. The crush pad is covered by the building's roof, and one side is left open for access. This design is based on a longitudinal layout and illustrates what can be done to accommodate a narrow site.

The 50,000-case winery is shown in Figure 104. It is also contained in a rectangular tilt-up concrete building. The ceiling clearance is 24 feet, in order to

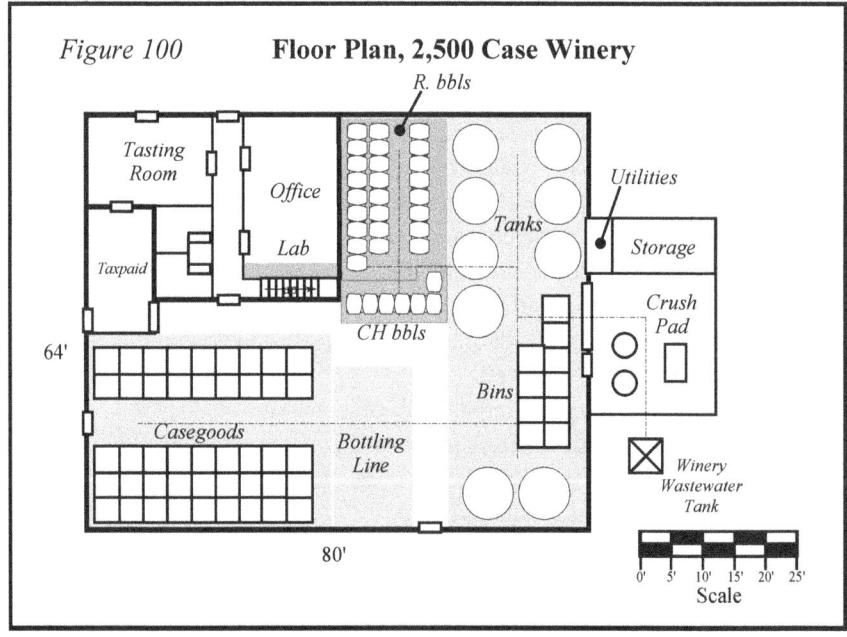

Figure 100 **Floor Plan, 2,500 Case Winery**

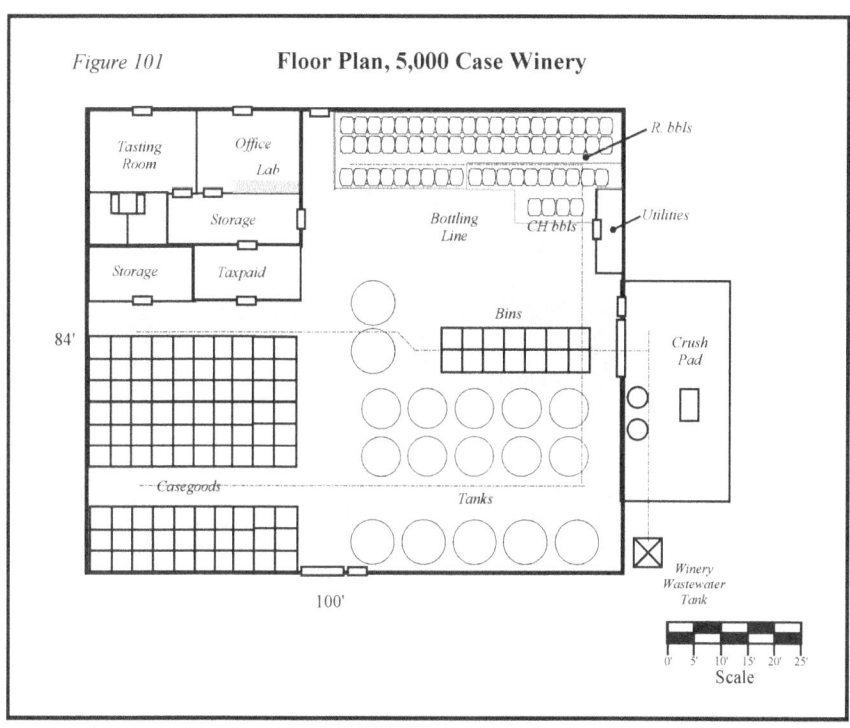

Figure 101   **Floor Plan, 5,000 Case Winery**

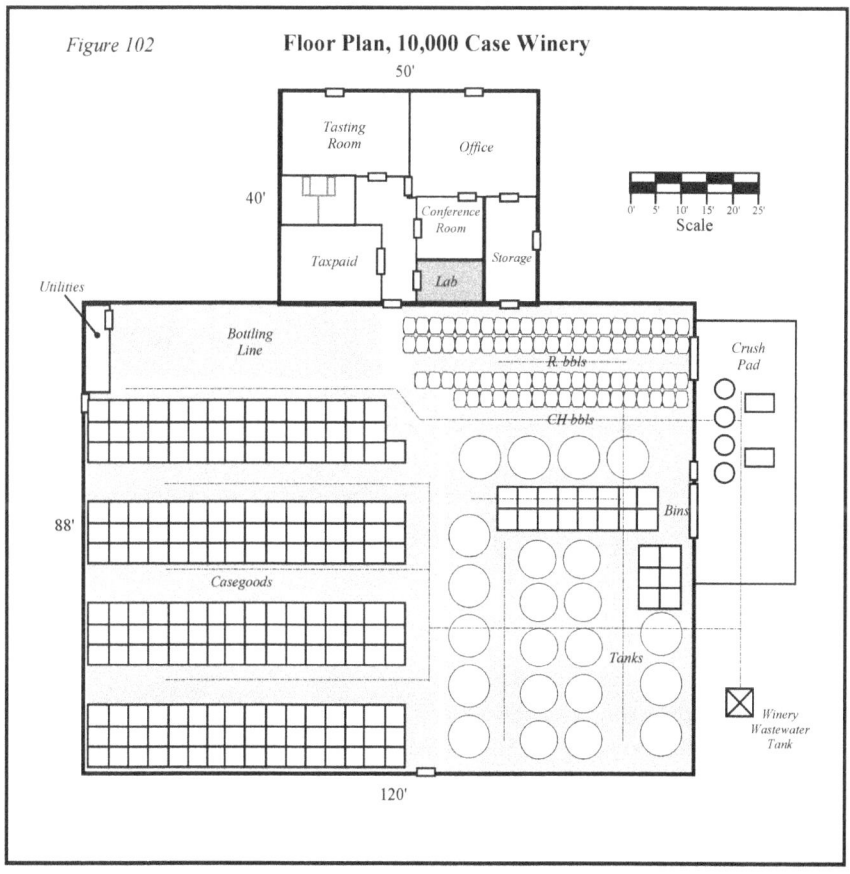

Figure 102   **Floor Plan, 10,000 Case Winery**

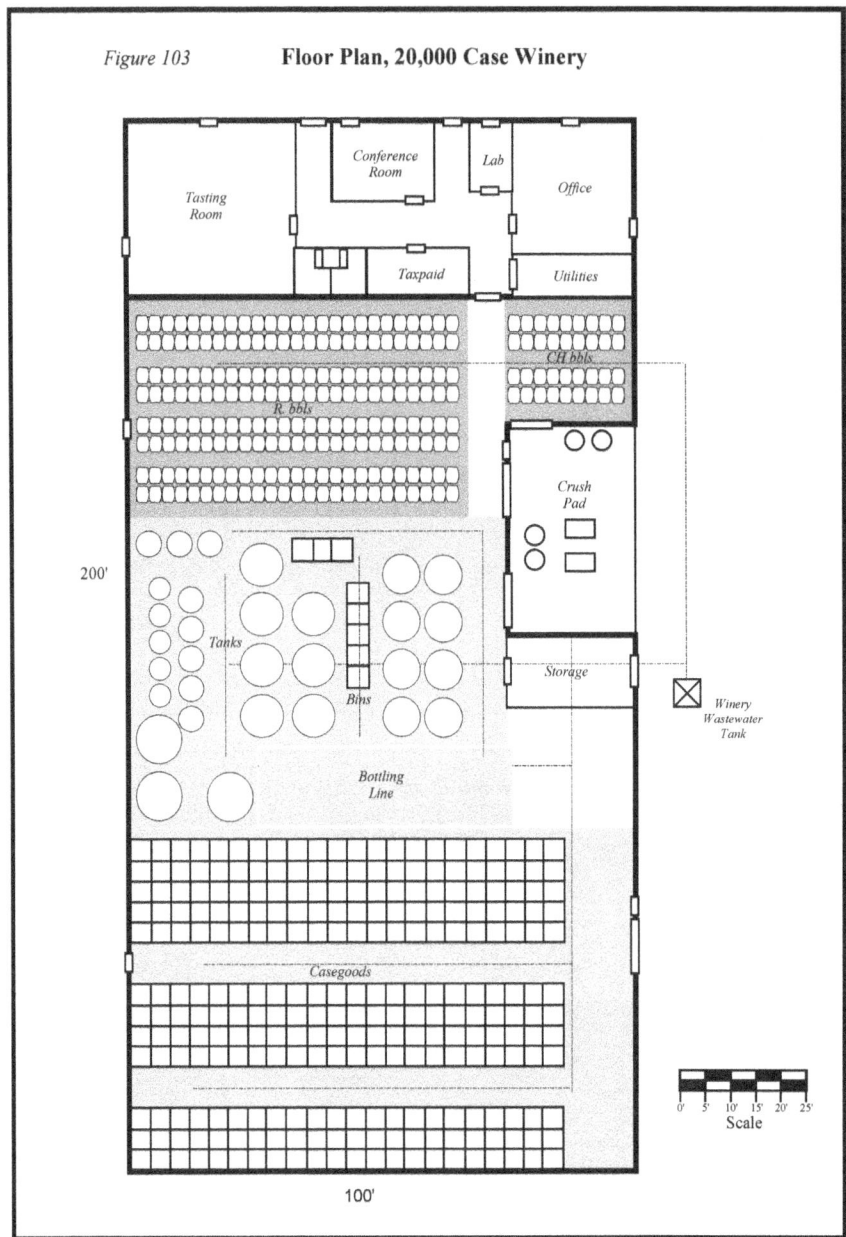

Figure 103　　　**Floor Plan, 20,000 Case Winery**

accommodate stacks of four pallets in casegoods storage and a 10,000-gallon tank. Again, the crush pad is inside the building perimeter, under the main roof, and one side is left open.

Actual floor space allocations

During the floor layout process, some opportunities for space efficiency became apparent, as did the need for more space for other functions. Accordingly, the finalized designations for floor space are revised in Table 69.

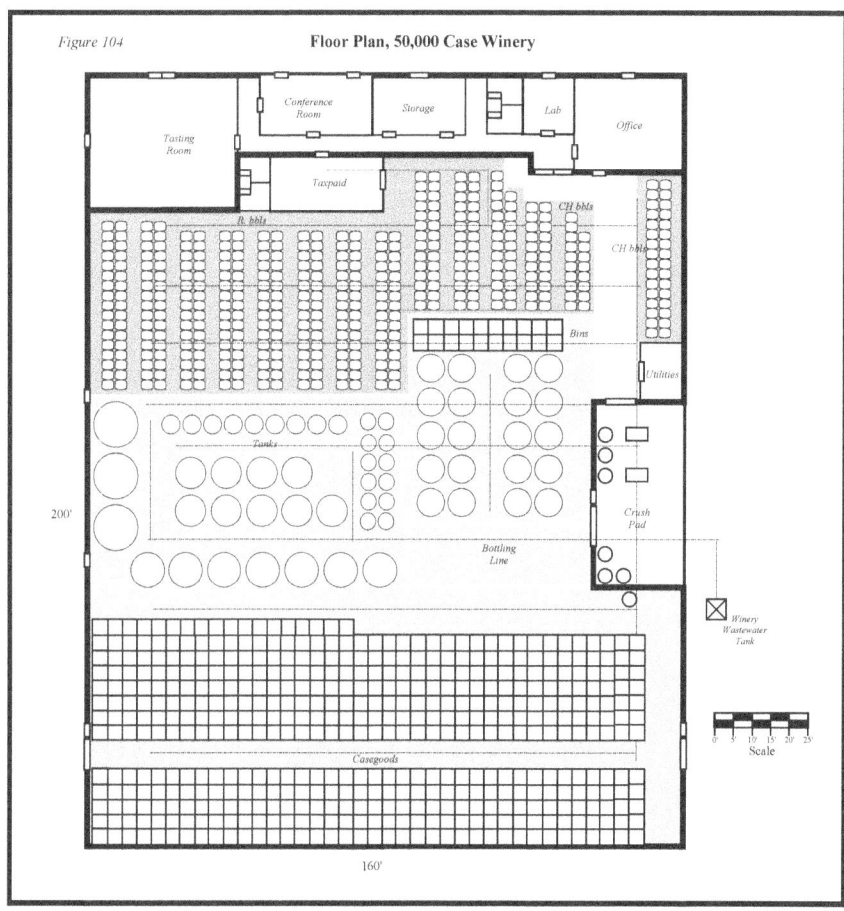

Figure 104   **Floor Plan, 50,000 Case Winery**

TABLE 69   **Actual Floor Space Allocations**

Five Example Winery Sizes

		Winery Production				
	Cases	2,500	5,000	10,000	20,000	50,000
	Gallons	5,946	11,893	23,785	47,570	118,925
Crush pad		440*	800*	1,000*	1,000	1,000
Tanks		1,320	2,860	3,350	3,760	7,050
Red wine barrels		425	561	897	2,835	5,354
Chardonnay barrels		135	145	294	624	1,235
Bottling line		300	750	800	800	800
Casegoods storage		960	2,000	5,075	6,500	10,720
Taxpaid storage		200	200	300	400	450
Laboratory		45	48	112	112	210
Office		330	360	500	600	750
Utilities & bathrooms		150	171	155	275	480
Tasting room		280	300	400	1,024	1,400
Conference room		—	—	168	300	450
Hallways		1,007	805	309	1,620	1,526
Miscellaneous storage		128	160	200	240	300
Total Floor Space, SF		**5,720***	**9,200***	**13,560***	**20,000**	**32,000**
Floor space/gallon produced						
Total floor space		0.962	0.774	0.570	0.420	0.269
*Production core space**		0.602	0.598	0.480	0.326	0.220

*Includes crush pad exterior to building.
**Includes crush pad, tanks, barrels, bottling and casegoods.

Winery construction cost

The construction costs for each of the example winery sizes were estimated using cost rates available from credible online construction cost services, as well as other direct sources. The results are shown in Table 70.

The progression of unit costs with increasing winery size is graphed in Figure 105.

The economies of scale are apparent, particularly when expressed in cost per gallon produced.

Twenty vineyard areas compared

Using the same methodology as in Table 68, total construction costs with markups are calculated in Table 71 for the same locations as used in the vineyard analysis. The estimates are adjusted for differences in the costs of labor, materials and equipment using several reliable indices.

TABLE 70   **Construction Costs***

Five Example Winery Sizes

		Winery Production				
	Cases	**2,500**	**5,000**	**10,000**	**20,000**	**50,000**
	Gallons	5,946	11,893	23,785	47,570	118,925
Site improvements**		26,830	42,020	85,140	154,500	235,440
Building walls & roof***		477,390	673,050	929,670	1,162,470	1,806,440
Floor						
Production		71,720	133,510	177,800	330,210	520,110
Tasting room/ office		14,230	11,830	32,090	37,300	43,920
Utilities		20,520	30,600	44,510	64,320	102,550
Laboratory cabinetry		1,650	1,650	1,640	2,100	5,740
Tasting room		19,000	22,240	30,950	85,570	130,140
Office		11,200	9,940	22,200	28,400	32,020
Bathrooms		2,490	2,490	2,480	2,420	4,840
Doors		3,400	4,010	12,020	14,400	43,470
Staircase, carport, shed		3,940	3,660	3,540	0	0
Wastewater tank		620	620	960	970	1,800
Total contractor costs		**653,030**	**935,660**	**1,343,070**	**1,882,690**	**2,926,520**
Contractor markup		163,250	233,910	335,760	470,670	731,630
Architect fees		39,180	56,130	80,570	112,960	175,590
Total project cost		**855,470**	**1,225,700**	**1,759,400**	**2,466,320**	**3,833,740**
$/sf		*167.08*	*145.92*	*129.75*	*123.32*	*$119.80*
$/gallon		*143.87*	*103.06*	*73.97*	*51.85*	*32.24*

*Values in mid-2014 dollars.
** Includes excavation, grading, backfill, parking and landscaping.
*** Includes foundation, walls and roof

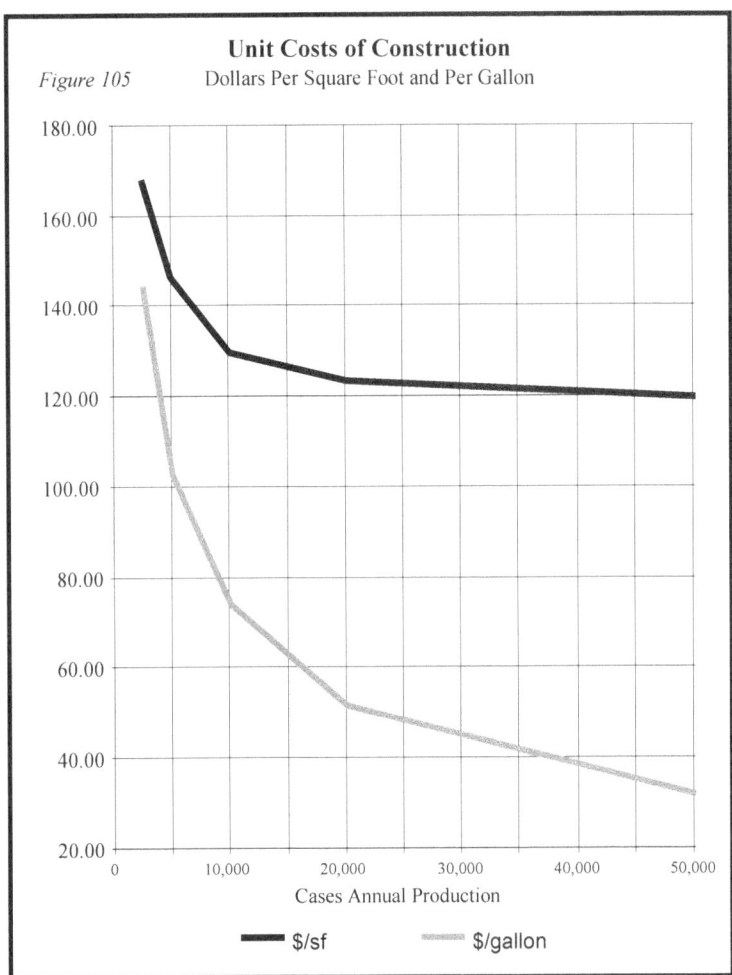

Unit Costs of Construction

Figure 105 Dollars Per Square Foot and Per Gallon

These estimates may appear high compared with some existing wineries, which have been built to minimize construction costs. However, the winery designs for these estimates assume better than average quality facilities, utilizing durable materials and energy conservation measures. All of the designs incorporate good floor design principles, and cost upwards of $15–18 per square foot, compared to a typical flat 4-inch thick slab at $8–10 a square foot.

A few concessions have been made to cost reduction. For example, we have used portable steel carports to cover the exterior crush pads in the three smaller wineries, rather than specifying permanent roof-over construction. Further, a ready-built garden shed is used for miscellaneous storage on the crush pad in the 2,500-case design.

A staircase has been shown in the 2,500-case plan, to access light-weight storage over the office space. Though not implemented in the other designs, second floor storage would be possible in all of them, above the office, conference room and tasting room spaces. Some adjustments in layout would be needed to locate the staircase.

TABLE 71   **Total Construction Costs, Five Example Winery Sizes**

20 Vineyard Areas in 18 States

		Winery Production				
	Cases	**2,500**	**5,000**	**10,000**	**20,000**	**50,000**
	Gallons	5,946	11,893	23,785	47,570	118,925
Columbia Valley, WA		890,100	1,275,300	1,830,700	2,566,200	3,989,000
Willamette Valley, OR		833,600	1,194,300	1,714,400	2,403,200	3,735,600
Southern Oregon		810,500	1,161,200	1,666,900	2,336,600	3,632,100
Snake River Valley, ID		797,700	1,143,000	1,640,600	2,299,800	3,575,000
Sonoma Valley, CA		907,100	1,299,600	1,865,500	2,615,000	4,064,900
Central Coast, CA		910,900	1,305,100	1,873,400	2,626,100	4,082,200
Sonoita, AZ		808,800	1,158,800	1,663,300	2,331,700	3,624,400
Grand Valley, CO		844,200	1,209,500	1,736,200	2,433,800	3,783,100
Texas Hill Country		843,900	1,209,200	1,735,600	2,433,000	3,782,000
Central Missouri		821,200	1,176,500	1,688,800	2,367,400	3,680,000
Shawnee Hills, IL		803,900	1,151,800	1,653,300	2,317,600	3,602,600
Leelanau Peninsula, MI		859,000	1,230,700	1,766,600	2,476,400	3,849,500
Ohio River Valley**		849,100	1,216,600	1,746,400	2,448,100	3,805,400
Lake Erie***		807,700	1,157,300	1,661,200	2,328,700	3,619,800
Finger Lakes, NY		830,500	1,189,900	1,708,000	2,394,300	3,721,800
Lancaster Valley, PA		854,300	1,224,000	1,756,900	2,462,900	3,828,400
SE New England****		892,300	1,278,500	1,835,200	2,572,600	3,999,000
Piedmont Plateau, MD		878,900	1,259,300	1,807,600	2,533,900	3,938,800
Central Blue Ridge Mt, VA		809,600	1,160,000	1,655,100	2,334,100	3,628,300
Yadkin Valley, NC		811,500	1,162,700	1,669,000	2,339,600	3,636,700
US Average		*855,470*	*1,225,700*	*1,759,400*	*2,466,320*	*3,833,740*

*Values in mid-2014 dollars.
**Ohio, Indiana, Kentucky, West Virginia.
***New York, Ohio, Pennsylvania

Cost of land

Land costs are not included in these estimates. They may vary from a low of $1,500–2,000 an acre in some newer vineyard areas, to a high of $50,000–60,000 an acre in Sonoma County, California.

Further reading

Get-a-Quote.net; online construction costs for contractors. Craftsman Books. Website: http://get-a-quote.net/

McGraw-Hill Construction Index. Website: http://dodge.construction.com/analytics/

Metal Building Comparison; *Metal Building vs. Wood Construction.* Website: http://www.metalbuildingcomparison.com/metal_vs_wood.html?id=

RadiantFoil; manufacturer of radiant barrier materials; Ketchum, ID. Website: http://www.radiantfoil.com/

RS Means/Reed Construction data; online construction cost information. Website: http://rsmeans.reedconstructiondata.com/

Tilt-Up Construction; Redimix Companies, Inc. Website: http://www.concretebuildings.org/

Why Do Design/Build Contractors Choose Tilt-up Construction?; Bob Moore Construction, Inc; Arlington, TX. Website: http://www.generalcontractor.com

೮ഗ

14

Winery revenues and expenses

Now, we are in position to calculate the financial returns possible from production of premium grape varieties by the example wineries detailed in Chapter 13.

Our first challenge will be to compute revenues, costs and returns for the five winery sizes, using typical wine types and national average costs.

Assumptions

1. **Separate legal entity.** The winery will be treated as a separate legal entity, apart from the vineyard. This is not done just to clarify financial analysis of the winery; it also reflects common practice. Vineyards are usually formed as partnerships or proprietorships for tax reasons.[1] For the vineyard, establishment costs of vines, trellis and cultural costs until the year of the first harvest must be capitalized, then amortized over a ten–year recovery period. In accounting, this is called *accrual accounting*. It is also a *tax shelter*, because acceleration of depreciation delays the payment of income taxes and time is money. Other vineyard costs are expensed at the time they are incurred, which is a *cash accounting* method.

2. Wineries, on the other hand, are usually formed under **corporate structure**, be it simple corporation, Subchapter S corporation or LLC, depending on the ownership pattern. Under IRS regulations, *all* wineries must use *UNICAP* (Uniform Capitalization rules) *accounting*. UNICAP requires that

---

1. Selection of the legal entity is a complex decision, and which form is chosen depends on the owner's other sources of taxable income. Consult your tax attorney, and perhaps your tax accountant, for guidance with this issue.

all direct and indirect production costs be capitalized during the production cycle.

3. **Winery size.** Five winery sizes been selected for financial analysis, a practice that has been applied beginning with the analysis of winery equipment costs in Chapter 12. The focus of this book is on small and medium–size wineries. The five sizes chosen include about 90 percent of the wineries in America.[2] Each winery produces 50 percent red wine, 25 percent Chardonnay and 25 percent another white wine, the last not requiring time in barrel.

4. **Grape cost.** The largest single cost of wine production is the cost of grapes. If the grapes are purchased from an independent grower or other winery, the cost is easy to figure. It is the amount spent to put the grapes on the crush pad. If transportation charges are incurred, they are included. If the winery pays for grapes on the basis of vineyard acres,[3] an increasingly employed method used for high-quality wines, then the winery will use the weights logged in at the crush pad or public scale.

5. If the winery produces the grapes in its own vineyard, the **appropriate transfer price** from vineyard to winery, for both entities, is the same as it is for any accounting of product transfers from subsidiary to parent corporation: fair market value.

6. **Grape costs** used in the following analyses are typical for the varieties and growing areas where the wine is made.

7. **Wine yields.** Measured in gallons of finished wine per ton of grapes, yields used are typical of the grape varieties employed. Red wines, which suffer some volume losses to evaporation while in barrel, are usually taken to be 150 gpt. Actual juice yields at the beginning of the process could run 165–168 gpt. For Chardonnay, the wine yield used is 155 gpt. Here, again, there are evaporation losses in barrel. Other white grape varieties could run 155–160 gpt of wine, depending on berry size. Grapes of extremely large berry size could yield as much as 180 gpt of juice and 175 gpt of finished wine.

8. **Retail wine prices.** The retail price of wine can depend on the volume of the winery's production, market demand for the variety, who is selling the wine, and distributor markups. If there is very strong demand for the wine, Oregon Pinot Noir is an example, there is no degradation of retail price with increasing winery size. For most grape varieties, though, there tends to be retail price reduction with increasing volume.

9. So, the **setting of wine retail prices is a market–driven phenomenon.** Whether the dominant retail outlet is the supermarkets or boutique wine shops will have a lot of influence, with higher prices related to the latter. Wine distributors differ in their markups, depending on the price level and dominant outlet. In spite of these tendencies, most states require distributors to charge the same wholesale price for a wine regardless of outlet. That's just to prevent any favoritism to one outlet versus another.

10. Retailers differ in regard to **wine markups.** Supermarkets may mark up 25 to 28 percent on selling price, boutique shops may mark up 35 percent or more on selling price. Restaurants and hotels typically mark up their prices at the rate of 2.5–3.5 times retail. That's why prices can vary widely for the same wine (Table 72):

The retail prices used here were determined by a survey of all growing areas.

---

2. From ATTTB data, 2004.

3. In this system, the winemaker contracts to take the grapes from a certain number of rows regardless of the tonnage. The method allows the winemaker to thin the crop by various actions without penalizing the grower. The amount paid per acre is usually based on a normal yield of 4 tpa, or whatever is common for the variety grown in the same location.

11. **Supermarket post–offs.** Ever wonder how the supermarkets choose wines for end stacks or free-standing stacks near the check stands . . . or even offer obviously large discounts on regular shelves? Those low prices are called post–offs. Post–offs result from pricing arrangements in which the winery sells to distributors at a discounted price, typically at something like $2–4 a case off the winery FOB. The distributor passes the discount per case along to retailers. The term *post–off* came from the old days, when wineries were required to post their prices with the state liquor authority in advance, and the prices had to apply for a minimum of thirty days. The state listings were available to competing wineries, who could follow immediately with matching prices. Challenges on charges of state–assisted price fixing sank the practice in the courts back around 1990.

12. **Tasting room sales.** The percentage of wine sold through the winery's tasting room, direct shipping and member clubs is a matter of opportunity and winery policy. To be sure, they offer the winery an opportunity to realize profit margins twice as large compared to selling only through distributors (Table 73). Among the additional costs to be considered in determining tasting room policy are: extra staffing, building space, display fixtures, and marketing expenditures needed to attract the extra sales to the tasting room.

For tasting room, direct shipment and member club sales, remember to add the cost of operating those programs. In this demonstration, the additional cost is estimated at 25 percent of selling price for those sales.

In some states, small wineries are self–distributed, meaning they deliver direct to retail accounts without the aid of a distributor. Some wineries are able to do this, but success depends on the winery's reputation and strength of loyal customer following. Some relatively small wineries are able to sell their entire output through the tasting room, direct shipment and member clubs. One prominent Oregon winery sells its entire production as wine futures sold at invitational tastings. That's a status to be desired by any hard–working winery owner.

Where should a winery price its tasting room sales? Well, no retailer likes to have his prices undercut by the winery at the tasting room. They might just respond by refusing to put your wine on their shelves, and

TABLE 72   **Price Structure (Dollars per 750ml Bottle)**

List price established by winery	16.00
Winery FOB price	8.64
Distributor wholesale price @28% MU	12.00
Supermarket price @25% MU	16.00
Boutique wine shop @35% MU	18.46
Restaurant price @3 times retail	36.00
Winery FOB as % of set retail price	*54.0%*

TABLE 73   **Profit Comparison, Distribution Channel vs. Tasting Room Tasting (in Dollars)**

	Distributor	Room
Sold through distributor	16.00	—
Winery revenue	8.19	16.00
Winery cost	4.27	8.27
Profit before taxes	3.92	7.73
Profit as percent of winery revenue	**24.5%**	**48.3%**

your distributor may not give your wines a best effort. Customers, too, don't react well if they see a wine priced at $9.00 when they just bought it at the winery for $7.50. So, if distributors are part of your marketing program, it is wise to sell the wine at the winery for the same price as local supermarkets.

Generally, it is permissible to offer substantial discounts at the tasting room for special events and industry wine–touring weekends. Further, although many retailers discount case sales by 10 percent, usually it is not considered obnoxious for the winery to go as high as 20 percent on case sales, particularly on big event weekends, if it's a wine you need to move.

13. **Labor costs.** Included in this category are the winemaker, "cellar rats" (winery assistants), and hourly labor brought in from the vineyard for crush and bottling operations. The estimation of these costs for the winemaker and cellar rats is compounded by the reality that both are frequently called upon for vineyard supervision and tasting room–related duty. The time spent in vineyard supervision should be separated from the winery and charged to vineyard operations.

    Further, simple distributions of salaries are complicated by the long hours worked in the winery. Our estimates for hours worked by the winemaker (who is also general manager) are in Table 74.

    Are you still interested in becoming a winemaker?

14. **Materials.** Most of the materials costs are in packaging: bottles, corks, capsules and labels. Among the others are costs for yeast, bacterial cultures, fining agents, filter sheets and cartridges, perhaps sugar and acid, laboratory supplies and propylene glycol for the refrigeration system.

15. **Depreciation.** Let's introduce a new way of looking at winery financial performance. At issue is the depreciation method used to calculate profits, specifically, the *recovery per*iod, or number of years used to calculate the annual depreciation amount in spreading the deduction over a service period. On the one hand, there is the Internal Revenue Service's **MACRS (Modified Accelerated Cost Recovery System) concept of life**. The allowable MACRS life is not based on how long the specific piece of equipment or building will be of practical use to the production process. It is a

TABLE 74   **Typical Weekly Hours Worked by Winemaker, by Month and Winery Size**

	Cases Produced				
	2,500	5,000	10,000	20,000	50,000
September	46	46	50	54	44
October	97	97	80	74	68
November	67	67	68	66	66
December	45	45	40	52	48
January	51	51	44	50	46
February	51	51	43	50	50
March	65	65	54	58	54
April	46	46	52	42	42
May	50	50	47	49	49
June	65	65	44	46	46
July	76	76	57	57	48
August	67	67	61	57	52
Average hrs/week	*60.5*	*60.5*	*53.3*	*54.6*	*51.1*

number derived for income tax purposes as a result of political pressure from the accounting and business communities, with an awareness of the economically stimulating effects of lower taxes and a goal of addressing the reality of trying to recapture the value of the item (i.e., replacement cost) during inflationary times . . .which is virtually always.

Being a government–contrived policy, MACRS depreciation is further complicated. It can be based on two differing rate schedules: GDS (General Depreciation System) and ADS (Alternative Depreciation System). The business is supposed to use GDS, unless the specific item being depreciated is required to use ADS, or the taxpayer elects to use ADS (when the item is placed in service) instead. In general, ADS lives are longer than GDS lives, which means ADS depreciation amounts will be less than those calculated under GDS.

Now, let's bring in the **economic life concept**. Under this concept, the entire useful life of the item is used. As a result, calculated profits are more realistically related to real operating costs. The method offers a more meaningful comparison of investment alternatives, rather than trying to base investment decisions on values that are distorted by government policy.

Table 75 is a comparison of depreciation lives under the two concepts.

Of course, the MACRS system still will be required to calculate taxable income.

16. **Administrative costs.** In this cost segment are salaries for accountants and other office employees, office supplies and equipment. Refer to the staffing chart in Chapter 7.

17. **Marketing.** Field salesmen and merchandisers, inside marketing support people, tasting room personnel, advertising and printed materials make up this category.

18. **Federal excise tax.** For all of the wineries under analysis except 50,000 cases, the federal excise tax is $0.17 per gallon. For larger wineries producing more than 100,000 gallons annually, the tax increases in increments to $1.07 per gallon. See *Title 26 U.S.C. 5041(a, b and c)* for the schedule.

TABLE 75   **Recovery Periods, Economic Life Compared with MACRS Life**

| Item | Economic life | MACRS life | | IRS Asset Class |
		GDS	ADS	
Crush pad	20	7	12	20.4
Tanks	30	7	12	20.4
Bins	15	3	4	20.5
Pumps, filters & hoses	15	7	12	20.4
Refrigeration system	20	7	12	20.4
Barrels	6	3	4	20.5
Bottling line	20	7	12	20.4
Laboratory equipment	15	7	10	00.11
Other equipment	10	7	12	20.4
Tasting room equipment	10	7	10	00.11
Building	40	7	12	20.4

States also impose excise taxes on wine, usually collected as the wine passes through distributors. Those state taxes are not included here because of their wide variety.

Financial analysis using economic life

Table 76 presents results of the financial analysis using the economic life concept for depreciation. The table covers two pages because there are three wine types and a consolidated statement for the whole winery. Red wine and Chardonnay are evaluated on the first page. "Other white wine" and the consolidation are on the second page.

Revenues and costs for the three wines and the consolidated totals are summarized in Table 77.

Financial analysis using MACRS depreciation life

The same analysis is performed in Table 78. Again, there are two pages for the same reason as in Table 76. The only differences from Table 76 are in depreciation and its effects on subtotals and total accounts. Cash flow and capitalized value are not affected.

Comparison of two depreciation systems

The effects of the difference in depreciation methods, economic life versus MACRS life, are compared in Table 79. Amounts are based on industry average costs, and are in 2014 dollars. The source Tables are 77 and 78.

In regard to tax shelter effect, MACRS is more favorable to the smaller wineries, and it's all because of the larger wineries' economies of scale in building and equipment.

Financial analyses for 20 locations in 18 states

Table 80 (four pages) shows the results of financial analyses of a 10,000–case winery in each of the 20 areas for which vineyards were evaluated in Chapter 6. In these financial statements, local production costs and wine prices are applied to one red wine and one white wine in each location.

Definitions

Bordeaux Reds means one or more of the five Bordeaux varieties: Cabernet Sauvignon, Merlot, Cabernet Franc, Malbec and Petit Verdot.

Rhône Reds means one or more of the Rhône varieties: Syrah, Marsanne, Roussanne and Grenache.

Fruit and berry wines

The financial profile of wineries would not be complete without considering fruit and berry wines. Many smaller wineries in the Midwest and East produce fruit and berry wines. As pointed out earlier, the marketplace does not support non–grape wines so well in the Western states.

Calculations for additions and adjustments are far more complicated than for grape wines. Federal regulations allow dilution of the juice with sugar and water. The raw juice may not comprise less than 65 percent of the finished wine

TABLE 77   **Financial Analysis by Wine Type Using Economic Life**

10,000 Cases Production—Industry Average Costs, 2014 Dollars

	Red Wine 1 yr in barrel	Chardonnay	Other White Wine	Consolidated Whole Winery
Grapes, $/ton	1,600	1,350	1,350	—
Yield, gals/ton	150	155	160	—
Retail, $/bottle	18.00	15.00	14.00	—
Net revenues, per gallon	**48.4726**	**40.3939**	**36.9103**	**43.5623**
Grapes	10.6667	8.7097	8.4375	9.5935
Other direct costs	18.0133	12.6924	12.5603	15.3198
Depreciation	3.8722	3.1388	2.7728	3.4140
Total production costs	**32.5521**	**24.5409**	**23.7707**	**28.3273**
Administration & marketing	1.3439	1.3439	1.3439	1.3439
Interest & excise tax	2.3132	2.3132	2.2390	2.2792
Net profit b/income taxes	**15.9205**	**15.8530**	**9.5567**	**11.6120**
% of revenues	32.8%	39.2%	25.9%	32.7%
Return on investment*	10.0%	11.3%	8.9%	10.4%
Average annual profit*	13.1%	17.4%	17.3%	16.2%
Total cash flow	**18.2788**	**17.4780**	**14.3986**	**17.1352**
Capitalized value per gallon**	182.79	174.78	143.99	171.09
Capitalized value**	**2,173,800**	**1,039,300**	**856,200**	**4,069,300**

Based on present worth values.
** *At 10% capitalization rate.*

TABLE 79   **Comparison of Taxable Incomes, Economic Life vs. MACRS Depreciation Life**

	Total Winery Production, Cases				
	2,500	5,000	10,000	20,000	50,000
Depreciation ($/gal):					
Economic life	$5.3889	$4.1854	$3.4140	$2.6255	$1.8953
MACRS	15.5279	11.7698	9.0173	6.9553	4.8825
Net profit before income taxes ($/gal):					
Economic life	6.4770	10.7714	11.6120	13.9057	17.0325
MACRS	(3.6620)	3.1870	6.0087	9.5759	14.0363
Profit % of Sales:					
Economic life	14.6%	24.4%	26.7%	32.6%	40.3%
MACRS	−8.3%	7.2%	13.8%	22.5%	33.2%
Return on Investment (ROI)					
Economic Life	2.9%	7.0%	10.4%	16.8%	32.5%
MACRS	−3.0%	1.4%	4.7%	10.9%	25.6%
Average Annual Profit					
Economic Life	5.5%	10.1%	11.2%	14.0%	17.7%
MACRS	−5.7%	2.0%	2.0%	5.1%	9.2%

TABLE 76   Financial Analysis—Economic Life, Example Winery, Total Winery Production, Cases (page 1 of 2)

	Red Wine – 1 year in barrel					Chardonnay				
	2,500	5,000	10,000	20,000	50,000	2,500	5,000	10,000	20,000	50,000
Grapes, $/ton	**1,600**	**1,600**	**1,600**	**1,552**	**1,520**	**1,350**	**1,350**	**1,350**	**1,310**	**1,283**
Yield, gals/ton	150	150	150	150	150	155	155	155	155	155
Retail, $/bottle	**$18.00**	**$18.00**	**$18.00**	**$18.00**	**$18.00**	**$15.00**	**$15.00**	**$15.00**	**$14.55**	**$14.25**
Retail MU%	30	30	28	25	25	30	30	28	25	25
Wholesale MU%	32	32	32	32	32	32	32	32	32	32
Tasting room % of sales	50	50	40	25	20	50	50	40	25	20
Net revenues, per gallon	**48.8577**	**48.8577**	**48.4726**	**48.3582**	**47.9495**	**40.7147**	**40.7147**	**40.3939**	**39.0896**	**37.9601**
Costs, $/gallon										
Grapes	10.6667	10.6667	10.6667	10.3467	10.1333	8.7097	8.7097	8.7097	8.1949	7.8605
Labor	5.7884	3.9725	5.6510	3.7241	1.7215	0.4959	0.3306	0.3301	0.2576	0.1060
Materials	12.9229	12.3355	11.7481	11.1607	10.5733	12.9229	12.3355	11.7481	11.1607	10.5733
Utilities	0.6756	0.6449	0.6142	0.5651	0.5221	0.6756	0.6449	0.6142	0.5651	0.5221
Total direct costs	**30.0536**	**27.6196**	**28.6799**	**25.7965**	**22.9502**	**22.8041**	**22.0207**	**21.4021**	**20.1783**	**19.0619**
Barrels	1.3817	0.9311	1.0993	0.9221	0.9732	0.4600	0.3100	0.3660	0.3070	0.3240
Crush pad	0.0897	0.1255	0.1791	0.1109	0.0842	0.0897	0.1255	0.1791	0.1109	0.0842
Tanks	0.2395	0.2693	0.2679	0.2136	0.1871	0.2395	0.2693	0.2679	0.2136	0.1871
Pumps & filters	0.0673	0.0367	0.0995	0.0517	0.0282	0.0673	0.0367	0.0995	0.0517	0.0282
Bottling line	0.0433	0.2613	0.2132	0.1427	0.0619	0.0433	0.2613	0.2132	0.1427	0.0619
Refrigeration system	0.1731	0.1393	0.0974	0.0712	0.0577	0.1731	0.1393	0.0974	0.0712	0.0577
Laboratory & other equipment	0.1906	0.0953	0.0855	0.0963	0.0398	0.1906	0.0953	0.0855	0.0963	0.0398
Tasting room equipment	0.0491	0.0271	0.0327	0.0177	0.0087	0.0491	0.0271	0.0327	0.0177	0.0087
Building & site improvements	3.7305	2.6878	1.7976	1.3835	0.8600	3.7305	2.6878	1.7976	1.3835	0.8600
Total depreciation	**5.9647**	**4.5734**	**3.8722**	**3.0098**	**2.3009**	**5.0430**	**3.9523**	**3.1388**	**2.3946**	**1.6517**
Total production costs	**36.0184**	**32.1931**	**32.5521**	**28.8063**	**25.2511**	**27.8471**	**25.9729**	**24.5409**	**22.5730**	**20.7136**
Gross margin	**12.8393**	**16.6646**	**15.9205**	**19.5519**	**22.6985**	**12.8676**	**14.7418**	**15.8530**	**16.5166**	**17.2465**
Administration	0.5039	0.4463	0.4391	0.4171	0.2836	0.5039	0.4463	0.4391	0.4171	0.2836
Marketing	1.6383	1.0650	0.9048	0.8595	0.5845	1.6383	1.0650	0.9048	0.8595	0.5845
Interest @4.5%	3.8078	2.9261	2.1432	1.6394	1.0762	3.7301	2.8737	2.0814	1.5875	1.0215
Federal excise tax	0.1700	0.1700	0.1700	0.1700	0.1700	0.1700	0.1700	0.1700	0.1700	0.1700
Net profit b/income tax	**6.7193**	**12.0573**	**12.2634**	**16.4659**	**20.4409**	**6.8254**	**10.1868**	**12.2578**	**13.4824**	**15.0437**
% of revenues	*13.8%*	*24.7%*	*25.3%*	*34.0%*	*42.6%*	*16.8%*	*25.0%*	*30.3%*	*34.5%*	*39.6%*
Present worth: (6.0% discount rate)										
Revenues	43.4832	43.4832	43.1405	43.0386	42.6749	36.7677	36.7677	36.4779	35.3001	34.2801
Costs	38.6117	33.7205	33.1788	29.2232	25.2063	31.5087	28.3834	26.1596	23.8083	21.3065
Net profit	**4.8715**	**9.7627**	**9.9617**	**13.8155**	**17.4686**	**5.2590**	**8.3843**	**10.3183**	**11.4917**	**12.9735**
Return on investment (ROI)	*2.8%*	*7.3%*	*10.0%*	*18.1%*	*34.2%*	*2.8%*	*6.6%*	*11.3%*	*16.5%*	*29.0%*
Average annual profit b/taxes	*4.5%*	*9.0%*	*9.2%*	*12.8%*	*16.4%*	*7.4%*	*13.1%*	*17.5%*	*21.5%*	*27.1%*
Net profit b/taxes	6.7193	12.0573	12.2634	16.4659	20.4409	6.8254	10.1868	12.2578	13.4824	15.0437
Plus depreciation	5.9647	4.5734	3.8722	3.0098	2.3009	5.0430	3.9523	3.1388	2.3946	1.6517
Plus interest	3.8078	2.9261	2.1432	1.6394	1.0762	3.7301	2.8737	2.0814	1.5875	1.0215
Total cash flow	**16.4919**	**19.5568**	**18.2788**	**21.1151**	**23.8180**	**15.9985**	**17.0128**	**17.4780**	**17.4646**	**17.7168**
Capitalized value per gallon @10%	164.92	195.57	182.79	211.15	238.18	155.99	170.13	174.78	174.65	177.17
Capitalized value (in 2014$)	**$490,300**	**$1,162,900**	**$2,173,800**	**$5,022,200**	**$14,162,800**	**$231,900**	**$505,800**	**$1,039,300**	**$2,077,000**	**$5,267,400**

TABLE 76   Financial Analysis—Economic Life, Example, Winery Total Winery Production, Cases (page 2 of 2)

	Other White Wine					Consolidated Statement – Total Winery				
	2,500	5,000	10,000	20,000	50,000	2,500	5,000	10,000	20,000	50,000
Grapes, $/ton	1,350	1,350	1,350	1,323	1,283					
Yield, gals/ton	160	160	160	160	160					
Retail, $/bottle	$14.00	$14.00	$13.50	$12.50	$12.50					
Retail MU%	28	28	26	24	24					
Wholesale MU%	32	32	32	30	28					
Tasting room % of sales	50	50	40	25	20					
Net revenues, per gallon	38.4807	38.4807	36.9103	34.6227	35.1751	44.2277	44.2277	43.5523	42.6072	42.2586
Costs, $/gallon										
Grapes	8.4375	8.4375	8.4375	8.2688	8.0156	9.5935	9.5935	9.5935	9.3276	9.1138
Labor	0.2975	0.1983	0.1980	0.1546	0.0636	3.0926	2.1185	2.9575	1.9651	0.9032
Materials	12.9229	12.3355	11.7481	11.1607	10.5733	12.9229	12.3355	11.7481	11.1607	10.5733
Utilities	0.6756	0.6449	0.6142	0.5651	0.5221	0.6756	0.6449	0.6142	0.5651	0.5221
Total direct costs	22.3335	21.6163	20.9978	20.1491	19.1746	26.2846	24.6924	24.9133	23.0185	21.1123
Barrels	0.0000	0.0000	0.0000	0.0000	0.0000	0.8058	0.5431	0.6412	0.5378	0.5676
Crush pad	0.0897	0.1255	0.1791	0.1109	0.0842	0.0897	0.1255	0.1791	0.1109	0.0842
Tanks	0.2395	0.2693	0.2679	0.2136	0.1871	0.2395	0.2693	0.2679	0.2136	0.1871
Pumps & filters	0.0673	0.0367	0.0995	0.0517	0.0282	0.0673	0.0367	0.0995	0.0517	0.0282
Bottling line	0.0433	0.2613	0.2132	0.1427	0.0619	0.0433	0.2613	0.2132	0.1427	0.0619
Refrigeration system	0.1731	0.1393	0.0974	0.0712	0.0577	0.1731	0.1393	0.0974	0.0712	0.0577
Laboratory & other equipment	0.1906	0.0953	0.0855	0.0963	0.0398	0.1906	0.0953	0.0855	0.0963	0.0398
Tasting room equipment	0.0491	0.0271	0.0327	0.0177	0.0087	0.0491	0.0271	0.0327	0.0177	0.0087
Building & site improvements	3.7305	2.6878	1.7976	1.3835	0.8600	3.7305	2.6878	1.7976	1.3835	0.8600
Total depreciation	4.5831	3.6423	2.7728	2.0877	1.3277	5.3889	4.1854	3.4140	2.6255	1.8953
Total production costs	26.9166	25.2586	23.7707	22.2368	20.5023	31.6735	28.8778	28.3273	25.6440	23.0076
Gross margin	11.5641	13.2222	13.1396	12.3859	14.6728	12.5542	15.3499	15.2250	16.9632	19.2509
Administration	0.5039	0.4463	0.4391	0.4171	0.2836	0.5039	0.4463	0.4391	0.4171	0.2836
Marketing	1.6383	1.0650	0.9048	0.8595	0.5845	1.6383	1.0650	0.9048	0.8595	0.5845
Interest @4.5%	3.7145	2.8633	2.0690	1.5772	1.0105	3.7650	2.8973	2.1092	1.6109	1.0461
Federal excise tax	0.1700	0.1700	0.1700	0.1700	0.3132	0.1700	0.1700	0.1700	0.1700	0.3132
Net profit b/income tax	5.5374	8.6777	9.5567	9.3621	12.4810	6.4770	10.7714	11.6120	13.9057	17.0235
% of revenues	*14.4%*	*22.6%*	*25.9%*	*27.0%*	*35.5%*	*14.6%*	*24.4%*	*26.7%*	*32.6%*	*40.3%*
Present worth (6% discount rate):										
Revenues	36.3026	36.3026	34.8210	32.6629	33.1841	40.0091	40.0091	39.3950	38.5101	38.2035
Costs	31.9974	28.9473	26.5681	24.5352	22.4205	35.1824	31.1929	29.7713	26.6975	23.4404
Net profit	**4.3052**	**7.3553**	**8.2529**	**8.1277**	**11.1415**	**4.8268**	**8.8162**	**9.6236**	**11.8126**	**14.7631**
Return on investment (ROI)	*2.6%*	*5.7%*	*8.9%*	*11.5%*	*24.7%*	*2.9%*	*7.0%*	*10.4%*	*16.8%*	*32.5%*
Average annual profit, b./taxes	*7.9%*	*13.5%*	*15.8%*	*16.6%*	*22.4%*	*5.5%*	*10.1%*	*11.2%*	*14.0%*	*17.7%*
Net profit b/taxes	5.5374	8.6777	9.5567	9.3621	12.4810	6.4770	10.7714	11.6120	13.9057	17.0235
Plus depreciation	4.5831	3.6423	2.7728	2.0877	1.3277	5.3889	4.1854	3.4140	2.6255	1.8953
Plus interest	3.7145	2.8633	2.0690	1.5772	1.0105	3.7650	2.8973	2.1092	1.6109	1.0461
Total cash flow	13.8350	15.1832	14.3986	13.0269	14.8192	15.6309	17.8540	17.1352	18.1420	19.9649
Capitalized value per gallon @10%	138.35	151.83	143.99	130.27	148.19	156.04	178.27	171.09	181.80	200.43
Capitalized value (in 2014$)	$205,700	$451,400	$856,200	$1,549,200	$4,405,900	$927,900	$2,120,100	$4,069,300	$8,648,400	$23,826,200

TABLE 78 Financial Analysis—MACRS Depreciation, Example Winery, Total Winery Production, Cases (page 1 of 2)

	Red Wine – 1 year in barrel					Chardonnay				
	2,500	5,000	10,000	20,000	50,000	2,500	5,000	10,000	20,000	50,000
Grapes, $/ton	**1,600**	**1,600**	**1,600**	**1,552**	**1,520**	**1,350**	**1,350**	**1,350**	**1,310**	**1,283**
Yield, gals/ton	150	150	150	150	150	155	155	155	155	155
Retail, $/bottle	**$18.00**	**$18.00**	**$18.00**	**$18.00**	**$18.00**	**$15.00**	**$15.00**	**$15.00**	**$14.55**	**$14.25**
Retail MU%	30	30	28	25	25	30	30	28	25	25
Wholesale MU%	32	32	32	32	32	32	32	32	32	32
Tasting room sales %	50	50	40	25	20	50	50	40	25	20
Net revenues, per gallon	**48.8577**	**48.8577**	**48.4726**	**48.3582**	**47.9495**	**40.7147**	**40.7147**	**40.3939**	**39.0896**	**37.9601**
Costs, $/gallon										
Grapes	10.6667	10.6667	10.6667	10.3467	10.1333	8.7097	8.7097	8.7097	8.1949	7.8605
Labor	5.7884	3.9725	5.6510	3.7241	1.7215	0.4959	0.3306	0.3301	0.2576	0.1060
Materials	12.9229	12.3355	11.7481	11.1607	10.5733	12.9229	12.3355	11.7481	11.1607	10.5733
Utilities	0.6756	0.6449	0.6142	0.5651	0.5221	0.6756	0.6449	0.6142	0.5651	0.5221
Total direct costs	**30.0536**	**27.6196**	**28.6799**	**25.7965**	**22.9502**	**22.8041**	**22.0207**	**21.4021**	**20.1783**	**19.0619**
Barrels	2.7634	1.8623	2.1987	1.8442	1.9464	0.9199	0.6200	0.7319	0.6140	0.6480
Crush pad	0.1495	0.2091	0.2985	0.1848	0.1403	0.1495	0.2091	0.2985	0.1848	0.1403
Tanks	0.5987	0.6733	0.6697	0.5341	0.4677	0.5987	0.6733	0.6697	0.5341	0.4677
Pumps & filters	0.0841	0.0459	0.1244	0.0647	0.0353	0.0841	0.0459	0.1244	0.0647	0.0353
Bottling line	0.0722	0.4355	0.3553	0.2378	0.1032	0.0722	0.4355	0.3553	0.2378	0.1032
Refrigeration system	0.2885	0.2321	0.1623	0.1187	0.0962	0.2885	0.2321	0.1623	0.01187	0.0962
Laboratory & other equipment	0.2711	0.1381	0.1374	0.1504	0.0626	0.2439	0.1219	0.1051	0.1062	0.0447
Tasting room equipment	0.0701	0.0387	0.0467	0.0252	0.0124	0.0701	0.0387	0.0467	0.0252	0.0124
Building & site improvements	12.4350	8.9594	5.9919	4.6118	2.8667	12.4350	8.9594	5.9919	4.6118	2.8677
Total depreciation	**16.7326**	**12.5944**	**9.9849**	**7.7717**	**5.7308**	**14.8619**	**11.3360**	**8.4859**	**6.4972**	**4.4145**
Total production costs	**46.7862**	**40.2140**	**38.6648**	**33.5682**	**28.6810**	**37.6660**	**33.3566**	**29.8879**	**26.6755**	**23.4764**
Gross margin	**2.0715**	**8.6436**	**9.8078**	**14.7900**	**19.2685**	**3.0487**	**7.3581**	**10.5060**	**12.4141**	**14.4837**
Administration	0.5039	0.4463	0.4391	0.4171	0.2836	0.5039	0.4463	0.4391	0.4171	0.2836
Marketing	1.6383	1.0650	0.9048	0.8595	0.5845	1.6383	1.0650	0.9048	0.8595	0.5845
Interest @4.5%	3.8078	2.9261	2.1432	1.6394	1.0762	3.7301	2.8737	2.0814	1.5875	1.0215
Federal excise tax	0.1700	0.1700	0.1700	0.1700	0.3132	0.1700	0.1700	0.1700	0.1700	0.3132
Taxable income	**(4.0485)**	**4.0363**	**6.1507**	**11.7040**	**17.0110**	**(2.9935)**	**2.8032**	**6.9107**	**9.3799**	**12.2809**
% of revenues	-8.3%	8.3%	12.7%	24.2%	35.5%	-7.4%	6.9%	17.1%	24.0%	32.4%
Present worth: (6.0% discount rate)										
Revenues	43.4832	43.4832	43.1405	43.0386	42.6749	36.7677	36.7677	36.4779	35.3001	34.2801
Costs	48.4783	41.0702	38.7799	33.5865	28.3492	40.6378	35.2484	31.1311	27.6226	23.8753
Net profit	(4.9951)	2.4130	4.3606	9.4521	14.3257	(3.8702)	1.5193	5.3469	7.6774	10.4048
Return on investment (ROI)	*-2.9%*	*1.8%*	*4.4%*	*12.4%*	*28.1%*	*-2.3%*	*1.2%*	*5.6%*	*10.6%*	*22.1%*
Average annual profit, b/taxes	*-4.6%*	*2.2%*	*4.0%*	*8.8%*	*13.4%*	*-4.7%*	*1.8%*	*6.5%*	*9.7%*	*13.5%*
Net profit b/taxes	(4.0485)	4.0363	6.1507	11.7040	17.0110	(2.9935)	2.8032	6.9107	9.3799	12.2809
Plus depreciation	16.7326	12.5944	9.9849	7.7717	5.7308	14.8619	11.3360	8.4859	6.4972	4.4145
Plus interest	3.8078	2.9261	2.1432	1.6394	1.0762	3.7301	2.8737	2.0814	1.5875	1.0215
Total cash flow	**16.4919**	**19.5568**	**18.2788**	**21.1151**	**23.8180**	**15.5985**	**17.0128**	**17.4780**	**17.4646**	**17.7168**
Capitalized value per gallon @10%	164.92	195.57	182.79	211.15	238.18	155.99	170.13	174.78	174.65	177.17
Capitalized value (in 2014$)	**$490,300**	**$1,162,900**	**$2,173,800**	**$5,022,200**	**$14,162,800**	**$231,900**	**$505,800**	**$1,039,300**	**$2,077,000**	**$5,267,400**

TABLE 78 Financial Analysis—MACRS Depreciation, Example Winery, Total Winery Production, Cases (page 2 of 2)

	Other White Wine					Consolidated Statement – Total Winery				
	2,500	5,000	10,000	20,000	50,000	2,500	5,000	10,000	20,000	50,000
Grapes, $/ton	**1,350**	**1,350**	**1,350**	**1,323**	**1,283**					
Yield, gals/ton	160	160	160	160	160					
Retail, $/bottle	**$14.00**	**$14.00**	**$13.50**	**$12.50**	**$12.50**					
Retail MU%	28	28	26	24	24					
Wholesale MU%	32	32	32	30	28					
Tasting room sales %	50	50	40	25	20					
Net revenues, per gallon	**38.4807**	**38.4807**	**36.9103**	**34.6227**	**35.1751**	**44.2277**	**44.2277**	**43.5623**	**42.6072**	**42.2586**
Costs, $/gallon										
Grapes	8.4375	8.4375	8.4375	8.2688	8.0156	9.5935	9.5935	9.5935	9.3276	9.1138
Labor	0.2975	0.1983	0.1980	0.1546	0.0636	3.0926	2.1185	2.9575	1.9651	0.9032
Materials	12.9229	12.3355	11.7481	11.1607	10.5733	12.9229	12.3355	11.7481	11.1607	10.5733
Utilities	0.6756	0.6449	0.6142	0.5651	0.5221	0.6756	0.6449	0.6142	0.5651	0.5221
Total direct costs	**22.3335**	**21.6163**	**20.9978**	**20.1491**	**19.1746**	**26.2846**	**24.6924**	**24.9133**	**23.0185**	**21.1123**
Barrels	0.0000	0.0000	0.0000	0.0000	0.0000	1.6117	1.0861	1.2823	1.0756	1.1352
Crush pad	0.1495	0.2510	0.3582	0.2218	0.1683	0.1495	0.2196	0.3134	0.1941	0.1473
Tanks	0.3991	0.4489	0.4465	0.3561	0.3118	0.5488	0.6172	0.6139	0.4896	0.4287
Pumps & filters	0.0841	0.0459	0.1244	0.0467	0.0353	0.0841	0.0459	0.1244	0.0647	0.0353
Bottling line	0.0722	0.4355	0.3553	0.2378	0.1032	0.0722	0.4355	0.3553	0.2378	0.1032
Refrigeration system	0.2885	0.2321	0.1623	0.1187	0.0962	0.2885	0.2321	0.1623	0.1187	0.0962
Laboratory & other equipment	0.2859	0.1429	0.1282	0.1445	0.0598	0.2680	0.1353	0.1270	0.1379	0.0574
Tasting room equipment	0.0701	0.0387	0.0467	0.0252	0.0124	0.0701	0.0387	0.0467	0.0252	0.0124
Building & site improvements	12.4350	8.9594	5.9919	4.6118	2.8667	12.4350	8.9594	5.9919	4.6118	2.8667
Total depreciation	**15.2769**	**10.5544**	**7.6135**	**5.7805**	**3.6538**	**15.5279**	**11.7698**	**9.0173**	**6.9553**	**4.8825**
Total production costs	**37.6104**	**32.1707**	**28.6114**	**25.9296**	**22.8284**	**41.8125**	**36.4622**	**33.9306**	**29.9737**	**25.9948**
Gross margin	**0.8703**	**6.3100**	**8.2989**	**8.6931**	**12.3467**	**2.4152**	**7.7655**	**9.6318**	**12.6334**	**16.2637**
Administration	0.5039	0.4463	0.4391	0.4171	0.2836	0.5039	0.4463	0.4391	0.4171	0.2836
Marketing	1.6383	1.0650	0.9048	0.8595	0.5845	1.6383	1.0650	0.9048	0.8595	0.5845
Interest @4.5%	3.7145	2.8633	2.0690	1.5772	1.0105	3.7650	2.8973	2.1092	1.6109	1.0461
Federal excise tax	0.1700	0.1700	0.1700	0.1700	0.3132	0.1700	0.1700	0.1700	0.1700	0.1700
Taxable income	**(5.1564)**	**1.7655**	**4.7160**	**5.6693**	**10.1549**	**(3.6620)**	**3.1870**	**6.0087**	**9.5759**	**14.0363**
% of revenues	*–13.4%*	*4.6%*	*12.8%*	*16.4%*	*28.9%*	*–8.3%*	*7.2%*	*13.8%*	*22.5%*	*33.2%*
Present worth (6% discount rate):										
Revenues	36.3026	36.3026	34.8210	32.6629	33.1841	40.0091	40.0091	39.3950	38.5101	38.2035
Costs	42.3841	35.6609	31.2698	28.1220	24.3018	44.9946	38.2624	34.9902	30.7294	26.2189
Net profit	**(6.0815)**	**0.6416**	**3.5512**	**4.5409**	**8.8823**	**(4.9855)**	**1.7467**	**4.4048**	**7.7806**	**11.9846**
Return on investment (ROI)	*–3.7%*	*0.5%*	*3.9%*	*6.6%*	*20.3%*	*–3.0%*	*1.4%*	*4.7%*	*4.7%*	*10.9%*
Average annual profit, b./taxes	*–11.2%*	*1.2%*	*6.8%*	*9.3%*	*17.8%*	*–5.7%*	*2.0%*	*2.0%*	*5.1%*	*9.2%*
Net profit b./taxes	(5.1564)	1.7655	4.7160	5.6693	10.1549	(3.6620)	3.1870	6.0087	9.5759	14.0363
Plus depreciation	15.2769	10.5544	7.6135	5.7805	3.6538	15.5279	11.7698	9.0173	6.9553	4.8825
Plus interest	3.7145	2.8633	2.0690	1.5772	1.0105	3.7650	2.8973	2.1092	1.6109	1.0461
Total cash flow	**13.8350**	**15.1832**	**14.3986**	**13.0269**	**14.8192**	**15.6309**	**17.8540**	**17.1352**	**18.1420**	**19.9649**
Capitalized value per gallon @10%	138.35	151.83	143.99	130.27	148.19	156.04	178.27	171.09	181.80	200.43
Capitalized value (in 2014$)	**$205,700**	**$451,400**	**$856,200**	**$1,549,200**	**$4,405,900**	**$927,900**	**$2,120,125**	**$4,069,300**	**$8,648,400**	**$23,836,200**

TABLE 80   Financial Analysis—Economic Life, 10,000 cases, 20 Selected Sites (page 1 of 4)

	Columbia Valley, WA		Willamette Valley, OR		Southern Oregon		Snake River Valley, ID		Sonoma Valley, CA	
	Syrah	Chardonnay	Pinot Noir	Pinot Gris	Syrah	Viognier	Rhône Reds	Chardonnay	Syrah	Chardonnay
Grapes, $/ton	**1,300**	**1,400**	**2,130**	**1,400**	**2,050**	**1,600**	**1,500**	**1,400**	**1,600**	**1,400**
Yield, gals/ton	150	155	150	160	150	160	150	155	150	155
Retail, $/bottle	**$20.00**	**$15.50**	**$24.00**	**$15.50**	**$22.00**	**$17.50**	**$19.50**	**$15.50**	**$20.00**	**$15.50**
Retail MU%	28	28	28	28	28	28	28	28	28	28
Wholesale MU%	32	32	32	32	32	32	32	32	32	32
Tasting room sales %	40	40	40	40	40	40	40	40	40	40
Revenues per gallon	**53.8585**	**39.0474**	**64.6302**	**41.7403**	**59.2443**	**47.1252**	**52.5120**	**41.7403**	**53.8585**	**48.4726**
Costs, $/gallon										
Grapes	8.6667	8.3871	14.2000	8.7500	13.6667	10.000	10.0000	8.3871	10.6667	10.6452
Labor	5.9335	0.3301	5.6510	0.1980	5.9355	0.1980	5.9335	0.3301	5.9355	0.3301
Materials	11.7481	11.7481	11.7481	11.7481	11.7481	11.7481	11.7481	11.7481	11.7481	11.7481
Utilities	0.3811	0.3700	0.3027	0.3027	0.3118	0.3027	0.3863	0.3750	0.7970	0.7738
Total direct costs	**26.7294**	**20.8353**	**31.9018**	**20.9988**	**31.6601**	**22.2488**	**28.0679**	**20.8403**	**29.1453**	**23.4971**
Barrels	2.1987	0.3660	1.0993	0.0000	2.1987	0.0000	2.1987	0.3660	2.1987	0.3660
All other equipment	0.9753	0.9753	0.9753	0.9753	0.9753	0.9753	0.9753	0.9753	0.9753	0.9753
Building & site improvements	1.8704	1.8704	1.7515	1.7515	1.7030	1.7030	1.6762	1.6762	1.9060	1.9060
Total depreciation	5.0443	2.2116	3.8261	2.7268	4.8769	2.6783	4.8502	3.0175	5.0799	3.2472
Total production cost	**31.7737**	**24.0469**	**35.7279**	**23.7257**	**36.5370**	**24.9271**	**32.9180**	**23.8577**	**34.2252**	**26.7443**
Gross margin	**22.0848**	**15.0005**	**29.9023**	**18.0147**	**22.7073**	**22.1991**	**19.5940**	**17.8826**	**19.6333**	**21.7283**
% of revenues	*41.0%*	*38.4%*	*44.7%*	*43.2%*	*38.3%*	*47.1%*	*37.3%*	*42.8%*	*36.5%*	*44.8%*
Administration & O/H	0.4347	0.4347	0.4285	0.4285	0.3816	0.3930	1.3925	1.3925	1.5559	1.5559
Marketing	0.9192	0.9192	0.8659	0.8659	0.8659	0.7862	3.0537	3.0537	3.5643	3.5643
Interest @4.5%	2.2830	2.1469	2.1018	2.0276	2.1324	1.9839	2.9591	2.6469	3.13340	2.8207
Federal excise tax	0.1700	0.1700	0.1700	0.1700	0.1700	0.1700	0.1700	0.1700	0.1700	0.1700
Net profit b/income tax	**18.2779**	**11.3297**	**25.3360**	**14.5226**	**19.1575**	**18.8659**	**16.2085**	**14.6332**	**15.8040**	**18.0351**
% of revenues	*33.9%*	*29.0%*	*39.2%*	*34.8%*	*32.3%*	*40.0%*	*30.9%*	*35.1%*	*29.3%*	*37.2%*
Present worth (6% discount rate):										
Revenues	45.2206	35.2620	57.5206	39.3777	49.7427	44.4587	44.0901	37.6939	45.2206	43.7735
Costs	30.7573	25.7706	36.0055	26.4362	34.6527	27.4488	31.3822	25.2029	36.8958	28.2994
Margin b/tax	14.4633	9.4914	21.5151	12.9415	15.0900	17.0098	12.7079	12.4909	12.3248	15.4741
Return on investment (ROI)	*13.3%*	*10.1%*	*13.3%*	*14.2%*	*14.8%*	*19.1%*	*12.6%*	*14.4%*	*11.2%*	*16.2%*
Average annual profit, b,/taxes	*9.1%*	*12.0%*	*15.0%*	*21.9%*	*8.7%*	*25.5%*	*11.5%*	*14.7%*	*7.8%*	*15.7%*
Net profit b/taxes	18.2779	11.3297	25.3360	14.5226	19.1575	18.8659	16.2085	14.6332	15.8040	18.0351
Plus depreciation	5.0443	3.2116	3.8261	2.7268	4.8769	2.6783	4.8502	3.0175	5.0799	3.2472
Plus interest	2.2830	2.1469	2.1018	2.0276	2.1324	1.9839	2.1082	1.9722	2.3150	2.1789
Total cash flow	**25.6051**	**16.6882**	**31.2640**	**19.2771**	**26.1668**	**23.5281**	**23.1669**	**19.6229**	**23.1989**	**23.4613**
Capitalized value per gallon @10%	256.05	166.88	312.64	192.77	261.67	235.28	231.67	196.23	231.99	234.61
Capitalized value (in 2014$)	**$3,045,100**	**$1,968,600**	**$3,718,100**	**$2,292,500**	**$3,111,900**	**$2,798,100**	**$2,755,100**	**$2,333,600**	**$2,758,900**	**$2,790,100**

TABLE 80 Financial Analysis—Economic Life, 10,000 cases, 20 Selected Sites (page 2 of 4)

	Central Coast, CA		Sonoita, AZ		Grand Valley, CO		Texas Hill Country		Central Missouri	
	Cabernet Sauvignon	White Viognier	Sangiovese	Sauvignon Blanc	Bordeaux Reds	Chardonnay	Syrah	Viognier	Norton	Vidal Blanc
Grapes, $/ton	2,025	1,650	1,800	1,500	1,600	1,400	1,650	1,600	1,620	1,200
Yield, gals/ton	150	160	160	160	150	155	150	160	150	160
Retail, $/bottle	$22.00	$20.00	$19.00	$18.00	$18.00	$15.50	$20.00	$18.00	$19.00	$15.50
Retail MU%	28	28	28	26	28	28	28	28	28	26
Wholesale MU%	32	32	32	32	32	32	32	32	32	32
Tasting room sales %	40	40	40	40	40	40	40	40	40	40
Revenues per gallon	59.2443	53.8585	51.1656	47.8466	48.4726	48.4726	53.8585	48.4726	51.1656	41.0114
Costs, $/gallon										
Grapes	13.5000	10.3156	11.2500	9.3750	10.6667	10.6452	11.0000	10.0000	10.8000	7.5000
Labor	5.9335	0.1980	5.6510	0.1980	5.6510	0.3301	5.9335	0.1980	5.6510	0.1980
Materials	11.7481	11.7481	11.7481	11.7481	11.7481	11.7481	11.7481	11.7481	11.7481	11.7481
Utilities	0.7970	0.7738	0.8285	0.8285	0.5669	0.5669	1.0339	1.0038	0.5343	0.5343
Total direct costs	31.9786	23.0324	30.2276	22.1496	28.6326	23.2902	29.7155	22.9499	28.7334	19.9804
Barrels	2.1987	0.0000	1.0993	0.0000	1.0993	0.3660	2.1987	0.0000	1.0993	0.0000
All other equipment	0.9753	0.9753	0.9753	0.9753	0.9753	0.9753	0.9753	0.9753	0.9753	0.9753
Building & site improvements	1.9140	1.9140	1.6994	1.6994	1.7738	1.7738	1.7733	1.7733	1.7255	1.7255
Total depreciation	5.0880	2.8893	3.7740	2.6747	3.8484	3.1151	4.9472	2.7486	3.8001	2.7007
Total production cost	37.0666	25.9218	34.0016	24.8243	32.4811	26.4053	34.6628	25.6985	32.5335	22.6812
Gross margin	22.1777	27.9367	17.1640	23.0223	15.9916	22.0673	19.1957	22.7741	18.6321	18.3302
% of revenues	37.4%	51.9%	33.5%	48.1%	33.0%	45.5%	35.6%	47.0%	36.4%	44.7%
Administration & O/H	0.3816	0.4290	0.3943	0.3816	0.3341	0.3341	0.3341	0.4417	0.3341	0.3341
Marketing	0.9292	0.9292	0.6768	0.6768	0.6768	0.6768	0.7817	0.7817	0.7111	0.7111
Interest @4.5%	2.3223	2.1739	2.0549	1.9807	2.1219	2.0600	2.1956	2.0472	2.0784	2.0042
Federal excise tax	0.1700	0.1700	0.1700	0.1700	0.1700	0.1700	0.1700	0.1700	0.1700	0.1700
Net profit b/income tax	18.3747	24.2347	13.8680	19.8133	12.6888	18.8264	15.7142	19.3335	15.3384	15.1107
% of revenues	31.0%	45.0%	27.1%	41.4%	26.2%	38.8%	29.2%	39.9%	30.0%	36.8%
Present worth (6% discount rate):										
Revenues	49.7427	50.8099	45.5372	45.1383	43.1405	43.7735	45.2206	45.7289	45.5372	38.6900
Costs	35.3294	28.7732	34.1760	27.2284	32.7890	27.5637	32.9734	28.3024	32.8287	25.1569
Margin b/tax	14.4133	22.0367	11.3611	17.9099	10.3514	16.2098	12.2472	17.4265	12.7085	13.5331
Return on investment (ROI)	13.0%	22.6%	11.9%	20.1%	10.5%	17.9%	11.7%	19.0%	13.2%	15.0%
Average annual profit, b/taxes	8.3%	28.9%	10.0%	26.5%	9.6%	16.5%	7.7%	25.4%	11.2%	23.3%
Net profit b/taxes	18.3747	24.2347	13.8680	19.8133	12.6888	18.8264	15.7142	19.3335	15.3384	15.1107
Plus depreciation	5.0880	2.8893	3.7740	2.6747	3.8484	3.1151	4.9472	2.7486	3.8001	2.7007
Plus interest	2.3223	2.1739	2.0549	2.1219	2.1219	2.0600	2.1956	2.0472	2.0784	2.0042
Total cash flow	25.7849	29.2979	19.6969	24.4686	18.6591	24.0015	22.8571	24.1292	21.2169	19.8157
Capitalized value per gallon @10%	257.85	292.98	196.97	244.69	186.59	240.02	228.57	241.29	212.17	198.16
Capitalized value (in 2014$)	$3,066,500	$3,484,200	$2,342,500	$2,909,900	$2,219,000	$2,854,400	$2,718,300	$2,869,600	$2,523,200	$2,356,600

TABLE 80   Financial Analysis—Economic Life, 10,000 cases, 20 Selected Sites (page 3 of 4)

	Shawnee Hills, IL		Peninsula, MI		Ohio River Valley		Lake Erie, OH-PA-NY		Finger Lakes, NY	
	Bordeaux Reds	Chardonel	Cabernet Franc	Pinot Gris	Bordeaux Reds	Chardonnay	Cabernet Franc	Chardonnay	Cabernet Franc	White Riesling
Grapes, $/ton	1,700	1,400	1,700	1,400	1,700	1,400	1,650	1,400	1,650	1,200
Yield, gals/ton	150	155	150	160	150	155	150	155	150	160
Retail, $/bottle	$18.50	$16.00	$19.00	$16.00	$19.00	$16.00	$18.00	$16.00	$18.00	$13.50
Retail MU%	28	28	28	28	28	28	28	28	28	23
Wholesale MU%	32	32	32	32	32	32	32	32	32	30
Tasting room sales %	40	40	40	40	40	40	40	40	40	40
Revenues per gallon	49.8191	40.3939	51.1656	43.0868	51.1656	44.4332	48.4726	47.1262	48.4726	36.9520
Costs, $/gallon										
Grapes	11.3333	6.7742	11.3333	8.7500	11.3333	9.6774	11.0000	9.6774	11.0000	7.5000
Labor	5.6510	0.3301	5.6510	0.1980	5.6510	0.3301	5.6510	0.3301	5.6510	0.1980
Materials	11.7481	11.7481	11.7481	11.7481	11.7481	11.7481	11.7481	11.7481	11.7481	11.7481
Utilities	0.7050	0.7050	0.4158	0.4158	0.5828	0.5828	0.5693	0.5693	0.5674	0.5674
Total direct costs	29.4374	19.5574	29.1482	21.1119	29.3152	22.3384	28.9684	22.3249	28.9665	20.0135
Barrels	1.0993	0.3660	1.0993	0.0000	1.0993	0.3660	1.0993	0.3660	1.0993	0.0000
All other equipment	0.9753	0.9753	0.9753	0.9753	0.9753	0.9753	0.9753	0.9753	0.9753	0.9753
Building & site improvements	1.6892	1.6892	1.8049	1.8049	1.7843	1.7843	1.6973	1.6973	1.7451	1.7451
Total depreciation	3.7638	3.0304	3.8795	2.7802	3.8589	3.1255	3.7719	3.0385	3.8197	2.7203
Total production cost	33.2012	22.5878	33.0277	23.8921	33.1741	25.4639	32.7402	25.3634	32.7862	22.7339
Gross margin	16.6179	17.8061	18.1378	19.1946	17.9915	18.9694	15.7324	21.7628	15.6865	14.2181
% of revenues	33.4%	44.1%	35.4%	44.5%	35.2%	42.7%	32.5%	46.2%	32.4%	38.5%
Administration & O/H	0.3983	0.3983	0.4343	0.4343	0.4180	0.4180	0.4180	0.4180	0.4470	0.4470
Marketing	0.6415	0.6415	0.7256	0.7256	0.6958	0.6958	0.6784	0.6784	0.8396	0.8396
Interest @4.5%	2.0457	1.9838	2.1499	2.0757	2.1313	2.0694	2.0530	1.9911	2.0960	2.0218
Federal excise tax	0.1700	0.1700	0.1700	0.1700	0.1700	0.1700	0.1700	0.1700	0.1700	0.1700
Net profit b/income tax	13.3625	14.6125	14.6581	15.7891	14.5764	15.6162	12.4130	18.5053	12.1339	10.7397
% of revenues	26.8%	36.2%	28.6%	36.6%	28.5%	35.1%	25.6%	39.3%	25.0%	29.1%
Present worth (6% discount rate):										
Revenues	44.3388	36.4779	45.5372	40.6479	45.5372	40.1257	43.1405	42.5576	43.1405	34.8604
Costs	33.4055	23.9703	33.4521	26.5139	33.5269	26.7928	33.0417	26.6104	33.2975	25.4596
Margin b/tax	10.9334	12.5076	12.0851	14.1340	12.0103	13.3329	10.0988	15.9472	9.8430	9.4008
Return on investment (ROI)	*11.5%*	*14.4%*	*12.1%*	*15.2%*	*12.1%*	*14.7%*	*10.6%*	*18.3%*	*10.1%*	*10.4%*
Average annual profit, b/taxes	*9.9%*	*22.9%*	*10.6%*	*23.2%*	*10.5%*	*14.8%*	*9.4%*	*16.7%*	*9.1%*	*18.0%*
Net profit b/taxes	13.3625	14.6125	14.6581	15.7891	14.5764	15.6162	12.4130	18.5053	12.1339	10.7397
Plus depreciation	3.7638	3.0304	3.8795	2.7802	3.8589	3.1255	3.7719	3.0385	3.8197	2.7203
Plus interest	2.0457	1.9838	2.1499	2.0757	2.1313	2.0694	2.0530	1.9911	2.0960	2.0218
Total cash flow	19.1719	19.6268	20.6875	20.6450	20.5666	20.8111	18.2378	23.5349	18.0495	15.4819
Capitalized value per gallon @10%	191.72	196.27	206.88	206.45	205.67	208.11	182.38	235.35	180.50	154.82
Capitalized value (in 2014$)	$2,280,000	$2,334,100	$2,460,300	$2,455,200	$2,445,900	$2,475,000	$2,168,900	$2,798,900	$2,146,500	$1,841,200

TABLE 80   Financial Analysis — Economic Life, 10,000 cases, 20 Selected Sites (page 4 of 4)

	Lancaster Valley, PA		SE New England Coast		Piedmont Plateau, MD		Central Blue Ridge Mountains, VA		Yadkin Valley, NC	
	Cabernet Sauvignon	Pinot Gris	Cabernet Franc	Vidal Blanc	Syrah	Chardonnay	Cabernet Sauvignon	Chardonnay	Cabernet Franc	Viognier
Grapes, $/ton	**1,700**	**1,600**	**1,500**	**1,100**	**1,400**	**1,600**	**1,600**	**1,600**	**1,650**	**1,600**
Yield, gals/ton	150	160	150	160	150	155	150	155	150	160
Retail, $/bottle	**$20.00**	**$18.00**	**$18.00**	**$14.00**	**$19.00**	**$18.00**	**$19.00**	**$18.00**	**$18.00**	**$18.50**
Retail MU%	28	28	28	26	28	28	28	28	28	28
Wholesale MU%	32	32	32	32	32	32	32	32	32	32
Tasting room sales %	40	40	40	40	40	40	40	40	40	40
Revenues per gallon	**53.8585**	**48.4726**	**48.4726**	**36.9103**	**51.1656**	**40.3939**	**51.1656**	**44.4332**	**48.4726**	**49.8191**
Costs, $/gallon										
Grapes	11.3333	10.0000	10.0000	6.8750	9.3333	9.0323	10.6667	9.3548	11.0000	10.0000
Labor	5.9335	0.1980	5.6510	0.1980	5.9335	0.3301	5.9335	0.3301	5.6510	0.1980
Materials	11.7481	11.7481	11.7481	11.7481	11.7481	11.7481	11.7481	11.7481	11.7481	11.7481
Utilities	0.5864	0.5693	0.6685	0.6685	1.0962	1.0643	0.7416	0.7200	0.5506	0.5506
Total direct costs	**29.6013**	**22.5154**	**28.0676**	**19.4896**	**28.1112**	**22.1747**	**29.0899**	**22.1530**	**28.9497**	**22.4967**
Barrels	2.1987	0.0000	1.0993	0.0000	2.1987	0.3660	2.1987	0.3660	1.0993	0.0000
All other equipment	0.9753	0.9753	0.9753	0.9753	0.9753	0.9753	0.9753	0.9753	0.9753	0.9753
Building & site improvements	1.7950	1.7950	1.8750	1.8750	1.8468	1.8468	1.7012	1.7012	1.7052	1.7052
Total depreciation	4.9690	2.7703	3.9496	2.8503	5.0207	3.1881	4.8751	3.0425	3.7798	2.6804
Total production cost	**34.5703**	**25.2858**	**32.0172**	**22.3399**	**33.1319**	**25.3628**	**33.9650**	**25.1955**	**32.7294**	**25.1772**
Gross margin	**19.2882**	**23.1869**	**16.4554**	**14.5703**	**18.0336**	**15.0311**	**17.2005**	**19.2378**	**15.7432**	**24.6419**
% of revenues	35.8%	47.8%	33.9%	39.5%	35.2%	37.2%	33.6%	43.3%	32.5%	49.5%
Administration & O/H	0.4264	0.4264	0.3750	0.3750	0.4770	0.4770	0.4255	0.4255	0.4101	0.4101
Marketing	0.6831	0.6831	0.7320	0.7320	0.7862	0.7862	0.7700	0.7700	0.6822	0.6822
Interest @4.5%	2.2152	2.0668	2.2130	2.1388	2.2618	2.1257	2.1307	1.9947	2.0601	1.9859
Federal excise tax	0.1700	0.1700	0.1700	0.1700	0.1700	0.1700	0.1700	0.1700	0.1700	0.1700
Net profit b/income tax	**15.7935**	**19.8407**	**12.9655**	**11.1546**	**14.3686**	**11.5021**	**13.7043**	**15.8777**	**12.4208**	**21.3937**
% of revenues	29.3%	40.9%	26.7%	30.2%	28.1%	28.5%	26.8%	35.7%	25.6%	42.9%
Present worth (6% discount rate):										
Revenues	45.2206	45.7289	43.1405	34.8210	42.9596	36.4779	42.9596	40.1257	43.1405	46.9991
Costs	32.9049	27.8098	32.5354	25.0161	31.8088	26.8622	32.3830	26.5496	33.0346	27.6092
Margin b/tax	12.3157	17.9191	10.6050	9.8049	11.1508	9.6157	10.5766	13.5761	10.1059	19.3900
Return on investment (ROI)	*11.6%*	*19.3%*	*10.3%*	*10.2%*	*10.3%*	*10.3%*	*10.4%*	*15.5%*	*10.6%*	*21.8%*
Average annual profit, b/taxes	*7.8%*	*26.1%*	*9.8%*	*18.8%*	*7.4%*	*11.7%*	*7.0%*	*15.0%*	*9.4%*	*27.5%*
Net profit b/taxes	15.7935	19.8407	12.9655	11.1546	14.3686	11.5021	13.7403	15.8777	12.4208	21.3937
Plus depreciation	4.9690	2.7703	3.9496	2.8503	5.0207	3.1881	4.8751	3.0425	3.7798	2.6804
Plus interest	2.2152	2.0668	2.2130	2.1388	2.2618	2.1257	2.1307	1.9947	2.0601	1.9859
Total cash flow	**22.9777**	**24.6777**	**19.1281**	**16.1437**	**21.6511**	**16.8159**	**20.7102**	**20.9148**	**18.2607**	**26.0600**
Capitalized value per gallon @10%	229.78	246.78	191.28	161.44	216.51	168.16	207.10	209.15	182.61	260.60
Capitalized value (in 2014$)	**$2,732,600**	**$2,934,800**	**$2,274,800**	**$1,919,900**	**$2,574,900**	**$1,999,800**	**$2,463,000**	**$2,487,300**	**$2,171,600**	**$3,099,200**

Table 81

Financial Analysis
Marionberry Wine
270 Cases* - 2014$

Fruit price, $/ton	**$1,300**
Gallons/ton**	322.2
Retail price/bottle	**$14.50**
Retail markup	28%
Wholesale markup	32%
Tasting room % of sales	75%
Revenues/gallon	**$41.8741**
FOB/retail	*57.2%*
Fruit cost, $/gallon	4.0354
Labor	0.1606
Materials	8.0981
Utilities	0.6449
Total direct cost	**12.9390**
Crush pad	0.1122
Tanks	0.2505
Pumps & filters	0.1054
Bottling line	0.2775
Refrigeration system	0.0708
Laboratory & other equipment	0.4129
Tasting room equipment	0.0640
Building	2.3656
Total depreciation	**3.6589**
Total production cost	**16.5979**
Administration & marketing	4.3588
Interest & federal excise tax	3.6825
Net income b/income tax	**17.2349**
% of revenues	*41.2%*
Revenues***	39.5039
Costs***	24.6393
Margin***	14.8646
ROI	*12.4%*
Average annual profit	*40.2%*
Net profit b/income tax	17.2349
Add depreciation	3.6589
Add interest	3.5125
Total cash flow	**24.4063**
Capitalized value/ gallon****	244.06
Total capitalized value**	**$39,050**

* In a 5,000-case winery.
** Finished wine, includes dilutions.
*** In present worth @6.0% discount rate.
**** @10% capitalization rate.

volume. The limitation allows production of a relatively concentrated final product. The dilution is significantly less than home winemakers do at 4-5 pounds of fruit per gallon.

Table 82 illustrates a spreadsheet calculation of wine adjustments for a Marionberry wine, one of the best fruit-based wines. The salient figures were

By applying the same methods as were used for grape wines, a financial analysis is performed in Table 81. Cost factors are based on a 270-case batch (644.3 gallons) of wine produced by a winery that makes a total of 5,000 cases of wine.

The cost of fruit is $0.65/lb., which was the average price for fresh Oregon Marionberries in 2009-2013. Freshly-picked, unfrozen fruit is the best economic alternative, as frozen Oregon Marionberries commanded a price of $1.00/lb. in the same crop year.

This wine yields an ROI (return on investment) of 12.4 percent, and an Average Annual Profit of 40.2 percent, results that are superior to typical white wines other than Chardonnay or Pinot Gris. Apparently, wineries in eastern and southern states can command as much as $17.50/bottle for a red raspberry wine. (Marionberry would be even better.)

Financial returns are very sensitive to the fruit cost. Some fruit prices are relatively volatile from year to year, much more so than winegrape prices, because some foreign countries are major players in the fruit market. Perhaps an even larger factor is that non-grape fruit prices are not normally subjected to multi-year contracts, so the price floats with the spot market. It is more volatile from year to year. In the case of red raspberries, Chile and

TABLE 82   Calculation of Adjustments, Oregon Marionberry Wine

Weight of fruit	2 tons	
Raw juice volume	418.80 gallons	
Finished wine volume	644.30 gallons	
Sugar additions:	Ounces	Pounds
Before fermentation	15,300.0	956.25
After fermentation	4,650.0	290.63
Total sugar additions	19,950.0	1,246.88
Deacidification	148.2 oz. of acid	
$CaCO_3$ used	98.8	6.18

China are distorting prices realized by U.S. producers. A winery would have to use frozen fruit from these other countries because of the long delivery time, and those prices are much higher than for freshly-picked fruit from nearby U.S. sources. Regardless, pricing goes up and down based on supply and demand.

To answer the protests from western winemakers who have sold into the berry wine market, it is illustrative to perform a sensitivity analysis in which the fruit cost is varied and the retail wine price is constant at $14.50 a bottle. The tolerance for fruit wine prices is much lower in western states compared with those in the East and South.

The wine may not be worth making at a retail price of $14.50 per 750 ml bottle.

Fruit cost $/lb	ROI, %	Average Annual Profit, %
0.65	12.4	40.2
1.00	10.6	31.6
1.25	9.3	26.2
1.50	8.0	21.4

Average annual profit, appearing high in this example, is not as useful as ROI in measuring financial returns. Winemaking is a capital-intensive business.

Interesting also is the escalation in retail wine price necessary to yield an ROI of 15.0 percent, depicted in Figure 106:

Fruit cost $/lb	ROI, %	Retail Bottle Price, $
0.65	15.0	15.65
1.00	15.0	16.45
1.25	15.0	17.00
1.50	15.0	17.56

Now, we can see how the fruit price affects the minimum retail price to support a 15 percent ROI. The numbers above provide a guideline to deciding whether or not to make the wine, depending on the raw fruit price available. The winery may decide not to produce it in a given year, but must also consider

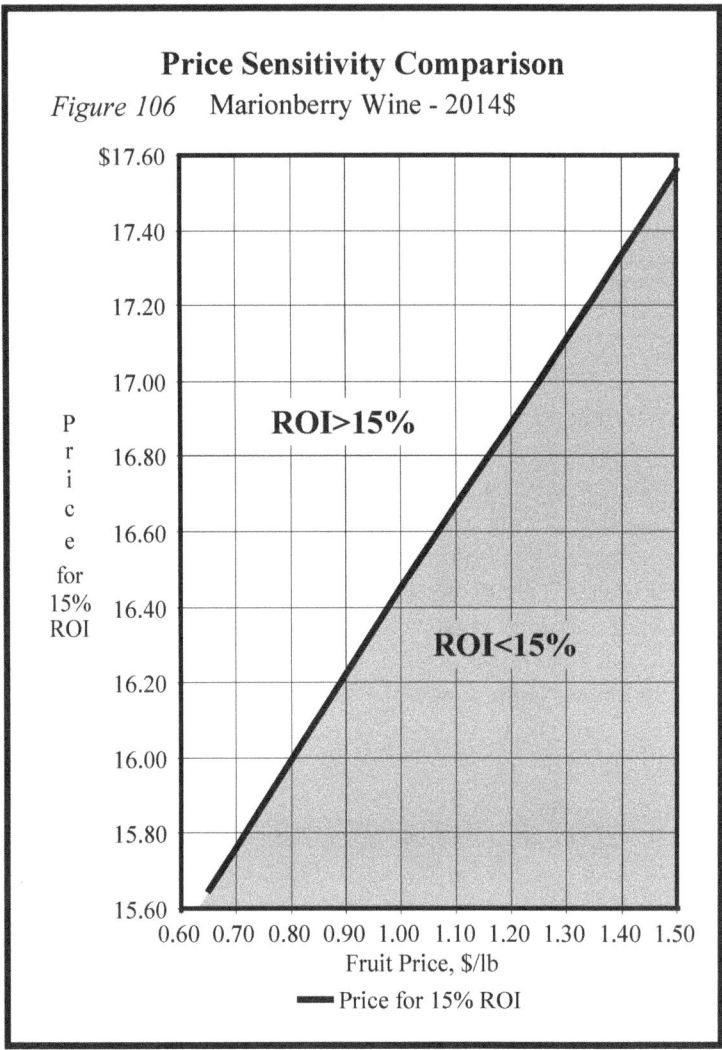

Price Sensitivity Comparison

Figure 106   Marionberry Wine - 2014$

the cost associated with fighting to regain the lost shelf position in the following year.

Sparkling wine

The same financial analysis can be performed for sparkling wine (Table 83). Revenues and costs will be significantly higher than they were for grape still wines and fruit wines. There are several reasons.

We have selected a premium quality brut sparkling wine for the analysis. It is made from 50 percent Pinot Noir and 50 percent Chardonnay. Although the fruit would be harvested earlier, i.e., with lower sugar and higher acidity, than those varieties would be for still wines, the tonnage can be greater and the price remains the same. The average of the two is $1,815 per ton.

The retail price is assumed to be $25.00 for a 750 ml bottle. Most of this wine would probably be sold in boutique wine shops and the winery's tasting room and direct shipping programs.

Production is taken at 1,000 cases annually in a winery that produces a total of 10,000 cases of all wine types a year.

The grapes are pressed "whole cluster," which means they are loaded into the press as intact clusters, stems and all. Juice yield is less than for still wines, mostly because the juice is divided into "cuts," or fractions, at the press. That is, the results from pressing at various pressure levels are kept separate for the first fermentation. This is done because the quality of the juice diminishes with each pressing, beginning with the best in the first squeeze and the worst in the last. Within the grape, the juice closest to the skin is higher in sugar, lower in acid, contains more aroma and taste esters, and is the first to be extracted by the press. The juice adjacent to the seeds is lower in sugar, higher in acid, tannins and harshness, and has much less body.

Winemakers in Champagne, France are much more exacting than typical American producers. Whereas French producers separate at least seven fractions from twenty pressings, you can probably succeed in a modern tank press with as few as four fractions. Those to be used for the sparkling wine cuvée are separated at 80, 30, and 20 gallons per ton of grapes. The total of the three fractions is 130 gallons per ton.

Costs are higher than for still wines because

- Smaller tanks are needed to accommodate the press fractions through the first fermentation;

- More laboratory analyses are needed to track more batches;

Table 83

Financial Analysis
Brut Sparkling Wine
1,000 Cases* - 2014$

Grape price, $/ton	**$1,815**
Gallons/ton	130
Retail price/bottle	**$25.00**
Retail markup	30%
Wholesale markup	32%
Tasting room % of sales	30%
Revenues/gallon	**$64.7299**
FOB/retail	*51.3%*
Grape cost, $/gallon	13.9615
Labor	0.2398
Materials	8.6336
Utilities	0.7370
Total direct cost	**23.5720**
Crush pad	0.1683
Tanks	0.2927
Pumps & filters	0.1256
Bottling line	0.4162
Refrigeration system	0.0708
Laboratory & other equipment	0.4629
Tasting room equipment	0.0640
Building	3.5483
Total depreciation	**5.1489**
Total production cost	**28.7208**
Administration & marketing	5.5292
Interest & federal excise tax	6.9125
Net income b/income tax	**23.5673**
% of revenues	*36.4%*
Revenues**	55.9552
Costs**	36.6346
Margin**	19.3206
ROI	*11.1%*
Average annual profit	*17.6%*
Net profit b/income tax	23.5673
Add depreciation	5.1489
Add interest	3.5125
Total cash flow	**32.2287**
Capitalized value/gallon***	322.29
Total capitalized value*	**$767,000**

* In a 10,000-case winery.
** In present worth @6.0% discount rate.
*** @10% capitalization rate.

- Assembling the cuvée requires much more time and effort than dealing with a still wine;
- Champagne pressure bottles are more expensive, as is the closure;
- Crown caps and plastic *bidules* are needed for the second fermentation and aging;
- Bottling for the second fermentation and disgorgement at finishing the wine, is more complicated;
- Champagne corks are more expensive than still wine corks and wire hoods are needed to safely secure the corks in place;
- Specially–designed equipment is needed.

The resulting ROI of 11.1 percent is lower than for other wine types. Average annual profit is 17.6 percent, also inferior to other wines.

In order to produce an ROI of 15.0 percent, a retail price of $28.00 would be needed, according to these cost estimates.

৪০গ্গ

—15—

Considerations relating to value in an acquisition

You know how the joke goes: "How do you make a small fortune in the wine business? Answer: start with a large one." That old saw notwithstanding, people do make money in this business. It's probably because they know what they are doing, in the winery and marketplace; they are dedicated to building the entity for the right reason, which is to make money by making good wine; and they treat the vineyard and winery like it's a business, rather than as an ego toy, or as a tax shelter grab-bag.

In preceding chapters, we explored some realities of assuming winery ownership; the importance of securing high-quality grapes; the crucial and pivotal role of the winemaker; the recordkeeping function; marketing; and equipment. Financial aspects of a vineyard or winery acquisition are reviewed in this chapter.

Considerations with large-value impacts that will be considered here include the following: winemaking staff, equipment, building, vineyard holdings, and cased goods inventory.

That winemaker, again

If you are purchasing a successful winery/vineyard, and the winemaker plus perhaps a vineyard manager are staying on, you may have the best of all worlds.

But, if the winery has not been notably successful in product quality, it is imperative to change the winemaker. If product quality has been good, but the winery has not been profitable, liberating the winemaker from the seller's control may be a good thing. In either of these two cases, valuation by capitalization of income probably won't yield enough value to cover the replacement cost of plant and equipment, plus the inventory valued at producer prices.

In such instances, the sales value may have to be based on depreciated value of facilities and realistic "winery FOB" values (the price at which wineries sell to distributors) for the wine inventory. In financial terms, the value attached to such a purchase is almost the same as starting a new operation by acquiring a vineyard, building and equipment, with no value attributed to the condition of a "going business concern" and goodwill.

Winery equipment and buildings

In the preceding chapter we reviewed typical values for winery building and equipment in some detail. So, we'll just summarize them here.

Approximate total **new equipment costs** (expressed as dollars per wine gallon produced) for the wineries evaluated in Chapter 12:

Winery Equipment Cost	
Winery Production in Cases	$/gallon Produced
2,500	19.68–21.68
5,000	22.86–24.92
10,000	22.96–24.84
20,000	17.27–18.70
50,000	13.40–14.43

The increased cost per gallon from the first to second sizes illustrates the transition from a lot of hand work in the smallest wineries to utilization of more mechanized methods, a substitution of machinery for labor.

Winery building construction costs vary according to materials as well as scale of production.

Building Construction Cost ($/gallon produced)		
Winery Production in cases	Construction Cost in $/gallon	Materials of Construction
2,500	141.77–156.69	wood frame
5,000	102.13–112.88	wood frame
10,000	68.31–75.50	wood frame & tilt-up
20,000	52.57–58.11	tilt-up concrete
50,000	32.68–36.12	tilt-up concrete

These cost figures apply to the completed building, appropriately insulated, with a properly sloped and drained floor, electrical service and plumbing. Additions have been made, as applicable, for coolant piping, special hot water system, extraordinary tasting room features, paved parking and landscaped grounds.

For used equipment and buildings, the values presented above have to be reduced by deducting estimated depreciation or applying the concept of *remaining economic life.*[1]

Vineyard holdings

Different wine varieties bring different profits. So, the varieties a vineyard grows have a strong effect on the overall vineyard value.

In addition to location and macroclimate (the general area, or neighborhood), the value of vineyard holdings depends on the grape varieties grown, vine density, trellis configuration and the vineyard's track record for prices received. Remember, too, the tractors and other vineyard equipment. Table 84 compares financial returns for the grape varieties most commonly grown in a selected vineyard area, Oregon's North Willamette Valley. Vine spacings and grape prices are typical for quality wine production in that area.

TABLE 84   Vineyard Financial Returns, Per Acre, by Grape Variety, Willamette Valley, 2014 Dollars

	Pinot Noir	Chardonnay	Pinot Gris/ Viognier	White Riesling	Sauvignon Blanc	Other Whites
Spacing, Row × Vine	9 × 7	9 × 7	9 × 7	9 × 5	10 × 8	9 × 7
Establishment Cost:	10,183	9,179	9,179	10,428	8,493	9,179
Grape Price, $/ton	1,700	1,500	1,700	1,100	1,200	1,300
Yield, tons/acre	3.8	4.0	4.0	5.0	5.0	4.0
Revenues/acre	6,460	6,000	6,800	5,500	6,000	5,200
Operating Costs	4,494	4,605	4,425	4,509	4,017	4,157
Net Profit, b/taxes	**1,966**	**1,395**	**2,375**	**991**	**1,988**	**1,043**
Percent of revenue	*30.4%*	*23.3%*	*34.9%*	*18.0%*	*33.1%*	*20.1%*
Add Depreciation, Interest & Amortization	1,513	1,419	1,413	1,537	1,335	1,406
Net Cash Flow	**3,479**	**2,814**	**3,789**	**2,528**	**3,319**	**2,449**
Capitalized Value @10%	**34,790**	**28,138**	**37,887**	**25,285**	**33,186**	**24,492**
Less Establishment Cost	10,183	9,179	9,179	10,428	8,493	9,179
Land Residual Value/acre	***23,917***	***18,121***	***27,921***	***14,172***	***23,907***	***14,621***

To simplify this comparison, we've applied the area's average prices and costs to each grape variety. The vineyard size is 20 gross acres, 17.6 net acres. There is no provision for irrigation, which would add another $3,000–3,500/acre to establishment costs and reduce the land residual value accordingly.

For all varieties, the value attributed to the vineyard would have to be adjusted downward if the vines are own-rooted. The deduction is based on the discounted present worth of replanting to grafted vines.

Vineyard equipment

In the vineyard financial profiles above the costs of vineyard equipment are treated as hourly charges. These rates per acre can provide a rough guide to estimating vineyard equipment cost.

---

1. For *remaining economic life*, deduct the building's age from estimated economic life. See Chapter 14 for application of the concept to financial performance.

Vineyard Equipment Cost	
Acres	Cost per Acre Mix New/Used
10	$6,500–7,200
20	4,850–5,350
40	2,600–2,900
60	1,800–1,950
80	1,550–1,700

There are substantial economies of scale in this business. These costs are mostly for new equipment. Some attachments are priced as used. If acquiring an existing vineyard with equipment, or purchasing used equipment, the amounts would have to be discounted according to their remaining economic life.

Winery value also reflects varieties produced

The same kind of financial analysis can be done with winery revenues and costs (Table 85).

In order to compare wine types objectively, we have to evaluate identical production volumes. We have selected a batch size of 5,000 cases (11,893 gallons) produced in a winery whose total production of all wines is 10,000 cases. It's a matter of comparing apples to apples rather than apples to oranges.

The winery location chosen is also the Willamette Valley, in order to provide continuity with the evaluated vineyard. Most grapes are grown at the winery. Some may be sourced in Oregon's Rogue Valley AVA and/or Washington's Columbia Valley AVA.

Pinot Noir wines comes out best in this comparison. That is not surprising, given that it is the state's flagship variety, favorable comparisons are made with Burgundy quality and acquisitions in Oregon have been made by prominent wine companies from Burgundy and California.

Further, the values derived in Table 85 may be applied to other varieties grown in other producing areas after adjustments for different wine prices, wages and utility costs, because of the similarity of production methods in the five categories as follows:

- **Red wine—1 year in barrel**: Cabernet Franc, Chambourcin, Grenache, Malbec, Merlot, Norton, Pinot Noir, Sangiovese.

- **Red wine—2 years in barrel**: Cabernet Sauvignon, Syrah.

- **Chardonnay**: in a class by itself by virtue of its intense use of barrels in comparison with other white wine varieties.

- **Other whites**: Aurore, Chenin Blanc, Gewürztraminer, Müller-Thurgau, Pinot Blanc, Sauvignon Blanc, Seyval Blanc, Traminette, Vidal Blanc, White Riesling. Most rosés and blush wines also fall into this category.

- **Sparkling wine**: *méthode champenoise* (fermented in the bottle in which it is sold) sparkling wines only. Charmat process (second fermentation in a tank) and wines injected with CO_2 at bottling are not included.

TABLE 85   Winery Financial Returns, 5,000 cases, by Grape Variety, 2014 Dollars

	Red Wine			Chardonnay	Pinot Gris	Viognier	White Riesling	Müller-Thurgau	Sparkling Wine
	Pinot Noir Super Premium	1 yr in bbl	2 yrs in bbl						
Grapes, $/ton	4,000	1,675	1,800	1,500	1,400	1,500	1,200	1,050	1,650
Wine yield, gals/ton	150	150	150	155	160	160	160	160	130
Retail price, 750 ml bottle	60.00	18.00	22.00	16.00	16.00	17.00	16.00	11.00	25.00
Retail markup, %	35	30	30	28	28	28	25	25	35
Wholesale markup, %	32	32	32	32	32	32	32	30	32
Tasting room sales, %	50	50	50	50	50	50	50	50	30
Revenues/gallon	157.7128	48.8577	59.7149	43.9780	43.9780	46.7266	36.8930	31.2172	61.7280
Total production costs	43.0250	27.5250	30.4785	20.8513	19.1870	19.8120	18.9560	16.9995	25.9495
Administration & marketing	4.8612	4.8612	4.8612	4.8612	4.8612	4.8612	4.8612	4.8612	4.8612
Interest & federal excise tax	3.0468	3.0468	3.2171	2.9048	2.8765	2.8765	2.8765	2.8765	6.9125
Net Profit b/taxes	106.7799	13.4247	21.1582	15.3607	17.0533	19.1770	11.2184	6.4800	24.0048
% of revenues	*67.7%*	*27.5%*	*35.4%*	*34.9%*	*38.8%*	*41.0%*	*30.4%*	*20.8*	*38.9%*
Return on investment, PW*	**90.6%**	**10.7%**	**14.6%**	**14.4%**	**16.7%**	**18.8%**	**10.7%**	**5.9%**	**12.5%**
Average annual profit, PW*	***26.7%***	***10.1%***	***9.6%***	***21.9%***	***39.1%***	***43.2%***	***26.4%***	***15.0%***	***19.6%***
Add depreciation and interest	7.6205	7.6205	9.6831	6.2162	5.5579	5.5579	5.5579	5.5579	8.0983
Cash flow/gallon	114.4004	21.0452	30.8412	21.5768	22.6112	24.7348	16.7762	12.0379	32.1031
Capitalized value/gallon	1,144.00	210.45	308.41	215.77	226.11	247.35	167.76	120.38	321.03
Capitalized value**	**13,605,100**	**2,502,800**	**3,667,800**	**2,566,000**	**2,689,000**	**2,941,600**	**1,995,100**	**1,431,600**	**3,817,900**

Note: Costs are 20-acre average,

* Calculated on present worth value @6% discount rates.

** At 5,000 cases (11,893 gallons) produced in a 10,000-case winery and 10% capitalization rate.

Cased goods inventory

Finished wine inventory is another element of value, and it relates importantly to continuity of the operation. If the inventory isn't included in the sale, or its quality is suspect, any goodwill value attached to established marketing and label will rapidly vanish. The production lead time for fine wines ranges from two to three years. Such a lengthy interruption in the flow of good product to the market means starting over again, with market share having to be wrested from eager competitors. It may also require establishing a new distributor network.

Before purchasing a winery's inventory, the prospective buyer should employ the services of an experienced winemaker to determine the wines' soundness and, perhaps, a capable brand manager of a wine distributor to determine the wines' marketability and price.

The price to be used for valuing a wine inventory is *winery FOB price*, the price at which the winery sells to a distributor. The amount will be 50–54 percent of retail shelf price in the supermarket setting.

Tasting room and sales events

In determining the value of wine and other sales through the tasting room and off-premise events, it is important to obtain the number of units that were removed from inventory. Cash revenues are sometimes distorted by shoplifting, pilferage and skimming of the till. The accuracy of the cash figures depends heavily on effective cost controls, and not all wineries have them. Obtain the number of cases for each type of wine, number of corkscrews, tee shirts, etc. Those numbers can be used to estimate dollar volumes based on price structure.

Some of the more egregious examples are

- Sales personnel who build huge home wine collections one bottle at a time;
- The occasional owner who backs his vehicle up to the tasting room door every Friday afternoon, opens the trunk, and says: "Fill 'er up!"

These are but a few of the value-related factors to be considered in acquiring or developing a winery.

❧☙

–16–

Minimum economic size

Most of us have seen the travelogues featuring small French wineries that work only 2–4 hectares (4.8–9.6 acres) of vineyard. How large does a vineyard or winery have to be in order to provide a reasonable income to its proprietor?

That French grower can make a satisfactory profit because, except for picking, he's doing all of the work himself; he's making the wine in bulk before selling it to a negoçiant; and the vineyard is located in an appellation area that commands a high price.

There is no universal answer to the question about minimum vineyard size. The variables are many: grape variety, vineyard design, development cost, grape price, wine price, management practices, operating costs and how much of the work is performed by the proprietor. The list goes on and on. However, what applies to red winegrapes in the vineyard generally applies to white winegrapes. For most vineyards, the methods do not change appreciably from red to white varieties. So, the finding of this analysis is more universal than winery breakeven for reds versus whites.

So, let's pick one wine, a red wine that is cropped at 4 tons/acre (tpa), barreled for one year, then aged in bottle for one year before release.

The vineyard costs are based on Oregon's Willamette Valley. The choice considered the overall labor and materials rates for the 20 growing areas, but averages tend to blur the distortion asserted by high-cost areas like California. A rank ordering of the 20 areas by wage rates and material costs shows Oregon in the middle of the pack. Choice of a specific area will simplify adaptation of the calculations to other producing areas.

These calculations do not apply to a vineyard owner who hires a vineyard management company to manage the vineyard, nor to a winery owner who hires someone else to do the winemaking. They do apply to an owner who maximizes his/her performance of production and management functions. In the vineyard, that means an owner who drives the tractor for the sprays, does most of the canopy management and personally supervises the picking. In the winery, it means an owner who runs the press, does the lab analyses and barrel work, operates the filters and personally participates in the bottling.

Independent grower

We'll start with the 10-acre vineyard evaluated in Chapter 6. Net vineyard acres are 8.8 after deducting avenues and headlands. The grapes sell for $1,700 per ton and yield is 4 tons/acre.

An important consideration is the crop load. In elite growing areas, we hear of grape prices at $4,000/ton and up. The grower's revenues per acre are the important number to focus on. It is likely that the winery is paying for the grapes by the row or acre. Perhaps the winemaker puts his own crew into the vineyard to thin the crop after veraison, leaving enough clusters for a 2.0–2.5 tpa crop load. Two tpa at $4,000/ton yields $8,000/acre to the grower, the same as 4.0 tpa at $2,000/ton.

Sources of income to the proprietor are the savings achieved by doing some of the work that would otherwise be done by hired employees, and the net profit from operations. We'll assume that income needed from the operation must be sufficient to earn $80,000 in annual income ($96,000 after adding payroll taxes and fringe benefits), plus a 10 percent return to investment (ROI) in plantings, building and equipment. Although an ROI of 15 percent would be preferable, we're seeking absolute minimums in this exercise.

First, the labor performed by the owner. Allocation of values between owner and hired help is shown in the columns for 8.8 net acres (Tables 86 and 87), and the percent will change with vineyard size. Totals for larger acreages are extended proportional to size, with allowances made for economies of scale. Then, the value of work performed by the owner is discounted to present worth as of July 1 at a rate of 6 percent. Pruning and tying tasks occur at the start of the calendar year. Spraying centers on mid-year. Harvest is in early October.

The value of credits for owner labor will not total the targeted $80,000 income. It is based on payroll savings for workers at lower pay rates who would otherwise have done the work.

Net profit from the operation is similarly extended to larger vineyard sizes and discounted to present worth as of July 1 at 6 percent (Table 88). Payments for grapes are made as follows: one-third at picking; one-third 30 days later; the remaining third on December 31, which is typical.

Return to investment (ROI) is calculated at 10 percent of the 50 percent of equipment and establishment costs that are financed by equity (Table 89). The other 50 percent is financed by loans.

Total income required by the owner at each size of vineyard is divided by the total labor savings and net profit received. The result is a multiplier that must be applied to the vineyard acres at each size (Table 90).

TABLE 86   Owner's Share of Tasks Performed, Vineyard Only, at 17.6 Net Acres, Performed by Owner

	Total Cost (dollars)	Amount (dollars)	Percent
Pruning & tying	791.24	474.75	60
Sprays	1,699.90	1,699.90	100
Canopy management	3,670.24	2,752.68	75
Floor management	339.98	339.98	100
Bird control	283.32	283.32	100
Frost control	0.00	0.00	100
Irrigation	0.00	0.00	100
Supervision	4,249.74	4,249.74	100
Pick	11,809.60	0.00	0
Load/haul	1,096.43	1,096.43	100
Supervision	1,359.92	1,359.92	100
Total labor items	**25,300.37**	**12,256.71**	**48.4**

TABLE 87   Value of Owner's Labor, Vineyard Only

	4.4 acres	8.8 acres	13.2 acres	17.6 acres	22.0 acres	26.4 acres	30.8 acres
Total labor items	6,005.77	10,500.55	11,378.63	12,256.71	13,127.16	13,993.79	14,813.85
Present worth @6%	**5,902.43**	**10,328.53**	**11,196.20**	**12,063.87**	**12,923.34**	**13,778.72**	**14,587.09**

TABLE 88   Net Profit from Operations, Vineyard Only

	4.4 acres	8.8 acres	13.2 acres	17.6 acres	22.0 acres	26.4 acres	30.8 acres
Net profit	11,518.60	23,037.19	34,678.36	46,442.09	58,205.82	69,969.55	81,610.71
Present worth @6%	**11,285.23**	**22,570.47**	**33,855.70**	**45,140.94**	**56,426.17**	**67,711.40**	**78,996.64**

TABLE 89   Return to Investment, Vineyard Only

	4.4 acres	8.8 acres	13.2 acres	17.6 acres	22.0 acres	26.4 acres	30.8 acres
Establishment costs @50%	41,649.70	48,465.10	66,639.50	80,775.20	100,969.00	121,162.80	141,356.60
ROI @10%	**4,164.97**	**4,846.51**	**6,663.95**	**8,077.52**	**10,096.90**	**12,116.28**	**14,135.66**

TABLE 90   Total Income and Minimum Gross Acres, Vineyard Only

	4.4 acres	8.8 acres	13.2 acres	17.6 acres	22.0 acres	26.4 acres	30.8 acres
Labor savings	5,902.43	10,328.53	11,196.20	12,063.87	13,923.34	13,778.72	14,587.09
Net Profit	11,285.23	22,570.47	33,855.70	45,140.94	56,426.17	67,711.40	78,996.64
Total returns	17,187.66	32,899.00	45,051.90	57,204.81	69,349.51	81,490.12	93,583.73
ROI needed @10%	4,164.97	4,846.51	6,663.95	8,077.52	10,096.90	12,116.28	14,135.66
Plus salary	92,243.44	92,243.44	92,243.44	92,243.44	92,243.44	92,243.44	92,243.44
Total needed	**97,408.41**	**97,089.95**	**99,907.40**	**101,320.96**	**103,340.34**	**105,359.72**	**107,379.10**
Multiplier	5.67	2.98	2.22	1.77	1.49	1.29	1.15
Minimum net acres	24.9	26.2	29.3	31.2	32.8	34.1	35.3

The method used for this analysis can be confusing. The reasons are twofold: economies of scale are available as vineyard size increases; and the compensation other than ROI is not constant. Better described, the number of acres needed is the number of acres calculated at the cost rates that apply to each size vineyard. More specifically, to generate the desired net income of $45,140.94, it takes 22.8 net acres at the costs associated with an 8.8-acre vineyard.

The minimum acreage for the independent grower is determined from Figure 107. It is 36.3 net acres, or 40.8 gross acres.

The minimum economic vineyard size is very sensitive to differences in grape price. For example, the same vineyard costs coupled with some increased prices per ton, would reduce the minimum economic size to:

Grape Price	Net Acres	Gross Acres
$1,700/ton	36.3	40.8
$2,000/ton	24.3	21.7
$2,500/ton	15.5	13.7

The acreage at each price is as accurate as the methodology permits.

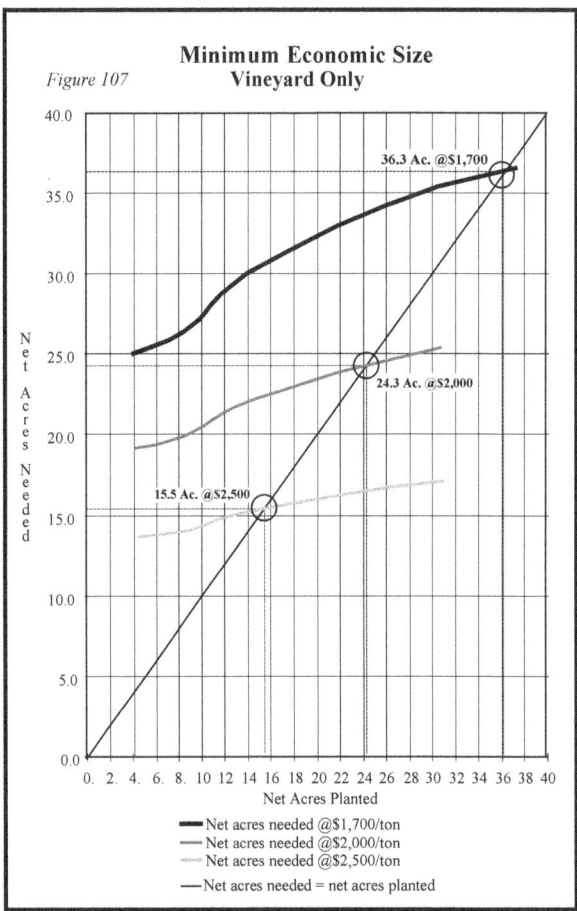

Figure 107

Minimum Economic Size Vineyard Only

Winery only

The same kind of analysis can be done for a winery, but using gallons of production as the measure of size. The winery buys all of its grapes. Grape cost is $1,700 per ton. Wine yield is 150 gallons per ton. The wine's retail price is $17.00 for a 750 ml bottle.

Labor performed by the owner. Total cost for the item and the amount performed by the owner are shown in the first two columns (Table 91). Economies of scale are built into the cost figures. The value of work performed by the owner is discounted to present worth as of July 1 at a rate of 6 percent. For labor, the weighted mid-point of the production year is December. Costs for administration and marketing are allocated and not specific to a crop year. Therefore, they are not discounted to obtain present worth.

TABLE 91   Value of Owner's Labor, Winery Only

	Cases	1,250	2,500	5,000			10,000	20,000
	Gallons	2,973	5,946	11,893			23,785	47,570
				Total	Performed by Owner	Percent		
Amounts per Gallon:								
Winemaking		2.9900	4.9833	1.1167	0.7817	60.0%	0.9082	0.5927
Administrative & O/H		0.0000	0.0000	0.1413	0.1271	75.0	0.0484	0.0242
Marketing		0.4565	0.7609	0.7119	0.4627	50.0%	0.4890	0.2168
Total Credits		**3.4465**	**5.7442**	**1.9698**	**1.3715**		**1.4456**	**0.8337**
Present worth, $/gal, at 6%		**6.7123**	**5.6011**	**1.9377**	**1.3491**		**0.8101**	**0.2966**
In dollars		**19,983**	**33,306**	**23,044**	**16,044**		**19,267**	**14,109**

Net profit is discounted to present worth over a period of 2.5 years, which is the average time from crush to sale. Economies of scale are already included in the amounts (Table 92).

TABLE 92   Net Profit from Operations, Winery Only

	Cases	1,250	2,500	5,000	10,000	20,000
	Gallons	2,973	5,946	11,893	23,785	47,570
Amounts per Gallon:						
Net profit		9.861	9.861	9.818	9.650	13.652
Present worth, $/gal, at 6%		**8.525**	**8.525**	**8.487**	**8.342**	**11.802**
In dollars		**23,345**	**50,689**	**100,933**	**198,415**	**561,402**

Again, **ROI** is placed at 10 percent of the equity invested in 50 percent of the equipment and development costs (Table 93).

Total income returned at each winery size, as well as the income needed, is summarized in Table 94.

The **minimum economic size winery** that produces the desired returns, determined from Figure 108, is **7,020 gallons**.

TABLE 93   **Return to Investment, Winery Only**

	Cases	1,250	2,500	5,000	10,000	20,000
	Gallons	2,973	5,946	11,893	23,785	47,570
Amounts per Gallon:						
Total equipment & development		34.6799	28.8999	33.2252	29.1272	36.3232
Equity investment @50%		17.3399	14.4499	16.6126	14.5636	18.1616
ROI needed @10%		**1.7340**	**1.4450**	**1.6613**	**1.4564**	**1.8162**
In dollars		**5,155**	**8,592**	**19,757**	**36,640**	**86,395**

TABLE 94   **Total Returns and Gallons Needed, Winery Only**

	Cases	1,250	2,500	5,000	10,000	20,000
	Gallons	2,973	5,946	11,893	23,785	47,570
Present worth dollar amounts:						
Owner credits		19,983	33,306	23,044	33,763	38,852
Profit		25,345	50,689	100,933	232,178	600,254
Total returns		45,328	83,995	123,978	246,878	617,744
ROI needed		5,155	8,592	19,757	34,640	86,395
Plus salary		82,956	82,956	82,956	82,956	82,956
Total return needed		88,142	91,579	102,743	117,626	169,381
Multiplier		1.9445	1.0903	0.8287	0.5066	0.2822
Minimum gallons		**5,781**	**6,483**	**9,856**	**12,050**	**13,423**

The minimum economic size for the winery is also very sensitive to the retail bottle price of the wine. If we increase the retail price by $1 and $2 per bottle, the minimum winery sizes are

7,020 gallons @ $17.00/bottle

4,500 gallons @ $18.00/bottle

3,520 gallons @ $19.00/bottle

Integrated vineyard/winery

In order to evaluate the integrated vineyard/winery operation, the **vineyard brackets have to be adjusted** (Table 95) so that vineyard output is synchronized with the winery's production.

TABLE 95   **Synchronization of Production Volumes, Integrated Operation**

	Cases	2,500	5,000	10,000
	Gallons	5,946	11,893	23,785
Tons of grapes at 150 gallons/ton:				
Grape tons		39.6	79.3	158.6
Vineyard acres at 4 tons/acre:				
Net acres		9.9	19.8	39.6

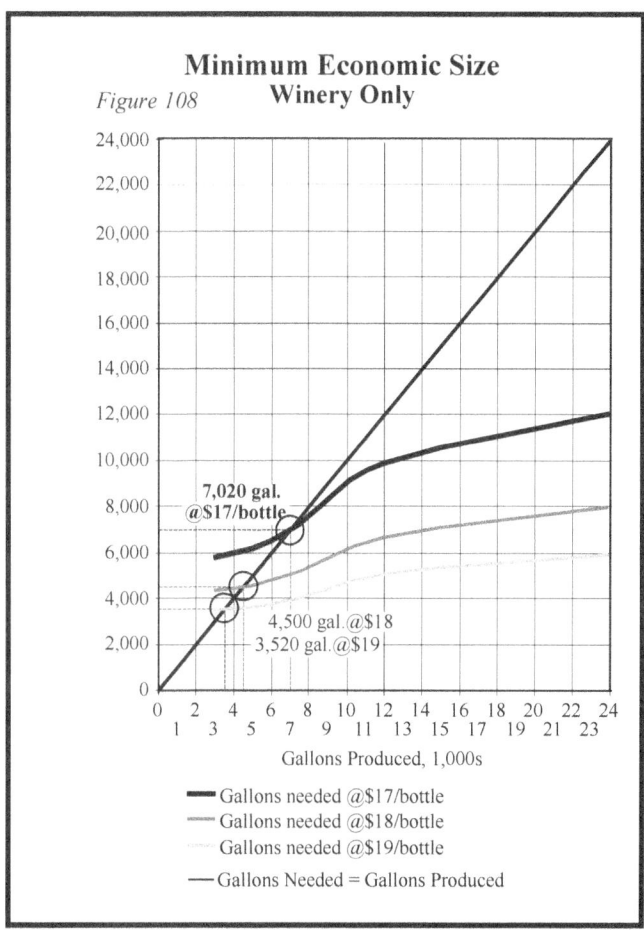

Minimum Economic Size

Figure 108   **Winery Only**

7,020 gal.
@$17/bottle

4,500 gal.@$18
3,520 gal.@$19

Gallons Produced, 1,000s

━━ Gallons needed @$17/bottle
── Gallons needed @$18/bottle
‥‥ Gallons needed @$19/bottle
── Gallons Needed = Gallons Produced

Further, the grape price is assumed at $1,700 per ton, as it was for the independent grower analysis. The wine's retail shelf price is set at $17.00 per 750 ml bottle, based on a bottle price multiplier (BPM) of 100.

20–30 years ago, a BPM of 100 represented a fair balance of winery and grower returns on the West Coast. Indeed, a BPM of 100 was used extensively for setting prices in grower contracts, particularly in California. In the course of reviewing current wine and grape pricing for this analysis, however, it is apparent that values of 85–90 percent are now typical of actual market conditions in other parts of America.

Owner labor savings

The winemaker-owner cannot expect to maintain the same level of effort in the parts of an integrated operation as he/she would have been able to do with either the vineyard or winery as separate ownerships. Net profit and ROI are unaffected by this adjustment. Further, the $80,000 threshold salary ($96,000 with payroll taxes and benefits) is earned only once in the integrated operation.

After applying the required adjustments, income and necessary income are summarized in Table 96 as follows:

TABLE 96   Returns and Minimum Gallons Needed, Integrated Operation

	Cases	2,500	5,000	10,000
	Gallons	**5,946**	**11,893**	**23,785**
	Net Acres	**9.9**	**19.8**	**39.6**
Present worth dollar amounts:				
Credits for Owner labor				
Winery		77,334	118,217	222,049
Vineyard		30,143	57,733	112,809
Net profit				
Winery		77,334	118,217	222,049
Vineyard		30,134	57,733	112,809
Total returns		107,468	175,949	334,858
ROI needed				
Winery		7,428	17,078	29,944
Vineyard		4,677	9,087	17,646
Plus salary, present worth		93,243	93,243	93,243
Total return needed		105,348	119,409	140,834
Multiplier		0.980	0.679	0.421
Minimum gallons		**5,829**	**8,071**	**10,003**

The resulting minimum economic size for the integrated winery, scaled from Figure 109, is:

> 5,840 Gallons
>
> 2,455 Cases
>
> 9.7 Net Acres
>
> 11.0 Gross Acres

The sensitivity to retail price of the wine is calculated by adding $1 and $2 per bottle:

Bottle Price	Gallons	Cases	Net Acres	Gross Acres
$17	5,840	2,465	9.7	11.0
$18	4,760	2,001	7.9	9.0
$19	4,050	1,703	6.8	7.6

The gallonage at each price is as accurate as the methodology permits.

Warehouse winery

A new phenomenon has developed over the past 20 years. Rather than being limited to siting wineries at vineyards, a significant number of entrepreneurs have developed wineries in urban industrial and business parks.

Of necessity, most of these operations are small in scale. But, the conditions make a lot of economic sense. The wineries are usually in urban areas and have excellent access to wine consumers. The buildings come with all of the

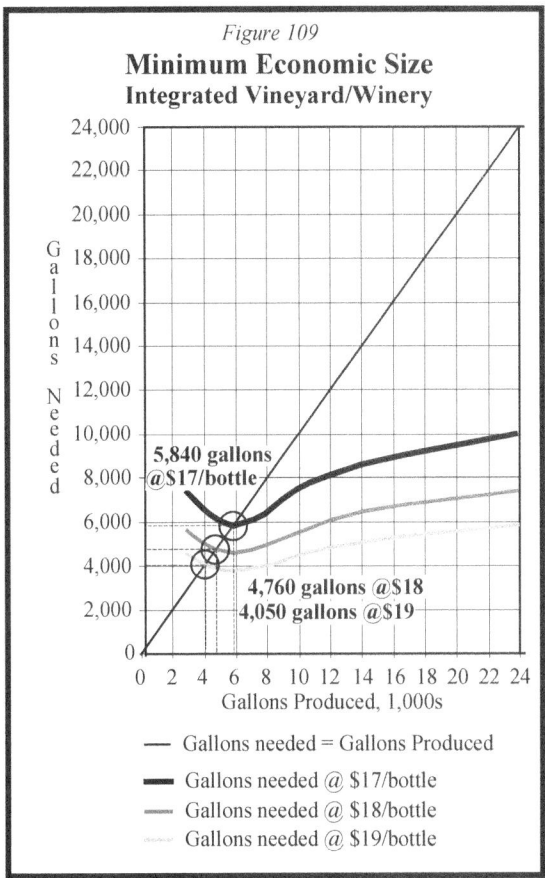

Figure 109
Minimum Economic Size
Integrated Vineyard/Winery

necessities . . . no need to drill a well for water, install an elaborate wastewater disposal system, run in a 3-phase 430-volt electrical supply or pave a large customer parking lot. Further, a lease is substituted for a large investment in building and grounds, which reduces the winery's need for capital among the startup costs. It even avoids the frequently onerous task of obtaining land use planning approvals.

Warehouse locations have served well as incubators for more ambitious entrepreneurs to take the operation through startup and a track record before having to raise capital for the jump to a vineyard location.

The example shown in Table 97's income statements is structured for a warehouse winery making 100 percent red wines in Washington's Puget Sound Area. The grapes are grown in the vicinity of the Horse Heaven Hills near Richland in the Columbia Valley AVA. The grape price of $2,450 per ton includes freight to the warehouse winery and is based on prices offered to small wineries. In general, prices reported in official Washington surveys are FOB vineyard and distorted downward by the purchasing leverage of Chateau Ste. Michelle/ Columbia Crest, who buy a majority of the state's vineyard production. The retail price of $21.00 is typical of premium red wines like Syrah and Cabernet Sauvignon made by small wineries in the area.

See Table 100 for the credit for owner labor.

TABLE 97　　Income Statements, Warehouse Winery Example

	2,500	5,000	10,000
Cases			
Gallons	5,946	11,893	23,785
Grapes, /ton	**2,475**	**2,475**	**2,475**
Yield, gallons/ton	150	150	150
Retail price/bottle	21.00	21.00	21.00
Retail markup %	30.0	30.0	28.0
Wholesale markup %	32.0	32.0	32.0
Tasting room sales %	80.0	70.0	50.0
Net revenues/gallon	**60.9419**	**59.6282**	**57.7211**
Revenues/case	144.95	141.83	137.29
Winery FOB/retail	*57.5%*	*56.3%*	*54.5%*
Grapes	16.5000	16.5000	16.5000
Labor	5.5928	3.8649	5.5479
Materials	7.4921	7.1516	6.8110
Rent & electric power	12.0059	8.8463	7.2612
Total direct costs	**41.5908**	**36.3627**	**36.1201**
Barrels	1.8022	1.8743	1.8923
Crush pad	0.0888	0.1122	0.1467
Tanks	0.2439	0.2505	0.2366
Pumps & filters	0.1256	0.1054	0.1050
Bottling line	0.0799	0.2775	0.2545
Refrigeration system	0.1183	0.0708	0.0509
Laboratory & other equipment	0.3086	0.0640	0.0338
Tasting room equipment	0.1183	0.0271	0.0327
Leasehold improvements	4.2043	2.1022	1.0511
Total depreciation	**7.0898**	**5.2697**	**4.0494**
Total production costs	**48.6806**	**41.6325**	**40.1695**
Gross margin	**12.2613**	**17.9957**	**17.5516**
% of Revenues	*20.1%*	*30.2%*	*30.4%*
Administration & O/H	0.0000	1.9979	1.4984
Marketing	0.8555	2.4498	3.6201
Interest	0.8670	0.9337	0.8423
Federal excise tax	0.17	0.17	0.17
Net profit b/income tax	**10.3688**	**12.4443**	**11.4208**
% of revenues	17.0%	20.9%	19.8%
Net profit/bottle	*2.06*	*2.47*	*2.26*
Production cycle, years	2.5	2.5	2.5
Revenues	54.2381	53.0689	57.3716
Costs	46.3405	43.2350	42.4253
Net profit (present worth @6%)	**7.8976**	**9.8339**	**8.9463**
Return on investment, ROI	*4.0%*	*8.2%*	*11.8%*
Average annual profit	*5.8%*	*7.4%*	*7.0%*
Net profit b/income tax	10.3688	12.4443	11.4208
Plus depreciation	7.0898	5.2697	4.0494
Plus interest	0.8670	0.9337	0.8423
Total cash flow	**18.3256**	**18.6477**	**16.3125**
Capitalized value/gallon @10%	183.26	186.48	163.13
Total Capitalized Value (2009 Dollars)	**544,800**	**1,108,800**	**1,940,000**

Net profit, again, is discounted by 6 percent annually over a 2.5-year period from crush to sale (see Table 98).

TABLE 98   Net Profit from Operations, Warehouse Winery

	Cases	1,250	2,500	5,000	10,000
	Gallons	2,973	5,946	11,893	23,785
Amounts per Gallon:					
Net profit		5.1844	10.3688	12.4443	11.4208
Present worth, $/gal, at 6%		**4.4816**	**8.9632**	**10.7573**	**9.8726**
In dollars		**13,324**	**53,298**	**127,932**	**234,820**

The **minimum return on investment (ROI)** is set at 10 percent of the equity invested in equipment plus $25,000 in leasehold improvements for the tasting room and office (Table 99).

TABLE 99   Return to Investment, Warehouse Winery

	Cases	1,250	2,500	5,000	10,000
	Gallons	2,973	5,946	11,893	23,785
Amounts per Gallon:					
Total equipment Cost		29.6340	24.6956	31.1231	28.0761
Leasehold improvements		5.0459	4.2043	2.1022	1.0511
Total capital investment		**34.6799**	**28.8999**	**33.2252**	**29.1272**
Equity investment @50%		17.3399	14.4499	16.6126	14.5636
ROI needed @10%		1.7340	1.4450	1.6613	1.4564
ROI discounted to PW @6%*		**1.4989**	**1.2491**	**1.4361**	**1.2589**
In dollars		**4,457**	**7,428**	**17,078**	**29,944**

*From time of sale of wine, 2.5 years.

Total income returned at each winery size, and the income needed, are summarized in Table 100.

TABLE 100   Total Returns and Minimum Gallons Needed, Warehouse Winery

	Cases	1,250	2,500	5,000	10,000
	Gallons	2,973	5,946	11,893	23,785
Present worth dollar amounts:					
Labor savings		8,710	26,516	16,468	22,649
Profit		13,324	53,298	127,932	234,820
Total returns		22,035	79,814	144,399	257,469
ROI needed		4,547	7,428	17,078	29,944
Plus salary		82,986	82,986	82,986	82,986
Total return needed		87,443	90,414	100,065	112,930
Multiplier		3.968	1.133	0.693	0.439
Minimum gallons		**11,799**	**6,736**	**8,241**	**10,433**

The minimum economic size winery that produces the desired returns, determined from Figure 110, is 6,790 gallons, or 2,855 cases.

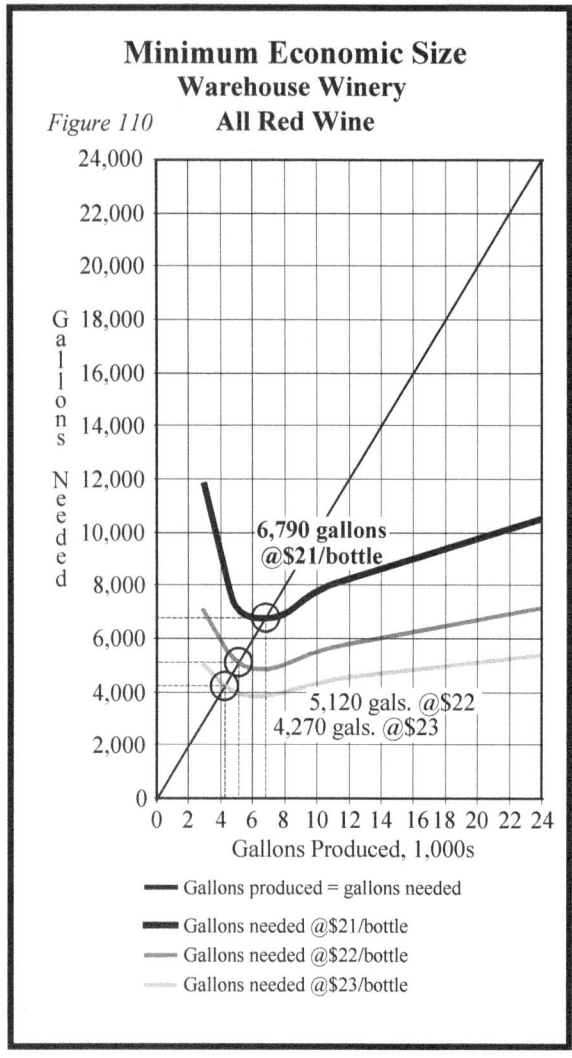

Sensitivity to the wine's retail price can be illustrated by increases of $1 and $2 per bottle.

Bottle Price	Gallons	Cases
$21	6,790	2,855
$22	5,120	2,153
$23	4,270	1,795

Recap of minimum economic sizes

The minimum economic size findings are recapitulated in Table 101. The apparent advantages presented by the Warehouse Winery are created by the exclusive offering of higher margin red wines, 100 percent self-distribution and improved customer access/visibility. Disadvantages are higher grape cost owing to transportation charges, and rent payments are larger than debt service would have been on an owned facility.

TABLE 101   Minimum Economic Size, Recap of Scenarios

	Winery Volume		Vineyard Acres	
	Gallons	Cases	Net	Gross
Vineyard only	—	—	36.3	40.8
Winery only	7,020	2,951	—	—
Integrated vineyard/winery	5,840	2,455	9.7	11.0
Warehouse winery	6,790	2,855	—	—

ഇൗരൂ

–17–

Where do you get the money?

Debt versus equity financing

If you are new to the world of finance, it's time to learn something. A lot of money is needed to start a vineyard or winery. **Debt financing** is money borrowed with the expectation of repayment (probably on a schedule) with **interest**. The lender will not loan you the money unless he/she is convinced that you will fulfill your obligation. Working capital loans, equipment financing, mortgages on buildings and trade credit are debt financing. So is accepting payment on credit cards in the tasting room, although the payback period is very short. You pay interest in the form of the credit card company's discount rate.

Why trade credit? If your supplier offers a discount for rapid payment, say 10 days, he is saying that you will pay interest if you take longer than 10 days.

Equity financing is the sale of partnerships or stock ownership to investors, who do not expect a return of their money on a schedule, but who forego interest in exchange for the expectation of higher returns in the form of **dividends and capital appreciation** over a longer period of time. Such investments entail much higher risk than simple loans, so the expected returns are higher.

Sources

It may come as a surprise to some that only a handful of wineries are financed by public stock offerings. The overwhelming majority are built with family money and other forms of ownership.

Here are the usual sources of capital:

- **Family money**, from inheritances, parents and siblings;
- **Personal wealth** earned in another line of work, like lawyers, doctors, stockbrokers, corporate executives and successful investors;
- **Friends** who are wealthy;
- **Other investors** through private placements of partnership interests or stock in limited quantities.

Like any new business enterprise, vineyard and winery projects require *venture capital,* also called *risk capital.* **Commercial banks** are not in the mix at this stage of vineyard/winery development because they do not exist to provide venture capital. Banks require a demonstrated track record and cash flow from the business that will repay a loan on time. A new vineyard/winery venture does not yet have an established stream of income. Bank borrowing will have to wait until the winery is established.

Institutional investors, such as pension funds, mutual funds, hedge funds, investment trusts and investment bankers also are generally not available sources for new vineyard/winery projects. To qualify for them, the developer would have to be a large, well-established business entity or someone who is considered to have a "slam dunk" prospect of success because of prominence and previous experience. Everyone else must look elsewhere. In general, a new vineyard/winery venture has too many unknowns and unpredictable variables for institutional investors to help by applying their usual expertise in management.

Farm Credit Bank

Formerly known as the "Federal Land Bank," the **Farm Credit Bank** is a federally chartered network of five regional banks and hundreds of retail businesses that exist to finance farm businesses, including processing facilities, in the form of long-term mortgages.

These associations are the contacts for borrowers:

- About 500 Federal Land Bank Associations (FLBA)—provide long-term mortgage credit for farmers to buy land and refinance debts.

- 9 Federal Land Credit Associations (FLCA)—long-term real estate and rural home mortgages only.

- 134 Production Credit Associations (PCA)—short- and intermediate-term loans for operating expenses, farm equipment, farm buildings and other capital improvements. Usually less than seven years in duration.

- More than 90 Agricultural Credit Associations (ACA)—short-, intermediate- and long-term loans to agricultural producers, rural homeowners and some agriculture-related businesses.

Borrowers from these associations must purchase ownership shares of the Bank amounting to 5 percent of the loan amount. The shares are cashed out when the loan is paid off.

Equipment loans

Tank manufacturers and distributors of other winery and vineyard equipment can direct the new vineyard/winery developer to sources of credit. In farm equipment there are manufacturer-related financing companies that are readily accessible to creditworthy buyers. Winery equipment dealers usually know of wealthy investors and other sources for equipment loans. Typical terms are 50–70 percent of the purchase price and seven to ten years duration. Some even offer lease-purchase agreements, which usually work out better for tax purposes.

Legal form of the business entity

You need to choose which legal entity form is best for your situation. Your attorney can help with this decision. Generally, a partnership or proprietorship form is best for the vineyard for tax reasons. The corporate form is usually best for the winery, for reasons of ownership structure, federal accounting requirements and liability protection.

Partnerships

A proprietorship is one owner. Partnerships are, simply put, two or more people with equal ownership in the vineyard or winery venture. One of them may be designated as *managing partner,* and admitted to the partnership at a lower initial investment than the others. As previously noted, the partnership form is usually of more use to vineyards than to wineries. Partnerships must use a *cash accounting system*, except for depreciation, where federal rules mandate the MACRS System. That means all costs incurred during the fiscal year, except for capital outlays, must be applied against revenues for income tax purposes. While that situation may be good for tax shelter benefits in the early years, it ends up in a walloping back-end tax problem.

The corporate form

The corporate form allows for multiple owners at different percentages of ownership, represented by the number of shares owned.

A corporation is usually funded by an Initial Public Offering (IPO) on the stock market, which is very expensive. Legal and underwriting fees are steep. But, as mentioned before, public ownership is rare in the wine industry. In most states, it is possible to do a limited private placement, not exceeding $1,000,000 of stock, without having to register it with the federal Securities and Exchange Commission. Shares are sold directly to people who can afford it. It is not unusual to set the share price at $20,000–30,000.

Federal regulations for wineries mandate that the *accrual method of accounting* be used. Essentially it is *job costing* when applied to production. All production costs are capitalized when incurred, then amortized against revenues when the wine is sold.

Subchapter S corporation

S corporations were created by the U.S. Congress to permit small business owners to use the corporate form for the protections it offers and the range of ownerships, and still be taxed as proprietorships. That is, the corporation is exempt from corporate income tax, although the shareholders still pay income tax on their dividends. To qualify for S corporation status, there must be no more than 35 owners. In an S corporation with a large per-share price, multiple owners of a single share each count as separate owners. For example, if Aunt Tillie and two of her friends partner up to buy one $25,000 share, they count as three owners.

Example of initial stock issue

As an example, a winery developer can raise $997,500 by selling 35 shares at $28,500 each and avoid SEC registration. Or, you could sell five shares at $199,000 each, totaling $995,000, or 99 shares at $10,000 each, totaling $990,000, and accomplish the same thing. The last alternative, 99 shares at $10,000 a share, would not be eligible for S corporation status, if it has more than 35 owners.

Someone who is qualified to be the winemaker and personally manage the business might take the $28,500/share route and keep some of the shares as his fee for developing the business enterprise.

	Shares	Percent of Total	Value
Winemaker organizing fee	10	29.4	$285,000
Net proceeds @$28,500 each	24	70.6	$684,000
Total issue @$28,500/share	34	100.0	$969,000

This funding, coupled with some equipment financing and able management, likely can be made to develop a 9,000–10,000 case winery that initially rents its facilities and buys all of its grapes, depending on the grape varieties and wine styles chosen, of course. Investment in a winery building and/or vineyard can be made later, even under a separate form of ownership and different owners. The corporation is eligible for S corporation treatment.

Choose your partners wisely

This is a warning to anyone who wishes to form a new winery or vineyard. Be careful to evaluate those who wish to invest in your project. There are ample stories around the wine industry about partners who decide to run the winery without the founding winemaker . . . after the hardship and grief of establishment are passed, of course. It seems there just are people who are motivated by opportunities to dominate and "take over" a business. It's like throwing a deer into the lions' cage . . . the takeover ambition appears to be instinctive for some.

And, then, there is another investor-related issue. The IRS regulations pertaining to *non-passive* expenditures are a financial incentive for owners who are otherwise unqualified to run a winery, to micromanage operations in an attempt to qualify extravagant lifestyle expenses as *non-passive* expenses. The winemaker or real manager has enough difficult things to do without having a quintessential 800-pound gorilla in his midst, "helping" with decisions and operations.

Make sure you don't serve yourself up as fodder for such swashbucklers.

The business plan

In order to communicate your vision and plans for the venture, you will need to write a business plan. There is a generally accepted format for such a document. The following is an outline for the business plan, modified to address characteristics of vineyard and winery ventures.

Make this document as attractive as possible but, most of all, it must be readily readable and understandable. Use graphics and photos to illustrate key points of the presentation. The winemaking business is a stranger to most investors and, although it is very enticing to many, it is not well understood by most. This is the place for the proposing winemaker to let his/her production and marketing expertise show through.

Business plan outline

1. Executive summary
2. Market analysis
   2.1 Wine industry growth trends (See Chapter 2)
   2.2 Projected growth
   2.3 Targeted market
   2.4 Production & lead time characteristics
   2.5 Profile of the competition
   2.6 Anticipated market share
   2.7 Regulatory issues (See Chapter 11)
3. Description of proposed vineyard/winery
   3.1 Site map
   3.2 Findings of independent vineyard site evaluation (See Chapter 3)
   3.3 Vineyard development plan (See Chapter 3)
   3.3 Plans for proposed winery facility (See Chapters 12 and 13)
   3.4 Off-premise tasting room
4. Organization and management
   4.1 Legal form, corporate versus partnership/proprietorship
   4.2 Organization chart (See Chapter 8)
   4.3 Licensing needed at federal and state levels (See Chapter 11)
   4.3 Key personnel: owners, general manager, winemaker, vineyard manager, marketing, accounting support. Background profiles as necessary. (See Chapter 18)
   4.4 Percentage of ownership retained by organizer.
   4.5 Board of directors—names and expertise, method of election

5.   Marketing & sales management (See Chapter 10)

    5.1   Marketing strategy, promotion and advertising

    5.2   Sales strategy—targeted market segments: restaurant, boutique wine shops, supermarkets, direct shipping, wine club

    5.2   Selling through distributors versus self-distribution

    5.3   Tasting room

    5.4   On-premise events

    5.5   Wine club and direct shipping

6.   Product mix

    6.1   Varieties to be produced (See Chapters 3, 14, 15 and 16))

    6.2   Wine styles

    6.3   Proposed price schedule

    6.4   Financial returns for each product

7.   Pro forma financial projections (See Chapters 6 and 14)

    7.1   Depreciation methods

    7.2   Income statements, cash flow statements, first ten years

    7.3   Balance sheets at key points

    7.4   Tax shelter aspects

8.   Requested funding (See Chapters 6, 14 and 17)

    8.1   Financial instruments—stock, partnership interest.

    8.2   Private placement versus registered public stock offering

    8.2   Common shares, preferred shares, long-term loans

9.   Appendix

    9.1   Credit history of proposer

    9.2   Resumes of key personnel

    9.3   Names of attorney, accountant, consultants

    9.3   Professional vineyard site evaluation report

    9.4   Preliminary winery development plan

In presentations to prospective investors, some convincing points need to be made:

1. The proposed business is capable of earning enough money to execute the business plan and make attractive returns to the shareholders;

2. You will be a good, compatible partner in the business venture;

3. You are capable, professionally and business-wise, to make it all work;

4. The high public profile that you will create for marketing purposes is compatible with the ego expectations of your investors.

Further reading

Farm Credit System. Website: http://www.farmcreditnetwork.com

Small Business Administration. *Create Your Business Plan.* Website: https://www.sba.gov/writing-business-plan

Smiley, Robert, and Kelly Grogan. "Global Recession Effects on the Wine Industry," *Practical Winery & Vineyard Journal* (November–December 2009), 51–61.

‮ℰℰ‭

—18—

Management, and expertise of the owner

The person who is contemplating the purchase of an existing winery, or development of a new one, stands at a crossroads. This is the point in time when decisions have the greatest impact on the future success of the winery. It is the best time to decide what the winery will produce, what equipment and facilities will be needed to produce it, what roles the owner and winemaker will play in the operation and who will be the winemaker. This is the last time such decisions can be made free of the taint of such influences as empathy for employees, competition with them for the spotlight and money already sunk in the operation with uncertain results.

In preceding chapters, we explored the realities of assuming winery ownership; the importance of securing high quality grapes; the crucial and pivotal role of the winemaker; the recordkeeping function; marketing; equipment; and financial considerations. In this chapter, we discuss the crucial role of the owners.

Are you suited for the challenge?

We have already mentioned how important it is to have the right person as the winemaker. Now, it's time for an owner's "gut check." Of course, we live in America and anyone who can find the money and pass the FBI's background check can get into the winemaking business. Even though you may feel it is none of their business, many people will pass judgment on whether or not this is where you belong. Competitors, wine writers, distributors, retailers, customers, your employees, your neighbors and even your friends, in time, all will render judgment on your ability to perform in the wine business.

Expertise of the owner

In the vineyard. Knowledge about the workings of the agricultural part of the wine business is essential to an understanding of the winery. The smaller the operation, the more important this relationship becomes. Without vineyard knowledge, the owner really is unable to comprehend the long-term implications of actions taken in the vineyard. If the objective is to improve wine quality, the vineyard is usually the first place to start looking for answers.

Where's another good place to start? *Vineyard & Winery Management* and *Wine Business Monthly* magazines will help. Many local growers have found *An Oregon Winegrape Grower's Guide* to be helpful. For advanced folks, the definitive text is *General Viticulture*, although much has been discovered since its writing. That's why those trade magazines are so important. Presentations by viticulture programs at colleges and cooperative extension services are very technical and academic, and will be specifically applicable to your climate.

For a wonderfully entertaining, and even technical, discourse on all of the grape varieties grown anywhere in the world, and the wines made from them, you cannot beat Jancis Robinson's *Vines, Grapes and Wines*.

You can purchase any of these texts through chain bookstores.

Wine production. Of course, anyone involved in an ownership position with a winery will benefit from a technical acquaintance with winery operations. Only then can you understand the relationships between investment and wine quality; why French barrels are important; why good crush pad and bottling equipment are necessary for wine quality; why it costs more to make one wine than another.

The same two trade magazines are good for learning about winery operations. Two technical texts dominate. The UC-Davis tome is *Table Wines*. A much more concise, usable and less academic book is *Knowing & Making Wine*.

University of California-Davis offers many short courses (one to five days) on winemaking, general and specific. Some other universities and colleges offer very helpful seminars on specific aspects of winemaking. They are highly technical and geared for the professional winemaker.

Marketing. Where the owner fits into the marketing work depends on the owner's abilities. Good wine knowledge and entertaining presentation go a long way in enabling an owner to help the marketing effort. So does the ability to work with distributors in a way that recognizes they have to make money for you to make money, and they hold all the face cards.

The purchaser of an existing winery should make an objective assessment of the strength of the winery's marketing program. How strong is it? Does the winery have good distributors who are getting the job done? Is the winery's sales manager effective? Does the winery have good relations with the wine media? Is the tasting room operation as productive as it can be? Is the price schedule where it should be?

If you plan to do **winemaker dinners**, here are six simple rules, the "Six A's" to achieve success and avoid embarrassment:

1. **A**rrive knowing which wines are being served.
2. **A**cknowledge that most dinner guests would rather hear from the wine-maker than the owner, since that's who they thought they were getting. If you occupy both positions, disregard this rule.
3. **A**bort your presentation gracefully when your audience is giving off vibes that they want you to shut up so they can get on with eating.
4. **A**nticipate that there's at least one wine geek present who has dedicated the evening to making a monkey out of you.
5. **A**void drinking more wine than your audience.
6. **A**lways make a hero out of the chef.

The wine cognoscenti can be tough on winery people . . . and sometimes ignorant. Within two months of the author's departure from one winery, a wine geek told a friend of his that "the wines have improved already." That sorry excuse for a wine snob knew too little about wine to realize that he'd still be pulling the corks on the author's wines, not his successor's, for the next two years.

Finance. This is your undisputed realm. Except, of course, you have to deal with your accountants. It is you who will have the challenge of convincing your banker that *your* piece of the wine business is worthy of getting in bed with . . . er, so to speak.

There are plenty of financing entities, eager to help with your equipment. Most of them are in California, where vineyards and wineries are viewed as real businesses by lending institutions. One California financing firm offers a credit card to use for acquiring equipment under their leasing program.

Commitment to quality

Commitment to success for the right reasons is essential in the winemaking business. Those "right reasons," in today's wine industry environment include quality, consistency of product, good working relations with competitors and suppliers and profit. One would hope, too, that today's enlightened winery owners also would establish a good working environment for employees.

"Commitment" means a willingness to see long-term strategies for product improvement through to their conclusions, and to spend the funds necessary for achieving those goals. Notice that pursuit of the highest possible product quality is not included among the list of essentials for all wineries. That's because production of average quality, affordable, everyday wines is also an honorable objective, indeed a marketplace necessity. It's a fact: more than 75 percent of the wine consumed by Americans is "jug" or "standard" in quality, sometimes called "generic."

The rest, which includes most wines made by new wineries, are made in pursuit of the Holy Grail. For those wineries who hold themselves out to be makers of "premium," "boutique," "superpremium" or "estate" wines, nothing less is demanded than maniacal dedication to production of the most exquisite wines possible.

There are two kinds of "quality":

1. One describes a clean wine (no hazes or particulate), without flaws like off-flavors, unpleasant aromas, excessively high or low acidity, high residual sugar not balanced with acidity, "volatile acidity" (acetic acid, acetaldehyde, and hydrogen sulfide) or "hot" (excessively high) alcohol. All wines should meet these basic standards.

2. The other type of "quality" encompasses all requirements of the first type and goes further by including pursuit of a varietal ideal. It relates to trueness to varietal character, reflection of growing site nuances (terroir), concentration (or intensity), depth, complexity and length on the palate. These are the standards for premium and superpremium wines.

Further reading

Amerine, M.A., and M.A. Joslyn. *Table Wines*. 2nd ed. Berkeley: University of California Press, 1970.

Casteel, Ted. *Oregon Winegrape Growers Guide*. 4th ed. Portland, OR: Oregon Winegrowers Association, 1992.

Peynaud, Emile. *Knowing and Making Wine*. New York: J. Wiley, 1984. Peynaud was France's dean of enologists.

Practical Winery & Vineyard Journal. Website: http://www.practicalwinery.com/

Robinson, Jancis. *Vines, Grapes and Wines*. New York: Alfred A. Knopf, 1986.

Vineyard and Winery Management Magazine. Website: http://www.vwmmedia.com/

Wine Business Monthly magazine. Website: http://www.winebusiness.com/wbm/

Wines & Vines magazine. Website: http://www.winesandvines.com/

Winkler, A.J., J.A. Cook, W.M. Kliewer, and L.A. Lider. *General Viticulture*. Rev. and enlarged ed. Berkeley: University of California Press, 1974.

A case study: Grand Eagle Estate Winery management meeting

Are you familiar with the "Harvard Business School case study" method of learning in the seminar environment? No, the author didn't go to Harvard, but the process is a winner. It entails the presentation of a hypothetical business case—a set of conditions and people in a business situation. Cases usually have their genesis in a real company's history, but the names may be fictional. Students discuss actions and remedies to resolve the challenges presented by the case.

So, here's a fictional case for you to ponder with your wine-loving friends. (Any similarity to actual wineries or their personnel in Oregon or elsewhere is purely coincidental.)

CAST OF CHARACTERS	
Rex LeGrande	owner
Dudley Brunnez	accountant
Gianni Tuscanini	wine broker/consultant
Huxley Vendor	vineyard consultant/supplier
Barry Batchelor	sales manager
Henri Vigneron	winemaker
Derek Farmer	vineyard manager
Grand Eagle Estate	the winery

Picture this hypothetical management meeting. Winery owner, Rex LeGrande—who has no expertise in the wine business—ask his accountant to arrange the meeting. Gathered around the conference table are three people besides Rex: Dudley Brunnez (his trusty accountant, who is an ace with computer spreadsheets and appears to be loyal to a fault in support of the owner, but is suspected of being a crafty behind-the-scenes manipulator and sycophant), Gianni Tuscanini (the winery's broker from the Midwest—a glib fellow in a silk shirt with a great line of patter relating to the romance of wine, who claims to move 125,000 cases of wine annually into Chicago, almost all of it for other wineries, of course), and Huxley Vendor (Rex's independent vineyard consultant, who also sells vineyard chemicals, vineyard management services and advice to the winery).

The four are tasting a pre-bottling sample of the barrel-selected Pinot that will be called *Oregon's Best Reserve 2002 Pinot Noir.*

Rex (the owner) says: "This is outstanding. Dudley, how much of this wine will we have to sell?"

Dudley (the accountant) replies: "Well, it isn't bottled yet, and we'll have to deduct the 90 cases you'll want to give to your friends for Christmas. Then, there's the 25 cases for the Unwed Mothers Charity Auction." Then, Dudley swallows hard and proceeds tentatively, almost in a whisper, "Uh, Boss, you'll probably want the usual 30–35 cases for your home wine cellar. That leaves about 650 cases for the market. Oh, and we'll go through about 50 cases of that for promotional tastings."

Gianni (the broker): His attention focused on his prospective commissions, bolts upright and declares, "Is that all? I can move at least 4,000 cases of that wine in Chicago and Milwaukee . . . at $39.95 retail . . . no post-offs. I've already promised 3,000 cases to distributors."

Rex: "Our winemaker, Henri, told me this is all he could put together that was good enough to be called *Oregon's Best Reserve.* Remember, it was a poor year. Huxley, is there anything we should be doing in the vineyard to increase our production of *Oregon's Best Reserve*?"

Huxley (the consultant) replies: "Well, Rex, we talked about this last year. You need to hedge more . . . I can sell you a hedging rig with all the right adjustment features for $21,000. Then, I can bring my leaf-pulling crew in for a few days after veraison, cost you about $3,600. Also, we can increase the yields to 4.5 tons next year by leaving more buds at pruning."

He continues, "Rex, I want to bring up something about this wine label that really upsets the winemakers over the county line. For what it's worth, they don't think you've earned the right to call this wine 'Oregon's *Best* Reserve.' They maintain that you can't just make a claim like that on a wine label. It's too cheeky. Maybe you can label a beer or whiskey that way, but not wine. I hear they're going to file a protest with TTB claiming it's a prohibited untrue claim"

Rex: Obviously irritated and pounding the table, "Well, you can just leave this meeting and not come back. I don't give a damn what those guys are saying!"

Huxley, somewhat chagrined, responds: "I only mentioned it because they're doing a real job on you with the wine writers, sommeliers and retailers. They even have wine writers referring to you as the proprietor of 'Grand **Ego** Estate Winery.' I think it's hurting your sales."

With that said, Huxley closes his briefcase and leaves the building. He knows Rex will probably call in a few days and act like the confrontation never happed.

Rex, shrugging off Huxley's departure, continues: "What does Derek (the vineyard manager) say? By the way, where is he?"

Dudley: "He's out in the vineyard. We don't need him for this. He says he's already doing everything necessary with that old hedging rig. I told him to cut back on the hedging to save you some money, Boss. I don't believe what Derek says about the benefits of hedging anyway."

Gianni: "How much of that non-reserve Pinot do we have? That was tolerable when we tasted a couple of barrels last month."

Dudley: "200 barrels, 12,000 gallons, about 5,000 cases."

Gianni: "That'll do it! Let's blend in 2,400 cases of that with the 800 cases and call it all *Oregon's Best Reserve*. Then, I can make my distributor commitments."

Rex: "What does Henri (the winemaker) think about this idea? By the way, where is Henri? And, where the heck is Barry (the sales manager)?"

Dudley: "Do you remember the last time we talked about dropping the standards for reserve wines? Henri said he'd quit if we did something like that. He doesn't think we should compromise our standards on reserve wines or the market will lose respect for *all* our wines. That's why I didn't invite him. He's down in the barrel cellar. We don't need to hear from him, anyway. Barry is on that sales call you set up with your close friend who owns the Hot Dog Emporium. I thought that was more important and he doesn't get along with Gianni, anyway. So, I didn't tell him about our meeting. By the way, the *Oregon's Best Reserve Pinot* brings twice as much profit as the regular stuff. That's about $100,000 more in your pocket, Rex."

Gianni, checking the trim on his fingernails: "Those French guys are too fussy anyway. They need to chill out."

Rex: "Good, good, good! It's time to wrap this up. Here's what we're going to do . . . ."

Well, dear reader, assume you are Rex. What action would you take? Here are a few questions to get you started.

- What would you do with Gianni's proposal to blend 2,400 cases of "average" Pinot Noir with the winemaker's selection of 800 cases for the reserve wine, in order to satisfy market demand?

- What do you think of Dudley's dismissal of the importance of bringing the sales manager, winemaker and vineyard manager into the discussion? Do you feel the same as Dudley about their knowledge, relevance, or lack of same?

- What do you think of Huxley's suggestion to leave more buds at next winter's pruning?

- In your opinion, what price will the "blended down" reserve Pinot Noir bring on the shelf? Will Midwest consumers snap it up at $39.95 a bottle? Do you think it really will bring an extra $100,000 profit for the winery, as Dudley has projected?

- How do you feel about the designation "Oregon's Best Reserve"?
- What do you think about the sales call on the Hot Dog Emporium? Is that a good prospect for wine sales?
- What do you think of Rex's management style?

ജ‍ൟ

Appendix A

Economic setting

The values expressed in this book represent mid-2014 levels.

At the time of this writing, the world is still experiencing the effects of an economic recession, and certain factors have an unusual influence on some winery and vineyard costs. Among them are:

1. Prices of fuel and agricultural chemicals are related to petroleum prices. Let's use gasoline prices as an example. Having just passed through a period of historically high prices over $4/gallon, prices have dropped to the as low as $2.00/gallon. The price situation can be described as "volatile" and should be expected to remain unstable into the near future.

2. Prices for steel, particularly stainless steel, have been at historic highs owing largely to two factors: (1) China has placed a very high demand on steel products because of their own economic expansion and (2) high labor costs have driven American steel production to other countries. Further, China is a major nickel producer and has been consuming 70 percent of the world's nickel supply. Without nickel, there is no stainless steel. So, prices for tanks, presses, filters, pumps and bottling equipment have risen dramatically. Demand for stainless steel remains strong owing to historically low, government-subsidized interest rates, which favor investment in fixed assets. China should not be ignored. They should be expected to continue their *hell-bent-for-leather* expansion of production.

3. Many agricultural economists render vineyard production pro forma operating statements, i.e., enterprise budgets, without disclosing the date to which the figures relate. Even more aggravating is the presentation of such statements to the public when they are so badly out of date that they are worse than no cost information at all.

4. The Federal Treasury diluted the money supply for seven years by a tactic they called "quantitative easing." Call it what you want, it was still artificial and intended to monetize the debt. That is, to repay the national debt with dollars of less value than they were when the debt was incurred.

   There's another effect of this dilution: inflation. Although the effect may be delayed, it will happen, driving up the real costs of construction, equipment and material for the wine industry.

5. The government's monetary policy has a considerable effect on interest rates. Banks are able to borrow funds at almost zero cost. For that reason, the financial analyses in this book is based on the rates below. (When the government returns to more normal money supply policies associated with a healthy economy, those rates should return to more normal levels, such as 6.0 percent, 6.5 percent, and 13.0 percent, respectively.)

Working capital and other short-term loans	4.5%
Discount rate for present worth calculations	6.0%
Capitalization rate for income property values	10.0%

To rectify this situation, price and cost rates that relate to the value of these estimates are given below. This is not a perfect solution, primarily because most of the new winery equipment purchased in America (except tanks) is built in Europe. But this data should enable those capable of doing so to adjust this book's costs to approximate the current levels. The numbers shown in parentheses in Table 102 are the product class numbers for the Producer Price Index, or other index, prepared by the Federal Bureau of Labor Statistics. PPIs are projected forward to mid-2014 values.

TABLE 102   **Producer Price and Other Indices**

Consumer Price Index (CPI), US City, adjusted	234.7
European euro	$1.35 USD
Nickel, London Metal Exchange, $USD/tonne	$13,750 USD
Producer price indices:	
Relating to vineyard development	
Treated wood & contract preserving (198506)	214.8
Preserved wood posts (3211141)	266.6
Wire & spring products (200312)	160.8
Farm machinery & equipment (333111)	207.5
Wheel tractors & attachments (3331111)	128.5
Relating to vineyard operation	
Bunker 2 diesel fuel (7303)	346.2
Agricultural chemicals (WPS065)	256.4
Pesticide & other farm chemicals (32532)	133.1
Relating to winery construction	
New industrial building construction (236211)	139.7
New warehouse building construction (NAICS236221)	139.7
New office building construction (PCU236223)	122.6
Concrete contractors, non-residential (PCU23811X)	108.0
Turner Construction Index	878.0
Relating to winery equipment	
Metal tanks fabricated at factory (332420E)	337.5
Custom tanks fabricated at factory & field erected (332420G)	191.6
Other plastic products (32619)	136.0
Industrial food production machinery (333241)	248.3
AC refrigeration compressor units (33341)	138.3
Analytical laboratory instruments (3345160)	145.0
Industrial trucks and stackers (33395421)	153.0
Relating to winery operation	
Electric power generation & transmission (2211)	127.7
Industrial electricity price, cents/kwhr (USEIA)	6.5
Electric power generation (221110)	100.2
Wineries (312130)	169.4
Glass containers (WPS138101)	194.7
Beverage manufacturing (312130)	169.4

Appendix B

Wage rates and power costs

Table 103 details the wage rates used for winery and vineyard employees, administrative and marketing personnel, and electric power costs.

TABLE 103 Wage Rates and Power Costs Used for Financial Analyses in 2014 Dollars

Location	Winery		Laborer	Vineyard Manager	Administrative Support	Sales Representatives	Power Cost		Season Degree-days
	Winemaker	Cellar Worker					Cents/kwhr*	$/bottle**	
Columbia Valley, WA	114,743	60,965	14.90	70,045	70,045	123,471	4.36	0.0733	2,826
Willamette Valley, OR	103,693	54,890	13.42	68,083	68,083	111,635	6.10	0.0600	2,370
Southern Oregon	100,564	58,852	14.38	56,490	56,490	94,150	6.10	0.0600	2,267
Snake River Valley, ID	96,840	58,746	14.36	67,250	67,250	80,700	6.95	0.0743	3,020
Sonoma Valley, CA	137,426	56,792	13.88	80,118	80,118	133,155	12.01	0.1533	3,034
Central Coast, CA	130,666	47,863	11.70	68,135	68,135	125,958	12.01	0.1533	3,019
Sonoita, AZ	92,966	47,521	12.41	56,813	56,813	69,725	7.47	0.1642	4,285
Grand Valley, CO	104,587	56,802	14.46	58,104	58,104	72,307	7.72	0.1123	3,593
Texas Hill Country	96,840	55,636	14.16	72,307	72,307	92,966	6.27	0.1989	5,248
Central Missouri	96,840	78,914	20.09	69,725	69,725	77,472	7.47	0.1059	3,679
Shawnee Hills, IL	92,966	46,304	11.79	58,104	58,104	61,978	5.76	0.1397	3,605
Leelanau Peninsula, MI	98,185	51,456	12.58	69,940	69,940	80,700	8.23	0.0824	2,269
Ohio River Valley	94,150	65,508	16.01	64,560	64,560	73,975	6.22	0.1155	3,212
Lake Erie	94,150	55,576	13.58	49,085	49,085	69,940	7.20	0.1128	2,420
Finger Lakes, NY	102,893	58,165	14.22	73,975	73,975	105,919	5.10	0.1124	2,255
Lancaster Valley, PA	96,840	68,044	16.63	67,250	67,250	71,285	7.20	0.1128	3,174
New England	91,047	47,546	11.62	50,620	50,620	82,045	14.54	0.1325	2,162
Piedmont Plateau, MD	110,290	64,188	15.69	73,975	73,975	94,150	8.42	0.2109	3,856
Blue Ridge, VA	98,777	69,633	17.73	67,067	67,067	90,384	6.71	0.1427	3,829
Yadkin Valley, NC	92,966	55,838	14.22	61,978	61,978	71,016	6.83	0.1091	3,552

Notes: Wage and labor costs include payroll taxes, fringe benefits and bonuses, where applicable.

*August, 2013. U.S. Energy Information Administration.

**Projected to mid-2014.

Procedures for titration of total acidity using a pH meter

The three measurements that are universal to all wines are sugar, pH and titratable acidity.

- **Sugar content** of juice is easily measured using a *refractometer* or *hydrometer*. Once there is some alcohol present, an accurate measurement is more difficult to obtain, but it may be approximated by using a hydrometer. A more accurate measurement can be made by using the Gold Coast method.

- **pH** is obtained directly by using a *pH meter*.

- **Titratable acidity**, or total acidity, is measured by the process of *acid titration*, where the acid level is determined by measuring how much sodium hydroxide (NaOH) is needed to bring the solution to neutral pH (8.0–8.2). The procedure is detailed after the equipment and supplies list below.

Equipment and supplies

50-ml burette with stopcock, mounted on a burette stand

0.1 Normal sodium hydroxide solution

Bench pH meter with probe

250-ml Pyrex beaker

Hotplate/stirrer

Teflon-coated stir bar

10-ml volumetric pipette

Sample of juice or wine to be tested

Procedure

1. **Calibrate.** If your pH meter hasn't been calibrated recently, now is a good time to do it. Follow manufacturer's directions. You will need fresh buffer solutions of 4 pH and 7 pH.

2. **Neutralize test solution.** Put about 25–50 ml of distilled water in the beaker. Use hotplate to bring temperature to 68°F, using magnetic stir bar. (If your pH meter is self-adjusting for temperature, this adjustment of the test solution temperature is unnecessary.) Add about 5 ml of juice or wine to the solution. Add NaOH (burette) to the solution to bring its pH to neutral, 8.0–8.2 pH. The reason for specifying a range is that a solution's pH becomes extremely sensitive to NaOH as the pH nears neutrality. One drop of NaOH can move the pH almost 0.2.

3. **Record NaOH level** from burette.

4. **Add juice or wine to be tested.** Add 10 ml to the test solution, using the 10-ml pipette.

5. **Titrate the solution.** Add NaOH from the burette. Proceed slowly as the solution approaches 8.0 pH.

6. **Record levels.** When the test solution reads 8.0–8.2 pH, record the NaOH level from the burette.

7. **Calculate.** Subtract beginning NaOH volume from ending level. Multiply the difference (the volume of NaOH that was required to neutralize the solution) by 0.075, or refer to Table 104 for the titratable acidity in 100 grams/100 ml. Multiply this figure by ten to obtain grams/liter.

8. **Repeat.** Additional samples may be tested using the ending solution from the previous test as the starting point. It's already at neutral pH. Just add the next 10-ml sample and begin titrating.

9. **Clean equipment.**

TABLE 104   Reference Chart for Acid Titration

Sodium Hydroxide 0.1 N	Total Acidity g/100 ml	Sodium Hydroxide 0.1 N	Total Acidity g/100 ml	Sodium Hydroxide 0.1 N	Total Acidity g/100 ml
6.0	0.450	10.0	0.750	14.0	1.050
6.1	0.458	10.1	0.758	14.1	1.058
6.2	0.465	10.2	0.765	14.2	1.065
6.3	0.473	10.3	0.773	14.3	1.073
6.4	0.480	10.4	0.780	14.4	1.080
6.5	0.488	10.5	0.788	14.5	1.088
6.6	0.495	10.6	0.795	14.6	1.096
6.7	0.503	10.7	0.803	14.7	1.103
6.8	0.510	10.8	0.810	14.8	1.110
6.9	0.518	10.9	0.818	14.9	1.118
7.0	0.525	11.0	0.825	14.0	1.125
7.1	0.533	11.1	0.833	15.1	1.133
7.2	0.540	11.2	0.840	15.2	1.140
7.3	0.548	11.3	0.848	15.3	1.148
7.4	0.555	11.4	0.855	15.4	1.155
7.5	0.563	11.5	0.863	15.5	1.163
7.6	0.570	11.6	0.870	15.6	1.170
7.7	0.578	11.7	0.878	15.7	1.178
7.8	0.585	11.8	0.885	15.8	1.185
7.9	0.593	11.9	0.893	15.9	1.193
8.0	0.600	12.0	0.900	16.0	1.200
8.1	0.608	12.1	0.908	16.1	1.208
8.2	0.615	12.2	0.915	16.2	1.215
8.3	0.623	12.3	0.923	16.3	1.223
8.4	0.630	12.4	0.930	16.4	1.230
8.5	0.638	12.5	0.938	16.5	1.238
8.6	0.645	12.6	0.945	16.6	1.245
8.7	0.653	12.7	0.953	16.7	1.253
8.8	0.660	12.8	0.960	16.8	1.260
8.9	0.668	12.9	0.968	16.9	1.268
9.0	0.675	13.0	0.975	17.0	1.275
9.1	0.683	13.1	0.983	17.1	1.283
9.2	0.690	13.2	0.990	17.2	1.290
9.3	0.698	13.3	0.998	17.3	1.298
9.4	0.705	13.4	1.005	17.4	1.305
9.5	0.713	13.5	1.013	17.5	1.313
9.6	0.720	13.6	1.020	17.6	1.320
9.7	0.728	13.7	1.028	17.7	1.328
9.8	0.735	13.8	1.035	17.8	1.335
9.9	0.743	13.9	1.043	17.9	1.353

Note: Total acidity = NaOH × 0.075

Source: The Business of Winemaking, Jeffrey L. Lamy, MS. Wine Appreciation Guild, 2014.

Jeffrey L. Lamy

1938–2014

Jeff Lamy's interest in wine began in 1972 as a hobby. As his knowledge of the field grew, his role evolved to winemaker, consultant and finally a known authority.

Jeff earned degrees in Industrial Administration, Mechanical Engineering and Business Management (MS) from Yale and the University of Idaho. Winery development became his second career; it spanned over 42 years of his life and he loved it, second only to his family.

As a consultant, Jeff evaluated vineyard sites, designed wineries, trained and guided new winery owners and their employees, and helped many make their own wines. During 1982–86, he taught courses in vineyard development and management; winemaking; and winery management at Portland College. He was a popular guest lecturer/featured speaker at universities, wine symposia, professional and business associations, radio and TV shows, and public hearings before legislative committees. Jeff tirelessly promoted Oregon wines and wineries.

Jeff was an accomplished winemaker. As general manager and winemaker, he took Oregon's then largest vineyard-winery project (Montinore Vineyards, 400+ acres) from feasibility study to national prominence.

Jeff always had a significant interest in books and learning and he wrote for several wine publications. He was extremely proud of his work on this book and the title "Author." Unfortunately, in May of 2014, he passed away just after finishing final updates on the manuscript.

It took a lot of hard work. Frequently, his family would describe his whereabouts as "he's working on the book" or "Dad's on his computer (working on the book)," but they had no idea how much work, professionalism and tenacity he devoted until he passed away and they finally read what he had written. Due to Guillain-Barre Syndrome, Jeff had only 30% of the use of his hands, he was in a wheelchair and his computer was slow, yet he worked tirelessly to complete the book and its final updates.

The Lamy family, Judy, Chris, Ann and Michelle, are very proud to honor Jeff in the final publication process.

Index

The Wine Business Library

ORGANIC WINE: A MARKETER'S GUIDE
Béatrice Cointreau

Building on detailed case studies, Cointreau presents an exhaustive analysis of global production and market trends, and provides clear insights on how to position one's product to the best effect.

$29.95
ISBN 978-1935879633
Pub Date: October 1, 2015
Paperback, 6 x 9 inches,
200 pp., graphs and charts

WINE MARKETING & SALES, 2ND EDITION
Paul Wagner, Janeen Olsen, Ph.D., and Liz Thach, Ph.D, foreword by Robert Mondavi

This completely revised and updated edition of the bestselling book puts new, practical, and powerful strategies into the hands of veteran brand managers and marketing professionals, and the vast bank of wine marketing knowledge within reach of the nascent winery owner.

$75.00
ISBN 978-1-934259-25-2
Hardcover, 7 x 10 inches,
400 pp., illustrations and
fully indexed

WINE BUSINESS CASE STUDIES: THIRTEEN CASES FROM THE REAL WORLD OF WINE BUSINESS MANAGEMENT
Pierre Mora, Editor

Published in association with the Bordeaux College of Business, this book applies business pedagogy's powerful learning tool to the unique challenges of wine business management. *Wine Business Case Studies* is written by an international group of respected wine business scholars.

$30.00
ISBN 978-1-935879-71-8
Paperback, 8.5 x 11 inches,
300 pp., graphs and charts

HOW TO IMPORT WINE: AN INSIDER'S GUIDE
Deborah M. Gray

Author and veteran importer Deborah M. Gray offers the benefit of her vast experience in this comprehensive guide. "I wish I had Deborah Gray's book at hand during my wine importing days; I might have saved myself time and money. This book is essential reading."—Thomas Matthews, *Wine Spectator*

$29.95
ISBN 978-1-934259-61-0
Paperback, 7 x 9 inches,
288 pp., 200 illustrations,
charts, and fully indexed

WINE MARKETING ONLINE
Brue McGechan

The whole wired realm of wine marketing is revealed in this encyclopedic yet readable and easy-to-follow guide.

$29.95
ISBN 978-1-935879-87-9
Paperback, 6 x 9 inches,
418 pp., illustrations and
fully indexed

HOW TO LAUNCH YOUR WINE CAREER
Liz Thach, Ph.D. & Brian D'Emilio, foreword by Michael Mondavi

Career coaching from two of wine's most respected professionals and scores of industry icons like winemaker Heidi Barrett and writer James Laube of the *Wine Spectator*.

$29.95
ISBN 978-1-934259-06-1
Paperback, 6 x 9 inches,
354 pp., fully indexed

The Viticulture and Enology Library

CONCEPTS IN WINE TECHNOLOGY, SMALL WINERY OPERATIONS
Yair Margalit, Ph.D.

Revised and updated, this detailed how-to guide, written by physical chemist and winemaker Yair Margalit, is organized in the sequence of winemaking, and is both an excellent text for the classroom and a concise guide for the practicing winemaker.

$40.00
ISBN 978-1-935879-80-0
Hardcover, 7 x 10 inches,
320 pp., illustrations, charts,
graphs, and fully indexed

WINE FAULTS: CAUSES, EFFECTS, CURES
John Hudelson, Ph.D., foreword by John Buechsenstein

A precise and comprehensive description of the problems encountered at times by all winemakers and wine judges. Every microbial infection found in today's wineries is fully described and arrayed in full-color slides.

$39.95
ISBN 978-1-934259-63-4
Paperback, 8.5 x 11 inches,
96 pp., full-color illustrations
and fully indexed

CONCEPTS IN WINE CHEMISTRY, 3RD EDITION
Yair Margalit, Ph.D.

In this new edition of his classic text, Yair Margalit gives complete and current pictures of the basic and advanced science behind the biochemistry of vilification, making the updated *Concepts in Wine Chemistry* the broadest and most meticulous book on the topic in print.

$89.95
ISBN 978-1-935879-81-7
Hardcover, 7 x 10 inches,
550 pp., illustrations, charts,
graphs, and fully indexed

BIODYNAMIC WINE, DEMYSTIFIED
Nicholas Joly, foreword by Mike Benziger & Joshua Greene

Joly shares the core philosophy behind biodynamic viticulture and explains why the use of foreign substances disrupt vineyard ecology and are ultimately counterproductive to a wine's best, consistent expression.

$24.95
ISBN 978-1-934259-02-3
Paperback, 6 x 9 inches,
180 pp., color plates and
fully indexed

UNDERSTANDING WINE TECHNOLOGY, 3RD EDITION
David Bird, foreword by Hugh Johnson

This completely revised and updated edition deciphers all the new scientific advances that have cropped up in the last several years and conveys them in Bird's typically clear and plainspoken style.

$44.95
ISBN 978-1-934259-60-3
Paperback, 6 x 8 inches,
328 pp., full-color
illustrations, charts, and
fully indexed

VIEW FROM THE VINEYARD: A PRACTICAL GUIDE TO SUSTAINABLE WINEGRAPE GROWING
Clifford P. Ohmart, Ph.D.

This comprehensive examination of the subject provides the farmer with a path to a sustainable vineyard and concludes with a self-assessment guide in which growers can easily track their progress.

$34.95
ISBN 978-1935879909
Hardcover, 7 x 10 inches,
240 pp., color and fully
indexed

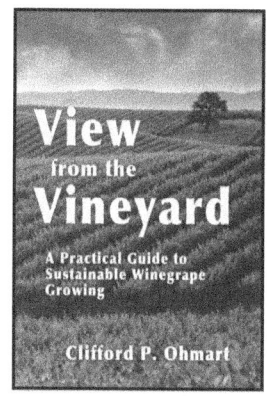